Refugees of the Revolution

Stanford Studies in Middle Eastern and Islamic Societies and Cultures

Refugees of the Revolution

EXPERIENCES OF PALESTINIAN EXILE

Diana Allan

Stanford University Press
Stanford, California

Stanford University Press
Stanford, California

Printed in the United States of America on acid-free, archival-quality paper

Library of Congress Cataloging-in-Publication Data

Allan, Diana (Diana Keown), author.
  Refugees of the revolution : experiences of Palestinian exile / Diana Allan.
    pages cm--(Stanford studies in Middle Eastern and Islamic societies and cultures)
  Includes bibliographical references and index.
  ISBN 978-0-8047-7491-8 (cloth : alk. paper)--ISBN 978-0-8047-7492-5 (pbk. : alk. paper)
  1. Refugees, Palestinian Arab--Lebanon--Social conditions. 2. Palestinian Arabs--Lebanon--Social conditions. 3. Israel-Arab War, 1948-1949--Refugees--Lebanon. 4. Shatila (Refugee camp) 5. Refugee camps--Lebanon. I. Title. II. Series: Stanford studies in Middle Eastern and Islamic societies and cultures.
  HV640.5.P36A45 2014
  305.892'7405692--dc23   2013028176

  ISBN 978-0-8047-8895-3 (electronic)

Typeset by Bruce Lundquist in 10/14 Minion

CONTENTS

ILLUSTRATIONS

ACKNOWLEDGMENTS

This book owes much to the support of many. Thanking those who have helped to bring it into being reveals the contours of its evolution and the constellation of felicitous circumstances that made it possible. My greatest debt is to the people whose lives it describes. The friendships I made in Shatila, and the extraordinary spiritedness, generosity, and humor of the people I have met there over the years, have inspired this work and enriched my own life in ways that extend far beyond this text. I would like to thank the many individuals who graciously opened their homes and their lives to me, shared their joys and sorrows, trusted me, and were willing to reflect on the complexities of their experience as Palestinians in Lebanon. Above all, I wish to thank Umm Mahmud, whose patience, perspicacity, and companionship during my fieldwork, and in the years since, have been critical to the realization of this work. I hope my friends in Shatila will accept this book as a small token of gratitude for all that they have given me.

Throughout the research and writing of this book I have received invaluable guidance and inspiration from professors in the Department of Anthropology at Harvard University. Steven Caton has been a generous and exacting reader, pushing me to think more carefully about the terms of my argument; Mary Steedly and Michael Herzfeld both gave insightful feedback on earlier incarnations of this text and spurred me on; Arthur Kleinman sharpened my interest in experience and the illuminating power of everyday life; and Lucien Castaing-Taylor awakened me to the possibilities of image and sound, which fundamentally changed my relationship to anthropology and my understanding of what ethnography can be: working in video has nurtured my interest in material worlds and the phenomenological registers of lived experience and has crystallized deeper movements within my written work. To all of them I am deeply grateful.

Among my colleagues and friends in Lebanon, I owe a special thanks to Rosemary Sayigh, whose pioneering research defines the field in which I work. She has been generous in sharing her knowledge about this community, remarkable for its depth and chronological breadth. I deeply respect the moral and political integrity of her work and value her friendship. I would also like to thank Mahmud Zeidan, who cofounded the Nakba Archive with me, for being such a superlative friend and partner. His charm and seemingly endless network of contacts continue to open many doors and made an infinite number of things possible for me during my field research. I would also like to thank Mustafa Abu Soueid, Jinan al-Amin, Saleh Demasi, Waseem Farhat, Sumaya Freiji, Nuhad Hamad, Monika Halkort, Sari Hanafi, Mohammed Kassem, Kholoud Hussein, Ali al-Khatib, Mohammed al-Khatib, Jamal al-Masri, Marcy Newman, Sandra al-Saleh, Nadia Sbaiti, Jaber Suleiman, Mayssun Sukarieh, Samia Tabari, Rabie al-Tayie, Livia Wick, Michelle Woodward, Rabie Zarroura, and the Zeidan family. The photos that provide visual touchstones for each chapter were taken by Hisham Ghuzlan, a brilliant young photographer from Shatila, whose images conjure up the world and life of the camp like no others I have seen. I am grateful to him for allowing me to use them, and to Yasmine al-Sabbagh for her meticulous care in preparing them.

Numerous other friends and colleagues have provided helpful comments and encouraged me along the way. Among them are Lori Allen, Negar Azimi, Amahl Bishara, Dawn Chatty, Alireza Doostdar, Beshara Doumani, Sarah Eltantawi, Munir Fasheh, Ilana Feldman, Michael Fischer, Nell Gabiam, Ghassan Hage, Clara Han, Sam Haselby, Jessica Hollows, Laleh Khalili, Nadia Latif, Toby Lee, Darryl Li, Nimco Mahamud-Hassan, Sreemati Mitter, Jessica Mulligan, Rebecca Murray, Karma Nabulsi, Verena Paravel, Laila Parsons, Wendy Pearlman, Sylvain Perdigon, Yousif Qasmiyeh, Mezna Qato, Maple Razsa, Anthony Shenoda, Sadia Shirazi, Bhrigu Singh, J. P. Sniadecki, Stephanie Spray, Ted Swedenburg, Salim Tamari, Emily Zeamer, and Souhad Zendah. I am especially grateful to Michael Jackson for his invaluable feedback on chapter drafts and for the inspiration of his scholarship. Laila Asser, Zaki Haidar, and Max Weiss assisted me with translation and transliteration, for which I am extremely grateful. Finally, I wish to thank Chantal Clarke and Douglas Hill for editorial assistance, and my editors at Stanford University Press, Kate Wahl, Frances Malcolm, and Cynthia Lindlof.

The research and writing of this book were made possible thanks to the support of a number of different institutions and grantors, including Harvard University, the Harry Frank Guggenheim Foundation, the Palestinian American Research Center, the Weatherhead Center for International Affairs, the Cora Du Bois Foundation, the Milton Fund, the Harvard Society of Fellows, and the Issam Fares Institute at the American University of Beirut, whose contributions are gratefully acknowledged.

It remains for me to thank my family, who have suffered through this endeavor with me and provided unwavering moral and material support. My husband, Curtis Brown, has encouraged me and patiently engaged with this project for over a decade in a way that leaves me at a loss for how to adequately thank him or acknowledge the many ways in which he has contributed to its realization. His intellectual and editorial input has been generous and unfaltering and has refined this work immeasurably. Our daughters, Layla and Freya, have also been loving and patient little supporters. My late father, Donald Allan, who lived and worked in the Middle East and cared deeply about the region, remains a constant inspiration; however, it was my mother, Belinda Allan, who nurtured my interest in Palestinians through her own work in Gaza and her commitment to the justness of their cause. She died as this book was going to print. Her unquestioning belief in me enabled this work, and it is to her that I wish to dedicate it.

NOTE ON TRANSLITERATION
AND TRANSLATIONS

I have minimized my inclusion of Arabic transliteration, both to simplify and to spare readers who do not know the language. The names of people and places remain the exception. Where no established convention exists for rendering proper nouns and terms in English, I have followed the pronunciation of Levantine dialect, which is what the speakers used. I have transliterated these names and terms using the simplified system recommended by the *International Journal of Middle East Studies*, with a few modifications to preserve some of the phonetic differences of Palestinian dialect. I do not use diacritics or long vowel markers and apply the standard convention of a single opening quotation mark to denote the *'ayn* ('), and a single closing quotation mark to denote the *hamza* ('); *ta marbuta* is transliterated as "a" and occasionally as "eh." While I sought some assistance in translating certain words and phrases, all translations are my own.

Refugees of the Revolution

Man and child in alley, Shatila camp. Photograph © Hisham Ghuzlan, 2008.

INTRODUCTION

"THERE WAS ONCE A KING who had a horse that he wanted trained to speak," Abu Ali began. "A refugee came forward and said, 'I'll teach your horse to speak, but it will be hard and it may take many years—forty, fifty, maybe more—and meanwhile I'll need a salary and shelter.'" Abu Ali paused, letting his poor refugee's cleverness sink in. "His friends said, 'Are you crazy? How can you teach a horse to talk? When the king finds out you lied, he'll kill you!' But the man responded, 'A lot can happen in forty years. The horse can die, the king can die, and in the meantime I'll eat, drink, and have a roof over my head.'"

I have listened to countless narratives, real and fantastical, of wiliness and survival in my years of research in Shatila, a Palestinian refugee camp in the southern suburbs of Beirut, Lebanon.[1] I was struck by what might be called the trickster element of such stories: the quick eye, audacity, and cunning that enable an underdog to outwit his masters. The business of survival in Shatila is often presented as one of stealth, mischief, willfulness, and an odd blend of humility and bravado. Shrewd resilience can be captured in set-piece narratives like Abu Ali's, ritually performed in everyday life or tactically deployed in response to the exclusions and privations of camp existence.

Such displays of cunning were not what I had expected to find. In the stereotypes of nationalist discourse, refugees are the stoic, "steadfast" (*sumud*) embodiment of a people who refuse to disappear; exiled subjects who would be citizens, upholding the right to return to their land.[2] The strugglers I encountered in Shatila seemed far more fractured and embattled, but also far more pragmatic. My interlocutors were more willing to question—and even subvert—the nationalist *doxa* of "perseverance and resistance" (*israr wa-muqawama*) than to adhere to it dutifully regardless of where it was taking them. Refugees' accounts of everyday survival strategies not only reveal tactical resistance to nationalist orthodoxy but also foreground the economic and existential—as opposed to purely political and cultural—dimensions of their struggle.

Shortly after moving to Shatila, in the context of a freewheeling discussion of camp politics, I heard another tale of mythic pragmatism. Before the advent of Islam, said Mahmud, a young man who lived in a neighboring building, the Bedouin tribe of Banu Hanifa created a pagan god. This deity, made of dates mixed with clarified butter, was worshipped for centuries as a source of power and oracular knowledge. When famine struck the tribe, they had no alternative but to eat their god. Mahmud related this story to illustrate why he no longer had time for politics. Extremity of circumstances, he said, was forcing him and his peers to adjust their aspirations and renounce certain closely held beliefs. The struggle to get by was now all-consuming, leaving little time for political or cultural life and muting nationalist aspiration. Refugees in Shatila had been left little choice but to "eat their god."

The image is both disturbing and paradoxical, evoking as it does not only disenchantment and defeat but also pragmatic agency and resourcefulness. It haunted me for the duration of my research and throughout the writing of this book, which aims to examine the interplay between canonical narratives of return to Palestine and local material realities of camp life. While Palestinian refugees in Lebanon have, in the last two decades, experienced new extremes of poverty, powerlessness, and political disillusionment, these conditions appear to be producing new forms of agency and subjectivity. This book is an attempt to understand how these everyday struggles affect Palestinian refugees in Shatila and to see the forces structuring social and political life through a phenomenological rather than ideological lens. Attending to what has been renascent in the wake of deprivation and disenfranchisement has been analytically central to my work.

The material and ideological crisis facing refugees today is often traced back to the departure of the Palestine Liberation Organization (PLO) in 1982, which marked the end of an unprecedented period of political ascendancy and institution building for Palestinians in Lebanon (Brynen 1990). The arrival of the Palestinian Resistance Movement (PRM) in Beirut in the 1970s had opened a new era—commonly referred to as "the revolution" (*al-thawra*)—transforming camps from poor, marginalized communities into politically active, vibrant economies.[3] Almost overnight, ostracized refugees were turned into major power brokers and political players, within both the Palestinian community and Lebanese society.

Despite the outbreak of the Lebanese civil war in 1975, what came to be known as the "Palestinian sector"—the committees and productive institutions established by the PLO—grew dramatically, soon absorbing 65 percent of the Palestinian workforce (Sayigh 1994, 17). The PLO's immense power and influence at that time afforded protection, and the wealth flowing into the organization funded a multitude of services. Shatila was the epicenter of these transformations, effectively functioning as the headquarters for the Palestinian leadership; residents who lived through this critical moment in the camp's history recall this period as a time of considerable prosperity and conviction.

All this ended in 1982, when the PLO was forcibly evacuated from Beirut in the wake of Israel's invasion of Lebanon. The Palestinian sector was dismantled, leaving the community vulnerable and jobless. The relocation of the leadership to Tunis has come to be seen as the turning point in the fortunes of refugees in Lebanon, marking the onset of radical political and economic instability and a collective crisis of faith whose effects have deepened with time. This watershed, which paved the way for the PLO's betrayals during the 1993 Oslo Accords—when refugees, formerly the core of the national movement, found themselves erased from the political arena—forms the historical context for this ethnography and is central for understanding the existential impasse that, for many, now characterizes camp life. The residents of Shatila today are refugees not only of "the catastrophe" (*al-Nakba*)—their 1948 expulsion from their homes in Palestine—but of *al-thawra*.[4]

The problem I am addressing, however, is more than a conflict between a nationalist metanarrative and local contingencies. It is something specific to Palestinians in Lebanon in the context of the Arab-Israeli conflict, where any form of assimilation is taboo, because it is seen as forsaking nationalist aspirations and legitimizing historical dispossession. In the discourses of both nationalism and international diplomacy, refugees have been reduced to symbols of a historical and political grievance awaiting redress, and their political and legal claims are almost always discussed with reference exclusively to Israel. The Lebanese government has exploited this situation as a pretext for withholding everything from health care, education, and social security to the basic right to work and own property. Lebanese politicians argue that extending civil, political, and economic rights to the Palestinian community will lead ineluctably to its naturalization, which they unanimously oppose. At the level of state rhetoric and policy, opposition to civil rights for Palestinian refugees in Lebanon is inextricably linked to support for their national rights in Israel/Palestine. Refugees, meanwhile, live lives existentially shaped, on the one hand, by their enduringly temporary status and, on the other, by the gathering infrastructural and institutional permanence of the camps.

A subtle version of this same logic has made its way into scholarship on Palestinians in Lebanon, ironically through the conduit of solidarity. In an effort to underscore the historical dimension of their case, much of the work on Palestinians in Lebanon addresses identity as a function of memory, a relation to the past. Remembrance is seen not only as central to contemporary Palestinian identity but also as constituting refugees' primary form of resistance (Abufarha 2009; Davis 2010; R. Khalidi 1997; Khalili 2007; Sa'di 2002; E. Said 2003; Slyomovics 1998; Swedenburg 1995). Camps are presented normatively as mnemonic communities held together by a shared memory of the villages and towns in what is now primarily Israel, from which they were ethnically cleansed during the Nakba, and by the collective demand for return. A physical reminder of the cataclysmic events of 1948, camps "represent the core of the problem as well as being the symbol of it" (Tuastad 1997, 105). Upholding the "right of return" (*haq al-'awda*) and "refugee" status over naturalization or permanent exile has become a core tenet of the community's political identity. The phrase "lest we forget" (*hatta la nansa*) encapsulates this sentiment and is often invoked both to express steadfastness and to forswear naturalization.

While oral narratives of the expulsion, the politics of memory, the right-of-return movement, and deracinated nationalism continue to figure prominently in ethnographies, the material conditions of refugee existence have tended to be occluded. Commemorative practices that invoke primordial attachments to land and cultural heritage are often viewed as central to maintaining membership within the Palestinian polity (Khalili 2004). Although this scholarship has enriched our understanding of the persistence of certain pre-1948 forms of social organization and cultural practice in exile, parallel transformations in the way identity and belonging are conceived and practiced locally—and the conflicting loyalties and attachments that have evolved after more than sixty years in exile—have been underestimated.[5]

This retrospective scholarly gaze has also been latently prescriptive, subsuming and replicating the ideological matrix of Palestinian nationalism. The pre-1948 Palestinian homeland is the normative focus of narratives of belonging, yearning, and political attachment. Refugees are presented as the living

remnants of a way of life that abruptly ended in 1948, the visible proof of cataclysmic events that drove an estimated 750,000 Palestinian Arabs from their
homes, the abject symbol of unrealized national claims, and the embodied reminder of a historical injustice awaiting redress. The ethical imperative that
many scholars feel often leads them to emphasize the continuities of attachment in exile rather than the discontinuities. By focusing on camps as temporary communities, where refugees ready themselves for return, scholarship has
tended to uncritically interpellate refugees as national subjects and to neglect
forms of social and political organization and identification that have developed in exile.

Within the implicit logic of this canonical account, moreover, the past is a
moral condition and a fixed inheritance rather than a sequence of events and
contingencies that have brought the Palestinians to where they are. Refugees
must inhabit the condition and pass on the inheritance in order to retain their
political identity. Meanwhile, the question of what it would mean for three generations born in exile to return to a place they never left is not explored, obvi-
ated as it is by the need for historical restitution. Throughout this book I attend
explicitly to the nuances and generational distinctions shaping discussion of
this issue among refugees themselves, and implicitly to what I think is a growing
gap between the maximalist positions of Palestinian (and Israeli) nationalists
and the pragmatism of refugees, who often distinguish between a symbolic recognition of the right of return and its actual implementation. Although home
and homeland are related concepts, they are not synonymous: dynamically
evolving solidarities and attachments that have developed in camp communities unsettle the alignment of people and place, complicating our understanding
of Palestinian identity and belonging in this context. Motivated by the need to
rethink solidarity rather than forsake it, this ethnography considers the various
ways in which refugees are pushing back against the assumptions and imposi-
tions of nationalist discourse.

Palestinian refugees in Lebanon and elsewhere are almost always discussed
in ideological terms, as if they dwelled entirely within a political realm, as if
their aspirations and inner lives lacked the fractured complexities of Western consciousness and identity, and as if their crucial needs were spiritual and
ethno-national but not material and economic. Everyday matters such as work,
health, and homemaking have received very little scholarly attention; even politically valenced issues such as power dynamics, grassroots action, and notions of futurity are recognized only when the frame of reference is large-scale,

national, and symbolic. An important aspect of my research has therefore been to study the dynamic material worlds refugees inhabit in Shatila, attending to the range of local factors and forces shaping existence at the granular level. I consider several interrelated questions: How do residents experience camp life and relate to one another? What are the dominant relations of power in the community? What forms of agency exist? How do individuals and households in the camp deal with the challenges they face? How do they plan for the future? How are continuity and social renewal conceived? Addressing—and redressing—this pattern of effacement in the literature on Palestinian refugees has been the principal aim of my work.

This book is not making a normative argument about the need to forget, to "let go" or "move on." Even as I critique the canonical emphasis on Palestinian identity as a function of collective memory and collective claims making, I am committed both to the importance of shoring up the historical—and oral-historical—record of 1948 and to augmenting rather than tamping down awareness of it. Specifically, I believe that preserving historical awareness of these events by recording refugee memories of 1948—at this point of transition from history as lived to history as text—is critical. Since 2002 I have worked on an archival project recording filmed testimonies with first-generation refugees in camps around Lebanon about their villages prior to the Nakba and their experiences during the expulsion. The Nakba Archive was initially to have been the subject of my research.[6] Based on the interviews I recorded in Shatila in 2001, I hypothesized that these narratives would shed light on the contingent processes by which displaced Palestinians in Lebanon construct a history and identity in exile, and how they articulate a sense of belonging, both to a diasporic community and to a Palestinian homeland. While I expected to find counternarratives of the 1948 war (narratives, for example, subversively inflected by gender, class, place of origin, and political division), I did not expect to question the essential originary power of eyewitness testimonies, much less their political and social significance within the community. I assumed that these stories were the primary means by which the paradigmatic motifs of Palestinian refugee identity—expulsion, collective dispossession, and displacement—as well as the sustaining structures of belonging and attachment, were transmitted to subsequent generations who had not lived the events of the Nakba.

Only a few months into my fieldwork I had already grown more critical of this view, and the experience of working on the archive while living in Shatila was to radically alter my understanding of the ways 1948 is remembered and forgotten, publicly and privately. Over the course of the next two years, the process of recording several hundred testimonies while I lived and conducted ethnographic research in the camp revealed stark discrepancies between how refugees recalled these experiences in the course of formal archival interviews and how they spoke of them in casual, everyday contexts. During informal conversations, nationalist imperatives would often give way to aspirations conceived in terms far more personal. The gravitational pull of the Palestinian nationalist master narrative became clearer, easier to discern, and I was able to track the trajectories of life stories as they fell into and out of discursive alignment with it.

More troubling were the residual experiences and local histories of several generations of refugees born in exile that seemed to have been silenced or left unassimilated by this renascent nationalist history. My friends and colleagues in Shatila tolerated, but did not always share my enthusiasm for, the salvage ethnography in which I was engaged. While elders were usually happy to be interviewed, often lamenting that we had not come sooner when their memories were sharper, second- and third-generation refugees were skeptical about the usefulness of such a project and cynical about the intentions that lay behind it. "Why are you documenting the problems of the past and not looking at how we are suffering *now*?" I was frequently asked, and many wondered why anyone would find these stories interesting after so many years. The most persistent question, framed more as a challenge, was how the archive would help the community. This I could not answer.

Such exchanges forced me to reevaluate certain assumptions that had informed my thinking about the archive and to think critically about the politics of what we do and do not witness in the field. What was at stake in these acts of remembrance for refugees in camps like Shatila? In making an archive that searched for certain kinds of national "truths," was I implicated in the structural forgetting of other, less usable pasts?[7] Was I engaged in a coercion of memory? Because I approached eyewitnesses as living links with Palestine, and their narratives as tools for regenerating collective meanings within a political field, did such quasi-institutionalized initiatives in some sense prevent elders from mourning their losses in more personal terms? By helping to codify this event as the core of national identity, were my colleagues and I making it harder for subsequent generations of refugees to articulate a sense of identity and belonging in their own terms? These and related questions haunted me. I have never been able to answer them, but the matrix of reflection, inquiry, and field-work they created form the critical substrate of this book.

As an anthropologist and activist, I was particularly unsettled to see how outsiders—not only ethnographers but also nongovernmental organizations (NGOs) and solidarity networks—play a key role in articulating and sustaining this metanarrative, often at the expense of more dynamic and diverse forms of remembering. In my interactions with local, civil, and political institutions, in Shatila as well as other camps, I became aware of the extent to which they have mobilized a nationalist narrative and minted its coin, often for the very prag-matic reason that cultural heritage projects invoking the right of return gener-ate investment and support from global solidarity networks.

To an activist committed to the right of Palestinians to national self-determination and to restitution and recognition for displaced refugees, an archive documenting the events of 1948 seemed compelling and important. Justice for Palestinians will inevitably entail a historical reckoning with and acknowledgment of past injustice: documenting the events of the expulsion is therefore of critical importance. However, the ethical obligation that those of us in sympathy with the aims of Palestinian nationalism may feel does not entitle us to speak politically for those whose lives have been determined by these events.

Empathy may draw us into history and nourish a desire that the Nakba be neither denied nor forgotten. Empathy may also cause us to lose sight of dis-tinctions—the ways the past does and does not continue to shape the present. Commemorative projects that peg remembrance to nationalist politics have created a hierarchy of events worthy of remembrance and witness. Occluded are the everyday forms of suffering experienced by refugees, and emergent sub-jectivities not conforming to the communitarian ideals of nationalism. Lack-ing the moral and political clarity of the 1948 expulsion, or the 1982 Sabra and Shatila massacre, everyday histories of grinding poverty are elided because they not only do not further but in some cases actively subvert the goals of Palestin-ian nationalism.[8]

There were several moments in the course of my fieldwork that highlighted tensions between nationalist orthodoxy and the irreducible particularity of local concerns. One such turning point for me occurred at a Civitas meeting con-vened in Shatila's main hall in July 2004. Funded by the European Union (EU), Civitas's stated aims were to examine the nature of relations between the Pal-estinian Authority (PA) and refugee communities living in exile; to bolster the credibility of the PLO as the primary institution responsible for representing Palestinian refugees; and to strengthen relations between the PA and the Palestinian diaspora (undermined as these had been by the 1993 Oslo Accords, which effectively removed refugees from the political arena).

Though the event was open to the entire community, the residents who attended were primarily men in their forties and fifties who had been former Fatah cadres and had helped organize the meeting. Almost no women or youth were present. The friend who accompanied me to the meeting speculated that Islamist groups and Syrian-backed opposition factions had intentionally not been invited, and it was clear that the event had not been widely publicized. When the audience was invited to respond, an elderly woman seated at the front named Umm Rabbiya stood up and after briefly asking the organizers to relay her greetings to Abu Ammar (Arafat's nom de guerre), launched into a narrative of personal loss and hardship beginning with the death of five sons and the loss of two homes, the first during the siege of Tel al-Za'tar camp in 1976, the second in Shatila during the 1982 Israeli invasion. She then described the harsh living conditions she faced as an elderly widow living alone. Offering a wish list for improvements, she said that Shatila needed a new transformer to solve the electricity problem, better health services for the elderly, money for schools, and free drinking water. "Our youth have no work; they have nothing to do." She concluded, "They sit and smoke nargileh outside my house the entire day. Their lives are being wasted—what can be done about this?"

When I spoke with Umm Rabbiya after the event, she was skeptical about the initiative's usefulness. "This kind of thing is talk without taste [*haki bala ta'meh*]. We can keep talking from now until the moment we die, and then what? We are on our own [*surna la-halna*]. It's like when a dog barks and no one responds [*zayy al-kalb 'amm bi'awwi—ma hada bi-ridd 'alayh*]," she told me. Her sharp intervention revealed the gap between refugee needs and institutional prerogatives, between the exigencies of camp life and a rhetoric of national unity and political participation. For Umm Rabbiya and others with whom I spoke, improving the mechanisms of political representation, while important, was less pressing than solving electricity problems, rebuilding camp sewers, and generating employment opportunities for youth, which were seen as imperative for communal survival and, in some ways, a more relevant form of national entitlement. These demands were directed not only to the national leadership but also to their host government, and claims to services and civic benefits in Lebanon were not regarded as incompatible with the right of return or with national liberation.

Other members of the audience shared Umm Rabbiya's reservations. "Every year we have these kinds of initiatives funded by the EU or others, and nothing changes for us," said one young man. "Why should we waste our time believing in them? They paint a nice picture, and that's it." As camp politics become increasingly mired in local struggles, these confidence-building measures seem ever more abstract.[9] Civitas's presumption of a stable continuity of national identity, belonging, and aspiration in the diaspora struck me as rooted in a fundamental misrecognition of the stakes—both political and existential—of life in Shatila.

The debate that Civitas generated within the Palestinian community in Lebanon revealed, more generally, the deep anxieties that foreign-funded initiatives provoke among refugees. Some said the lack of a clear statement in support of the right of return indicated that Civitas was part of an EU proposal to settle refugees in Lebanon. Others said Civitas was undermining rather than underscoring the relevance of the PLO, that if they truly wanted to strengthen the institution, they could have funded the PLO to conduct the survey. Many I spoke with in Shatila, however, saw it as yet another well-funded scheme that would enrich its organizers but bring no significant improvement for refugees. The range of speculation and rumor Civitas generated is symptomatic of the vulnerability refugees experience, cognizant as they are that their fates are decided for them behind closed doors.

PALESTINIAN REFUGEES IN LEBANON

By the early summer of 1948, about 750,000 Palestinians had been displaced from their homes by Jewish militias and forced into neighboring Arab states; about 110,000 people, mainly from the Upper Galilee and from the coastal towns of Mandate Palestine, sought refuge in Lebanon.[10] Most of these refugees registered with the United Nations Relief and Works Agency (UNRWA), the UN apparatus established in 1950 to provide relief and work for Palestinian refugees, and were admitted to one of the dozen camps operated by the organization around the country.[11] The most recent population estimate provided by UNRWA (2012) suggests that there are currently 465,798 Palestinians living in Lebanon,[12] of which 233,509 are registered as living in camps.[13] This community hovers in an ill-defined space, out of place and between states, as Lebanon denies their naturalization and Israel rejects their return. The "peace process" has reinforced the view prevalent among international actors that the right of refugees to return to their homeland is expendable in the service of statehood; indeed, the international community has increasingly viewed forfeit of this right as a precondition for peace. Meanwhile, the majority of Palestinian refugees residing in Lebanon have no citizenship of any kind and hold only temporary travel documents issued by the Lebanese authorities.[14] As objects of political negotiation, speculation, and back-room deals, refugees—and the intractable "refugee problem" they have come synecdochically to represent—cast a stark light on Israeli, Palestinian, and international intransigence as well as Lebanese discrimination.[15]

Their vulnerability in Lebanon is complicated by a history of troubled relations with their hosts, a history of extreme violence in which Palestinians have been at once witnesses, perpetrators, and victims. Few Lebanese can forgive or forget the PLO's role in their fifteen-year civil war in 1975–1990 (Fisk 1991; Hudson 1997; Picard 2002), and Palestinians are regularly blamed for the political turmoil of this period. The 1969 Cairo Agreement, brokered between the PLO and Lebanese authorities, saw the lifting of the repressive policies of the Lebanese Sûreté Générale, and later the Deuxième Bureau (al-Maktab al-Thani, the office of military intelligence), which had banned everything from political activity to professional work to arms possession. Many Lebanese chafed at the political and military power Palestinians accrued during this period and accused them of creating "a state within a state." Their sudden prominence was also regarded as having destabilized the fragile sectarian balance in the country and precipitated the civil war (in which they sided with the Lebanese Nationalist Movement against the Lebanese Forces [LF] and Christian militias backed by Syria).

In 1978 Israel invaded South Lebanon, intent on destroying the PLO's military bases, and established therein a "security zone." The attempted assassination of the Israeli ambassador Shlomo Argov in London on June 4, 1982, provided the casus belli for the Israeli invasion (Operation Peace in the Galilee).[16] After six weeks of heavy shelling, much of the PLO's infrastructure had been destroyed, several camps had been wiped out, and thousands of civilians had been killed. The PLO agreed to evacuate on condition that international protection be provided for Palestinian civilians. On September 16, two weeks after the PLO's leaders and cadres had been evacuated to Tunis, Lebanese Christian militias carried out the massacre of Sabra and Shatila under the passive watch of Israeli forces, murdering at least thirteen hundred Palestinian and

Lebanese civilians in retaliation for the assassination of Bashir Gemayel, the leader of the LF and newly elected president.[17] This was followed by a period of internecine fighting between Palestinian factions, fueled by Syria as part of its bid to gain control of the Palestinian national movement. In 1985 the Shi'ite militia Amal—with Syrian support—attacked and besieged the camps in Beirut in an effort to root out forces loyal to PLO chairman Yasser Arafat, igniting what came to be known as the "War of the Camps" (*Harb al-Mukhayamat*), which raged until 1988.[18] The departure of the PLO and the fedayeen forces in 1982 is therefore viewed as a critical turning point for Palestinian refugees in Lebanon; it deprived them of an important source of employment and protection, marking the beginning of a period of political, economic, and humanitarian instability continuing through the present day.[19]

The other defining moment in the history of Palestinian refugees in the Near East was the 1993 Oslo Accords between Israel and the PLO. When Yasser Arafat and Yitzhak Rabin signed the Declaration of Principles on the White House lawn, Palestinians living in the Occupied Palestinian Territories (OPT) imagined themselves a step closer to self-rule and statehood, but the agreement turned out to put off the discussion of the fate of refugees displaced in 1948 to a later date (Brynen 1997). The right of return was never even on the table.

For Palestinians in Lebanon, the majority of whom trace their displacement to 1948, the sense of betrayal and exclusion from the national movement—after years of struggle and sacrifice—was acute. Quick to exploit the rift between the national leadership and Palestinian refugees in the camps in Lebanon, the Lebanese government justified its policies of nonintegration and exclusion through a renewed commitment to the right of return and Palestinian nationalist aspirations (Tamari 1996). The maximalist demands of the international right-of-return movement, which gathered momentum in the late 1990s in the wake of Oslo, unwittingly helped reinforce the claim that naturalizing Palestinians would undermine their national rights. The government's pro-return stance has shaped not only the legal status of refugees in Lebanon but also the physical environment of camps. Until 2005, there was strict regulation of infrastructural development and camp rehabilitation, as the government sought to limit residents' social and spatial assimilation and underscore their temporary status.[20] Ironically, the discourses of Palestinian nationalism and Lebanese sovereignty have, with respect to the refugee question, increasingly come to resemble one another. Both understand the identity of Palestinians in historical terms and champion return as the only durable solution.

LEGAL DISCRIMINATION IN POSTWAR LEBANON

The Ta'if Accords that ended the civil war in 1989 did so at the expense of Palestinians, who were—and continue to be—cast as the principal troublemakers.
Within postwar Lebanese politics, Palestinians have remained the indigestible
element—in the words of one minister, Michel Murr, "human waste"—a "sect"
without a place in a sectarian system (Sayigh 1995, 42). Animated by fear that
absorbing the refugees, who are overwhelmingly Sunni, would destabilize the
sectarian balance, successive governments have opposed "nationalization," colloquially referred to as "implantation" (*tawtin*), on the grounds that it would
infringe on Lebanese sovereignty. This anti-*tawtin* position, which is shared by
the majority of Lebanese and regarded as a "national constant" (*al-thawabit
al-wataniyya*), precludes Palestinians from access to basic civil rights, which are
obtained through nationality.[21]

In 1990, the Lebanese constitution was modified to include formal rejection
of permanent resettlement of Palestinians in Lebanon, a stance that has enjoyed unprecedented consensus within Lebanon's various sectarian communities. A 2001 law forbade Palestinians from owning property outside the camps
(Law 261).[22] The tenacity of the *tawtin* taboo was also manifest in the near hys-
teria generated by reconstruction of Nahr al-Bared camp and the debates surrounding proposed changes to the labor law in 2010, both of which have been
interpreted by Lebanese commentators as precursors to naturalization.[23] Some
even argue that persistent refusal to naturalize Palestinian refugees, along with
the tendency to view them as a fifth column, has itself become a constitutive
element in the formation of postwar Lebanese identity (Peteet 2005, 174; Sfeir
2010). As a friend from Shatila put it, "When the Lebanese civil war ended, all
the Lebanese who were left behind were angels, and the only ones with dirty
hands were the Palestinians. All hung their bloodstained clothes on us."

In the wake of the Ta'if Accords Palestinians were without a military presence, and subject to laws that curtailed their freedom of movement and restricted their participation in the labor market. Suhail al-Natour, a legal
theorist in Beirut, described Ta'if as having marked the end of civil war and
the start of the legal war against the Palestinians: "What we now face is a war
of hunger. . . . The idea is not to allow Palestinians to work or make money
because then they'll settle and forget Palestine—keep them poor and they'll
want to return."[24] Since then, Palestinians have been treated as stateless foreigners, requiring a permit to work in almost all professions except agriculture and
construction.[25] Palestinians fortunate enough to obtain permits are not com-

pensated in the event of injury or layoffs, are not eligible for social security, but nonetheless pay taxes from their salary for social welfare services they do not receive. Various efforts to promote economic integration of refugees have met with considerable resistance, not only from Lebanese but also, initially at least, from refugees themselves, who feared that such measures might lend permanency to their condition (Peteet 2005, 63). These structures of legal exclusion, by which the Lebanese government has sought to marginalize refugees from social and economic life and confine them to camps, are seen by most as part of a concerted effort to force refugees out of Lebanon (Peteet 1996; Sayigh 2001).

Despite massive budget deficits during the last decade, UNRWA has continued to be the primary aid institution for refugees in the camps. Its role is fraught with contradiction. Because UNRWA's work is explicitly humanitarian rather than political, it is often accused of being "an avatar of colonialism" (Schiff 1995, 6), of depoliticizing the status of Palestinian refugees by deflecting attention from their current political and legal crises as well as from the historical cause of their mass displacement.[26] While the PLO used social welfare to promote political mobilization and galvanize collective military resistance, UNRWA draws on a politically neutralized discourse of "empowerment" through social development.[27] Although credited with enabling the continuity of camp communities, UNRWA is also blamed for undermining their will and initiative through a regime of "management and containment."[28] The ongoing resistance of the Lebanese government to economic projects for refugees has effectively removed the "W" from the United Nations Relief and Works Agency mandate, reducing camps to spaces of bureaucracy rather than production.[29] As the camp economy continues to worsen and emergency conditions become the norm, relief programs have eclipsed investment in "development" and microcredit schemes.[30]

Anyone who has spent time in a Palestinian camp will be familiar with the dissatisfaction elicited by discussion of UNRWA services, particularly in the field of health and education. Overcrowded classrooms, lack of resources, decaying infrastructure, and poor instruction have led to high dropout rates and encouraged many families to invest meager resources in private tutoring. Similarly, the perceived inadequacy of UNRWA clinics and distrust of local doctors have created a strong preference for private health care, an expense well beyond the reach of most. Dependency has engendered frustration and humiliation. Friends of mine described their elderly neighbor greeting the arrival of the UNRWA ration van with a mixture of relief and outrage. Holding up the bag of flour so all could see its UNRWA logo, she exclaimed bitterly, "This is the price of Palestine, a kilo of flour!" (*hay haq filastin, kilo tahin*), a reminder of what might be called the moral cost of aid.[31] While refugees regard UNRWA's operations as determined by the political interests of third parties pursuing their resettlement,[32] they also fear cessation of its services, not only because it would leave them without any safety net but because UNRWA, for all its flaws, represents the last vestiges of international recognition of refugee status and rights.[33]

The growing number of NGOs in Shatila during the last three decades is similarly seen as ineffectual, as compromised by the political interests and agendas of foreign donors and invariably corrupt.[34] The very term "NGO" may be misleading insofar as it presupposes the existence of governmental or quasi-governmental institutions, which do not in fact exist in the camps in Lebanon.[35] This goes some way toward explaining the overlap between NGOs as social providers and promoters of civil society, on the one hand, and actors in the political arena, on the other. Although a small number of local Lebanese-registered NGOs are independent, the majority are affiliated with leftist political factions and were established in the post-Oslo period as part of a bid to create a separate institutional power base in relation to the PA, and many are run by former faction leaders.[36] This has led to considerable blurring of the lines between the social, economic, and political activities carried out by such organizations. Although many of the NGOs in Shatila are run by sincere and dedicated staff and provide important services in the fields of culture, vocational training, and education (particularly for women and children), access to these resources will often depend on membership in affiliated political factions, making welfare a thinly disguised "means to a political end" (Hammami 1995, 55). This has undermined their credibility as charitable societies serving the broader community and hampered the development of civil society.[37]

A cursory review of recent statistics for the Palestinian camps in Lebanon reveals the extent of economic duress in these communities. Unemployment levels in all camps are now extremely high. It is estimated that approximately 56 percent of Palestinians are unemployed and more than a quarter of refugee households are without any employed members (UNRWA 2011b). Approximately two-thirds of Palestinian refugees subsist on less than $6.00 per day, and 6.6 percent of the population on less than $2.17 per day (UNRWA 2011b).

Poverty rates among Palestinians are considerably higher than those of their Lebanese neighbors, and the occurrence of extreme poverty is four times as great within the Palestinian community (Chaaban et al. 2010, 12). Palestinian refugees living in Lebanon are now considered the poorest and most deprived Palestinian community worldwide, a fact reflected in the growing numbers of refugees classified by UNRWA as "Special Hardship Cases" (SHCs), most recently estimated at 12.1 percent, exceeding Gaza's 8.7 percent.[38] The gradual removal in recent years of subsidies for basic foodstuffs, gasoline, and transport, and the increase in regressive indirect taxation, have benefited the wealthy at the expense of poorer Lebanese and Palestinians.[39]

The socioeconomic vulnerability of refugees has been compounded by their lack of legal protection (Knudsen 2009). Placed outside the international protection system afforded to most refugees through the United Nations High Commissioner for Refugees (UNHCR), the Palestinian case represents a striking exception to the "refugee regime." UNHCR conventionally presents refugee status as determined by actual contemporary circumstances, primarily the fear of persecution. United Nations General Assembly (UNGA) Article 194, however, defines the Palestinian refugee condition in terms of a specific historical event ("persons whose normal place of residence was Palestine between June 1946 and May 1948, who lost both their homes and means of livelihood as a result of the 1948 Arab-Israeli conflict"). Transmitted through patrilineal descent to four generations in exile, the status of refugee has thus come to be regarded as a social and collective identity as much as a legal category (Tuastad 1997). While international refugee law privileges the "durable solution" of voluntary repatriation, in this instance the country to which refugees are meant to return does not exist. The Lebanese government has nonetheless interpreted international refugee law as sanctioning the abandonment of integrative policies in favor of temporary solutions oriented toward ultimate repatriation.

Since Palestinians are technically considered to be receiving assistance from UNRWA, they are not subject to the protections and safeguards of the 1951 Convention Relating to the Status of Refugees, or to the 1967 Protocol (W. Said 2003). UNRWA, however, is not mandated to provide legal or political protection for Palestinian refugees, creating what is known as "the Protection Gap" (Akram 2002; Gabiam 2006; Knudsen 2009). If UNHCR's legal protection functions as a proxy for a home state's protection, then the lack of any international body with responsibility for the legal protection of Palestinian refugees further underscores that they have no country to return to. The ostensible reasoning behind this policy choice is that Palestinians, unlike most refugees, are assumed to seek repatriation only and not the option of asylum in a third country.

SHATILA CAMP: CONTEXT AND FIELDWORK METHODOLOGY

Shatila is one of twelve Palestinian camps in Lebanon and one of three in the southern suburbs of Beirut. Located in the interstices between the wealthy residential neighborhoods of West Beirut and the predominantly Shi'ite southern suburbs, Shatila occupies a liminal space in the city's imaginary—a site of neglect and political violence that has been stenciled out of postwar urban renewal. Infrastructural decay marks and separates Shatila, but like other urban refugee camps it has become increasingly integrated with surrounding neighborhoods. While parts of Beirut are designated areas of productivity, economic power, and luxury living, the camps now serve as human dumping grounds for Palestinian refugees and the urban poor and represent a hodgepodge of nationalities brought together by poverty. Only those working as cleaners, chauffeurs, or itinerant laborers now circulate within the wealthy residential areas, shopping districts, and financial sectors of the city.

Languishing in the shadow of unattainable wealth has reinforced the stigma of deprivation among Shatila's residents and is an important dimension of their experience of poverty and exclusion. The sociologist Pierre Bourdieu (2000) observed that socioeconomic marginalization is conditioned as much by the denial of symbolic capital—respect, freedom, and opportunity—afforded those within the imaginary bounds of "civil society" as by material want. The camp, and the modern housing complexes that border it to the north, sit side by side like alternative realities. These differences can be felt as temporal disjunctions: after twenty years in Canada, Fadi (a relative of my host family) likened his journey from Beirut's International Airport to his uncle's home in Shatila to time travel. "Walking into the camp after you've been driving down the new highways of Beirut feels like going backwards. . . . It's like returning to the past, only now it's worse."

Residents of Shatila live in poorly built and insecure homes with little or no access to essential services. The lack of resources for camp improvement programs, and the politically sensitive nature of such work, has meant that the camp's infrastructure is old and inadequate, in need of radical repair.[40] The average size of dwellings in the camp is 131 square feet, 2.2 rooms with a population density of 5.6 inhabitants per unit (Tiltnes 2005). Lacking proper infrastructure, garbage collection is sporadic, and the streets and alleyways of the camp are often littered with the overspill from the mounds of waste that accumulate.

In recent years, the plot of land allocated for refugee families in 1948, which is less than one square kilometer, has been the site of rapid development, and the camp is now home to around 22,000 people, of which Palestinians represent the minority. The most recent population estimate provided by UNRWA (2011a) suggests that there are currently 9,154 registered Palestinians living in Shatila. While camps have always been home to non-Palestinian residents, over the past two decades the population of Shatila has become increasingly mixed and now includes a large number of foreign service workers from South Asia, as well as Egyptians, Syrians, Turks, Kurds, and Lebanese: non-Palestinians who now represent the majority. A high percentage of the Palestinians living in the camp were displaced from other camps (at least once) before settling in Shatila. For its Palestinian residents, particularly those from the founding families, Shatila is no longer a camp in the sense that it was in the 1960s and 1970s, when it was essentially a closed community with a relatively homogeneous population. Now it is viewed by many as an extension of the poor urban neighborhoods in the southern suburbs.

Originally one- or two-story buildings have grown by as many as six or seven floors, as families add additional rooms to accommodate married children or even renters. Much of the construction in Shatila is informal, carried out without permission or plans and often with the most basic building materials. Buildings lean precariously into one another, and the haphazard vertical expansion has reduced the amount of natural light that penetrates the camp, leaving homes and walkways in semidarkness and creating health problems due to poor ventilation. The few remaining open spaces in the camp are being rapidly consumed; Shatila's principal thoroughfares have been halved in width since the camp was first established, and a growing number of alleys can now be navigated only by a slender person walking sideways.

This frenzied development has created the paradoxical situation in which there are neither public spaces nor privacy. As one friend aptly put it, "Shatila is now one house with many rooms." Neighbors are privy to the intimate details of each other's lives, and buildings are so close that one often sees people handing things to one another from stairwells and rooftops. Children play in the alleys, while their mothers converse through windows above them. The impression of a community collapsing in on itself is also reflected in chronically inadequate provision of electricity and water, a problem further compounded by factional disputes over control of camp services. Health care and education have become luxuries.[41] Rumors circulate that the very land on which Shatila is built will be bulldozed to make space for a leisure center.

When I arrived in Lebanon in July 2002, I rented an apartment in Sanayeh, a neighborhood in West Beirut—twenty minutes by bus from Shatila. I made this my base, keeping my computer, books, and camera equipment there. I then set about finding a room in the camp where I could spend the week, planning to return to Sanayeh on weekends to type up notes, read, and go for walks (I had learned from my stay in Shatila the year before that finding time alone there is next to impossible). I was put in touch with Umm Mahmud, the sister of a woman I had met while volunteering at a women's NGO in the camp the previous year. I was told she had a room I might be able to rent. When I introduced myself and inquired about the room, I sensed her reservations about having a foreigner living with her.[42] That I was British and studying at an American university did not help. The previous occupant of the room, she explained, had been a young man from a camp in the north who had taught at an UNRWA school in Shatila; he was clearly much beloved by Umm Mahmud and her family. She let me rent the room with the understanding that I would vacate it should the teacher decide to return.

Umm Mahmud, I discovered, was quite unlike her sister, a charismatic, larger-than-life woman in her late forties well known for her big heart and forceful personality. By contrast, Umm Mahmud appeared reticent and less easy to gauge. She was physically slight, with shoulder-length dark hair, and— apart from a wonderfully loud and explosive laugh, like a burst of celebratory gunfire—her demeanor was quiet and reserved. Despite her gracious hospitality, from the moment I set foot in her home, I felt her watchful eyes assessing whether I was to be trusted and if she could afford to admit me into her care. She asked questions about my research, to which I gave embarrassingly vague and long-winded answers, not knowing what exactly I was doing or even how to describe what I thought I might be doing. Like many I came to know in the camp, Umm Mahmud had never heard of anthropology and was patently skeptical of its usefulness. My poor grasp of Palestinian dialect when I began my fieldwork—and the awkward formality of the little modern standard Arabic (*fusha*) I had mastered—gave my responses a clumsiness that, I imagine, could only have added to her impression that I would be a burden and a liability. She showed me the room—perched like a crow's nest on the top of their building with an uncommonly panoptic view of the camp—and explained that her husband, Munir, had built it himself several years earlier. It was a small breeze-block structure that took up half of the roof, the remaining space functioning as a modest terrace on which to sit and hang washing. She gave me a key, and we agreed that I would return the following day with my belongings. At the time I remember feeling unnerved by her astute gaze that gave nothing away, and by her probing questions that had made visible my own limitations—linguistic and otherwise. It was, in fact, precisely these qualities that were to make her friendship and guidance so valuable to me over the course of my field research.

Though I was initially introduced as "our friend, the British woman living on the roof who is studying the Nakba," or a variant of this formula, after several years of living and working in Shatila, I came to be known by Umm Mahmud—and by the Hasan family more generally—as auntie (*khalti*), sister (*ukhti*), or as being from "our house" (*min baytna*). Extending the line of fictive kinship still further, I was jokingly referred to as a native of Sufsaf, their village in the northern Galilee, hence whose loyalties should be to their clan. Over time I was absorbed into family life to such a degree that I could no longer easily occupy the position of "observer" but was expected to be an active participant in family debates and disputes. When a row broke out between Umm Mahmud and her father, Abu Ali, over a disagreement with one of her elder sisters, I became her confidant and it was clear that I was not to spend time in her father's house. When fences were mended, I was once again permitted to go and have afternoon tea with him, as I had done in the past. When her mother fell ill, it seemed natural that I should offer moral and material support, as other relatives were doing, and I helped with domestic chores and took care of her four-year-old son while she tended to her mother.

While my outsider status could never be completely transcended—I was, after all, a foreigner who would eventually leave the camp and return only for periodic visits—the immense warmth, hospitality, and trust of my hosts often made me forget this fact. I was and remain deeply grateful for the privilege. Umm Mahmud was tolerant of my endless and often obscure questions, and I learned more from her about the difficulties, despairs, and joys of life in Shatila than from any other person, and she enriched my field experience immeasurably. She shared her friendships and opinions with me liberally, occasionally helped me with interviews, and argued with me continuously over my research.

It was above all Umm Mahmud's willful optimism, resilience, and forbearance, in spite of the obstacles she faced, that inspired me to shift my research focus away from narrative re-creation of pre-1948 Palestine to the local pragmatics—individual and communal—of survival, identity, and continuity. Shifting sympathetic and analytical attention away from the discursive continuities of nationalism toward the contingencies of everyday experience, I turned my attention to the camp's political economy and the ad hoc coping strategies of refugees. Living in Shatila was invaluable because it allowed me not only to immerse myself in the values and opinions of the community but also to better understand its daily predicaments—poor provision of electricity, lack of water, the endless struggle to make ends meet. Analyzing what people actually did from day to day in the local environment of the camp shifted my attention from the purely verbal and performative to the existential. In many ways this book is an attempt to respond to the challenges Umm Mahmud set me in the course of our conversations about camp life, and I have no doubt that she will continue to take issue with much of what I have to say here.

Living with the Hasan family yielded many useful contacts who were to prove important for my research, and Abu Ali's house, a stone's throw from my crow's nest, remained the hearth of my fieldwork. I also spent a lot of time in a store belonging to Fatima, a woman in her late fifties who lived alone. We became friends during my first month in Shatila when she invited me into her shop to escape a downpour, and I regularly kept her company while she worked. It was in her store that I came to better understand the workings of the camp economy; the social ties formed through debts, loans, and savings clubs; and the increasingly prominent economic role women play in brokering these alternative support networks. Another important family network was that of the Nassers, whom I met while conducting preliminary research in 2001: Umm Yusuf and Abu Yusuf figure prominently in several chapters. Through my work on the archive I also formed a number of friendships with elders like Abu Ali, who deepened my understanding of the intergenerational dynamics of camp life.

To protect the privacy of friends and colleagues, I have used pseudonyms throughout, except in the case of certain informants interviewed in their capacity as public figures and spokespersons for the community. In some cases this is a courtesy, sparing those who have shared intimate details about their lives with me unnecessary embarrassment. In other instances, as in the case of Abu Sadan, who is discussed in Chapter 3, or Naji, the protagonist of Chapter 5, it has been to protect people who are engaged in illegal activities or who have expressed political opinions that could put them at personal risk.

In an effort to question some of the reified categories and political stereotypes used to describe this community, I have tried to hew closely to the particulars of people's experience and to the terms they use to describe their lives and account for their actions, hoping to produce what Lila Abu Lughod calls "ethnographies of the particular" (1991, 158). My research methodology combined participant observation, detailed field diaries, and extensive interviews—both formal structured interviews, conducted while working on the archive and independently, and informal discussions recorded in the course of everyday interactions. In the first few months of research I used a digital recorder during many interviews and conversations, allowing me to go back over parts I had not understood and receive help with translation. As I became more proficient in Palestinian dialect, I relied less on the recorder and began taking detailed notes in shorthand while people were speaking—a habit friends quickly grew accustomed to, seeing the notebook that I always carried as a kind of prosthetic extension of my person. In situations where it was uncomfortable or inappropriate to be scribbling notes, I reconstructed these conversations with as much precision as I could in my field notes afterward. The conversations and interview excerpts quoted in the book are therefore sometimes recollections of scenes that I observed and, in other cases, direct word-for-word transcriptions of recorded interviews.

In my use of these source materials, I have tried to foreground the voices of my informants, erring on the side of unnecessarily extensive quotation rather than manipulative cherry picking. Excerpted passages, of course, inevitably represent a tiny and idiosyncratic selection of the total material gathered, but my intention has been to establish a dialectic between their voices and my own; I hope this will not only make the subjects, and the local worlds they inhabit, more vivid for the reader but also allow the latter to find meanings in my ethnographic material beyond what I highlight for the trajectory of my argument.

My network of friends and informants has defined the contours of my field interests, creating unavoidable gaps and biases. Gender codes being what they are, my relationships with men were fewer and more formal than those with women, which were often quite close. Notably absent from my fieldwork is attention to the role played by religion in the social and political life of Shatila. While camp populations have historically been fairly secular, the past decade has witnessed their growing radicalization and increased support for Hamas and Islamic Jihad. Since the time I began working in Shatila, an eclectic assortment of Islamist forces, many espousing jihadist ideologies, have begun to operate in the camp. This is conventionally attributed to a combination of political discontent, growing deprivation, divergent views on national liberation, and rejection of the corruption and incompetence now associated with secular factions (Knudsen 2005; Rougier 2007). Two of Shatila's three local mosques have been built in the last decade. One is run by Hamas, another by Islamic Jihad, while the third and oldest is used by followers of the al-Ahbash movement.[43] The number of Qur'anic reading groups and religious classes offered for women and children has increased, and the mosques provide places for women to gather. Though neither Hamas nor Islamic Jihad has political offices in the camps in Lebanon, both enjoy widespread grassroots support for the social services and welfare they provide to refugees.

The minor role religion plays in my analysis reflects the contingent fact that my host family and many of my friends identified themselves as religiously moderate and politically secular. When I began my fieldwork, few of my male friends prayed daily at their mosque, and many of my female friends were not veiled (and among those who were, it was not always for religious reasons). Many expressed respect for Hamas and Jihad, however, despite their own political leanings, because they admired these groups' commitments to military resistance and to social services.[44]

In outlining the practical and social setting of my fieldwork, it is important to factor in its particular historic moment. I entered the field in the wake of two events that profoundly affected the Palestinian refugee community in Lebanon, the liberation of South Lebanon and the beginning of the al-Aqsa Intifada, and I left it shortly after the assassination of Prime Minister Rafiq Hariri, an event with far-reaching consequences for politics in Lebanon and the region.

When the Israelis ended twenty-two years of occupation in May 2000, it was widely regarded as an unprecedented victory for the Lebanese Shi'ite resistance movement and political party, Hezbollah. The border immediately became a site of pilgrimage both for Lebanese and for Palestinians—especially those born after 1978, who had never seen Palestine with their own eyes. It renewed a sense of connection to Palestine and raised hopes (at least temporarily) for an imminent return. Busloads of refugees from camps all over Lebanon were escorted by Hezbollah commandos through Lebanese army checkpoints to join groups of Lebanese demonstrating along the border. They threw rocks at Israeli checkpoints, filled their pockets with Palestinian earth, and saw relatives from the OPT through barbed wire, after decades of separation.

In September 2000, when the al-Aqsa Intifada began, satellite television's intensive live coverage allowed Palestinians living in Lebanon to feel involved— in an unprecedented way—in the daily struggles on the ground. Large protests in support of the Palestinian resistance brought tens of thousands of refugees and Lebanese into the streets of Beirut's Central District, colloquially known as "downtown," in a rare display of solidarity.[45] Both the liberation of the south and the Intifada radicalized the community, and refugees often describe this period as a time when the political factions were—however briefly— reinvested with importance and credibility, as a moment, moreover, when an end to their struggle seemed to be in sight.

By July 2002, when I arrived in Beirut, it was clear that the collective euphoria would be short-lived, and the sense of optimism that the Intifada had nourished had already begun to crumble. During the three years I lived and worked in Shatila, the number of demonstrations and acts of solidarity dwindled noticeably, and people began to express exhaustion and despair at the news of daily tragedy from Palestine, finding their own powerlessness increasingly hard to bear. Anger at the negligence and partiality of the international community regarding the Israeli-Palestinian conflict intensified considerably during the buildup to the US invasion of Iraq, an event that irreparably damaged UN credibility in the eyes of Palestinians. Friends in Shatila regarded the weapons-of-mass-destruction red herring as symptomatic of the duplicity with which international institutions had always treated the Middle East. For many it recalled their own history of injustice at the hands of the UN, whose 1947 call for partition of Palestine gave international recognition to the State of Israel while failing to protect the rights of Palestinians. The Arab League's impotence and complicity in the Iraq War sounded for many the death knell of Arab nationalism, in turn extinguishing remaining hope for a just solution for Palestinians.

This moment of hopes precipitously raised and dashed forms the context for this study. The bitter sense of disappointment that followed the collapse of the Intifada made feelings of vulnerability and despair more intolerable than ever. Prospects for a just resolution for refugees in the diaspora were receding; not only had the "peace process" revealed the duplicity of a national leadership willing to sideline refugees from the political arena but it had also set in motion a steady reallocation of PLO assistance from Lebanon to the self-rule areas of the West Bank and Gaza.[46] The radical fluctuation of political mobilization and nationalist conviction I witnessed between my stays in Shatila in the summers of 2001 and 2005, and more recently between 2010 and 2012, underscores the protean nature of camp politics, while serving as a reminder that ethnographic knowledge is contingent, always built on the shifting sands of the historical moment. More particularly, the reverberative shifts and swings set in motion by these seminal events help explain discrepancies between my own findings and those of researchers who worked in the camps during the outbreak of the Intifada, when there was a greater sense of political conviction and hope (Khalili 2007).

STRUCTURE AND METHOD

This is a study of daily life and survival in Shatila. I use a loosely phenomenological approach to explore how camp life is understood and experienced by refugees. My approach builds on recent work in the social sciences exploring the existential dimension of refugee experience as well as the nexus between social, economic, political, and spatial marginalization (Ager 1999; Agier 2008; Bauman 2002, 2007; Chatty 2010; Latif 2008; Malkki 1995a; Nyers 2006; Sanyal 2010). Despite the increasing permanence of many camps,[47] the refugee condition is still conceptualized as temporary, with the camps themselves too often thought of as provisional spaces people occupy rather than worlds they inhabit.[48] This notion has only been reinforced by recent formulations—produced under the spell of the Italian theorist Giorgio Agamben—of the camp as an extraterritorial space of exception and "bare life."[49] The cost of all this has been a set of ethnographic blind spots regarding social life, rootedness, and agency in the camps.

This ethnography examines questions of identity and belonging less through discursive formulations than through lived experience. It takes as its starting point the everyday practices and processes that enable people to navigate poverty and uncertainty and create a meaningful existence. For obvious reasons, the field of Palestine studies has been dominated by scholarship about Palestinians as political actors and agents of resistance. Less attention has been given to the social, material, and affective worlds that refugees inhabit and negotiate from day to day. In the context of the camps in Lebanon, refugees have tended to be viewed in politically reified terms—as victims, symbols, statistics, or bargaining chips in interminable peace negotiations but rarely, for example, as economic agents invested in satisfying their material needs and generating security for themselves and their families.[50] The studies that do address material conditions in the camps today have tended to be multisite, policy-oriented surveys, conducted by research institutes and institutional providers (Abdulrahim and Khawaja 2011; Chaaban et al. 2010; Khawaja and Blome Jacobsen 2003; Tiltnes 2005; Ugland and al-Madi 2003); valuable as these are in other respects, they provide no ethnographic understanding of how marginality and poverty are experienced or how material and existential conditions affect social and political life. Combining ethnographic analysis with a study of history and political economy allows one to explore the means by which refugees subvert and make porous the spatial, legal, social, and political quarantines imposed upon them.

Relations and solidarities in Shatila are often bound up with coping strategies and built around need: accessing electricity and other basic services; soliciting financial support in times of crisis; forming support networks and alliances through emigration and the speculation that surrounds it; performing everyday routines that provide relief from the daily grind—having morning coffee with a neighbor, flying pigeons, or interpreting dreams with friends, and so on. It was these activities, at first sight often unremarkable, that I found sustained refugees and held the community together. In addition to generating meaning and continuity in extreme conditions, these practices also shape social and political relations and form the ground on which moral life and an everyday ethics of care are built. The contingencies of prolonged exile are producing new forms of subjectivity and belonging rooted in the local environment of Shatila. These emergent forms of identification and community point to dynamically evolving attachments that cut against the grain of officially sanctioned nationalism.

A number of excellent studies of the Palestinian refugee community in Lebanon have produced rich analyses of the formation of national identity, attentive to the matrices of historical memory, narrative, political symbolism, and practice that have enabled the continuity of Palestinian traditions, beliefs, and political attachments in exile.[51] My work departs from this existing scholarship in its emphasis, both rhetorical and conceptual, on the contingencies and ambiguities of everyday life that also structure the social field in which identities are lived, negotiated, and resisted. This partly reflects the fact that my research has taken as its explicit focus the interrogation of nationalism in this context. Drawing on the pragmatist philosophy of John Dewey, Michael Jackson argues that preoccupation with the regularity and stability of knowledge may constitute an attempt to "buy off contingency, to get us above the world of materiality and change and magically bring us a kind of immortality" (1989, 15). Within this worldview the conceptual order of ideology— nation, religion, justice, and so on—trumps the practical matters of economy, health, or security. Focusing on the continuity of cultural forms and antecedent truths, however, can cause one to lose sight of the significance of disruption, contradiction, and ambivalence. To shy away from the complexities of practice that elude clear exegesis—or depart from tradition—is to ignore what is "existentially most imperative" (Jackson 2005a, xxix). Cultural forms forged through action map what is at stake and reveal the changing priorities of a community.

In exploring the pragmatics of daily life in Shatila—what Jackson elsewhere calls the "precarious and perilous character of existence" (1989, 15)— this ethnography contributes to a body of anthropological literature that explores the central role that doubt, uncertainty, and misfortune play in structuring social and moral life (Beck 1999; Biehl 2005; Bourdieu 1977, 2000; Das 2007; Desjarlais 1997, 2003; Han 2012; Kapferer 1997; Kleinman 1995, 2006; Lindquist 2006; Malaby 2002; al-Mohammad 2010; Whyte 1997). Foregrounding the centrality of "lived experience," anthropologists like Robert Desjarlais, Jackson, and Arthur Kleinman have drawn inspiration from the phenomenological and pragmatist traditions, as means of exploring the intimacies and "felt immediacies" of people's lives (Desjarlais 1997, 223). For Shatila's residents, coming to terms with radical exclusion, alienation, and the indignities of refugee existence, or the daily struggle with poverty, loss, and political disenchantment, necessarily entails evaluation and questioning. Asking questions about why things are the way they are creates in turn the conditions in which people find themselves searching for solutions—developing compensatory tactics (affective and material), tentatively exploring the various options available to them. Susan Reynolds Whyte makes the important point that in thinking about uncertainty, one must be careful to distinguish between uncertainty as a vaguely existential condition and uncertainty as "an aspect of specific experience and practice" (1997, 19). I have tried to adhere to this distinction in my own work, where I take contingency to be a productive condition that people engage rather than simply something they passively endure. The significance of adopting a pragmatist stance is that it allows one to understand uncertainty not only as a condition of experience and orientation to the future but also as a way of being and operating in the world (Jackson 2005a).

One of the tenets of pragmatism that has proved critical to my thinking is the notion that reality is always in the process of becoming and that the structures of knowledge are continuously being reinscribed through experience and practice.[52] Identity and community remain inert, schematic concepts so long as they are detached from lived experience. Individuals are not objects of knowledge but active practitioners. I argue that in contexts of radical uncertainty, people seek to understand and alleviate the problems they face through purposeful action. Ethnographies that focus on an anthropology of practice in contexts of insecurity and transition often demonstrate how contingency itself develops the capacities of humans to imagine, plan, and exert control over what is not yet known (Kleinman 1980; Lindquist 2006; Whyte 1997). By focusing on action rather than discourse, pragmatism finds social meaning deriving from critical engagement, from "belief and intelligent inquiry, rather than knowledge and reasoned recognition of an existing order" (Whyte 1997, 19). While the Palestinian refugee condition is freighted with great historic and political significance, this is not something that people apprehend directly: they experience it as it is inscribed in and through everyday practice in the local context of the camp.

In attending to the strategies of survival and quotidian practice over discourse and culture as "text," I have also drawn on Pierre Bourdieu's (1990, 2000) theory of practice, and more specifically on his notion of *illusio*, the ability to invest oneself in a meaningful life. Bourdieu (2000) argues that although people may find themselves constrained by historical power relations that structure what he calls their *habitus*, their embodied dispositions, they will seek to maximize their yield within any given social field. Action and perception, he suggests, are therefore ontologically future-oriented, and shaped by an investment in the "forthcoming" (1977, 76). In framing cultural forms as protean and unstable, and in exploring the ways in which refugees orient themselves to the future, Bourdieu's theory of *illusio* becomes particularly useful because it introduces a proleptic dimension to cultural practice and daily life. Bourdieu's work has also been foundational to my understanding of how refugees experience the passage of time in conditions of seemingly permanent temporariness.

Similarly, I have found social phenomenology theoretically compelling in its recognition that "*who* you are is very much about *where* you are" (Frykman and Gilje 2003, 37) and in its conception of identity as having a dispositional relationship to a material life-world. I am wary, however, of redressing one imbalance with another. Focusing on everyday experience and practice to the exclusion of historical and political contexts can disguise the role these larger forces play in setting the parameters of individual agency and subjectivity. In Chapter 3, for instance, the significance of electrical theft in the camp becomes meaningful only when one examines the hierarchies and exclusions that necessitate it in the first place. Similarly, the idiom of interpretive possibility that finds expression in "dream talk" becomes more resonant when one considers how other, normative avenues of anticipation and planning have been foreclosed. In adopting socially embedded, "experience-near categories" to explore the particularities of refugee life and what is at stake "for survival, for coherence, for transcendence" in this community (Kleinman 1995, 272), I have therefore tried to situate my analysis of experience as rigorously as possible within its historical and political context. Bourdieu's theory of practice, which tacks back and forth between the micro and the macro, between external structures of power, habitual dispositions, and social being, has been a valuable model in this regard.[53] Finally, in questioning the relevance of certain categories of nationalist discourse, I am not suggesting that all ideology in this context is reified or false or that it plays an insignificant role in giving meaning to people's lives.

. . .

The opening chapter considers the politics of commemorative practice in Shatila and critiques the almost Lamarckian conceptual model acccording to which memories of the 1948 expulsion are passed down seamlessly from one generation to the next. The strength of Palestinian tradition and collective memory is often presented as the primary weapon of resistance in this transgenerational conflict—a motif at the center of many ethnographies of refugee life. Historic claims—and the continuity of Palestine itself—are understood to be contingent on communal memory across time and space. I examine how memories of the Nakba are structured by narrative conventions, and I ask to what extent refugees born in exile invest this past with social and political significance, teasing out generational distinctions in this investment. Do refugees in Shatila in fact constitute a "mnemonic community"? What is suggested by dissonance between the official, publicly performed nationalist narrative of 1948 and more subjective forms of personal remembrance?

Examining what is normatively considered an ideological practice in materialist terms, I look at the ways local NGOs and factions employ commemoration of 1948 to generate international support and funding for camp institutions. Public remembrance, I suggest, is not simply or primarily a medium of political claims making or cultural transmission but also has a practical function in the camp economy. My case studies indicate the workings of a pragmatic agency on the part of refugees, who use commemoration to generate investment in the very institutions that have come to form the locus of social agency in the camps—schools, NGOs, cultural centers, libraries, and so on. The chapter concludes by considering the extent to which these forms of solidarity may be contributing to a trivialization of memory and cultural practice.

If the primordial attachment to land and to an idealized pre-1948 existence is waning, what now forms the basis of group solidarity? How is the ideology of collective belonging—so critical to Palestinian nationalist sentiment and political identity—sustained? In Chapter 2, I attend to the relations of social life, exploring the affective and material practices through which people connect themselves to one another, mapping the interdependencies that exist among the social, economic, and political dimensions of the life of the camp.

The departure of the PLO in 1982 led to deprivation and disillusionment, and the long shadow it cast over the life of the camp forms the backdrop of this chapter. In the last three decades refugees have found themselves increasingly marginalized from national politics, looking back over fruitless careers and a failed liberation movement, all the while facing tightening legal restrictions. Rising unemployment, UNRWA's diminishing budget, and the redefinition of need have meant scarce resources are now fought over more furiously. As scarcity and debt have become facts of life, how have deteriorating material conditions affected Shatila's moral and political economy? Examining the economic histories of three individuals and their families, I explore how traditional social structures—kin relations, village ties, and factional allegiances—are being reconfigured by poverty and political duress.

A politics and practice of daily subsistence—privileging temporary and flexible forms of association, primarily between friends and neighbors—appears to be taking hold, supplementing the "moral familism" that was viewed as central to a culture of resistance during the revolution (Sayigh 1979, 1994). The analysis focuses in particular on alliances formed through loans, "gifts," credit relations, and the growing importance of informal savings collectives (*jam'iyya*) within the camp economy. I argue that these evolving techniques of solidarity and everyday care not only make visible the means by which refugees negotiate poverty and gain temporary relief; they also illustrate the ways in which traditional kin structures—both social and political—are being absorbed into wider and more strategic networks of dependency.

One of the primary aims of this book is not only to consider refugees as economic subjects (rather than simply as national ones) but also to broaden our notion of the political in this context. Chapter 3 examines how structures of power have become enmeshed in battles over electricity provision in the camp; this case study illustrates the struggle for power (in this instance, literal and metaphorical) between Shatila's residents and local governing institutions, and between the camp and the Lebanese state. As an example of how ad hoc strategies for acquiring basic amenities are redefining the nature and practice of politics in Shatila, I examine new skills, embodied practices, and uninstitutionalized forms of political mobilization that have evolved to meet shortfalls in electricity. Electricity distribution also highlights the shifting boundaries between deviance and propriety, as refugees find themselves forced to resort to "illegal" methods of securing services. With the nationalist dimension decentered, this informal politics becomes visible, revealing how refugees contest their marginalization and make claims upon the Lebanese state despite their exclusion from civil society.

In a context in which local politics have moved away from the representational structure of formal parties, and in which refugees are often wary of openly challenging the corrupt local leadership for fear of rekindling the factional strife of the civil war years, I consider how an informal, ostensibly nonpolitical collective founded in response to Shatila's electricity crisis in 2004 became the basis for sustained suprafactional mobilization, culminating in the first democratic elections in the camp's history the following year. The events leading up to the 2005 election demonstrated how political subjectivity is being remade in light of these everyday tactics for making do. Though these practices are not self-consciously ideological or politically self-formulating, I suggest that they are latently political; they create structures of affiliation that can be mobilized in moments of political crisis.[54]

Much has been written on the ways refugees relate to the past, and very little on how they orient themselves to the future. Barred as they are from ordinary means of personal development and advancement, how do they remain invested in the future? What generates for them a sense of hope and prospective momentum? Chapters 4 and 5 examine a range of strategies—by turns material and social, imaginative and spiritual—used by refugees to generate what Ghassan Hage calls "societal hope" (2003, 15) and to compensate for inadequate distribution of opportunity in official contexts by activating it in others.

Chapter 4 widens the scope of everyday survival to consider "dream talk"—the practice of dream narration and interpretation, most often engaged in by women—as a modality of anticipation and imagination that weaves futurity and possibility back into everyday experience. Dream talk is a hermeneutically rich narrative practice; it creates opportunity for self-reflection and meaning making. As an activity that helps individuals make psychological investments, it is on a continuum with the other pragmatic activities and coping strategies I address. Just as Chapter 3 revealed how inventiveness can compensate for marginality in the field of service provision, allowing refugees to bridge the gap between need and access, Chapter 4 considers how dream talk—with its aesthetics of narrative integration, transcendence, and renewal—can help refugees think and act prospectively in contexts where the future is shrouded in uncertainty. The experiences of several women I talked with are suggestive of the way uncertainty itself can refine people's abilities to imagine, hope, and exert control over the unknown.

At some point in the course of my research it struck me, with the force of delayed revelation, that refugees in Shatila have two distinct registers for thinking and talking about the future. They seem contradictory but are in fact contrapuntal. One—the discourse of steadfastness and an eventual return to Palestine—is roundly and publicly declaimed and is rhetorically so familiar to outsiders that they regard it as a kind of shorthand for the Palestinian condition. The other—the language of emigration (*hijra*) and assimilation elsewhere—is murmured in intimate settings, in strategic huddles where candor and pragmatic individualism hold sway. It includes talk of forged documents, human smugglers and their fees, variations in asylum law by country, and the prospects for employment, debt repayment, and family reunification in the target country. The former looks forward unwaveringly to the consummation of national claims that the latter seems quietly to retire. Many refugees I knew spoke both languages fluently.

Planning for emigration may be active, passive, or vicarious, but it is ubiquitous. Drawing on a number of detailed case histories of young men who have left, or tried to leave, Chapter 5 considers the complex interplay of structural and subjective forces involved in the migratory project. While the depredations of camp life clearly inform refugees' sense of urgency, the desire to emigrate arises from a sense of impasse as existential as it is economic. In its planning and execution, the goal of emigration creates space for fantasy, speculation, and the promise of a meaningful life; as such, it represents an arena in which aspirations are cultivated and acted upon. To understand migration, one must recognize that it is not only about attaining financial security; it is also about reclaiming agency, about connecting the sphere of action in the present to the prospect of a future yield. Even for those who lack the resources to realize this goal, the idea itself has become a powerfully motivating force. It is redirecting community aspirations and complicating the relationship between citizenship and nationality, "home" and "return."

Chapter 6 returns to the "consecration" of the right of return—and rights discourse more generally—and examines how it has been placed beyond interpretation or reevaluation on the part of those whose interests it aims to protect. The discussion considers how nationalist discourse, presenting the right of return as central to refugee identity, presupposes fixed relations to the past and to place, as well as to conceptions of nation and home—idées fixes that belie the evolving nature of identity and belonging. Through conversations with several generations of refugees living in Shatila, and by examining the "March of Return" direct action held at the border on May 15, 2011, I address the growing gap between the durable solutions discussed in the arena of international policy and nationalist politics, and the pragmatic alternatives proposed by refugees themselves. The range of viewpoints reveals a level of complexity often obscured by the absolutism with which the right of return is publicly discussed. What constitutes home and community for refugees has evolved during their sixty-five years in exile, and new forms of identification and belonging have been forged in the crucible of camp life. I consider how the very anomalousness of camp life and refugee experience—placelessness, provisionality, and poverty—may be producing its own form of "Palestinianness," distinct from a national identity tied to ancestral land and return.

. . .

The cruel economic realities of life in Shatila are unmaking the social and political structures that once formed the basis of collective belonging. As refugees wrestle with their everyday difficulties and struggle to survive extraordinary deprivation, new forms of solidarity and belonging arise, informed by a sharpened awareness of what is at stake. In light of these shifts, "Palestine" has taken on almost metaphysical status for refugees living in the camps. Merely suggesting that Palestinian nationalism has become a contested category, or asking what now constitutes collective belonging in this context, places one in an acute ethical quandary. Israeli policy regarding the Palestinians has often been described in terms of establishing "facts on the ground"; such facts can be military and strategic but also cultural and historical. The depth of attachment of the Palestinian refugee diaspora to the land of Palestine, and to their right to return to it, is obviously an iconic centerpiece of this struggle, so the risk exists that bringing it into the light of scrutiny may be miscast as a concession. I am also aware that those who have shared their experiences with me in the context of personal friendships and work, expressing critiques and reservations about the trajectory of Palestinian nationalism and the fate of their community, might not, as one put it, "want dirty laundry washed in public." Others may not recognize themselves in my depictions of their lives. Not to include the nuanced positions adopted by refugees living in Shatila, however, is to deny the agency expressed through critical reflection.

Though I have tried not to give undue weight to the personal, the idiosyncratic, and the ephemeral, I have felt compelled to foreground the ambivalence and anxieties people shared with me. I hope that this will not be taken as a breach of trust. The intensity of despair and frustration experienced by refugees in Shatila has not been fully acknowledged in the literature on them, nor have the causes to which many of them attribute their suffering. These omissions represent a distortion of their lived experience and thus introduce obligations for the ethnographer. The extraordinary resilience and resourcefulness I encountered, moreover, cannot simply be understood in national terms, through concepts like *sumud*. Rather, these qualities form part of a material pragmatism that keeps these communities going against all odds and is producing new forms of subjectivity and belonging.

In a context in which refugees have regularly found themselves excluded and silenced, there is a pressing need to represent the complex and sometimes contradictory terms in which refugees explain the adversities they face, their frustrations and anger with the international community, and their aspirations for the future. This is particularly important in the case of second-, third-, and fourth-generation refugees whose lives will be determined by any political solution reached. In my capacity as ethnographer I cannot advance or detract from the ethical or political claims of Palestinian nationalism and, more particularly, of the right of return. My mandate is to describe and analyze people in their social and material environments; it is not to prescribe political solutions. I proceed with certain misgivings and concerns about the way in which my work may be interpreted and used, but also with a sense of necessity, and I remind readers that what is under scrutiny is as much the politics of solidarity as the politics of Palestinian nationalism. To critique solidarity is not to erode it but rather to strengthen and reaffirm it.

Woman hanging washing, Shatila camp. Photograph © Hisham Ghuzlan, 2009.

1 COMMEMORATIVE ECONOMIES

ONE MORNING IN EARLY MAY 2004, at the start of what some residents of Shatila jokingly refer to as "the tourist season," I stopped by Najdeh, a women's NGO, to see Samar, a friend who worked there.[1] During the summer months Najdeh becomes home to a steady flow of foreigners, principally activist delegations and volunteers working with children. On this particular day, a battered minibus was parked outside the entrance, and I could hear foreign voices over the early-morning din of the camp. Inside, a group of middle-aged Americans, mainly women, were seated around a small table littered with pamphlets about Najdeh's work. Mazen, a young Palestinian American man working with a US-based right-of-return organization, was midway through a presentation on the history of the 1948 expulsion. I found a chair at the back of the room and sat with Umm Qasim, one of the center's coordinators. She explained that the group was part of a New York coalition that had come to Shatila to learn about the problems Palestinians faced in the Lebanese camps.

After coffee was served, Mazen recounted to the group a story my friend Samar had just told him about her father. "I want to share with you Samar's story," Mazen began:

> When her family first came to the camp in the early 1950s from Tripoli, where they had been living since they were forced out of Palestine in 1948, her father planted the same trees and plants they had in Palestine. . . . He also planted a grape vine that he tended every day. During the 1982 Israeli invasion his house was destroyed and so were the plants and the vine. . . . Afterwards he rebuilt his house and planted another vine that he calls the symbol of his future and of his hope.

This narrative, as related by Mazen, sought to highlight the continuity of Palestinian culture, the tenacity of peasant traditions, and localized structures of belonging in exile. The hope alluded to is, implicitly, that of return. Mazen's peroration made this explicit: "The right of return and the desire to go back to Palestine, to our villages, is at the center of every refugee's identity. The real Nakba was not just the loss of our land but the total destruction of the social fabric." The director of Najdeh, who had chaperoned the group, then added, "It is very important that you tell your communities in America how refugees in Shatila are suffering and how we still remember our villages in Palestine and want to return to them." Deeply moved, a member of the group responded: "Please tell Samar and your colleagues here that we haven't given up on them."

For the next few hours I accompanied the delegation as they were escorted by Samar through the camp, first to the mosque to see the tombs of refugees buried during the sieges of the War of the Camps, and then to the burial ground for the victims of the 1982 massacre, just south of the camp.[2] The group wandered around the memorial site, taking photos and looking at the graphic images erected on large billboards around the periphery: montages of black and bloated bodies piled in the streets and in the foreground a woman screaming. The display was framed by a quote: "What is . . . the Guilt She Committed to be Murdered?"[3] As we stood in the shade of one of the trees near the entrance, Samar recalled her own memories of the massacre for the visitors. About half an hour later the same dusty minibus pulled up outside the gate of the grounds to take the group back to their hotel.

As I reflected on the day's events, I was struck by the almost total absence of any discussion of the quotidian concerns of camp residents. Shatila, when it was discussed at all, was presented as the negation of everything believed to constitute an authentic Palestinian community. The discussion had been thematically dominated by an idealized pre–1948 Palestine, a backdrop of cultural and political wholeness against which the camp—temporary, fragmentary, defined by abnormality and lack, without cultural integrity or intrinsic worth—figured as a pathological foil. Mazen's talk, structured as it was around nostalgic descriptions of life in Palestine, interwoven with accounts of refugee steadfastness in Lebanon, presented identity as a function of memory and a relation to the past, animated by what had been lost rather than what has been created. Mazen had effectively glossed over the history of the camp itself, the material conditions shaping the lives of Palestinians in Shatila today, and the fraught relations that refugees have with their host society. It was as if attending to the complex support structures that have kept the community going, or local forms of affiliation that have taken root after generations in exile, would somehow compromise or contaminate a continuity of attachment to a Palestinian homeland.

Commemorative activities such as these are increasingly important for NGOs and other local institutions, and I attended a great many of them in the course of living and working in Shatila. After the 1993 Oslo Accords revealed the Palestinian Authority's willingness to sign away the right of return, commemorating 1948 became a way for refugees to counter their political marginalization, resist normalization of the expulsion, and underscore that they were not willing to concede the right of return. The Palestinian scholar Lena Jayyusi noted that foregrounding the Nakba was understood to be central to the preservation of Palestinian identity: "Our narrative of dispossession, so fundamental to our moral condition, and to our national and collective claims, and to the possibility of genuine restitution, still needs to be spoken and insisted upon" (quoted in Sayigh 2006, 134). As Palestinians in Lebanon found themselves marginalized and excluded from negotiations, the political and institutional value placed on Nakba commemoration increased. Nakba-themed plays, films, art exhibits, oral history projects, and memorial books documenting personal histories of villages and cities in Palestine proliferated.[4]

The 1998 celebrations of Israeli independence further raised the historical stakes. In stark contrast to previous years, the fiftieth-anniversary commemorations of the Nakba were accompanied by demonstrations in downtown Beirut, widely circulated right-of-return petitions, and public debates.[5] Such events, supported by local and international right-of-return groups, NGOs, and political factions in the camps, focused discussion of the "refugee problem" and the suffering of Palestinians in Lebanon around the issue of historical responsibility, foregrounding that of Israel and deflecting that of the Lebanese government and its discriminatory policies (al-Hout 1998; Khalili 2007; Sayigh 1998b). Both explicitly and implicitly, these commemorative events also reinforced the nationalist argument that when refugees reject naturalization in Lebanon, they are not acquiescing to a Lebanese caste system tantamount to a second, contemporary phase of their dispossession but rather are adopting a position of principled agency regarding their historical dispossession by Israel.

That this campaign of commemoration was at its height when I began working in Shatila in 2002 has had profound implications for the original conception and final argument of this book. Just as the moral imperative to bear witness to 1948 felt by camp institutions representing refugee interests—as well as by academic and international activist networks—was decisively shaped by a particular political moment, so, too, is my analysis of the politics of commemoration. And, if anything, this interest of NGOs, activists, and scholars in documenting and publicly commemorating the 1948 expulsion has gained momentum over the past decade.

The growing prominence of camp NGOs and solidarity networks as mediators of national claims and cultivators of nationalist sensibility, moreover, is representative of a broader shift in the nature of Palestinian resistance in Lebanon. After the PLO departed in 1982, marking the end of the military struggle for national liberation among Palestinians in Lebanon, refugees increasingly addressed their claims to the international community, framing their struggle in terms of human rights and international law (Allen 2009; Khalili 2007). A consequence of this shift has been the evolution of a rights-based approach to activism, promoted in large part by civil institutions in the camps. Like Najdeh, many Palestinian NGOs have turned to commemoration and testimonial as a way of attracting attention and support from the international human rights community.[6] While institutional investment in commemoration remains strong, the last few years have witnessed a sharp fall in communal participation;[7] refugees increasingly see these events and practices as directed at an international audience and motivated by the funding considerations of NGOs.

In Shatila, this cottage industry of commemoration has cropped up around not only the Nakba but also the other instantly recognizable symbol of collective Palestinian victimization, the 1982 Sabra and Shatila massacre. Demonstrations and rallies are organized on May 15 to mark the anniversary of the Nakba, to which foreign donor organizations are invited, and a committee of local and foreign activists now organizes an annual march to the Sabra and Shatila memorial site. In the course of these events, foreign visitors are often taken to the homes of camp elders to hear personal accounts of the 1948 expulsion or to visit survivors of the 1982 massacre. Those with firsthand knowledge of these events are increasingly called upon to inhabit the valued roles of victim or survivor because their narratives merge individual recollection with a collective memory of persecution in a way that resonates with the moral and political goals of Palestinian nationalism.

Though elegiac in tone, elders' narratives invoke a form of reminiscence in which evidentiary claims and causal explanations take precedence over more ephemeral, idiosyncratic, or trace elements of memory and experience. It often seems as if the rhetorical power of these types of narrative, which have become synecdochic of the Palestinian struggle, has subsumed a plurality of memories and stories into a singular narrative of loss, erasing less starkly political strata of experience. This politics of commemoration has also created a hierarchy of experiences deemed worthy of retention and fostered the belief that daily life in Palestinian communities—in all its minutiae—is always a direct reflection of larger political forces. The net result is that macrohistories masquerade as microhistories.

COLLECTIVIZING MEMORY

During the early years of exile, the term *Nakba* had not yet acquired symbolic currency, and the expulsion more often represented a moment of weakness and humiliation to be exorcized than an event to be actively commemorated. Refugees expected that their exile would be temporary; they referred to themselves as "returnees" and actively resisted using the term *Nakba*, fearing that it lent permanency to their situation.[8] In the 1950s and early 1960s other, more euphemistic terms were employed to describe the events of 1948, including "the rape" (*al-ightisab*), "the events" (*al-ahdath*), "the exodus" (*al-hijra*), and "when we blackened our faces and left" (*lamma tsakhamna wa tla'na*).[9] While Palestinian nationalism thrived in Lebanon in the 1970s under the leadership of the PLO, the focus was on revolution and renewal, making the invocation of 1948 memory neither desirable nor appropriate.[10] It was not until the 1990s, largely in response to the perception that Yasser Arafat was on the point of signing away the right of return in exchange for Palestinian statehood, that a renewed interest in commemorating the Nakba developed among institutions representing Palestinian refugees in Lebanon, in large part as a signal to the international community that this right was not negotiable.[11]

Narratives about the Nakba have since emerged as the symbolic linchpin of collective identity and the bedrock of nationalism.[12] Personal histories that memorialize villages and cities and lay claim to the land are both an assertion of ownership in the face of dispossession and a challenge to the erasures of a hegemonic Israeli narrative. Rashid Khalidi notes that "an attachment to place, a love of country and a local patriotism"—in short, parochial loyalties—constituted "the crucial elements in the construction of nation-state nationalism" among Palestinians (1997, 21). Mass displacement and the creation of a diaspora were key to Palestinian nation formation, and Palestinian nationalism continues to draw on idioms of home and homelessness. Alienation and exile deepen the need to reconstruct a homeland; they generate acts of imagination believed to be essential to the forging of national identity. Edward Said described the Palestinian diaspora's impulse to cultural creativity as deriving from this "perilous territory of not-belonging" (1984a, 50). Indeed, the very absence of a state and national institutions has increased the prestige of Palestinian intellectuals, activists, and scholars in the field of Palestine studies, whose work has collectively consolidated this nationalist discourse and helped to fashion a vocabulary of cultural authenticity and belonging.[13]

The writings of Mahmoud Darwish—Palestine's most beloved poet—are the best example of this phenomenon, transforming Palestine and the collective suffering of its people into lyrical archetypes of *sumud*. In his classic prose poem *Memory for Forgetfulness* (*Dhakira li-l-nisyan*) Darwish addresses an imagined Israeli reader: "The true homeland is not that which is known or proved. . . . Your insistent need to demonstrate the history of stones and your ability to invent proofs does not give you prior membership over him who knows the time of the rain from the smell of the stone. The stone for you is an intellectual effort. For its owner it is a roof and walls" (1995, 72). The image of the Palestinian as viscerally attached to—even synonymous with—the land is set against the abstract, intellectual, or archeological claims of Zionism. The struggle is framed in terms of two kinds of knowledge, one ontic and the other epistemic, with the former lived and the latter learned. While the poem's narrator claims to remember in order to forget and to reconcile, the work is clearly about the need not to forget. Underwriting this need is a perception that for Palestinians, individual forgetting is tantamount to an erasure of self; collective forgetting, in the words of the Palestinian psychologist George Awad, to "psychic genocide."[14]

The power of collective memory and the existential threat posed by forgetting are indeed pervasive themes in much Palestinian scholarship and literature.[15] The continued existence of Palestine and its people, it is assumed, now depends on a consciously remembered history and cultural tradition. By extension of this logic, it is thanks to their mnemonic tenacity that Palestinian refugees in the diaspora, despite the long years of exile, have defied all predictions that they would eventually become Lebanese, Syrian, Jordanian, or other nationalities. This refusal to forget or disappear symbolically imparts to their suffering and marginality a "latent form of power" (Sayigh 2006, 134).

By a further extension of this logic, nowhere is memory claimed to be—or rhetorically constructed to be—more authentic or vital than in the camps. The camps are where, in spite of the poverty and powerlessness of refugees—or perhaps because of it—"the Palestinian national spirit was, and still is, burning. *They are the real Palestinians*" (Klaus 2003, 129, emphasis added).[16] The memorializing consciousness believed to structure refugee experience in exile is often characterized as a compulsive desire to map, through narrative, "every tree, every stone fence, every grave, house, mosque, every street and village square [the refugees] had left behind."[17] Cartographic naming practices and the creation of intimate records of a lost past "make the absent present."[18]

Palestinian historian Elias Sanbar goes one step further, describing this experience in terms of radical substitution and synecdoche: "To rescue their land," he writes, "the refugees would gamble everything on taking it with them, gradually becoming the temporary replacement of their homeland. . . . They would live as if they were everything—Palestine and Palestinians, a people and its land" (2001, 90). Tellingly, Sanbar collapses the distinctions between memory as recollection and memory as cultural reproduction, making it almost indistinguishable from culture or identity. In other words, for refugees, the memory of 1948 is presented as the essence of their identity and humanity.

The rhetorical power of memory and cultural transmission in the context of the camps also draws upon the belief that disempowered communities are preternaturally oriented toward remembering and have a rich, spontaneous oral tradition—the "social glue" of identity politics—through which they record the injustices and suffering of the past.[19] The claim that Sanbar and others appear to be making—that the identity of refugees from different generations, with different experiences, remains an enduring constant—does not account for the passage of time, for the disparateness of individual memory, or, most controversially, for the fact that new avenues of aspiration and belonging may be decoupling the nationalist dyad of territory and home.

The mounting pressure on refugees in Shatila to give voice to traumatic memories of the expulsion and the 1982 massacre may result partly from a Western model of traumatic memory and a "politics of blame" (Antze and Lambek 1996, xxi), where authority and authenticity are grounded in stories of extreme suffering and the voicing of pain is viewed as redemptive and empowering.[20] Informed by a transnational discourse of rights, commemoration has become a form of political expression for refugees that "on the one hand legitimates their claim to membership in the Palestinian national polity and, on the other hand, appeals to the international community for recognition and justice" (Khalili 2005, 32).

One of the consequences of this valorization of traumatic memories of the Nakba, and the need to bear public witness to them for political ends, is the mirroring of the Holocaust paradigm of remembrance. The similarities are obviously not coincidental, given that the sense of urgency motivating much of the work on 1948 has been Israel's ongoing denial that it engaged in deliberate acts of ethnic cleansing.[21] The symbolic power that emerges from the remembrance of both events does not depend on inquiry into the historical conditions that might better explain how or why they occurred or, for that matter, the contradictory ways in which they are remembered; on the contrary, it depends on minimizing historical investigation.[22] In much of the testimonial work with Holocaust survivors and first-generation Palestinian refugees, there is a sense that the *fact* of transmission is a priori validating, while the *act* of speaking exceeds any questions of "truth" (Felman and Laub 1992). Elegiac remembrance, as an unproblematic form of truth telling, has also effectively obscured the political contexts and relations of power in which these histories are being produced.[23]

Historical trauma and suffering in the case of the Holocaust, according to the historian Dominick LaCapra, has been made "sublime," altered and elevated from historical event to something like doctrinal faith.[24] I would argue that a similar process has occurred with regard to the Nakba. In both cases traumatic memory is presented as a pure form of experiential knowledge—like the "real" of poststructuralist discourse, it is the always absent signified, which escapes our grasp yet retains the status of an absolute that cannot be questioned (Douglass and Vogler 2003, 5). In both cases the authority and authenticity of eyewitness narratives derive from proximity to traumatic experience.[25] For Israelis and Palestinians, victimhood has become a crucial component of national narrative, in which each side vies for the position of "true" victim, making history the means to "enshrine grievances" (Maier 1993, 147). Like the Shoah, which Israel internalized as constitutive of national identity only in the 1980s, the Nakba became a point of historical and political orientation toward the future—as founding myth and teleology—only at a relatively late stage in national consciousness.[26] An official address by Mahmoud Darwish at a fiftieth-anniversary event in Ramallah exemplifies the semantic shift in nationalist rhetoric that has taken place in relation to 1948: "The Palestinian people have launched a redemptive journey into the future. From the ashes of our sorrow and loss, we are resurrecting a nation celebrating life and hope."[27] Whereas in the context of Holocaust commemoration the injunction to "never forget" does not entail trying to reverse the never-to-be-forgotten event, in the context of the Nakba the equivalent injunction usually does.

The authenticity and legitimacy enacted and often controlled by this increasingly institutionalized understanding of 1948 history come at a cost. This monument to an idealized past, to which subsequent generations are expected to bear witness and even claim as their own, and which many of us working in the field of Palestine studies may be unintentionally co-constructing, can be both alienating and oppressive. It supplants an understanding of history and identity as lived experience, as practice, that might evolve organically into future possibility. The irony is that the expedient reframing of memory and identity in starkly political terms, with refugees as the human remnants of historic tragedy striving in their very being for return, puts the burden of remembrance on those with the least resources to bear it. Not only does a heroic narrative of suffering obscure localized, less legible legacies of 1948 currently existing in the memories, experiences, and hopes of refugees in the diaspora; it also conceals the fact that the intensity of longing for nation may now be coming more from the elite echelons of the Palestinian diaspora than from its impoverished base.

One of the broader questions I address here and throughout this book is whether the quest for political agency among refugees might be better served by arguments rooted in the present-day realities of life in the camps rather than those conceived in terms that imply an undoing of history. One consequence of the political appropriation of 1948 in the context of camp activism is that the search for recognition of refugee rights under international law is often conflated with the existential imperative of not forgetting. While commemorative practice highlights the historical origins of refugee suffering and challenges the proverbial Israeli claim that Palestine was a land without people, it does not address the more immediate threat facing these communities: the discriminatory and repressive policies of the Lebanese government. Remembering 1948 has come to be seen as one of the few "legitimate" ways in which refugees can make visible their present suffering to a larger audience. What is at stake in these acts of political commemoration for refugees living in Shatila, and how do different generations of refugees remember and forget 1948 in public and private settings? To what extent are they able to weave everyday concerns and experiences back into official commemorative discourse and practice?[28] The multi-faceted modes of remembering and forgetting 1948 I encountered gesture to the existence of more nuanced forms of remembering and mourning the past, often predicated on a distinction between personal experience and national claims. My attempt to give deserved and long-overdue attention to the former should not be understood as compromising the latter.

NAKBA ARCHIVE: TEMPLATES FOR REMEMBERING

I have not been a neutral observer of commemoration. Since 2002 I have worked on an archival project to record testimonies on film with first-generation refugees in camps around Lebanon about their villages prior to 1948 and their experiences during the expulsion.[29] The idea for the project came in 2001 while I was working on a documentary with a group of Palestinian teenagers in Shatila, for which we interviewed a number of their grandparents. Elders who had left Palestine as teenagers or young adults were in their seventies, and it was clear that within a few years there would be no more witnesses with memories of Mandate Palestine or the events of the expulsion. It was the experience of working on this documentary that convinced me of the importance of recording these narratives.

In hindsight, the conceit that we would in some sense be capturing the transmission of memory itself seems naïve, not least in its assumptions about the transparency of video. The project, as it was then conceived, was highly idealistic: to create an audiovisual archive that would document historic claims and serve both as a resource for future scholars, activists, and filmmakers working on pre-1948 Palestine and the expulsion and as a record for Palestinian refugees in Lebanon. In the wake of the fiftieth-anniversary celebrations of the State of Israel, amid growing awareness that the living ranks of the 1948 generation were thinning, the initiative appeared timely and generated considerable interest and support.

When I began conducting interviews for the archive in Shatila, I was taken to elders widely recognized to have good or "important" (*muhim*) memories. Among the first of these local sages I came to know well was Abu Nayef from Majd al-Krum, a village in the northern Galilee. After brief introductions we were seated, and without prompting he launched into a poignant narrative about his village. This oral memoir seemed practiced, even stylized. There were signs of prescriptive plotting, for instance, in the invocation of key political tropes: close relations with local Jewish communities prior to 1948, British duplicity, escalating acts of violence, air raids, a perilous journey into exile, the hardship of early years in Lebanon, and the establishment of the camp, in which his father had played a major role. It was as if an interpretive template had been laid over Abu Nayef's personal experiences. This is not to belittle his account or cast doubt over its veracity but more to note the ways in which the form and content of his story appeared to have internalized the protocols of testimony by foregrounding a rhetoric of authenticity and moral edification. It was as if Abu Nayef, anticipating the sympathies of his audience, emphasized those elements of his own history that fit the nationalist paradigm of remembrance and spoke to collective political interests. This was also suggested by the way in which his story was structured around episodes marked for some kind of future redemption. As he brought his narrative to a close, he turned and gave us a penetrating look: "If I could go to my village tomorrow, I would leave everything I have and walk," he said, raising his voice a notch; "I would be happy to live under a tree with the sky as my roof. It would be enough just to die in Palestine." Then finally: "The right of return is our most important right—we will not give it up for anything."

Over bitter coffee after the interview, Abu Nayef showed me a photograph album of images of himself with various visiting delegations, foreign officials, and volunteers from a host of different countries and joked that his house had become "like the United Nations." He was clearly proud that representatives from local NGOs regularly take their visitors to see him as part of their tour of Shatila. A respected camp elder, he has fashioned his identity as a narrator of the Nakba. Through these acts of witness he is both a representative of the community and an agent of collective identity and experience. This might be understood as an indexical maneuver that allows the "I" to speak for the "we," that constructs the subject as a collective voice. Through narrative, Abu Nayef tries to evoke the identification and empathy of his audience, interpellating the viewer as secondary witness in this "rhetorical space of intersubjectivity" (Hesford 2004, 105). On the various occasions I saw him talking with visitors to the camp, the form his narrative took was almost identical; his guests were usually invited to ask questions at the end, sometimes prompted by the "guide"—what, for instance, does Abu Nayef think about the right of return? To which his resounding answer would be, "If I could go to my village tomorrow, I would leave everything I have and walk." These strategies of performance and persuasion point to an economy of memory in which particular versions of the past become standardized and circulate almost as commodities, often governed by the need to generate political support and emotional identification with the Palestinian cause. These narrative conventions also illustrate the ways in which a transnational discourse of testimony may be shaping local practice, informing the processes by which individual experience becomes social text and public past.[30]

As I came to know Abu Nayef better in the course of living in the camp, I began to notice how the same events could be discussed in radically different terms in other contexts. His niece became a close friend, and I would often find Abu Nayef talking with her husband when I called to visit. In these informal family settings his memories (built almost entirely around his experiences in Shatila and rarely straying as far afield as Majd al-Krum) took on a fluidity and depth—at times a sharp humor—largely absent in the more stately narrations given to visitors. After the Geneva Accords (the unofficial Palestinian-Israeli peace plan) were made public in December 2003, he refused to come with us to a demonstration outside the UN building, telling me—with a certain impatience—that it was a waste of time and that everyone "knows" that the right of return is impossible. Through these interactions with Abu Nayef and other elders in Shatila, I became more aware of the ways in which the rhetorical language of collective dispossession, struggle, and return that has come to index "Palestinianness" in these more "official" contexts has lost its resonance, not only in the minds of elders like Abu Nayef but also, as I came to discover, among younger generations of refugees in Shatila.

When the subject of Palestine and the events of the expulsion arose in the course of my daily interactions with elders, it did so as supple, anecdotal, associative reminiscence, more deeply concerned with commenting on the present than memorializing the past. These stories were rarely relayed to convey anger or cast blame (though I would occasionally receive a sharp comment or reproachful look when it was discovered that I was British), and I was struck by their elliptical quality, which stood in stark contrast to the rhetorical flourishes accompanying any institutional mention of the Nakba or pre-1948 Palestine. Recollections were often sparked by sensory associations—the taste of a particular dish, the smell of herbs. One elderly woman from the village of Tarshiha told me of a recurring dream she had about a fig tree that had grown outside their house, and how she felt she could taste the figs in her sleep—a flavor never matched by any fig available from Sabra souk nearby. "I feel this is my body telling me that it wants to go back," she told me. At other times it was through memories of work and daily routines that lost homes and ways of life found expression. When I asked Said, a fisherman from Acre, if he had ever visited the border with Palestine in his boat, imagining that he might have tried to return by sea, he responded that he did not have the right nets to fish in those waters, implying that it would be pointless. "Palestine" for him signified a constellation of material practices as much as a geographical or iconic space.[31]

These memories seemed unrehearsed, vanishing as quickly as they surfaced, as the contingent moment of their telling passed. Unlike reified and institutionally sanctioned forms of remembrance, these memories form part of an unsegmented continuum of lived experience.[32] For Umm Saleh it was the aroma of wild thyme (za'tar) that sparked a series of interconnected memories that took her first to Jish and the memory of picking wild za'tar in the mountains with her grandmother, then to its use in cooking, and the memory of seeing a snake in their courtyard as a child, then finally to a recent visit with her sister in Ayn al-Hilweh camp, where she had seen, and smelled, families pounding their own za'tar—a practice she said was now rare in Shatila. These recollections were addressed to her daughter and grandson over breakfast one morning. That this unsystematic weaving of events and places at first appeared to me as passing anecdote rather than a narrative about the Nakba points to my own biases and limits of imagination about what constitutes a historical narrative. In hindsight, it illustrates for me the extent to which prescribed conventions of bearing witness influenced what I listened for, giving primacy, for example, to emotionally charged moments in which national narrative and self-narrative intertwine. Umm Saleh's stories, like many I have heard since, suggest a refusal to force fragmentary memories into an interpretative scheme. Fragmentary memories may indeed enact a doubling of witness, transmitting not only histories but also their shattering effects on those who lived them.[33]

While these Proustian moments may form points of reference for elders, do they have any impact across generational lines? My encounters with children and adolescents in the camp suggest that few know more than the name of, and the most generic facts about, their ancestral village. Most identify as Palestinian and from Shatila rather than as coming from a particular village or region. This finding stands in contrast to the claims of many scholars and sympathetic commentators that the identity of refugees—even those born in the diaspora, with no direct knowledge of Palestine—remains inseparable from their specific places of origin.[34] Both Rosemary Sayigh (2005) and Laleh Khalili (2007) argue that there has been a resurgence of interest in places of origin occluded by the nationalist rhetoric of the 1970s and 1980s, which emphasized the unity of Palestinian identity over its particularities. They suggest that after Oslo, when the collective claims of Palestinian nationalism were shown not to extend to refugee communities in the diaspora, reviving village ties became a way of insisting on membership in a Palestinian nation.[35]

Mahmud, the grandson of Abu Ali, who was thirteen when I began my fieldwork, knew almost nothing about his grandfather's experiences in Palestine. Abu Ali, who originated from Sufsaf, had witnessed the massacre perpetrated by Jewish Haganah forces in his village in October 1948 and was able to name all seventy men who were murdered—a feat given the numbers involved.[36] Yet, somewhat surprisingly, Mahmud knew only that his relatives in Palestine had not needed money: "People didn't even know what money looked like in those days—they were farmers and grew everything they needed—not like now." When I later asked Abu Ali if he had ever described his experiences in detail, he admitted that his grandchildren were more interested in watching television or chatting on the Internet. "Every day my friend Abu Waseem comes to visit me—we sit and have coffee and sometimes we talk about Palestine, but my grandchildren don't like to sit with us—they'd rather be playing pinball with their friends." Many times when I stopped by Abu Ali's house in the afternoon, I would find him sitting with Abu Waseem, often in silence. This at first struck me as odd. Over time, however, it became clear that this ritual meeting that structured their days was a form of exchange and solidarity. These silences—which at times seemed to me agonizingly long but which they clearly both felt comfortable with—expressed something deliberate and shared.

Umm Mahmud, who had been sitting with us and had overheard my discussion with her father, later privately acknowledged that she had not encouraged her son to ask her parents about the past:

> Although my parents used to speak a lot about Palestine when we were young, I don't like hearing these stories now. . . . Sometimes my mother sings to my children about Bint Jbeil and how families were separated when they first came to Lebanon, and it makes us cry. . . . These memories are too painful for her, and for us. . . . I realize it is important for the children to know about Palestine, but I feel that it's good for us to think about how to make their future better rather than to live in the past.[37]

In the context of my fieldwork, this family's experience is representative. Among younger generations of refugees, historical awareness seems to be diminishing, as is historical transmission through the public performance of personal narrative. In place of the latter, one finds more intimate—and less easily transmitted—forms of cultural retrieval: stories may no longer be a retentive milieu for communal memory.[38] Silent practice, gestures, and repetitive rituals—meeting for coffee, a lullaby—seem to be supplanting narrative as the semiotic site of communal solidarity. I am duly alert to the risk of overstating my argument here. Institutionalized and subjective forms of remembrance have no doubt always coexisted in camp life and will doubtless continue to do so, but as more formal modes of remembrance appear increasingly forced and detached from the experiences of the community, more contingent forms of memory gain visibility and relevance.

Remembering Palestine and the events surrounding the expulsion now appears to be unconsciously performed where it may once have been actively relayed. As Karima, a young woman who works in a youth center in the camp succinctly expressed it: "I *know* about the Nakba because I live in Shatila." Another friend, Fatima, who owned a small grocery store, recounted conversations she had had with her father about the humiliating legacy of 1948:

I used to ask my father, "Why did you leave Palestine?" If you don't have a country, you have nothing. He was a simple person who didn't really understand politics and would say, "We left our world behind when we were forced to come to this foreign place." But now when I think of it, I think *we* are the ones who paid for it, not our parents—we carry the pain of the Nakba—the daily suffering, the humiliation, and social oppression—*we're* the ones who have suffered this. I used to tell him, "You didn't know the real value of Palestine—it's we who know this."

Vincent Crapanzano's (2011) study of the "mnemonic communities" of the Algerian Harkis in France, with its analysis of the "wound" passed on to children and grandchildren, is relevant to the Palestinian case in Lebanon. As it became clear that the Harkis would not be able to return to Algeria, due to their collaboration with the French in the Algerian war, memories of this event took on a constitutive role in the construction of a community in exile. Crapanzano argues that the affective dimension of trauma continues to shape the lives of generations that did not suffer it directly. For children and grandchildren, the original "wound" of having been forced to flee is acknowledged yet simultaneously marked by an absence since there is no experiential counterpart for this memory. Similarly, the suffering that second- and third-generation Palestinians experience is of a different order, rooted in the indignities of daily poverty and exclusion. What it means to be Palestinian may be now understood more in terms of existential bonds of suffering than through a connection to the place itself. Memories of the Nakba seem closer to a lived condition, experienced as a process of survival rather than as historical possession.

REMEMBERING AGAINST THE NATIONALIST GRAIN

In the same way that I had expected to find an active narrative tradition of the Nakba (in which, following Sanbar, the intensity of verbal recollection compensates for suffering), I was also surprised to discover that many life stories began in the present and worked their way back to the past and involved a constant shifting of historical registers.[39] At times this took the form of simple comparison—like Umm Saleh's of what Shatila is now with what it used to be. In other instances the temporal shuttling was more complex. When I would sit with Umm Jamal in her son's cake shop on the edge of the camp, she would begin most recollections about her childhood in Jaffa with a pointed qualification: "But as you know, my dear, I am one of those who say enough! Let's put our hand in the hand of Israel—we've suffered too much and we're tired. Let's be realistic. If I'm not going to go back to Jaffa, then at least I want the right to live well here or somewhere else." She rarely spoke to me about the specific events leading to her family's expulsion, or the death of relatives, which I learned about from her niece. Instead, she luxuriated in detailed descriptions of her family's wealth and status in Jaffa. For Umm Jamal, the desire to construct a normative picture of her past, as if to somehow draw it back into her present, trumped the need for accusation and exculpation:[40]

> I remember how in our house we had two different kinds of bathrooms—we had a foreign one and an Arab one—we had lots of rooms. My grandfather was the president of the port, and my father worked with him, and they had three ships and traded with many countries from Addis Ababa to Britain—one time when my father was in England, he had a pain in his head, and he went to the doctor—he couldn't speak much English, so he said "my head hurt" or something like that, and they said he should remove all his teeth and put in false ones, so he did—it cost a lot of money! If only Jamal could fix his teeth, but we don't have the money—look at them; it's awful!

Jamal, her son, has had ongoing problems with his teeth, most of which were broken when the butt of a rifle was smashed into his mouth at an Amal-manned checkpoint during the War of the Camps. He jokingly told me once that he was afraid of going to the dentist in the camp, "because they're so cheap they'd use dogs' teeth for dentures!" Umm Jamal continued:

> But my uncle, now he was *very* educated—he went to the American University in Beirut and studied in schools in Jaffa—he was one of the first people to work at UNRWA. We came here on one of my father's boats—we brought everything with us in boxes the size of this room—the only thing we left behind was the stone for grinding wheat [*jarusheh*] because it was so heavy. We had all our chairs, the old lights—chandeliers—and we had all the pots, from this big to this small [gesturing with her hands]. One cooking pot from my grandfather's wedding was so big you could put two whole sheep in it—his wedding lasted for forty days, and my grandmother wore a *badleh* [wedding costume]—she had five different ones and I would iron them and wear them on the Eid and dance like Cinderella! . . . There were many people on the boat with us—one woman gave birth onboard, so they called the boy Bahr [sea]. They were shooting at us from the port. I still remember how the bullets fell on our heads like stars and the sound they made as they hit the water, like this [she gently taps the table].[41]

In Umm Jamal's stories, references to life in Palestine surfaced as disconnected fragments, and her account of the events of the expulsion hovered awkwardly at the edge of our conversations. Her narrative unfolds with an absence of blame: the Jewish forces attacking Jaffa are not named, and the shooting is mentioned almost as an afterthought. The experience of expulsion seems contingent, even inexplicable, the suffering it entailed deriving from chaotic forces and without meaning. She normalizes and neutralizes a tragic past, lamenting rather than blaming. Indeed, Umm Jamal's emphasis on transformation and continuity seems to outweigh memories of death and violence.[42] It not only falls short of the legal requirements of testimony that focuses on particular events, like Abu Nayef's, but also seems to go against the genre of testimony in which the rhetorical appeal of the particular, of the "self," is given meaning through its relation to the collective.

This ambivalent relation of the "I" to the "we" was a feature of a number of interviews I conducted, both for the video archive and in the course of fieldwork. The Palestinian saying "my story is the story of my people" is subtly undermined by more intimate and circumscribed forms of cultural retrieval. As a point of convergence of collective memory and commemoration, 1948 necessarily becomes a site "in which individuals must come to terms not only with a *prêt-à-porter* past, but also with their relationship to the collectivity in which they find themselves" (Crapanzano 2004, 172). Umm Jamal's experience emphasizes elements of her family's history that are unique; the metaphorical association of the "I" and "we," which appeared so forceful in Abu Nayef's narrative, has been sundered. It suggests a growing ambivalence about practices that salvage Palestinian cultural heritage and align political subjectivities with nationalist goals. The extent to which new forms of collective representation may be emerging is a question I return to later when discussing how younger generations facing different pressures forge their own discourse of identity and belonging.

When I later mentioned the absence of detail about the Nakba in Umm Jamal's stories to Umm Hasan, a mutual friend, she laughed and said that it was because Umm Jamal was from the families of Jaffa (*ahl Yafa*). Umm Hasan, who was then in her late thirties, several generations younger than Umm Jamal, elaborated as follows:

> These people are good at forgetting the past—throwing it away and starting a new life. They live only for the present without thinking about the future. . . . We have a proverb about Jaffa people: "If you have money in your pocket, spend it and God will provide later." . . . Farmers worry about the future and plan for it. City dwellers have different habits from us—I know a woman from Manshiyya who married someone from Jaffa, and she told me that when they had meat— this was during the invasion, so it was hard to get—her husband would say, "Let's eat it all now; don't ration it." But she would always hide some away. One day her husband died while he was working at the port, and she was beside herself because she hadn't made him a big meal the day before. She'd hidden some of the meat away. She always tells me this, saying, "He was right—better to enjoy what you have when you have it." There are differences between us. In 1982 it was the families from Jaffa who were the first to leave the camp. Everyone tried to persuade them to stay—"Who will liberate Palestine if you leave the resistance?" we'd say. The people who stayed to fight were farmers.

Relations between peasants and urbanites, defined by mutual mistrust and prejudice, ultimately shaped even the spatial arrangement of the camps. Julie Peteet has described this mapping of former regional and social divisions into camp space as creating "a physical and social geography of trust" (1995, 174). Few families or village networks, however, have the space or resources to maintain a meeting place (*diwan*) or village hall. These structures of kinship and the cartographic links to Palestine, which organized the camp around "houses" and pre-1948 village boundaries, were largely eroded and replaced by factional spheres of influence, which in turn are now also diminishing. In Umm Hasan's comments we see that the perceived contrast between rural and urban mentalities persists, even taking on a temporal dimension, with urban Jaffans living in the moment, recklessly forgetting past and future, while rural farmers—the true nationalists—conserve the heritage of the past and struggle for future liberation.

The perception that nationalist nostalgia has become increasingly anachronistic and irrelevant to the present hardships of camp life also shaped the way elders responded to the archival project and the invitation to be interviewed. While some were delighted to speak and be filmed, many were unwilling. Their misgivings were sometimes rooted in fear; other times, in what seemed to be a weariness of the duty to recall.[43] "What's the point?" said one eighty-year-old woman I spoke with in Baddawi Camp. "I've done so many interviews now— I've even been on television—what good has it done?" Many we interviewed assumed we were journalists and would begin by berating us for profiting from their stories and for not doing enough to make their voices heard. Our reassurances elicited incredulity ("We've heard that before!" "You'll go back to America and make a film about us and make lots of money," etc.). Such comments reflect a growing impatience with testimonial practices in the camp, and form part of a broader skepticism about researchers and journalists seen to be circulating refugees' stories in arenas beyond their control.

More often, however, reluctance to bear witness reflected a sense that the experiences in question have been cordoned off. A friend's mother who had fled her prosperous home outside Haifa at the age of eleven could not be persuaded to be interviewed. She listened patiently as we tried to justify the importance of the archive—for future generations, for justice, for historical truth—before politely but firmly refusing. Her son, Abu Farah, who was visiting from abroad, was not surprised:

> Whenever I ask her about what happened, she says, "One day, when I am more comfortable." She doesn't want to remember or talk about what happened. Eventually I had to ask my wife's family, who are from the same village. They live near Saida, but outside the camp. It's more relaxed there, so they can talk about things; here every single part of this house or alley reminds my parents of what's gone—a reminder that they try to bury. . . . My mother focuses on us; she worries about us. That's her escape from thinking about the past and maybe the future too. . . .

My grandfather had a huge amount of land, near Haifa, on the side of a mountain, very fertile land, and they built huge houses. Even my mother got an equal share of it along with her brothers because there was such plenty. And then suddenly in one hit they left, leaving everything. And since then my mother has remained an eleven-year-old girl, in a frame, and whatever happens to her now is outside that frame. She brings us inside the frame, but that past is something . . . how to put it. It is the biggest trauma for her. It's like she is looking at the world through a screen, which filters out color and reality—sometimes when I look at her, I feel she is in constant pain.[44]

The paradox at the heart of traumatic experience is that forgetfulness and the breakdown of witnessing are intimately linked to the act of remembrance, since the event is neither fully recalled nor erased.[45] Abu Farah describes how the condition of inhabiting a world made strange by violence—in which one can never again feel "comfortable"—stifles memory, creating what Veena Das describes as a "kind of atmosphere that cannot be expelled to an 'outside'" (2007, 62). For Abu Farah's mother, it is as if the work of mourning cannot be realized, her experiences caught somewhere between memory and forgetting, in a shadowland without distance or perspective. To refuse to speak is to refuse the implicit substitution of words for experience; it also preserves the intimacy of memory by resisting the nationalist imperative to bear public witness.[46]

Abu Farah's account of his mother's silence is synchronic and associative; historical consciousness is embedded in a scarred physical landscape blending past and present.[47] His words reveal the extent to which Shatila's fraught history—and the structures of social and political exclusion that shape refugee existence—have become a continuation of the erasure that began in 1948, blurring the distinctions between past and present suffering: *Every single part of this house or alley reminds my parents of what's gone.* The context of narration inflects memories of 1948, which in turn are filtered through local histories that shape communal life. The Nakba has come to seem more existential than historical, memories of it more lived than stored, and one can begin to see how Sanbar's formulation about the refugees having "gambled everything on taking [Palestine] with them, gradually becoming the temporary replacement of their homeland," is both true and untrue.

Vanished public spaces and increasingly cramped living conditions have affected other shifts in memory practices in the camp, as elders find themselves isolated from their friends and the rest of the community. I would sometimes encounter Abu Nayef sitting by himself on a stool at the entrance of the narrow alley that led to his home, hoping someone he knew would walk by so that he could engage the person in conversation. Whenever I dropped in to see him, he berated me for not visiting more and complained generally of loneliness.

The experience of Abu Aziz, the eighty-three-year-old uncle of a friend, offers another example. After the War of the Camps, his family moved in with other former camp residents in a building outside the camp. Abu Aziz soon grew bored and depressed living away from his friends and began to meet with other elders living in the building; they would sit on the wall facing the street and talk. Within two years, three members of this impromptu sidewalk *diwan* had died, and my friend recounted that, throughout the summer, his uncle had started to sit on the opposite side of the street from the remaining two, outside a barber's shop, on a borrowed chair. Every day Abu Aziz would hang his kaffiyeh over a nearby bush and sit in silence. When his nephew one day asked why he no longer sat with the others, he said that he was tired of listening to them reminisce about Palestine: "No amount of talking will ever bring it back." It is as if the collapse of the social context of memory had precipitated recognition of the impossibility of returning to his village, leaving him to enact remembrance through private ritual, defiantly unattached to any political agenda. The expression of willed forgetting relies, paradoxically, on remembrance, since one can consciously forget only that which has been recuperated from oblivion.[48] Remembrance is neither opposed to forgetfulness (since they are interwoven), nor is it the solution to his predicament. Although Abu Aziz may refuse to speak about the past, he is not "forgiving and forgetting" and believes that justice—to his mind, the true opposite of oblivion—will be done. "There will come a day when all this has to stop," he told me. "It can't go on as it is now; God will see to it."

In much of the recent literature on memory, forgetting is a weakness, and commemoration—with its attendant practices of intergenerational transmission, storytelling, and so on—ennobling, richly symbolic, and associated with well-being and recovery. In her study of mortuary exchanges among the Sabarl Islanders of Papua New Guinea, Debbora Battaglia argues that theories of memory need to accommodate "forgetting as willed transformation of memory"—in terms not of loss but of its own constructive force.[49] Battaglia describes how Sabarl funerary rites deliberately forget the dead in order to allow for creation of new memories and identities, unburdened by the weight of ancestors. The forms of "forgetting" I encountered in Shatila differed in that they were private and noninstitutional, a response to the erosion of the social and spatial environment that invested particular memories with meaning. The cumulative effect of these acts, however, is no less significant than the ritual displays Battaglia encountered, because they contribute to the restructuring of collective memory and identity in the community and to the way refugees orient themselves toward past and future.

I was struck by a similar willingness to forget when I joined a group from Shatila in 2004—all originally from Khalisa—when they went to the border to celebrate and mark the liberation of the south. Khalisa, now called Kiriyat Shmona, is clearly visible from various vantage points near Fatima's Gate, and at one point we made out what may have been the home of one elderly woman in our group. It was the first time she had been to the border, having been too ill to travel in 2000, and I was surprised to note that the experience evoked not sad memories but joy. She was delighted to see her house and village, and in the car on the way home she kept smiling and saying that Palestine was even more beautiful than she had remembered. Later, when describing the outing to her granddaughter, she said she felt she could now die in peace, having seen her home again. It was as if in saying this, she was commenting on her relation to the past, to her village, to Palestine as something very important but also, quietly, finished. What seems at first resigned acceptance, or forgetting, might better be understood as the serenity that marks the completion of mourning. Experiences like this trip to the border, or Abu Aziz's enacted ritual, appear to free energies previously invested in marking absence and prolonging "poisonous knowledge" within the community (Das 2007, 76).

The sheer variety of mnemonic stances in relation to Palestine casts doubt on the familiar notion of a community held together by the imperative to transmit, preserve, and restore the homeland in memory while holding fast for retributive justice. These stances are "antiphonal" (A. Feldman 2004, 176), alternating between individual and collective, between duty to recall and desire to forget, between speech and silence, sorrow and joy. These ambivalent discourses of memory and collective meaning making do not fit extant paradigms for public witness, which presume that a narrative of "what happened" can be communicated and documented. My initial concern that the suffering and loss of 1948 needed to be measured and documented—transmuted into material for political advocacy—presupposed an ontological and existential consensus about the past and the need to bear witness to it. I was surprised—initially even disappointed—when I discovered that this need to bear witness to 1948 was not foregrounded in refugee narratives, but I came to see that be-

neath this apparent lacuna lay a richness of mnemonic alternatives, complicating the binary of victimization and agency, prompting recognition of more
complex and ambiguous processes of semiosis and social action. These alternative registers of remembrance suggest other means of coming to terms with
the past, and other ways of imagining the future, than those that our own desires for justice might envisage.

TRANSMISSION AND TRANSFORMATION AMONG SHATILA'S YOUTH

What of the younger generations of refugees in Shatila? What role does the
Nakba play in their lives? The dialectical tensions at the heart of renascent nationalist interest in the history of 1948 were laid bare during an event I helped
organize in Shatila to mark Nakba Day in May 2004. With the help of a local
NGO we mounted a screen against one of the buildings near the main entrance
to the camp, squeezed between large posters of two Hamas leaders, Shaykh
Ahmad Yassine and Abdel Aziz Rantisi, put up after their assassinations by the
Israelis in March and April of that year. The proximity of the screen to these
images proved confusing, with passersby initially thinking the event was organized by Hamas.

The films we had selected—a collection of documentaries, interviews, and
features about Palestine and the history of 1948—were to be shown over two
evenings. For the opening night we had chosen a series of six 15-minute excerpts
from interviews that we had filmed with elders in the camp about their memories of Palestine. The elders had enthusiastically encouraged us, and we thought
the interviews would be of interest to their families and the community more
generally. A small group of about twenty people gathered—mainly the stars of
the show and their friends—perched on plastic chairs or watching from the balconies that overlooked the street. Kids sat on the hoods of parked cars, enjoying the novelty of street cinema, if not altogether gripped by the subject matter.

About ten minutes into the first interview with Umm Waseem, Muhammad
Hasanayn—the brother of Hasan Hasanayn, who, with Shadi Anas of Burj al-
Barajneh Camp, was killed in a demonstration at the border in October 2000—
approached me and asked when we were planning to show "the film about
Hasan." I explained that the idea of the event was to commemorate the events
of 1948. At this point I had to leave to get an extension cable for the projector.
When I returned five minutes later, I found that a large crowd had gathered
and that the tape had been changed. Instead of Umm Waseem talking about
the air attack on her village of Sufsaf, we were now watching news footage from

Al-Manar (Hezbollah's TV station) of the demonstration in which Hasan was killed. Among the chanting protesters projected above our heads were recognizable faces from the camp—lobbing stones and scurrying away from the clouds of tear gas; some of the more fearless could be seen trying to climb the wire fence. Panicking Israeli soldiers on the other side fired bullets, and in the ensuing confusion of running bodies and blood two protestors were killed and about fifteen wounded. The footage then cut to images from the camp: Hasan's distraught mother and grieving family, lines of people coming to pay their respects, a funeral procession in which several thousand mourners marched, carrying Hasan's coffin through the streets on a wave of anger.

Among those gathered, some were animatedly pointing out friends and relatives, while others cursed the Israeli jeeps darting across the screen; many were moved to tears. The mood was somber and focused, in stark contrast to the distraction of the crowd when we projected the first interview. The tension and grief were palpable, and it was clear that both practically and symbolically, the Nakba had been upstaged by more recent events in the camp's memory. "Look how many more people there are now," Mohammed said to me as I returned. "People are not interested in watching old people talk about the past—besides, we've heard all these stories before." Turning to Mahmud, a friend who had helped organize the event, he added, "I'd rather be watching Umm Kulthoum than these old guys!" After the event I hung around talking with friends who, as they put it, had "come to support me" because of my involvement with the screening. They were not surprised that the event had not drawn a crowd, noting how few people had even remarked on the significance of the day.

The screening deepened my doubts regarding the significance of institutional commemoration of 1948, suggesting that it may be widening rather than narrowing the gap between nationalist history and subjective memory in the community. The overall response to the event was mildly factionalized boredom. The hijacking of the evening's program, however, suggests how acts of public remembrance bring personal and collective memory into dialogue. The solidarity generated by scenes of riot and demonstration was presumably a function of the audience's active involvement in those events, in contrast to its heavily mediated—and overdetermined—historical distance from the Nakba. One friend said to me after the screening, "People like to remember how they felt at this time. There was a lot of hope in the camp then."

Younger generations born and raised in the diaspora are finding it difficult to absorb originary narratives as part of their own identity or as a frame for national belonging. Commemoration's political impetus—the felt need to be seen to be salvaging the histories and cultural heritage of Palestine (particularly in the presence of foreign researchers and journalists)—now exceeds the community's appetite for it. I came to appreciate this growing disconnect through my friendships with second- and third-generation refugees. Nidal, a young man working as a teacher in an UNRWA school in Shatila, expressed a feeling of historical claustrophobia he associates with the demand for commemoration:

> Although we are still living the results of the Nakba, my generation didn't experience it, and I refuse to inherit it. . . . When I think of the Nakba and how Palestine used to be, I don't think of it as just some beautiful place where people sat under the trees eating fruit; I think of it as a normal life that I was not part of. When I hear elders who lived the Nakba talk about it, and the things they experienced, I sympathize with them, but sympathy changes. My memories are different from my father's, and my problems are different from his also. It's as if all we need know is the slogan "Palestine is ours"—but to really feel that you are from a place, you need to know it. I've learned about Palestine, but I know and love Lebanon—there's a difference of experience. There is much about our history here that remains hidden and ignored—for instance, why did it take us so long to start a resistance here? We have to ask ourselves this. Why, even after the revolution [PLO] came here, did we fail to liberate Palestine?

The expectation that younger generations should keenly miss something they themselves have not lost firsthand has affected them in unacknowledged ways; it is producing flickers of quiet personal resistance ("I refuse to inherit it"). Recognition of this throws into question the efficacy of reviving nationalist discourse through idealized descriptions of life in Palestine, what Mohammed Bamyeh calls a mythological "deep time" (2003, 836). Nidal suggests that this highlighting of 1948 may provoke a sense of frustration among second- and third-generation refugees who have developed their own forms of rootedness and belonging in Lebanon.[50] For younger generations wary of it, fetishization of the national entity as a "beautiful place where people sat under the trees eating fruit," with Palestine signified synecdochically through a kind of prelapsarian pastoralism, has produced a different, albeit derivative and self-conscious, sense of solidarity.[51] Here again one senses the referential dissonance of a nationalist discourse out of sync with local and national realities. Nidal's reference to the PLO's failure to liberate Palestine also points to an intellectual shift taking place, in which critical assessment of the past supersedes nostalgic reminiscence. There is a generational backlash in the making, against a Palestinian history that has obscured politically sensitive chapters of violence and loss in Lebanon, especially those that foreground the divisive ineptitude of the PLO.[52]

Nidal went on to note that parents of some of his UNRWA students had expressed similar concerns that the emphasis on what Palestine *was* and what Shatila *is not* in many school- and NGO-organized activities—intended to ensure generational continuity of identity in relation to lost homeland—is making it harder for children to acknowledge or appreciate the strengths of their own community:

> In the NGO where my wife was working in Shatila, children were being told to draw pictures of Palestine rather than things from their own experiences, because these are the kind of activities that get money. . . . It is as if all Palestinians here have to have the same memory, and the same perspective on who we are or how to resist. Now when I talk about Palestine, it makes me sad, because I start to feel as if I am lying too.

A further unsettling aspect of the factional and NGO-fed Nakba industry is that it effectively bypasses the very members of the community who directly experienced the event in question. Most commemorative activities in the camp are directed at youth and rarely involve the participation of camp elders (the home visits to Abu Nayef and other residents mentioned earlier are exceptional in this regard, and more often for the benefit of visitors to the camp). Instead of catalyzing critical discussion of the past across generations, these cultural activities appear to be transmitting a static and reified historical inheritance, one in which "imagined nostalgia" trumps the messiness of lived experience (Appadurai 1996, 77). Although the phenomenon of internationally subsidized activities in the camps is viewed by many refugees as a troubling form of business, it is one that reveals their pragmatic economic agency. The simplified narrative of 1948 works far better than the ethical quagmire of present reality in attracting foreign investment in the very institutions—schools, cultural centers, local NGOs, and so on—that have come to form the locus of social agency for refugees. While these commemorations clearly do have resonance for refugees, they should also be understood in materialist terms, as part of the economic pragmatics of everyday life, and not merely as a form of political claims making and cultural transmission.

Palestinians of Nidal's generation often do not "refuse" the legacy of the Nakba so much as transform it. The introduction of the Internet and satellite television to the camp, which roughly coincided with the start of the Al-Aqsa Intifada in 2000, has enabled diverse forms of community to be created online, less bound by village or kin or even nation. The rise of Islamism has also contributed to this shift from village and land to a form of supranationalism. While social media has provided Palestinian youth across the diaspora with virtual *diwan*s, it is less clear that online communities are establishing durable new forms of transnational belonging within the Palestinian diaspora, as is sometimes claimed (Khalili 2004, 11). My own (albeit infrequent) forays into Shatila's Internet cafés suggest that the online networks camp youth create are more concerned with consolidating their local social networks within the camp; indeed, Internet cafés represent one of the few places where teenagers meet and hang out, suggesting that they may be more like real *diwan*s than virtual ones. This is not to suggest that the Internet is not mediating the formation and expression of political identity but rather to guard against wide-eyed claims that it has ushered in a new era of cross-border political activism and transnational identification among camp youth.[53]

That said, the friendships formed online are sometimes surprising. Hasan, a young man in his twenties, spends much of his day in a Yahoo chat room and is in regular contact with an Israeli man, his peer, living in Haifa—the city from which his family originates. Through this relationship, and others formed with Palestinians in Brazil, London, and Detroit, as well as the OPT, Hasan has established his own complex and idiosyncratic form of attachment to a Palestinian community, the keynote of which is apolitical, and the tenor far removed from the territorial attachments of his grandparents' generation.

The role of new media suggests the emergence of a more synchronic and associative form of historical consciousness. Satellite television, like the Internet, is not simply a new mode of transmitting history and memory but seems actually to be reshaping them. A television program produced by Al-Manar, *Yatadhakkarun* (They remember), which invited first-generation refugees to recall their lives in Palestine, would often provoke discussion and debate and, in a few cases, actually encouraged youths to revisit this period of history by directly engaging the memories of their grandparents. I noted with some irony, however, that friends' children often appeared more at ease watching these narratives on the television than listening to them in their own homes. If the kind of richly embodied transmission of history traditionally assumed to be the core of Palestinian refugee experience is in fact on the wane, it is being rapidly replaced by an iconic shorthand, one that more often than not finds its locus in mass media. While televising these narratives on programs like *Yatadhakkarun* may—by removing them from their "natural" familial setting—create new mass communities around them, questions arise about the depth and durability of these communities (Allan 2005).

THE POLITICS OF WITNESS

I return briefly to the house of Umm Jamal. During one of my last visits before returning to the United States, I met her youngest son, Mahmud, who was sitting drinking coffee with his friend Faruq. Twenty-two years old at the time, Mahmud worked in a factory about an hour outside Beirut. He had just returned from work and invited me to join him for coffee while I waited for his mother to return. Having heard about the archival project, he asked several questions and then burst in on my reply with barely concealed frustration: "What's the point of your research?" As I tried to stumble into an answer, he cut me off:

> What will come of this for us? Foreigners like you come to the camp and do research. They ask us questions about the past, about the Nakba, who died, what we felt, about the massacre, about our sadness, and it's like it's a thrill for them. We cry and they profit from our tears, but things stay the same for us. The electricity is still shit, we have no rights, and this kind of thing just makes us suffer more. For this reason I don't think any research people like you do will make a difference. Okay, so it's true that many people here don't know the history of Palestine; I think we should try to solve this through better education. But the problem is that people don't really care anymore, and they don't have the time to care. All we do now is think about survival—this kills our desire to improve ourselves. We don't have time to think about our culture or our history; we are dying in this struggle simply to exist. . . . I believe that after two years there will be no more Palestinians here. I am taking an Australian passport [through a recent marriage to an Australo-Lebanese living there, whom he met online], and my friend Faruq is getting a German passport through his marriage to his cousin there—so you see, soon it will all be gone.

Like Nidal, Mahmud has both intellectual and visceral misgivings about the voyeurism of much institutionalized engagement with the community's past suffering, what might be called "an unwanted parody of genuine witnessing" (Weine 1999, 183). I heard many versions of this claim that focusing on the Nakba obscures both the suffering presently experienced by refugees and the source of that suffering. The expectation that increased interest on the part of the international community leads ineluctably to amelioration of conditions is being supplanted by cynicism about "empty talk" (*haki fadi*) with foreign researchers and activists. There is a perception that much of the research on the camps has created an economy of victimhood, one in which suffering associated with the expulsion in 1948 and the massacre in 1982 are legal tender, indeed, earn interest, while everyday suffering linked to poverty, political disenfranchisement, and social exclusion in Lebanon are of ephemeral value, like stamp scrip.

These angry interventions by Nidal, Mahmud, and others forced me to reconsider the implications—for their generation in particular—of producing an archive in which remembrance and witnessing are framed in such exclusive terms. Not only does it necessarily create a hierarchy of admissible and inadmissible memory; it also assumes a set of criteria for what forms of suffering have the power to interpellate witnesses. What struck me most forcibly about their comments were the uncomfortable questions they raise about what I—as a privileged Westerner—was doing recording these traumatic pasts or trying to bring subaltern histories into view. Both Nidal and Mahmud suggest that in Shatila people do not have the luxury to judge or blame; their duty is survival. If we probe the origins of the "thrill" Mahmud speaks of, what do we find? He suggests that the very people who purport to be trying to alleviate their suffering—activists, scholars, researchers, NGO and aid workers—may be the very ones minting and circulating this currency of symbolic violence. The use of testimony as a means of mobilizing solidarity has created a troubling situation in which intimate and painful memories are authenticated by "making their interiority ever more present, as if experiences were commodities that were being advertised" (Kleinman and Kleinman 1997, 4). By documenting histories of violence and suffering in marginalized communities, are we—as we often claim—introducing the possibility of real change in people's lives? Or are we just easing our own consciences, indulging in what Luc Boltanski calls a "politics of pity" (1999, 3)? Allen Feldman (2004), in his analysis of the role violence plays in "theaters" of witnessing, argues that the validity of these acts depends as much on the violence of the signifier as the signified; it depends, in other words, upon the processes by which we, as activists, scholars, and public intellectuals, authenticate certain moments of historical memory, or rank some forms of violence and suffering above others, through expert knowledge, truth-claiming procedures, and mass media.

Faruq, who had been sitting silently, playing with Mahmud's niece, joined the discussion:

> Ever since I was young, I wanted to be a poet—and I can realize this dream, not like Mahmud who wanted to be a doctor but is not permitted to practice here. I keep my strength by going on. I have tried to focus on my education because I feel that I will get another nationality. I don't want to ignore my nationality as a Palestinian, but I know that it is impossible for me to return to Jaffa, and I don't want to go to the West Bank or Gaza, so why keep talking about this? I am sure that I can do many things if I get German citizenship.

Faruq's comments, like Mahmud's, suggest that the potential for change generated by an increasingly heterogeneous community has been left untapped by a moribund form of communal solidarity invoking a monolithic, reified culture and past. Both Mahmud and Faruq are clearly invested in the lives they hope are about to begin for them elsewhere. (It is as if the idea of emigration has become a new myth of wholeness replacing the one with which they were brought up.) The form of refugee identity and aspiration codified in slogans like al-ʿAwda (return) is reductive, effacing agency and diversity of opinion. While for first-generation refugees "return" means return to a physical place that has been experienced and lost, Faruq's generation appears to understand it in more abstract terms: the restoration of dignity and justice, the right to respect oneself and to be respected (Bamyeh 2003, 841). Remembrance and bearing witness, oriented as it is toward "truth telling," must accommodate these new political identities and conflicting viewpoints.

While the political objectives of legal accountability, justice, and restitution may lie at the heart of much of the work being done on memories of the Nakba, collective memory cannot be reduced to formula. It necessarily comprises a constellation of personal experiences, and as such is dynamic, consisting of conflicting temporalities and impulses. In the case of Palestinians in Shatila, memory is configured both within and between generations, creating spaces of remembrance marked by renewal and adaptation. Comments by Umm Mahmud, Nidal, Mahmud, Faruq, Abu Farah, and countless others I have not quoted, have forced me to reflect on my own interest in documenting the history of the catastrophe, what it means to bear witness, and the politics that inform commemorative practice in this context. There is clearly a need for scholars and activists working in camp communities to move beyond the coercive harmony of a national identity rooted in past history in order to include emergent forms of subjectivity, and there is a need to recognize that these new forms may privilege individual aspiration over collective, nationalist imperatives. Exclusively fore-grounding the need to bear witness to the violent history of 1948 threatens not only to obscure from view seemingly more mundane though equally devastat-ing present-day suffering; it also elides the creative ways in which refugees deal with a traumatic past, their hopes for the future, and the new subject positions they are articulating in relation to it. All of these were memorably expressed by Nidal during the twentieth-anniversary commemorations for the Sabra and Shatila massacre in September 2002, when he led a group of students in the march to the burial grounds, wearing T-shirts that read, "We are still alive."

The perceived need to revivify attachments to a Palestinian homeland through political commemoration comes, not coincidentally, at a time when the connection between refugees within the diaspora and Palestinians within the territories is at its most tenuous. The palpable ambivalence about ritualized remembrance, particularly among younger generations, suggests growing un-certainty about what binds them to a lost homeland, as well as about fundamen-tal issues of kinship and belonging within Shatila, the subject of the next chapter.

Morning coffee, Shatila camp. Photograph © Hisham Ghuzlan, 2008.

2 ECONOMIC SUBJECTIVITY AND EVERYDAY SOLIDARITIES

IN FEBRUARY 2005, several months after I had returned to the United States, I received a call from a friend in Shatila telling me that Umm Ali, the mother of Umm Mahmud, had died. This was sad news but not wholly unexpected. While I had lodged with the Hasan family, Umm Ali had contracted a severe kidney infection that left her dependent on dialysis and weekly visits to a clinic in Sidon, some forty kilometers south of Beirut. Her illness proved a huge strain on the family, who struggled with the costs of her treatment. Although the financial burden was ultimately borne by siblings living abroad, the labor of looking after Umm Ali fell largely to Umm Mahmud, who tended to her mother with great diligence and care.

When I called Umm Mahmud to offer my condolences, she described the difficulties she and her siblings had experienced as they tried to gather funds for Umm Ali's hospitalization and burial. Her grief was mixed with anger at the logistical and financial hurdles they had faced securing care for their mother in those final weeks. Because Umm Ali was in her late seventies when she became ill, she was ineligible for financial aid from UNRWA, which assists only those under sixty in situations of chronic illness. "We say here sixty is the year of death," Umm Mahmud explained bitterly. "If you get sick and you're elderly, you're done for." The task of paying medical bills therefore fell to family members, who were compelled to draw on various overlapping support networks.

Even though the family was fortunate in having wealthier relatives abroad who were willing to cover the bulk of Umm Ali's hospital fees, the bills for her biweekly outpatient dialysis sessions, medications, and specialist referrals were paid by her immediate kin in Lebanon. Those who had savings drew on them, and others took loans from friends, employers, and neighbors. A number of strategic visits were made to the offices of various political factions and NGOs to which the family had ties, in the hopes that they might also contribute. This search for funds in the end produced complex, overlapping webs of support, linking individuals to institutions, and family and friends in Shatila to relatives in other camps in Lebanon, and as far afield as Ohio, Denmark, and Germany— a reminder that long-distance attachments and the flow of remittances from abroad both extend and destabilize clear-cut boundaries of communal solidarity.

Umm Ali's illness and death reactivated kinship ties within the extended family but also exposed latent tensions and the burden of kin obligations for poor households. The various efforts to procure resources culminated in a confrontation between different branches of the family when opposing networks allied to rival political factions both claimed credit for securing financial support. The rift over the form of care Umm Ali should receive and the hospital in which she should be treated fueled other family tensions, as the opinions of wealthier siblings contributing more from abroad appeared to take precedence over those of family in Lebanon.[1] The instances of prevarication and resistance Umm Mahmud and her two sisters encountered as they sought aid from relatives were evidence of the strain that prolonged insecurity and destitution place on both the discursive and material fabric of kinship; in circumstances like these, poor relatives often find themselves unable to behave in ways consistent with the cultural norms and social obligations expected of kin. Umm Mahmud's account of the preceding months cast doubt not only on the presumptive primacy of kinship networks in dealing with unexpected crises such as illness and death but also on their efficacy for day-to-day survival in Shatila.

With scarcity necessitating a greater degree of financial calculation, even among relatives, economic considerations sometimes seemed as important as moral and affective ones. Having kin no longer assured everyday survival and, in some instances, even seemed to increase vulnerability. Umm Mahmud's experiences were by no means unique. In the course of my research I was often told of the strategies by which relatives would try to avoid financial obligations to each other; of disputes between family members about the allocation of scarce resources; of wives who concealed savings from their spouses, fearing they might be squandered or that their husbands would contribute less to household expenses.

Competing claims on dwindling reserves have introduced difficult choices: Should one treat an ailing father who cannot work or the injury of a son who can? Should one put money aside to pay for the university education of the child who is gifted, and whose earning potential might improve the family's security in the long-term, or spread limited resources over several children? Because family and kin have been for so long the unquestioned foundation of communal life (idealized as Palestinian culture's source of strength and resilience in the face of displacement and dispossession, and inextricably intertwined with nationalist ideology), these trade-offs and tensions revolving around the distribution of resources in kin networks vividly underscore the precariousness of existence and the uncertainties of moral life.[2]

The perception that poverty is undermining the customs that once allowed communal ties and traditional solidarities to be maintained and publicly performed is widespread, and many regard the social, moral, and political costs as unacceptable. Friends described the feeling of being a stranger in the camp, with familiar faces and ways of life having disappeared. The displacement of Shatila's founding families (*ahl al-mukhayyam*) during the civil war in the 1980s, high rates of emigration, and a majority non-Palestinian presence together have contributed to the view that Shatila is no longer a camp in the sense that it was in the 1960s and 1970s, when everyone knew everyone else. As one friend put it, the camp has been transmogrified into a "jungle." While life in Shatila has always been shaped by uncertainty and economic strain, the chaos and precariousness today are often compared to the relative stability and plenty of the civil war years when the PLO leadership was based in Beirut.

Even for younger generations who did not experience the heady days of revolution, the PLO's departure in 1982 continues to be seen as the turning point in the fortunes of refugees in Lebanon, marking the onset of radical political and economic instability. A decade of institution building, prosperity, and intoxicating possibility ended in a bitter hangover. Refugees found themselves without support and subject to ever-tightening legal restrictions and diminished job prospects. In the post-Oslo period refugees in Lebanon were dealt a further blow with the reallocation of resources to the self-rule areas of the West Bank and Gaza under the newly created Palestinian Authority, which along with UNRWA's growing budget deficit diminished the safety nets on which refugees could count.

The fate of Shatila's village associations is symptomatic of the impact these macrolevel changes have had on the microdomains of everyday life. Once considered an important economic safety net and mechanism of social control, particularly in the wake of the PLO's evacuation from Beirut, only two of the six associations now remain. These belong to the families of Majd al-Krum and Dayr al-Qasi; only the former continues to have a fund (*sanduq al-balad*) to which members can apply for support in times of need.[3] Up until the War of the Camps (1985–1988), these associations and "committees" (*lijan*) provided economic security for village members and represented a powerful political force in the camp. Built on kin ties, they were an effective mechanism for redistributing resources, solving disputes, and providing public spaces for funerals and marriages (Sayigh 1994; J. Suleiman 1999). Similarly, there are no longer any functioning public meeting places where male elders can gather to socialize. Like village associations, the *diwan* helped to preserve the authority of family elders and village notables (*wujaha*), and fellaheen values more generally. When I asked why there were no functioning *diwan*s, one man responded jokingly that now people only talk about each other and not to each other. He explained that the cost of renting a hall (*qa'a*) and maintaining a meetinghouse was too great and there were no longer enough members to make it viable. The demise of these cultural institutions is one example of the ways that transformations in Shatila's political economy—and its increasingly diverse and transient population—have weakened the ethos of "moral familism" that formed the basis for social and political cohesion, tethering individuals to kin and community.[4]

My conversations with Umm Mahmud in the following months were revealing for what they said not only about the contours of kinship and care within the Hasan family but also about communal solidarity in the camp more generally. "How can we spend our days thinking about our village [in Palestine] when we do not know if we can feed our children?" Umm Mahmud asked me, twisting her hands together nervously. "My mother told me when there was nothing to eat, people would put rocks in the pot and stir them so the children would think there was food. This is how we are living. Many people don't have money to buy bread." Then, pointing to a woman passing in the street below, she added, "Give this woman $1,000 and she'll forget she's a Palestinian. Offer her a visa to Denmark and she'll leave the camp without looking back."

Admittedly, comments that pitted collective national struggle against the exigencies of everyday survival were often made for rhetorical effect. Refugees do not see the solution to their predicament in purely economic terms; they have political aspirations and seek recognition of their rights and their identity as Palestinians, and to suggest otherwise diminishes the significance of their long struggle for self-determination and their deep attachment to Palestine. However, these sentiments point to a zero-sum logic taking hold, as refugees find themselves compelled to balance the material needs of family against the claims of the national movement, which since the relocation of the Palestinian political leadership—first to Tunis and then to the OPT—seems increasingly distant and abstract.[5]

Umm Mahmud was not alone in her efforts to reorient my attention to the pressing material struggles of refugees. Most of my close friends lived on incomes below the official poverty line (estimated at roughly $2 per day in 2005), and for them deprivation was a way of life. "We are alive for want of death" ('ayishin min illit al-mawt), one often hears uttered with ironic resignation. I was struck by the pervasive talk of money, ranging from anxious discussion of a price hike in basic foods to the more desperate question of how to fund an emergency operation for a sick relative. Preoccupation with household expenses, savings strategies, access to resources, and establishment of reliable support networks represented more than a general comment on economic insecurity; it shed light on the extent to which the struggle to subsist has become part of the fabric of social, political, and moral life. Economic exclusion and poverty represent more than an austere backdrop to camp life; they are, arguably, the conditions that now constitute it. The various forms of material and monetary exchange (gifts, loans, credit, charity, and so on), which poor families in Shatila have come to rely on, delimit both positively and negatively how refugees sustain different forms of community and inform how continuity is realized (rather than idealized). They also reveal the extent to which the persons central to these relations of dependency and mutual support are increasingly not family members but friends and neighbors.

This chapter discusses how refugees in Shatila meet basic needs and secure material and emotional support, both day to day and in moments of crisis. While transformations in Shatila's political economy may be undermining certain customary relations, these conditions are also generating new forms of sociality and support motivated by the imperative of economic survival and by an ethics of care rooted in the shared experience of privation. With kin ties no longer ipso facto integrated into networks of reciprocal exchange, households are cultivating wider networks of dependency that provide material and affective support—a transformation with wide-ranging implications for how we understand both coping strategies in camp communities and identity and belonging in this context. On the one hand, it seems that traditional mechanisms of support—centered on village and clan ties—are being superseded by something inchoate. On the other hand, within this inchoateness, older structures of relatedness and solidarity linger like an afterimage and continue to inform social relations and moral life. Drawing on the experiences of three individuals in Shatila, I consider how refugees are responding to these changes, the means by which they negotiate inclusion in economic and moral support networks, and the social and political relations emerging at this intersection of need.

RELUCTANT RECIPROCITY

In the months following Umm Ali's death the conflicts between Umm Mahmud and her sisters escalated as they quarreled over how their mother's illness had been treated and over care for their father, who now lived alone. Because Umm Mahmud lived closest to Abu Ali—within shouting distance—she invariably tended to his daily needs. Umm Mahmud cleaned and cooked for Abu Ali every day, made sure to bring him foods he liked, made coffee for visitors, and kept him company for long stretches in the afternoons and evenings. From the vantage point of my room on the roof, I would often see them sitting together in the early evening or standing on the adjoining balcony conversing with neighbors. Her care entailed a sacrifice of time and resources she felt went unappreciated by her siblings, including a sister who seldom saw their father even though her workplace was near his house, and even by Abu Ali himself, who seemed to expect more than she could give.

By the time I returned in the summer, Umm Mahmud had begun to chafe at the mounting responsibilities and complained she had no time for herself or her children. Friction over family obligations had grown in the intervening months, and she blamed her sisters for not taking their duties seriously, preferring instead to leave the work to her. "There is no feeling of honor [*ma fi nakhwa*] or reciprocity [*al-tabaduliyya*] between us anymore," she lamented, gesturing vaguely in the direction of her father's house. "Before, people would say a family who cooks and eats together is blessed. Each person would bring something and help the others [*al-baraka aktar iza bnakul ma' ba' d. Kul wahad lazim yijib*]." Her perception that an ethic of reciprocal care had disappeared from family life was intensified by the critical remarks her sisters made about her four-year-old son, Saleh, who they believed was being corrupted by days spent playing with older boys in Shatila's alleys. "How can they say these things to me when it is *my* hard work that permits them to work and spend more time with their own families?" she protested.

Although Umm Mahmud's critique of her sisters' negligence was largely defensive, and a way of rhetorically distinguishing her own commitment to

family, it pointed to the particular pressures brought to bear by kin obligations and a desire to set limits on investment in family relations. It also highlighted the perceived tension between idealized depictions of modern family
life and more traditional renderings of kin relations associated with clan and
home (*dar, bayt*). Her frustration was not directed only at siblings who did not
give enough but also at herself. Privately, she questioned why, unlike her sisters,
she did not put her own interests and those of her immediate family first. She
did not have the time to search for work to supplement the family's income and
was envious of both the career her elder sister had made for herself as an NGO
coordinator and the security and independence this brought. It was clear Umm
Mahmud saw this conflict with her sisters as part of a broader shift in social
and familial relations in the camp: she felt that trust and reciprocity between
relatives was being undermined by self-interest, and the obligations of kinship
often seemed exploitative, serving to deepen rather than alleviate vulnerability.
Elders were no longer able to exert control or resolve family feuds as they once
had, which for her was both a symptom and cause of friction in her own family. "Before, people used to look after one another [*'abal al-nas kanu ymunu 'ala
ba'd*]," she explained, emphasizing the important role elders had played in mediating family disputes and the protection and support they afforded.

Given that kin ties have, historically, been fraught with antagonisms (Peteet
1987; Sayigh 1979), Umm Mahmud's perception that harmonious family relations were unraveling was perhaps in part nostalgia for an ideal that has never
existed. Indeed, her comments often seemed paradoxical: sometimes she ex-
tolled the virtues of the "modern" nuclear family, where emancipated women
worked, emphasizing the need for greater autonomy from coercive kin ties that
hampered social advancement; at other times, she spoke of feeling a keen ethical obligation to care for her father and yearned for a lost harmony in familial
relations, when bonds appeared strong and uncompromised. Her ambivalence
seemed to reflect her own uncertainty of how to be an independent woman,
good daughter, wife, and mother and the difficulties involved in navigating the
contradictions between these different roles and responsibilities.[6]

As Umm Mahmud's relations with her siblings and father grew more
fraught, Shatila itself came to seem like a morally inert space that was deplet-
ing her resources. She felt it had become unlivable and would wander bordering neighborhoods looking for apartments she could ill afford. She longed for
greater privacy, and the idea of home as a space free from the interference of extended family, where she could focus on the needs of her children, had become

something of an obsession. Umm Mahmud began to depend more heavily on friends and neighbors and for about three months stopped visiting family altogether—a move clearly intended to reestablish boundaries of expectation between her and her siblings. When she went to the market, she would leave her youngest son in the care of her neighbor Huda; in return she would buy groceries for Huda or stop by later in the day with food she had cooked. They would often have morning coffee, when they sought advice or helped each other with household chores. Choosing to spend time with friends and neighbors was also a method of asserting greater autonomy and withdrawing—albeit temporarily—from the seemingly infinite duties of caring for her father. She felt she could talk openly about her concerns with friends in a way that had come to seem impossible with family and was confident in the advice and support she received. On one occasion, her spirits buoyed by a visit from a neighbor, she exclaimed, exuberantly, "True friends [sadaqa mazbuta] are dearer than brothers [a'zz min al-ikhweh]; they aren't opportunistic [ma fi maslaha], and there are no false compliments [ma fi mujamalat]. Friends help you in ways family can't."

Clearly, neighborly relations have always played an important role in camp life. However, Umm Mahmud's conscious retreat to this type of relation, as a way of renegotiating the limits of familial responsibility, offered insight into the room for maneuver and critical reflection these alternative networks create. The affective and material support Umm Mahmud received during this period sustained her and renewed her faith in community, as the knots in ethical relations with family were worked out. Everyday reciprocal gestures, and the subtle ethic of care that informed them, were made meaningful again through relatedness and belonging. While the assistance of friends and neighbors seemed to promise deliverance from the suffocating entanglements of kin, it was also clear these relationships were themselves modeled on family ties. Indeed, Umm Mahmud would often use the idiom of kin when speaking of them, reintroducing the affective dimension of kinship at the very moment when, in her mind, these ties were being superseded. Referring to her female friends as ukhti (sister) generated intimacy and allegiance and lent weight to friendships that, in actuality, were far more provisional. Although khalti (aunt) and ukhti are common terms of endearment in Arab culture, her use of them not only strengthened ties and facilitated a more liberal exchange of resources in moments of need but also gestured to the way in which these relations were sanctified through the ideal of kin.[7]

During the months that followed, Umm Mahmud's small living room was frequently filled with women who had stopped by, some simply to chat and drink coffee and others with a specific request—often the use of her refrigerator or washing machine. The loosening of established structures of relation and support had allowed new ones to form and flourish. Umm Mahmud's door was always open, and women would drift in and out with what seemed to me, at times, a relentless regularity. On busy days as many as five women might gather and linger for the better part of the morning, as conversation moved seamlessly from local gossip and marital problems, to dreams, camp politics, assistance programs, employment opportunities, or where the best deals were to be had in Sabra market. These gatherings also functioned as conduits for detailed knowledge about the financial status of different households in the neighborhood and the needs of specific families as they arose. It enabled women to learn more about each other's resources, to solicit assistance, and to gauge the willingness of friends and neighbors to lend support.[8] Moments of crisis tested the efficacy of these networks, their responsiveness, and reach. Unexpected events— the onset of illness, death, or job loss—revealed who could be relied upon, as seemingly slight social ties rapidly thickened into more substantial forms of assistance, or fell away.

When the child of Umm Mahmud's neighbor was hospitalized with a severe gastrointestinal infection, she and women from her diffuse network of friends discussed where funds might be found for his treatment. Initially, around $200 was gathered, with some giving as little as $5 and others as much as $50—an amount beyond what I had imagined people could afford. When I asked Umm Mahmud what motivated people to give so generously, she initially invoked the Islamic ideal of charity as a moral duty, adding, "We give because we feel with others." Allocating income in this way, however, was also a form of insurance against unforeseen expenses in the future. "Those who give," she continued, folding her hands in her lap, "take comfort in the thought that were some misfortune to befall them, they would be similarly supported." Because these contributions (*sadaqat*) are given as a collected sum and not as individual donations, they are perceived less as individual gifts to be reciprocated by a countergift (implying a closed transaction) than as part of an everyday ethics of give and take that establishes relations of solidarity and dependence through mutual indebtedness.[9] Allocating money in this way is not strictly opposed to saving, because it carries the expectation—if not the assurance—of reciprocal support.

Additional funds were also raised through the local mosque. At Umm Mahmud's suggestion, a public announcement was made through the loudspeaker, encouraging the community to give alms (*zakat*) for a sick, unnamed child. Donations are called for and given anonymously to protect the recipient from feelings of shame or indebtedness. Although this practice (*yizi'*, or *bynadi b-i-l jami'*) has appeared relatively recently in Shatila, it is increasingly common. Anonymous and indirect, this form of assistance is not motivated by reciprocity per se but rather by Islamic ideals and the need to perform an ethos of collective care. Both forms of support suggest that an ethic of communal solidarity, formerly activated through village committees, kin networks, and customary ties, continues to animate social relations—but at a distance, and now as part of a broader coping strategy rooted in the particularities of camp life. Especially striking was the way these acts of solidarity could extend beyond traditional ethnic divides to include Syrian and Lebanese neighbors, suggesting that forms of everyday cooperation and sharing may help promote social cohesion in an increasingly diverse and densely populated community.

The growing preoccupation with day-to-day survival has resulted in a greater emphasis on flexible and negotiated relations and informal alliances oriented toward meeting short-term needs as they arise.[10] Friends and neighbors are increasingly relied upon over extended kin and village ties, which typically entail long-term obligations of open-ended reciprocity few can afford. Most informal networks I encountered were brokered by women and had little, if anything, to do with principles of village or clan but were shaped instead by knowledge of particular households and neighborhoods accumulated over time and by proximity.[11] These networks, which are chosen rather than given, offer moral and economic support based on a careful assessment of the costs and benefits of different forms of material and nonmaterial exchange; they are understood to be provisional and can therefore be created and dissolved with relative ease.[12] To note these changes is not to claim that traditional solidarities are defunct: most people I knew relied on family for some kind of assistance. However, the means by which residents of Shatila navigate the vicissitudes of poverty and diversify their sources of income to meet their needs and deal with emergencies suggest that the ethic of kinship is absorbed into larger, more provisional and strategic, networks of association.

TALKING SHOP WITH FATIMA

I first met Fatima, a woman in her late fifties, when she invited me into her small grocery store to escape a downpour. She was short and stout with a halo of black curly hair and expressive dark eyes, accentuated by a thick line of kohl. We became friends, and I would often sit with her while she worked in the evenings. Located on the western edge of the camp, Fatima's store—a kiosk-type shop selling sweets and basic household goods—was a hub of economic activity, speculation, and banter. Her hospitality made her store a gathering place for elders, unemployed youth, and a constant stream of children who kept her solvent through their insatiable appetite for chips and sodas. She regularly spent the entire day behind the counter, giving her ample time to socialize with clients. When I dropped by, I often found Fatima bent over her accounts, assessing what goods needed to be restocked, or reading *al-Safir* (a rare sight in Shatila, where literacy levels are low and newspapers represent an expense few can afford). Other times, I found her deep in discussion with camp elders, perched awkwardly on empty produce boxes around her counter while drinking coffee from small disposable cups or on stools in the street outside—a habit that transgressed codes of conduct between men and women. This ambiguity about whether Fatima's shop was a place one went to buy goods, gossip, or talk shop was one she worked to her advantage.

Most businesses and institutions in Shatila are run by men. As an unmarried Ghawarni Bedouin woman originally from Nabatiyyeh camp, Fatima saw herself—and was treated by others—as something of an outsider, which in her mind brought us closer together.[13] The angularities of her character had not been smoothed by family life, and many of my friends were wary of her, seeing her as a fiery-tempered eccentric and a little "odd." I loved spending time with her and enjoyed listening to her scathing, if somewhat scattershot, critiques of camp politics. She was articulate and opinionated and quick to share with me her views about social and political life in Shatila, which she felt she observed from a vantage point not unlike mine. Her lack of formal ties to political factions and virtual independence from reciprocal kin relations made her more resourceful in identifying alternative forms of support; in this respect, even in her anomalousness, she revealed forms of economic agency increasingly available to women as traditional structures of social and political organization in the camp weaken.

Because Fatima lived on her own, her store was an entirely independent enterprise. She recalled the skepticism with which people had viewed her proposal to start a business in the mid-1990s and the initial difficulties she had faced trying to raise money. The only assistance she received was from Nabil, a childhood friend from Nabatiyyeh also living in Shatila (again suggestive of how attachments rooted in camp life appear to be superseding ancestral ones). Nabil rented her a room on the ground floor of his building and gave her a small loan, which she paid back in installments that could be adjusted according to her weekly profit margin. These initial obstacles, however, dampened neither her resolve nor her nerve: she worked hard, dressed in provocatively short skirts, and generally caused a stir. On one occasion, soon after she had opened her store, a neighbor broke in and put a curtain around her counter in an effort to conceal her bare legs from customers; the curtain was immediately removed, and the skirts got shorter. Running a local store gave her a sense of social standing and purpose:

> People here do not think it is right for a woman to be confident and successful in business; they become jealous. . . . When one of my neighbors realized I made more money than he did, he said—with great surprise—"So you've really succeeded, Fatima!" And I responded, "Of course, why shouldn't I?" . . . In our religion, work is a form of worship and I work all the time. Even in Ramadan I open my shop at Iftar [when people break fast]. . . . Last year someone complained this was not appropriate. They thought I was Christian and didn't understand the ways of Islam because of the way I dress. I said, "Listen, you know my name is Fatima, which is the name of the daughter of the Prophet (Peace be upon Him), so why do you ask me this? You've stopped recognizing the signs of your own religion!"

The terms with which she described her business revealed the transformation it had wrought in her life, turning her marginality into a source of economic strength and independence. Her store allowed her to reinvent herself as a successful businesswoman, which gave her greater latitude in forging productive relationships—with suppliers, clients, neighbors, local officials—circumventing many of the restrictions normally faced by single women in the camp.

When I asked Fatima what had motivated her to open a shop, she told me it was born of need and that without the safety net provided by a spouse or kin, or ties to a political faction, she could think of no other way to generate a regular income. She was clearly proud of the fact that she did not rely on handouts, and the role of entrepreneur allowed her to set herself apart from the political clientelism she believed was undermining camp society:

> Sometimes I feel representatives in the factions are frightened of me because I am not on their payroll and they know they have no hold over me. . . . When one man from the Popular Front for the Liberation of Palestine saw me writing . . . I teased him and said, "I am writing a report about you!" I was not afraid. . . .

I said, "You [the factions] are killing me slowly anyway; what do I have to fear?" Who benefits from the money given to these organizations for the general good of the community? . . . They pocket the money and don't improve conditions. . . . I don't have to answer to anyone; I can say what I want, and no one will threaten me.

Fatima used her financial independence to underwrite her critique of the clientelism of political factions, which used limited resources to recruit members and extend their influence rather than to work for the collective good of the community. The fact that Fatima, like many camp residents, sought to distance herself from political parties says much about the parties' loss of prestige amid the general perception of their corruption.

COFFINS AND CASTLES: A CRITIQUE OF UNSANCTIONED GAIN

"We used to be as one hand [*kunna 'id wahdeh*], though now people can only afford to think of themselves," Fatima told me, shortly after our first meeting. Sipping her coffee and nervously tapping cigarette ash into the saucer, she described how during the revolution, with the PLO still based in Lebanon, the community had been bound together by political conviction and confidence in the future, but also by an ethic of mutual care:

Despite the difficulties of this period [the civil war] our lives were better because we lived in each other's hearts and in each other's houses. We shared everything! We had hope in what the revolution would bring, and we were a lot better off; we had our fill and were happy [*kaffayna wa-inbasatna*]. That all ended when the PLO left in 1982, and we saw things clearly. Some wars bring coffins; and some wars, castles [*fi hurub bit'ammir 'ubur, wa fi hurub bit'ammir qusur*].

Shatila, she told me, was no longer a place of caring or trust; people had become stingy, calculating, and opportunistic. From the vantage point of the precarious present, the revolution is remembered as a time of relative wealth, wellbeing, and opportunity, within structures of welfare provided by the PLO—a time when refugees enjoyed a good and "normal" life. Like many, Fatima saw the weakening of communal relations that followed the post-1982 changes in exchange and distribution structures in terms of a failure to uphold the cherished practice of sharing and giving. "Everyone says, I have nothing because they don't want to give!" she exclaimed, with exasperation. Such expressions of "structural nostalgia" (Herzfeld 1997) reveal a collective perception that the struggle to generate enough income to subsist has eroded reciprocal relations and the moral economy that once prevailed.

A striking feature of this narrative of social and moral entropy is the way people invariably placed themselves outside the transformative process, presenting the changes as happening to them and not through them. Even Fatima, who claimed (perhaps somewhat disingenuously) not to be interested in profit but only in being able to pay her bills and buy her blood pressure medicines, always set her own financial preoccupations apart from what she saw going on around her. However, Umm Mahmud's experience demonstrates that camp residents were far more willing to support each other in adversity than Fatima's comments suggest, and she herself was constantly engaged in acts of kindness and care for those around her. Such instances of solidarity, like the reciprocal networks in which Umm Mahmud participated, form part of a pragmatics of daily survival and reflect a shift toward negotiating (rather than presupposing) not only relations of exchange and charity but also the ethics of communal care. The collective chorus of complaint I encountered might therefore be better understood as awareness of the need to consciously maintain community and reconstitute the moral order, and as a reminder that wealth is meaningful only when embedded in social relations that enrich the collective.

Although Fatima spoke reverentially about "the days of the revolution" (*ayyam al-thawra*), she continued to be haunted by the leadership's lack of concern for the refugees left behind. A conversation we had about the 1976 siege of Tel al-Za'tar camp, where her family had moved after being displaced from Nabatiyyeh camp in 1974, exemplifies this:

> During the revolution people believed Arafat would take care of us and they gave freely to him because they believed the reward would be great. He was like a father for us. . . . Before the resistance came, we were living . . . in poverty and were repressed, so the PLO was something wonderful—this is how people saw them, because we were less politically aware then. . . .
>
> At that time I was working in Ras Beirut as a nanny. . . . Leaders from the resistance would come to the house to drink and talk politics. I remember one of the leaders visited the house; it was during the siege in Tel al-Za'tar. . . . I was very worried for the safety of my family who were caught inside the camp. I asked him whether they [the PLO] were providing people with enough food and assistance. I told him I would kiss the ground if my family got out alive, and he told me they were doing everything they could. . . . When the siege broke and

I first saw my sister and her four children, they looked like the pictures you see of starving people in Africa. Skin and bone! So I went to him and said, "You're a liar! How could you say you were providing food and water and arms when people had only dirty water to drink?" While they were starving, he was sitting in his air-conditioned office in a padded chair. In reality they [PLO leaders] had abandoned the people to their fate.[14]

Using the idiom of kinship, Fatima viewed the PLO leadership as subject to the same responsibilities and moral standards expected of kin. While Fatima cursed the ineptitude of the national movement, she acknowledged the importance of key political figures within it: "After Tel al-Za'tar, people were angry with Arafat. We would drink our coffee bitter and say, 'For the souls of the martyrs.' Then when his compound in Ramallah was besieged, everyone felt with him, and we'd drink our coffee bitter and say, 'For Arafat.' . . .[15]Abu Ammar [Arafat] may have made mistakes, but he is still our only hope, politically, and George Habbash [the leader of the PFLP] will always be our conscience," she conceded.

In Fatima's mind the wealth of the revolution both created and destroyed community. Shuttling between heady nostalgia for the golden days of the resistance and lingering anger over the corruption and neglect that characterized its leadership, Fatima's narrative about Tel al-Za'tar illustrates that feelings of loyalty exist in tension with a demystifying view of authority. The leadership's apparent indifference to the needs of camp refugees languishing after years of loyalty and sacrifice constituted for her a scandal. This discourse of social and political distrust in the wake of the PLO's departure is similar to the crisis of faith in family and kin relations described by Umm Mahmud. Just as an era of political solidarity rooted in nationalism is thought to have given way to one fractured by self-interest, familial solidarity and reciprocity are seen to be weakening, superseded by more instrumental relations.

"THE NEIGHBOR CLOSE BY IS BETTER THAN THE BROTHER FAR AWAY" (JAR 'ARIB AHSAN MIN AKH BA'ID)

Although Fatima would regularly remind me that "neighbors are precious," she was less forthcoming about her family. The only relatives she spoke about were her parents and six siblings and their families, who were killed in the 1982 Shatila massacre yet remain vividly present for her. For a long time I therefore assumed she had no living relatives in the camp. However, during a conversation about a heart operation she had undergone several years earlier, it emerged she had an aunt and several cousins living nearby:

> When I had my heart operation, I did not get the help I expected, neither from my relatives nor from UNRWA. . . . Now I have to go for a checkup twice a year, but none of my family here will help me, so how am I meant to pay? Even UNRWA doesn't help now; when they discovered I had a shop, they stopped giving me benefits. I said to the representative, "It's okay, take your money; what can I do with LBP 10,000 [$7] a month anyway?"

Fatima recalled that after her illness her relatives regarded her as a burden. They claimed not to have the means to help her, but Fatima had another explanation: "They don't help me because they think my medical expenses will use up their savings, and once they start, they will have to continue. They imagine if something similar should happen to them in the future, I would not be able to help them in the same way." When I asked her if she had ever tried to borrow money from them, she explained that loans between family members are frowned upon. "They say, 'If you lend to your brother, you've lost him'" (*iza bitdayyin akhuk btikhsaru*). A loan from a family member is read as an admission that reciprocal ties of kin have collapsed. She went on to note that it is not uncommon for relatives to hide money and resources from one another.[16] Concealing wealth, Fatima suggested, offered a strategy for withdrawing from kin duties, avoiding the awkwardness of refusing the petition of a needy relative.

Fatima's feelings of resentment were accentuated by her past role as primary provider for her family. Some of the same aunts and cousins who were now refusing to lend support had taken refuge in her home during the civil war:

> After we left Nabatiyyeh in 1974 and moved to Beirut, I got a job in Hamra. . . . I was the one who paid all the expenses for my family at that time. . . . During the siege in 1982, they all came and lived with me. My house was filled with people for whom I had suddenly become responsible, and there were children everywhere. I began to feel taken advantage of. . . . This is a problem in our society: if they [family] feel you have initiative and you can earn money for them, they will sit back and wait to be supported. Even though I was angry at their opportunism, as a woman I felt for them, and I couldn't bring myself to throw them out.

Just as Fatima never censored her critique of the national movement, often naming and shaming particular individuals, she did not shy away from the question of kin obligations and family loyalty. Recalling the comfort of family life as a child in Nabatiyyeh did not prevent her from addressing the cumulative cost of kin relations. She also spoke about the ways familial ties can limit the possibilities available to women, whose individual aspirations are always expected to come after their duties as caregivers and providers for their families.

The stress Fatima placed on quid pro quo equivalence—that her eligibility to receive relatives' help would depend on the future likelihood of her returning equivalent favor—marks a departure from what Marilyn Strathern calls the "distinguishing asymmetry" of gift exchange, in which accepting the debt of a "gift" is the precondition for continued social relations (1988, 178). Value here is conceived in largely calculative and instrumental terms rather than in those of moral obligation to maintain kin relations or underwrite traditional structures of sociality in the community. The fact that Fatima's medical expenses were ultimately covered by an unexpected gift from the Lebanese family for whom she had worked as a nanny years before lent further credence to her belief that "fictive" kin were more dependable than blood relatives.[17]

LONG-TERM CREDIT AND PARTIAL PRICING

Over time, I came to understand that the popularity of Fatima's store was partly a result of her payment policies. Knowing that many of her clients had small and unpredictable incomes, she adopted a credit system of payment at the end of the month, or periodically in small installments (*taqsit*), allowing customers to buy basic necessities during fallow periods. "Though people may be poor here, no one dies of hunger," she remarked with some pride. A small sign behind her counter read, "Cash today, and tomorrow a loan" (*yawm al-naqdi, wa ghadan dayn*—the use of the term *dayn* [loan] is significant since it normally refers to the give and take of everyday life—conceived as a social favor—in contrast to *qard*, which is used for contractual loans). Credit is not unusual among Shatila's stores, but unlike other shopkeepers with whom I spoke, Fatima usually left the terms of repayment to be determined by the debtor.[18] (Her store credit hence qualified, according to established Islamic practice, as a "benevolent loan" [*qard al-hasan*].)[19]

If a debt became too great or went unpaid too long, Fatima might refuse further credit or even threaten to report the delinquent to the Popular Committee.[20] Her strategy for determining the credit limit for each customer was usually based on a rudimentary assessment of the person's living expenses. "You have to have an idea of what people earn and what they spend before you decide how much credit to give," Fatima told me. "If someone is renting an apartment for LBP 300,000 [approximately $200], they won't be able to afford more than LBP 50,000 [$34] a month. If you work only with your heart, it'll kill you." Her reasons for refusing credit, however, could also seem arbitrary and capricious. On one occasion, Fatima explained to me why she chose not to give more credit to a particular client: "She spends all her money on junk food [*shabra*] and buys small amounts of labne and bread. She could live more cheaply and feed her family better if she were to buy a kilo of yogurt instead of biscuits and chocolates. I don't like to give credit for these kinds of things."[21] However, Fatima was critical of shopkeepers who bullied or humiliated clients into paying their bills on time and recounted with distaste that one store had posted notices of a family's outstanding debt all along the main street to shame them into swift repayment. She was also against levying fines in cases of late payment. "This is like giving a loan and charging interest," she explained disapprovingly. "The one who charges interest, whether through sanctioned or crooked means, benefits from it" (*bidayyin bi fa'ideh halal haram, biddu yistafid minha*).

Fatima's studied forbearance, however, concealed more complex motivations and economic calculations. Because she cultivated her store as a social space and played shopkeeper, friend, and host, the distinction between social and material exchange was often blurred, with the result that gifts and favors were regularly introduced into what would normally be straightforward commodity exchange.[22] Gifts, along with her tolerance for long delays in the repayment of loans, created conditions for new forms of sociability, allowing her to extend her own social networks.[23] This policy not only increased her sense of self-worth, enabling her to establish herself as an ethical, friendly person, but also increased others' feelings of indebtedness to her.[24]

Strategic patience could be accompanied by an idiosyncratic pricing system that varied according to Fatima's assessment of a debtor's finances or the nature of her relationship with the individual. If she knew the person to be in a precarious financial position or without adequate support—a widow, an elderly person, or a single mother, for example—she might choose to sell certain goods (normally basic household necessities) at a cheaper rate or give the person a little extra. When she was feeling empathetic, she might say it was a shame not to help those worse off than herself, though it often seemed that her care for the suffering of others extended to those whose situation was comparable to her own.

This charitable disposition was far from constant, however, depending both on her mood and the state of her own finances. Like her credit system, variable pricing allowed her to disrupt structures of economic equivalence. Though never articulating this as a specific aim, Fatima used the debts of others to construct a safety net for herself, mindful as she was of her own vulnerability. The significance of her habit of "giving extra" (*bazid shway*) was ambiguous because it was framed more often as a gesture than clearly as a gift that would incur a debt. In this respect, these acts of generosity—the moments of recognition that renew faith in the social—could be interpreted as an effort to delineate and re-affirm boundaries of moral community and networks of allegiance in her own life. In her mind, the relations of give and take established through this "economy of favors" represented a support network that might be activated at some point in the future (Ledeneva 1998). Lending and borrowing came to inscribe her relations with others as well as produce a sense of security.

JAM'IYYAT: SAVINGS ASSOCIATIONS

During my last year in Shatila, Fatima embarked on an ambitious project to remodel her store, which involved knocking down one of the exterior walls and replacing it with a garage door. Her immediate kin were unable or un-willing to help with the cost of materials and labor, forcing her to raise the money elsewhere. Like most refugees, Fatima had neither a bank account nor the prerequisites for a bank loan. "I try to save, but daily needs intervene," she explained. "I have no will power. I put money aside and then I spend it" (*bihaji a'mil tahwisheh . . . ma andi 'iradeh. Badubb masareh wa ba'dayn busruf*). One of Fatima's proposed strategies for raising the funds was to join an informal savings collective (*jam'iyya*). These rotating credit schemes are usually initiated by neighbors or coworkers rather than relatives, thereby avoiding some of the pressures associated with loans within families. Typically, group members give a set amount of money every week or month and take turns collecting the sum of the contributions (*madkhul*). Although Fatima was ultimately able to secure a loan from a friend, the time spent discussing the pros and cons of the system alerted me to its growing importance within the camp economy. It turned out that many of my friends had participated in savings groups at one time or another. Since these collectives allow members to diversify their sources of income and extend their networks of support and reciprocal exchange, they have become a useful tool for economic survival, allowing households to reduce the risks of poverty.

While both men and women participate in *jamʿiyyat*, I encountered the practice mainly among women.[25] Because women are often responsible for balancing everyday expenses for electricity, water, and food against long-term investments such as children's schooling, university fees, or the purchase of expensive household items, they tend to have a better grasp of how money flows within the domestic economy and how to plan for large expenditures.[26] Women are often given the task of banking the family's wealth because they are viewed as less likely to gamble it away or misallocate it.

Umm Walid, a friend of Fatima's who had run a number of *jamʿiyyat* and had a reputation for being an adept and skillful facilitator, regarded savings groups as particularly important for women because they enabled mothers to provide for their children, since fathers were unreliable.[27] Because Umm Walid was a mother of four and the sole breadwinner in her household, *jamʿiyyat* represented an important safety net for her and enabled her to pay for the university education of two of her children. Looking back over the previous decade, Umm Walid observed, "The number of *jamʿiyyat* has gone up as the money in the camp has gone down." She regards them as more effective than unregulated modes of lending and borrowing because they are interest-free and allow members swiftly to mobilize significant sums of money. Moreover, they compel participants to abide by fixed rules that determine in advance both how often contributions can be made and when each person will receive payment. In the case of an emergency, when funds are unexpectedly needed earlier than anticipated, the order of payouts can be altered.

Most members of *jamʿiyyat* I spoke with told me they had joined either to meet an unexpected expense—most often sudden illness or the death of a relative—or to plan for a significant future expenditure. Like Fatima, many described the difficulty of saving on their own, with funds appropriated by relatives or dissipated in everyday spending; ad hoc saving rarely allowed individuals to reach a point where the money saved could be turned into tangible assets. In this sense, participating in *jamʿiyyat* offered a way to set aside money for future needs and, in some cases, to avoid certain kin duties—by cordoning off resources—as well as the obligation to share.[28] By the same token, it also offered a way of minimizing the need to borrow from relatives and friends.

I did, however, encounter instances where family members formed a *jamʿiyya* in order to raise money for a sibling or parent. In one instance, five siblings created a savings group to raise the money needed for their mother's pilgrimage to Mecca. Establishing a *jamʿiyya* became a way of forcing family members to give, when otherwise they might not have. When I asked Umm Walid what had prompted her to join a *jam'iyya* five years earlier, she responded:

> Before [the late 1980s and early 1990s] . . . things weren't so expensive, so everyone had more money then, and it was easier to borrow or lend and not to think too much about it. . . . Now, since fewer and fewer people have work, it becomes harder to know whether you will ever get money back if you lend to someone. . . . I found myself fighting with neighbors and family about how much I had borrowed or what I had loaned. I would have disagreements about when the money needed to be repaid; I would ask them to repay me in a month, and they would return the money after a year. . . . I first joined a *jam'iyya* when I needed to raise money for my daughter's university entrance fee. The following year I bought new chairs and several gold bracelets, which I was able to sell for a profit this year because the price of gold has doubled. If I didn't have the obligation to pay LBP 50,000 [$33] every month, I wouldn't have been able to save anything and I couldn't have managed any of these expenses. The *jam'iyya* is good because it is clear from the beginning we all depend on each other if we are to benefit.

Although there is always a risk members will stop contributing once they receive their payout, moral obligation and fear of being excluded from future savings groups appear to dissuade potential defaulters. Since the system depends on the reliability and commitment of all participants, it is believed to encourage fair dealing while helping to forge new networks of solidarity. The importance of maintaining good relations with other members in the savings association is underscored by the fact people will often participate without a particular goal in mind, simply to retain a presence in the network or establish better "credit" relations with a respected *jam'iyya* leader in anticipation of future need.

What is so effective about these associations is that they provide credit based on carefully negotiated terms, making indebtedness manageable and mutually beneficial through reciprocal guarantees. By regulating and controlling relations of credit and debt, *jam'iyyat* function like a form of insurance, allowing households to borrow significant sums of money without the burden of having to repay the entire sum at once. Conditions for membership also establish reassuring boundaries for inclusion and exclusion. The chronically unemployed are not usually permitted to join because of the high risk of default, making it not an option for the truly destitute or those believed to be making money illicitly (through the sale of drugs, gambling, etc.), on the grounds that *jam'iyyat* are meant to abide by the principles of *takaful* (the Islamic alternative to commercial insurance) in which money cannot be used to further sin and transgression. The fact that savings associations do not involve interest—the payouts are not even conceived as loans—reinforces the view they are more ethically and religiously sound than formal banking institutions or debts. In practice, however, the rules governing membership and use of funds in *jam'iyyat* are malleable, and the belief that money should be sourced through moral means often coexists with a readiness not to inquire too closely where it comes from.[29]

PUSHING LIFE: THE STRUGGLES OF ABU YUSUF

While Umm Mahmud, Fatima, and Umm Walid have developed viable structures of support outside family, village, or faction networks, many of their male peers, whose social ties continue to be bound up with political affiliations, have found it harder to reinvent roles for themselves in Shatila's postwar economy. For Abu Yusuf and the Nasser household, the economic deterioration that followed the PLO's departure and intensified after the implementation of the 1989 Ta'if peace agreement (which increased the legal vulnerability and social marginality of Palestinians, particularly in the field of employment) has been decisive.

Now in his fifties, Abu Yusuf lives hand to mouth. He is tall and thin, with an open face, thinning hair, and humorous dark eyes that seem to give nothing away. Born and brought up in Shatila, Abu Yusuf fought for the DFLP between 1978 and 1988. In 1996 he cut all ties after faction officials refused to cover treatment for injuries he sustained during the civil war. He now maintains minimal contact with his former cadres, which has increased his sense of vulnerability and isolation. Like many from his generation who fought during the revolution and found themselves unemployed and underqualified after the departure of its leadership, Abu Yusuf has limited job options, and he forms part of Shatila's growing cohort of low-paid, informal workers.[30] While admitting that, as a vegetable vendor, he no longer enjoys the same protections and support, he says it is a sacrifice he is willing to make to avoid degrading clientelist relations.

The Nassers were among the first people I met on my initial visit to Shatila in the summer of 2001. During the time I have known them, Abu Yusuf and Umm Yusuf have lived with their three children, Yusuf, Ahmed, and Salma, in a two-room apartment bordering the Tel al-Za'tar quarter on the eastern side of the camp. Umm Yusuf moved to Shatila from Tel al-Za'tar camp in the late 1970s; she was in her late thirties and working as a cleaner at a Red Crescent

Hospital in Beirut's southern suburbs when I first met her. Although Abu Yusuf has irregular work in Sabra market, his earnings are small and Umm Yusuf is the primary provider. That the Nassers receive neither factional support nor remittances from relatives abroad deepens their financial strain during Abu Yusuf's periods of unemployment. Although Umm Yusuf's aunt and uncle live in Germany, they do not provide assistance. When Umm Yusuf's father was hospitalized in the early 1990s, the extended family abroad did not rally (as Umm Ali's did when she fell ill). A small portion of the hospital bills were paid by UNRWA, and the remainder were covered by a patchwork of handouts from NGOs and loans from friends and neighbors, which Umm Yusuf and her brother paid off over the course of several years. Umm Yusuf regarded her uncle and aunt's indifference as proof that her relatives in Germany had chosen to sever ties with the family they left behind. Citing the sole exception of her brother, Umm Yusuf would often tell me she no longer had family. "You're doing research on the Nakba? Well, note this," she would say. "This is our Nakba. No one cares for anyone, even in our own families. If you asked my aunt about me, she would probably say, 'I know no one by that name.'"[31]

When I returned to Shatila in 2002, Abu Yusuf had been without work for several months. A spate of poor health had left him bedridden, making it impossible for him to keep his job at the market. "I'm pushing life" (*'am daffish hayati*) Abu Yusuf told me, ruefully. Initially he had borrowed small amounts of money from his former employer and subsequently from neighbors and friends to help cover household expenses. Sometimes these small sums were given as loans, but oftentimes as charity. When I visited, he told me about his most recent search for work, always optimistic that something would soon turn up.

As his unemployment continued, frustration was heightened by a sense of shame that the family had come to rely entirely on his wife's salary. "Some people say men who are supported by their wives are controlled by their wives [*mahkumin*], and soon they'll be wearing aprons and washing the carpets," he joked, deflecting my questions with characteristic good humor. "They say women should stay home, while men spend their days working and their nights being treated like Harun al-Rashid [the famous literary character from *A Thousand and One Nights*]. But life is not like this. Now it's every rooster on his own pile of garbage [*kul dik ilu mazbaltu*]."

Abu Yusuf was acutely aware he could not provide for his family in the way he would have liked, and for all his lightness of spirit it depressed him. During Eid he expressed regret at not having the money to buy new shoes for his son and wished he could take his family to a restaurant, adding it had not always been this way. "During the civil war everyone was in the same situation; the rich had left, and the rest of us lived together. When the rich came back, we began to feel poor again. . . . You start to feel you need a car or a trip to Raoche [a popular tourist destination in Beirut] rather than food and a place to sleep." While material conditions in Shatila were undoubtedly worse during the latter stages of the civil war, Abu Yusuf's perception that he has become poorer is due both to deteriorating economic conditions in the camp during the last decade and the changing needs within his family. The experience of poverty and social exclusion in postwar Beirut is felt more keenly as the disparities of wealth and privilege grow more pronounced, and its culture of consumption ever more conspicuous.[32]

Although Abu Yusuf remembers the relative prosperity and political conviction of the revolution, like Fatima he has also come to see it as a time of missed opportunities. "Living off the *thawra* was a mistake," he told me. "They encouraged us to leave school and fight. Then when they left and told us to help ourselves, what could we do? We are the generation without skills." With their primary provider and employer gone, many from his generation have found themselves looking back over fruitless careers and a failed liberation movement:

> In the 1950s and 1960s people still struggled for an idea, and from the late 1970s it became about money. It is not about politics or nationalist ideals anymore. People join factions for the salary, which is why poor factions have fewer members. We have become mercenaries [*murtazaqa*]. . . . We haven't forgotten Palestine—how could we; it's in our hearts. If we could go back to our country, we would eat grass and that would be enough. Give us peace! Like in the songs of Fairuz. Give us our childhood! Oh Jerusalem, city of peace. No one forgets this. . . . But now it is about day-to-day survival. In the camps in Gaza and the West Bank they think differently because they hope to live in their own nation, on their own land, and they are fighting Israel; this is a big difference. We have a saying here about those inside: we say their blood is mixed with Palestinian soil [*dam majbul bi-turab Filastin*]. We can never be like them because our blood is mixed with the water and soil of Lebanon. . . . If there is ever another revolution among Palestinians in Lebanon, it will be a revolution against hunger, sickness, and deprivation. Why? Because these are the conditions we live in.

The claim that money rather than political conviction drives camp politics, that ideological differences have been collapsed into highly localized struggles over resources, animated the political disenchantment of many with whom I spoke.[33] The crisis of political representation that followed the PLO's departure, and their failure to define the role of political groups in exile or to provide adequate material support to camp communities, further undermined the political faith of refugees, who found themselves marginalized from the political process and without purpose.

This sense of disillusionment deepened with the PLO's endorsement of the Oslo Accords in the 1990s, leading to increased factional conflict and infighting. As clientelism and factionalism have become entrenched over the past two decades, political loyalties are often presented as bereft of ideological conviction and vulnerable to the vicissitudes of wealth distribution.[34] This in turn fosters the view that factions, mired as they are in petty squabbles over spheres of influence in the camp, have lost sight of national goals and collective interests. This has undermined the legitimacy of and transformed the nature and practice of politics in Shatila, shifting the center of gravity from ideological questions to a politics of everyday existence. As with family relations, in short, political kinship is being reconfigured by local material realities.

AID AND DEPENDENCY

To what extent have the proliferation of NGOs in Shatila compensated for the shortfall in material support after the departure of the PLO? Abu Yusuf, like many, sees little improvement and believes funds intended for the community have been siphoned off by those in charge, producing a handful of wealthy entrepreneurs at the expense of the collective. "How is it that the directors of these organizations all live outside the camp and send their children to private schools?" he asked. "Now everything is business here [kull shi tijara]; everything has a price." Skepticism about the work of charities is common; NGOs are accused of being paternalistic and insensitive to the needs and priorities of the community, driven instead by the interests of the political factions to which they are allied or by the agendas of foreign funders. UNRWA, the main provider of relief to Palestinian camps, remains the primary target of people's criticism and is routinely accused of corruption, incompetence, and subordination to the political agendas of Western donors through the largely foreign executive branch.

While Abu Yusuf would try to distance himself from local institutions he believed were squandering funds, he was not above accepting the odd handout and even displayed a grudging respect for those adept at working the system.

"There are those who eat chicken and those who get stuck on the fence," he explained, aware that he fell squarely into the latter category. While rumors about the financial impropriety and opportunism of NGO employees are often exaggerated or the product of personal grudges, they reveal the distrust characterizing relations between refugees and the institutions distributing aid. This is particularly true in the case of UNRWA, most employees of which are from the camps, "blur[ring] the boundary between benefactor and beneficiary" (Farah 2010, 391). Far from bringing greater security or diminishing clientelism, relief programs are frequently accused of generating greater disparities of wealth and influence by creating divisions between those who benefit on the strength of their political or social connections and those, like Abu Yusuf, who lack institutional leverage and are left to fend for themselves.

Another aspect of NGO culture troubling Abu Yusuf is the normalization of dependency. "Little drops may keep you alive, but it makes people lazy and there is less will to work," he told me. On one occasion, after a neighbor with ties to an Islamic charity procured a ration card for Abu Yusuf, he deliberated about whether to accept: "I was reluctant, but he [his neighbor] said, 'Everyone is taking, so why not you?'" When Abu Yusuf eventually went to the center, he was shocked by what he found:

> The street was filled with people shouting and pushing one another. The center had erected a barrier to prevent people from entering the building. It was a disgrace [*shi bahdaleh*]. A woman was sent back because the man distributing the food said she had already received meat, but she protested and swore by God she hadn't. I began to worry he might say the same to me and almost turned back. But he handed me a plastic bag with one kilo of flour and some frozen meat. Do you know where it came from? From Saudi Arabia! It had been frozen since the Eid al-Adha [several months before]. It was clear this meat was rotten—a dog wouldn't touch it! It had been stored in a room, not in a refrigerator, because the camp had been without electricity for the past week. This meat had been donated by a wealthy Saudi. . . . I am poor, but I am not an animal, and I want to eat healthy food. If I want to eat meat, I'll buy my own from the market when I have the means.

Recalling the way the woman in the queue had continued to plead with the employee distributing the meat after being insulted, Abu Yusuf said people had grown thick skin, or, as he put it, had become "like crocodiles [*tamasih*]." Ad hoc aid parcels, like the one described here, are a fraught category for many, and people were often embarrassed to admit they had accepted them or dismissed them as inadequate and ill-conceived.[35] Refugee frustration with NGOs seems to be a product of both the perceived disregard for local needs and the feelings of humiliation that accompany dependency. Necessity has allowed an unhappy pragmatism to take hold, as acts of charity are recast as something refugees are entitled to, "less as a gift and more their just due, although certainly not adequate to compensate for their loss" (Peteet 2005, 80). Conceding "a drowning man cannot refuse the straw held out to him," Abu Yusuf said he too felt he was left with little choice but to accept any help offered, however inadequate or degrading.[36]

In 2005 Abu Yusuf became involved in a protracted struggle with the Shahid Foundation, an organization funded by Fatah that assists the families of martyrs and the wounded. His Kafkaesque descriptions of trying to secure benefits cast a harsh light on the difficulties families without strong institutional ties can face. He described for me his conversation with a representative from the foundation, in which he was informed he would not be eligible for assistance:

> Even though I had fought for the PLO during the resistance, they claimed they didn't have my name in their files, so I said to the official, "Well register me in your files; I fought for you!" He told me he wasn't empowered to do this and I needed to get a special report from Fatah headquarters in Rashidiyyeh, with Sultan Abu al-Aynayn's signature [then a leading Fatah official in Lebanon] proving my status. This angered me, so I said to him, "What's the point of this report? All this begging so I can receive LBP 40,000 [$26] a month!" When I thought about this, my whole body felt tired and I left his office. To be honest, I was disgusted.

When I asked him if he had tried to procure the necessary paperwork from Sultan Abu al-Ayayn, he explained that he subsequently discovered this would be possible only if he attended Fatah's monthly rallies in Ayn al-Hilweh camp (since at that time Fatah had no office in Shatila), something he was not prepared to do. At this point Umm Yusuf, who had been sitting with us, joined the discussion:

> None of the factions have money to give anyone now except Abu Ammar [Arafat]. They pay LBP 100,000 [$65], or LBP 90,000 [$60] a month for youth. . . . You see the same women who meet with Amneh Jibril [the head of Fatah's Women's Union] for coffee in the morning going to Hamas rallies in the af-

ternoon. Everyone here is bought; no one is independent even if they claim to be. You'll hear them at the demonstrations chanting "qulu Allah, qulu Allah, nihna rijal al-haq walla"; they'll tell you they're walking for God, but they are walking for a salary. . . . Women go to the religious classes organized by Sheikh Abu Qudah in the community hall in the camp because they are being paid to do so.

Both comments challenge the view that aid is given unconditionally or that it is symbolically opposed to economic exchange. Material assistance is understood to be a form of patronage, and political ties are often determined by strategic assessments of wealth and influence at any given time.[37] As Umm Yusuf observed, the reluctance to acknowledge political ties very often conceals more complicated relations with political factions. By the same token, I regularly encountered people who had claimed to be "independent" but were carrying flags in demonstrations, attending political rallies, or engaging in other duties expected of salaried members. Indeed, as an employee of the Red Crescent Hospital (an institution funded by Fatah), Umm Yusuf was not free of such ties either. However, the reticence with which faction membership tended to be discussed, and the way in which people often shifted between "us" and "them" when speaking about these issues, revealed a deep-seated ambivalence. More generally, the cynicism with which camp politics is discussed says much about the changing structures of power relations and the attribution of agency and morality in the camp.[38]

During the time I have known Abu Yusuf, his social relations have been periodically compromised by unpaid debts, and the effects of prolonged unemployment have been cruel. Economic uncertainty has made it impossible to save, and money set aside for his children's education has been gradually reappropriated for everyday expenditures, foreshortening the temporal horizon to that of daily subsistence. His irregular income also limits his borrowing credit with friends and shopkeepers, further weakening his support structures and deepening his sense of isolation.[39] Producing LBP 1,000 ($0.60) from his pocket, he once wryly remarked, "Here you're worth what you earn. If you have LBP 1,000 in your pocket, that's what you're worth: that's who you are. If you have nothing, you're worth nothing." Against the backdrop of Lebanon's voracious consumer culture, where social status increasingly appears to be determined by one's capacity to purchase commodities and brand-name goods, the inability to participate in these market-based identities can be experienced as a personal failing and existential crisis.[40]

Unemployment has narrowed the domain in which Abu Yusuf feels morally and materially alive. A conversation I had with him when I returned to Shatila in the summer of 2005 captured the corrosive effects of prolonged joblessness and the shift in affective attachments triggered by changes in the camp's political economy:

> If you ask me where I am from, I'll tell you "Lebanon." I was born and raised here. What should I think? That I am from Jaffa? Or I can say, "I'm a Palestinian living in Lebanon." If you were then to ask me where I am from in Palestine, I would respond, "My father was from Jaffa, but I am from Shatila." Now, as you ask me this question, all I can say is, "I am the dust under your feet [*ana zift min tahtak*]."

As the unified pluralism and integrative politics of the revolution yield to divisive factionalism, social and political relations are again being reconfigured, this time by political duress and economic precariousness. Prior to the questions, who am I? or where do I belong? comes the question, can I exist? Life itself has become uncertain. Paying for food, amenities, and basic medical care often seems impossible, creating a mind-set in which ideological struggles are superseded by material ones. "All we want is a normal life," Abu Yusuf told me. "We want the same things you want: a good education for our children, good health, a home, food. The government says keeping us poor strengthens our resolve to struggle for our [national] rights. But how can we think about resistance when we spend our days running after work?" he asked, voicing growing resentment of policies that pit economic rights against political ones and challenging the claim that economic and social integration and the right to a dignified life are necessarily incompatible with the right of return. "In the end, what good has this done? We have become experts in survival and that is all. We can buy Eid clothes for three children with $50 or cook a meal on a gas stove with a single flame."[41]

Abu Yusuf's comments reveal transformations in his sense of self and his relation to the camp. Like Umm Mahmud's and Fatima's, Abu Yusuf's experience suggests that family life, and the material arrangements that sustain it, are far more complex and unstable than is often assumed. These vignettes offer salutary reminders that in our thinking about refugee identity and the role of family in the struggle for survival, and more generally, in our conceptualization of camp communities, we need to bear more rigorously in mind the radical material transformations that have occurred over more than six decades. We need, above all, to acknowledge the primacy of economic subjectivity and the decisive shaping influence it is having on what it means to be a Palestinian, and on once-sacred notions of kin, nation, and even return itself.

THE AFTERLIFE OF KINSHIP

In August 2004, Fatima had a heart attack and fell into a coma. None of her immediate family came forward to pay her medical bills, and UNRWA gave her only minimal support because she was on the cusp of her sixtieth year. Nabil (her ever-benevolent landlord) and several friends and neighbors collected around $1,800, guaranteeing her a bed in the Palestinian Red Crescent Hospital south of the camp. Although the doors to her store remained padlocked for a week, Nabil's wife reopened the shop to help cover Fatima's mounting medical bills, and others soon joined her. When I spoke with mutual friends about her precipitous decline, their grief was mixed with anxiety over how they could continue to find sufficient funds for her to remain in the intensive care unit. She died two weeks later. After considerable effort, Nabil managed to locate a distant cousin living in Sidon, who agreed to help with the costs and logistics of her burial. The manner of Fatima's death—in which an unseemly scramble for funds alternated with bracing shows of solidarity from a kind of virtual, provisional kin network—seemed to make suddenly visible the stakes of her long campaign to create, sustain, and extend webs of allegiance and reciprocity.

The case studies I have discussed are suggestive of how different forms of solidarity and community are simultaneously being created and subverted by deepening poverty. Although deprivation limits the capacity to engage in open-ended circuits of reciprocal exchange associated with kin and village, refugees continue to show great resourcefulness in generating alternative networks. As traditional support structures weaken, moral and social relations have become increasingly imbricated with a pragmatics of survival. While the support of family is no longer assured, the obverse of this is that neighbors and friends are often moved to offer assistance, becoming bound together through a socially mediated ethics grounded in the experience of everyday exigency.

Clearly, some are better able to adapt to these changing conditions than others: while Fatima's commercial enterprise allowed her to establish diverse networks of support, Abu Yusuf has struggled to make ends meet in Shatila's postwar economy. Their experiences suggest that those whose positions were already marginal within the previous and more stable economy are better suited to adapt to its erosion. Attention to what has been renascent in the wake of deprivation and disenfranchisement reveals emergent forms of agency, subjectivity, and sociality that enable camp refugees to get by and create some semblance of stability in increasingly uncertain conditions.

By shifting sympathetic and analytical attention away from the continuities of cultural forms in exile toward the contingencies of everyday practice, I do not wish to suggest traditional support structures have become inoperative or obsolete. Indeed, even as they are acknowledged to be onerous or dysfunctional, they continue to be invoked and represent—in theory if not always in practice—the ideal form of practical and moral support. Family continues to anchor existence and to shape how refugees inhabit the world: to dwell on the attenuation of kin ties is also to memorialize them and to signify their ongoing importance, albeit in altered form. Clearly, to be without these familiar forms of emotional and material support is to be extremely vulnerable, and in an emergency it is still to family that one will turn first. Had the Hasan family not received help from siblings abroad or from relatives in Lebanon, they would have been unable to meet the expense of Umm Ali's treatment. It is also significant that Fatima's funeral costs were born by a distant cousin, though it is perhaps even more significant that the cousin had to be tracked down by her landlord. The solidarities that Sayigh described as the bedrock of the camp politics and nationalist sentiment still underwrite the normative ethical vocabulary with which refugees conceptualize familial, communal, and political responsibility, even in the breach. While the ideological charge associated with the primordial ties of kin and village is increasingly overtaken by pragmatic considerations, these structures have an afterlife and are being newly inhabited.

Electrical wires and political posters, Shatila camp. Photograph © Hisham
Ghuzlan, 2009.

3 STEALING POWER

You look up at the sky,
Electric wires everywhere
If you don't steal electricity
How can you see?

Katibeh Khamseh, "Welcome to the Camps"

Everyday life invents itself by poaching in countless ways on the
property of others.

Michel de Certeau, The Practice of Everyday Life

A FEW MONTHS AFTER I had moved in with Umm Mahmud and her family, as we were sitting down to dinner, there was a power cut—a common occurrence in Shatila, where people have learned to plan their days around unpredictable supplies of electricity. Instinctively, I got up and fumbled my way through the dark to the kitchen, carrying out the routine I had seen performed by Umm Mahmud and her husband, Munir, countless times. Decreasing the voltage on the gauge in the kitchen, I leaned out the window to check our connection to the supply of "stolen electricity" (*kahraba masruqa*) channeled from a neighborhood bordering the camp through the apartment below. I then plugged in a low-watt bicycle bulb, kept in readiness under a chair in the front room. With a look of delight Munir leaned over and gave me an approving pat on the back: "You've become Palestinian; you've become one of us!" (*surti Filistiniyyeh, surti minna!*).

While this throwaway remark was intended to put me at ease, it also illustrated the degree to which coping strategies shape the boundaries of Shatila's communal solidarity. Munir's comment was a salutary reminder that individuals are constituted as national subjects not only through the symbolic order of discourse and ideas but also through everyday material practices. As the iconic image of the Palestinian resistance fighter has been superseded by the more prosaic figure struggling to make a living and access basic services, this shift from revolution to everyday material survival is reconfiguring the nature and practice of camp politics.

The canopy of tangled electrical wire hanging over every alley of Shatila maps complex political and socioeconomic struggles taking place both within the camp and between residents and the surrounding city. In recent years extreme overcrowding has placed enormous pressure on provision of services, particularly electricity and water. Because camps in Lebanon are excluded from state and municipal development schemes and services and have, until recently, been without any form of rehabilitation program, environmental conditions have become increasingly hazardous and dysfunctional.[1]

As the experiences described in the previous chapter make clear, the credibility of factions, local institutions, and other representative bodies in the camp has been undermined by mistrust and accusations of corruption. The Popular Committee (PC) and its associated security committee, which were created by the PLO in 1973 to govern and oversee the management of the camp—"the small government" of the camp (*al-hukuma al-saghira*)—are now largely regarded by residents as illegitimate and incapable of offering concrete solutions to the community's problems. Lacking effective institutional mechanisms for expressing grievances and effecting change, camp residents have had to resort to direct action and "illegal" practices in order to deal with the increasingly erratic provision of electricity.[2] The chaos of jerry-rigged wire is testimony to the energy and ingenuity with which local residents have taken matters into their own hands; it also makes visible new strains of political activity forged in the crucible of material necessity.

In the preceding chapters I have been arguing for the need to develop alternative paradigms for conceptualizing camp communities and Palestinian identity, shifting analytical attention away from the discursive continuities of nationalism toward the contingencies of lived experience and material practice in local environments. Here I build on this by examining the dynamics at work in the field of electricity distribution—a medium at first glance free of symbolic resonance, materialist in the most literal sense, but in fact rich with political significance.

The practice of siphoning electricity from municipal supplies outside Shatila and sharing it within the camp has created a complex topography of social interdependency, one that is reordering political practice in the camp. Tracking the sourcing and distribution of electricity, I suggest, broadens our understanding of what forms the basis of political life in the camp and reveals the struggles for power—literal and metaphorical—now animating relations between camp residents, the PC, and the Lebanese state. As the sociologist Ulrich Beck (1994, 18–20) argues, political life—what he calls "sub politics"—is for the most part dominated by issues that concern people's immediate future, such as welfare, health, security, public services, and only occasionally deals with collective existential issues truly transcending these local frames of reference.Moving beyond the binaries discursively identified with the Palestinian struggle (for instance, the revolutionary resistance fighter versus the passive victim) and political analyses that foreground national issues over community ones, this discussion considers refugees as pragmatic opportunists engaged in complex struggles to access essential resources and improve their lives.

Between 2002 and 2005, dwindling supplies of electricity emerged as a primary site of tension between residents and the pro-Syrian PC that has controlled the camp since the PLO's departure in 1982. In a context where political control continues to be divided between pro-Syrian and pro-Fatah factions, and where refugees are wary of challenging the PC for fear of rekindling the factional strife of the civil war years, questioning representation and leadership can be particularly fraught. In this particular instance, informal and ostensibly nonpolitical collectives formed to deal with the crisis, which subsequently became the basis for more sustained forms of suprafactional mobilization, and in 2005 the first democratic elections in the camp's history were held. As a case study, it illustrates how refugees overcame, albeit temporarily, the problems of factionalism and clientelist politics.

STATE-CAMP RELATIONS: EXCLUSION AND ENCROACHMENT

Discriminatory and politically partisan distribution of resources in Beirut and the surrounding suburbs has left it a motley postwar patchwork of dereliction and development, prosperity and abject poverty. Since the allocation of state resources is essentially clientelist, with services bartered for electoral support, Palestinians in the camps are doubly disenfranchised, both politically and with regard to infrastructure. The organizational power to disrupt—through strikes, demonstrations, or street protests, tactics often employed by the urban poor to make demands on the state or municipal authorities or to express discontent—is a negotiating tool unavailable to stateless refugees. Historically, the institutional reluctance to develop camp infrastructure—on the part of both UNRWA and the state—is part of a policy of nonintegration intended to underscore their temporary and transitory nature. This absence of state largesse and political support has nourished factionalism and patron-client relations within the camp itself.

Once-porous borders between the camp and surrounding districts have in recent years become increasingly demarcated. Infrastructural decay visibly separates Shatila from the urban development surrounding it, but like other refugee camps located in cities, it continues to be integrated with bordering neighborhoods through everyday social and economic exchange. The ghetto-ization of the camps, which was pronounced under the Deuxième Bureau during the 1950s and early 1960s, resumed after the departure of the PLO and the 1987 abrogation of the Cairo Agreement, and there is a sentiment, pervasive among Lebanese, that the camps should be subject to even stricter control and spatial segregation. Through discriminatory laws, the government has sought to regulate how camps are organized as well as prevent their sociopolitical and spatial assimilation.[3] These policies have enabled the government to divest itself of responsibility for the well-being and security of Palestinians, while at the same time condemning camps as zones of deviance beyond its control. Communities like Shatila, which do not appear on official maps and are absent from discourses of state welfare, remain highly visible in political discourse, as malignant spaces that need to be contained.[4] Rumors of lawlessness deployed by the government to foment anti-Palestinian sentiment have calcified into fixed beliefs about the "pseudo-clandestineness" of camp communities.[5] Refugees have no rights as citydwellers, and state policy toward their community combines prophylactic containment with malign neglect.[6]

Refugees, however, continue to find creative ways to navigate official policies governing access to services. Just as the material and social marginality of camp communities is a political condition, the tactics residents employ to acquire amenities constitute a politics. Munir's tapping power from Electricité du Liban (EdL, Lebanon's state-run power company) through an illegal outside connection serves daily practical needs but also carries a subversive, secondary reward: in a discriminatory system, it is an expressive act, an act of sabotage and an assertion of his right to basic everyday amenities. Ranged against repressive state policies, electrical piracy is a form of resistance. By effecting a more equitable distribution of resources, thefts sustaining the camp complicate idealized notions of law and order, questioning the conflation of illegality with illegitimacy.[7] We might invoke the urban theorist Edgar Pieterse to recast such acts as provocative questions: "Who is the city for? Whose identities and cultures are embodied by representations of the city? How can the futures of the city be reimagined?" (2005, 160).

In the field of electricity provision, the majority of Shatila's residents regard illicit practices as justified because of the Lebanese government's unwillingness to ensure proper services. Friends who relied on stolen supplies were remarkably candid about their illegal or quasi-legal practices. "What can we do? This is our life," Munir would say as he devised another illegal connection from his roof. Like the "quiet encroachment" Asef Bayat encountered among the urban poor in Cairo and Tehran, involving the "silent, protracted and pervasive advancement of ordinary people on the propertied and powerful in order to survive hardships and better their lives," camp residents see electricity theft as a natural, even righteous, response to deprivation (1997, 57).[8] Bayat argues that habitual routines, like Munir's daily hookups, are significant by virtue both of their regularity and their power to condition how individuals experience and interact with their environment. Unburdened as they are by ideology or institutional ties, strategies of survival and circumvention remain dynamically productive, capable of disrupting established social and political logics.[9]

Although spontaneous practices for dealing with scarcity are rarely consciously political or collectively organized—what Bayat calls a "non-movement"—they represent a kind of "street politics" in marginalized communities without institutional power or influence (2010, 14).[10] Though they lack an ideological framework or the formal structure of a protest movement, these practices are almost always "surreptitiously offensive" and represent a means by which the poor and disenfranchised effect a redistribution of material and symbolic capital, imposing "restraint upon the privileges of the dominant groups, allocating constituents of the life chances of those groups . . . to themselves" (Bayat 1997, 6).The illegal cables now knitting the buildings and walkways of Shatila together represent an assertion of need as well as a form of collective mobilization—a compensatory and provisional local power structure.

In recent years, the demolition of illegal housing on the camp's periphery has produced another arena of contestation. These periodic acts of counter-encroachment by government authorities have deepened uncertainty about Shatila's future and fueled rumors that the government intends to evict the community and redevelop the land.[11] In the spring of 2003, an illegal housing complex on the eastern edge of the camp, housing eight squatter families (primarily Lebanese migrants from the south), was demolished. One morning, a group of well-armed policemen turned up, unannounced, accompanied by a truck and a bulldozer. When the families refused to leave, the workers began to break down the outer wall of the building. I watched the scene unfold from an apartment in a nearby building. My host, Salim, pointed out that the squatters were not Palestinian, as if to say there was little reason to get exercised about the demolition.

Despite Salim's indifference, groups of youths gathered on rooftops began hurling bottles and rocks at the bulldozer, and within minutes a barricade of blazing tires had been erected to block its path. Residents in neighboring buildings rained verbal abuse on the heads of the policemen, while women in the street below, more diplomatically, tried to plead with them. "You see we have our own Intifada here!" Salim joked, pointing to the tires and the bottle-wielding youths. "Just wait and see what they say on LBC news [a Christian TV station] tonight," he continued, less optimistically. "They'll say, 'Palestinians in Shatila living on illegally occupied land were evicted.' For the Lebanese, we're a bunch of criminals and the camps are warrens of corruption [*awkar al-fasidin*]. These policemen are the same. They think the squatters are Palestinian; they don't realize most of them are Lebanese and Syrian."

The incident revealed technologies of state power, as well as the forms of political mobilization that can rise up in response to them. The incremental "quiet encroachment" of residents, which hitherto had not been viewed as a gain needing to be collectively defended, swiftly registered as such in the course of confrontations with government officials. The shared threat of eviction catalyzed a vigorous defense of the squatters by other camp residents, revealing latent solidarities that were neither explicitly ideological nor defined by ethnic, racial, or sectarian difference.

Such moments of sporadic, collective mobilization are both occasioned and conditioned by the shared experience of poverty and marginalization and by the recognition of common interests at stake. They reveal forms of agency and activism that lie outside normative categories for thinking about political practice in this context. As Bayat argues, the urban poor represent a collective force by virtue less of their intentions than their way of life, engaging as they do in a "politics not of protest but of redress."[12] Like Munir's hookups, practices that address concrete material concerns and seek to improve the quality of life in small but significant ways increasingly represent the ground on which political life is built. Despite their limitations, engaging them as a form of agency allows us to explore other, less obvious forms of political activity in Shatila and to recognize "illegality" as a resource and form of activism.[13]

THE HISTORY OF ELECTRICITY PROVISION IN SHATILA

Since the camps were first established, one of the ways the Lebanese state has sought to control and marginalize camp communities has been through the strict regulation of development and service provision. Abu Nayef, who comes from one of the founding families of Majd al-Krum who ran the camp prior to the establishment of PLO institutions in the 1970s, recalls the years when it was illegal to bring building materials into Shatila and the camp was without running water and power. Shatila was not connected to the grid until the mid-1950s, when two families from his village purchased meters. "It was then that the camp was first supplied with electricity from Sabra [a bordering neighborhood], and suddenly we were illuminated [*nawwaritna*], 'enlightened!'" he quips. This initiative to bring electricity to Shatila was spearheaded by Abu Turki, who came to be known as the "feudalist of electricity," supplying power to his neighbors from six o'clock in the evening until midnight for a small monthly fee (Sayigh 1994, 40).

Even though the absence of electricity up until that point was due, in part, to UNRWA's funding constraints and limited resources for such expenditures within the community itself, access to electricity was also highly political, dependent as much on influence and contacts as on wealth. Abu Turki's description of persuading EdL's director to extend a cable from Sabra to his home and provide him with four electric meters is revealing about the politics of service provision at that time: "I think it was in 1956—I went to the city and contacted the prime minister, Sami Solh. He gave me his card, and I took it to the director of the electricity company. He said, 'We have no instructions from the authorities to supply electricity to the camp. But because you have a card from the prime minister, I will give you a meter'" (Sayigh 1994, 40). Although Abu Turki was given a line, thanks to a number of hefty down payments and the deft introduction of the prime minister's business card at the opportune moment, state directives prohibited the EdL from connecting Palestinian camps to the grid.[14]

After the 1969 Cairo Agreement and the arrival of the PLO, living conditions in the camps improved dramatically.[15] A number of generators were installed in and around Shatila, providing free electricity for the growing Palestinian economy and for the personal use of camp residents. Flush with petrodollars from the Gulf, the PLO was able to fund an ambitious program of development in the camps, securing the provision of services UNRWA had lacked the means and influence to implement. This infrastructural safety net created in the 1970s and early 1980s—connecting camps to the grid and supplying them with potable water—was largely destroyed during the civil war. During the War of the Camps, Shatila was essentially razed: well systems were badly damaged, and the provision of electricity all but stopped, as generators outside the camps were hijacked or destroyed by the Shi'ite militia, Amal. The cables from neighboring districts supplying power to the camp were cut, while

shortages of diesel fuel and intensive shelling rendered the few remaining privately run generators largely unworkable (Sayigh 1994, 271–277). Recalling the
almost total absence of power during the sieges, friends recounted that dwindling supplies were carefully rationed to maintain essential services: the pump
for the main well, the bakery, and the UNRWA clinic. With less than four hours
of electricity per day, operations in the clinic were often performed by candlelight or by a lamp powered by a car battery (Giannou 1992).

With the departure of the PLO, the responsibility for providing water,
electricity, and sanitation services fell once more to UNRWA, which, along
with a number of local NGOs, financed much of the repair and reconstruction of Shatila's infrastructure in the late 1980s and early 1990s. Hampered by
ongoing building restrictions and a severe budget deficit, UNRWA was unable to complete much of the work needed to ensure the reliable provision of
services.[16] Although free electricity ended with the PLO's departure, UNRWA
subsidized the cost of reconnecting the camp to the grid in the early 1990s.
Since the end of the civil war, the electricity supplied by the EdL (as with all
other services in Shatila) has been administered by the PC, and all six neighborhoods in the camp are provided with electricity through a single transformer substation.

In order to receive electricity, individual subscribers are technically required
to install a meter. Monthly fees, which also include a service tax of around $7,
are paid to the EdL through the PC, which acts as the liaison between camp
residents and the company. Many of those receiving EdL electricity in Shatila,
however, do not have meters and source their supplies either by sharing a line
with others who do or by making illegal connections often arranged through
the PC for a small fee, which EdL officials are paid to ignore. It is now widely acknowledged that the PC and lower-level EdL employees have lucrative working
relations, with the former selling electricity at inflated rates (both within and
outside the camp) and accruing income through "fees" for illegal connections,
and the latter receiving hefty bribes and payoffs. Camp residents, state officials,
EdL inspectors, and PC representatives are increasingly entangled in webs of illegal or quasi-legal association.

Power lines officially intended to provide electricity to about eleven hundred households now supply close to five thousand. Unmetered "hookups"
clearly visible throughout the camp bear witness to the active redistribution
of electricity and to the inaccuracy of official statistics. Even though each
line should technically be able to carry a load of about one thousand watts—

enough to run an incandescent light, a small fan, and a television—the amount residents actually receive is often considerably less, because a single source may be shared by several families and there are an increasing number of illegal connections created, with or without the helping hand of the PC.[17] The increased strain on the camp's electricity supply has led to severe shortages and frequent power cuts from overloaded lines, but rather than reduce the number of illegal connections, the PC—in conjunction with the EdL—introduced "shifts" (*taqnin*) rationing electricity. When a friend once explained the concept of *taqnin*, which derives from the word for "law" (*qanun*), he speculated that it was an attempt by the PC to generate the impression of lawful regularity precisely where it was lacking.

Shatila's other main source of electricity comes from privately owned generators, for which subscribers pay a fixed monthly rate of between LBP 40,000 and LBP 60,000 (between $26 and $40) for a relatively stable supply of power. A number of local entrepreneurs—Abu Turki's roguish heirs—now manage these generators and sell electricity, either as a supplement to or substitute for EdL supplies. As with the EdL supply managed by the PC, these lines may be shared by several families living in close proximity. Wealthier families and businesses in the camp tend to rely on privately generated power supplies, which are regarded as more dependable and better maintained.[18]

When I asked friends to describe how they accessed electricity, most would preface their response by condemning the state neglect and PC corruption that had led to a growing number of illegal connections. Their own illicit dealings were often presented as unavoidable in context. While candor about electricity theft from municipal supplies was the norm, furtive hookups to a neighbor's supply, or the bribing of local brokers with ties to the PC, were more rarely acknowledged. Stealing electricity from outside the camp to supplement inadequate supplies within is viewed as a morally justified response to the state's policy of neglect, one that keeps power circulating in more than one sense. Electricity stolen from within the camp, by contrast, is regarded as enriching a corrupt group of PC members at the expense of the community. The moral consensus regarding electricity theft, however, is protean, shaped by contingencies, not absolutes. The assignment of blame in the event of a power cut therefore brings into relief shifting ontologies of power and offers entry points for understanding camp politics and the fraught dynamics of opposition, as they have become folded into everyday struggles over resources.

WHEN THE EDL CAME TO SHATILA

Although encounters between state officials and camp residents are relatively infrequent, EdL representatives are occasionally dispatched to Shatila to monitor local usage, dismantle illegal connections, conduct surveys, and extract subscription fees and fines from residents, usually with the assistance of PC representatives or, in some cases, the Lebanese police. Like the demolitions described previously, EdL visits number among the intrusive instruments of governmentality. Their sudden appearance reveals gaps between the letter of the law and everyday practice—gaps that residents, for their part, are quick to exploit.

One such visit took place in 1993. Despite the fact that Shatila was effectively without power between 1985 and 1993, Umm Mahmud remembers EdL officials turning up, demanding that houses with meters pay the service tax for the previous eight years; the bill in the case of her family came to almost $1,000. Officials also used this as an opportunity to impose fines on those without meters found to be accessing electricity from friends and neighbors. "Many disputed the fines, while others refused to pay to have meters installed, tearing up the paper in front of the authorities, arguing that it was a government scam to raise money to meet reconstruction costs after the war," recalled Umm Mahmud. "My father paid the bill because the meter was registered in the name of Ali [her elder brother who left in the late 1970s and was living abroad]. At the time, people warned us the officials would take down Ali's name and make trouble for him when he came back to visit." In particular, her family feared the government might take away Ali's refugee documents or make it difficult for him to reenter the country. Accounts of encounters between EdL staff and camp residents reveal the vulnerability of the latter, who are at the mercy of arbitrary changes in government policy.

This anecdote was recounted to me following an almost identical encounter with EdL officials in June 2003. One morning, without warning, company representatives returned to Shatila for the first time in several years, accompanied by a number of heavily armed police officers. The small group toured the camp, trying, with limited success, to extort heavy fines from those who, unlike Abu Ali, had chosen not to pay their bills or install official EdL meters when the camp's electrical supply had been reconnected in 1993. The EdL's halfhearted show of strength, which was stretched over several visits, was precipitated by a severe energy crisis in Lebanon that left the southern suburbs of Beirut without electricity for extended periods. This led to a series of investigations that revealed institutionalized corruption reaching up to the highest echelons of the company and the state: it was discovered that several prominent ministers had not paid their bills for years. Despite various proposals to radically reform the system, root and branch, few changes were implemented, which many speculated was the result of backroom deals by corrupt government ministers and EdL officials.[19]

The EdL's impromptu visit was clearly intended as a warning to the growing number of people engaged in stealing and selling electricity in and around Shatila. Rumors began to circulate that this visit was a clandestine information-gathering exercise and that a list of names of those who stole electricity from bordering neighborhoods was being compiled.[20] The uniformed officers and a handful of EdL staff, carrying files bulging with proof of unpaid bills, paraded up and down the main streets of Shatila. People watched their progress from windows and balconies with a mixture of interest and alarm, relishing the inevitable clashes. For many, the face-to-face encounter with despised state bureaucrats afforded the opportunity to complain about the inadequacy of camp services. Abu Ali, emboldened by his foresight years before, banged his cane on the wall of the balcony and nervously shouted curses as the group passed by in the street below: "Nabih Berri [the speaker of the Lebanese Parliament and leader of Amal, the Shi'ite political party] hasn't paid his bill for years, and you come to the camps first to take from us! Shame on you!"

Even after the last gray uniform had disappeared from view and we returned to Abu Ali's front room, the abject state of Shatila's services remained the subject of conversation. The small space soon filled to capacity, as neighbors, drawn by the rising decibels, joined in. There was a sense of irrepressible, almost euphoric, outrage that EdL officials had dared to set foot in the camp and demand payment for nonexistent and poorly maintained services. The visit heightened collective awareness of the community's unjust treatment at the hands of the state, lending further legitimacy to the unlicensed activities supplying the camp with power. The fact that the EdL had chosen to tackle its deficit by extorting money from its poorest clients (instead of addressing the corruption of ministers and unpaid bills in wealthy neighborhoods) blurred distinctions between the legality of the state and the criminality of the street. People also noted the differential treatment poor Shi'a communities living in Dahiyya received, where Hezbollah officials had swiftly intervened on behalf of their constituents. By contrast, when Shatila's power supply was capped at one or two hours a day—or cut off completely—so that wealthy residential neighborhoods might enjoy an uninterrupted supply, neither the PC nor any other body interceded. Moreover, the camp's unauthorized consumption of power was not quietly regularized in the weeks running up to elections, as had happened in neighboring districts in the southern suburbs.[21]

Umm Nabil, a passerby who had joined the discussion, described her encounter that morning with the same officials accompanied by representatives from the PC trying to impose a hefty fine on an elderly woman in her building who did not have a meter:

> The EdL official came with a policeman, and they had a receipt for LBP 450,000 ($300) [the cost to install a meter] and asked this woman—a cripple and in a wheelchair, shame!—for the money. Then Maher [a neighbor] came and defended her, shouting, "Either I kill you or you can kill me, but this woman cannot pay." Maher may be a drinker, but by God he's an honorable man. So the policeman arrested Maher and took him to the PC office to question him. It's a shame when you see how they [the EdL and the PC] are working in this business together.

While the unexpected arrival of EdL officials and policemen was unsettling for residents, it brought together—like the squatter eviction several months before—disparate groups in the camp, revealing common interests at stake. Elders I had heard make disparaging remarks about electricity brokers bringing the camp into disrepute became the first to commend the clandestine work of their neighborhood electricians; drunkards were redeemed as local heroes, and condemnation of PC corruption and complicity was unanimous.

The various small-scale conflicts that took place around the camp sorted the wheat from the chaff, good neighbor from bad. Acts of courage and resistance in the face of institutional power, like Maher's defense of his elderly neighbor, were counterbalanced by descriptions of cowardice and fear. Umm Nabil went on to note that she heard another neighbor providing EdL officials with information about who relied on stolen electricity in their building. "I heard him say, 'My *Palestinian* neighbor buys his electricity from this person, who steals from that person . . .' I couldn't believe it! In this moment, when he was facing these officials, he forgot that he too was Palestinian."

The climax came, however, when Abu Faruq, a friend and neighbor of Abu Ali's with the air of an elder statesman and a reputation for rhetorical flare, launched into an imaginary confrontation with the then prime minister, Rafiq Hariri, to the delight and amusement of all gathered:

> I shall say to him, "Forgive me your majesty, Mr. Prime Minister; my words are not lies. I speak on behalf of the dispossessed. At least you cannot tax my words!

I speak for the poor who have been canceled from the world map. We are souls, and we have respected you. . . . Have you sent your officials to mock us? The rich who have factories do not pay a franc for the power they use [he is referring here to Nabil Berri]. I told the official you sent I could not pay the fine—how can I, Mr. Prime Minister? Can't you see how we are living? Wake up! It's enough! If I don't die from darkness, I'll die from heat, and if I don't die from heat, I'll die from rottenness and suffocation. Are you laughing at us? You believe that because of the heat we have become pickles and can't think. We are surviving through our faith in God, and this is what enables us to still live in God's Qur'an."

This richly ironic speech, heavily abbreviated here, inspired a number of similar, if less rousing, critiques of Hariri and state cronyism. All shared a deep resentment of the rapacious hypocrisy of state officials who protect the rich at the expense of the poor. For Abu Faruq, the predicament of Palestinians in Shatila was shared with their poor Lebanese and Syrian neighbors. Residents clearly felt humiliated being treated as dupes—or "pickles," to use Abu Faruq's memorable metaphor—that could be preyed upon and pushed around, while the wealthy could buy their way out of any fix.[22] Others echoed his demand that the state provide for the poor and underprivileged. Since refugees cannot invoke the rights of citizens, these claims were framed as the moral entitlement of a subject population.[23] Just as appropriation of electric lines around the camp can be read as challenging the state's inequitable distribution of resources and its policy of neglect and denial, these angry critiques of corruption and extortion allowed residents to reframe their marginality as the moral high ground, all the while shoring up justifications for their own illicit dealings.

What was particularly poignant about these displays of defiance was that they often seemed directed at no one in particular or conjured up some fictive or absent subject to whom frustrations might be addressed. The powerlessness of the audience—whether a handful of elders sitting on a street corner, a gathering of friends and relatives, or neighbors complaining about the frequency or length of power cuts over morning coffee—lent these intermittent outbursts an air of added desperation and circularity. The EdL's visit made the absence of institutional mechanisms of grievance and redress abundantly clear.

HERDS AND MOBS: CAMP RESIDENTS AND THE POPULAR COMMITTEE

The name "Popular Committee" is clearly misleading on a number of levels. Most of Shatila's residents now contend that the hardships they experience have been exacerbated, rather than alleviated, by the institution meant to be serving their interests. "There is no authority!" (*ma fi marja'iyyeh*) is a frequent lament. As corruption scandals, rampant factionalism, and the inept management of camp resources have brought the credibility and legitimacy of factions and camp institutions under scrutiny, the trust that once characterized relations between residents and committee members has all but gone.

When the PC was first established in 1973, following the 1969 Cairo Agreement, it symbolized Palestinian autonomy in the camps and deliverance from the repressive policies of the office of military intelligence, the Deuxième Bureau. Between 1970 and the departure of the PLO, Lebanese security forces were not able to enter the camps without first negotiating with the PC, with permission granted on a case-by-case basis. During this time the PC also acted as mediator between the PRM leadership (where real political power lay) and camp residents. It represented a broad cross section of camp politics, with members from different political factions in the PLO appointed by the PRM (Sayigh 1994, 95). A number of additional posts were held by independents and camp elders (*wujaha*), who were expected to remain politically neutral and promote the interests of "the families of the camp" (*ahali al-mukhayyam*). Rather than challenge traditional structures of authority, the PRM sought, wherever possible, to accommodate and integrate them (Peteet 1987).

While the PLO leadership was based in Lebanon, the duties of the PC were primarily social and environmental, concerned with improving services and camp infrastructure. In the wake of the political fragmentation and realignments following the PLO's relocation to Tunis, the profile and role of the PC changed dramatically, with far-reaching consequences for the social and political organization of the camp. In the void left by the PLO leadership, the PC's role became more political, as it found itself also responsible for maintaining law and order and acting as a point of contact with Lebanese authorities. Although Lebanese military intelligence expect the PC to deliver wanted persons to them, they provide no resources for doing so, effectively extracting favors from the PC while offering nothing in return (Hanafi and Long 2010, 142). Following the abrogation of the Cairo Agreement, refugees lost the right to bear arms, and the authority of the Lebanese state over the camps was partially reinstated. Since this time the camps have continued to function outside the purview of Lebanese law as semiautonomous bodies, within which the PC is essentially responsible for policing and managing conflict resolution and arbitration. The net result is that there is no independent body to hold the PC accountable.

Although the PC has never been strictly democratic (its representatives have always been appointed by faction leaders rather than elected), a number of significant changes in the political landscape of the camp in the last two decades have altered its composition and undermined its legitimacy as a representative body. From the end of civil war in 1989 until the Syrian withdrawal after Prime Minister Hariri's assassination in 2005, Lebanese intelligence reasserted control over the camps with Syrian backing and blocked the reestablishment of a Palestinian United Front.[24] Fatah and the PLO were effectively prevented from building any power base in the camps in Beirut and northern Lebanon, and Syrian sponsorship of proxy factions fueled conflict between Arafatist factions and "the Alliance" (al-Tahaluf), a coalition of ten pro-Syrian factions (non-Fatah members of the PLO).[25]

In Shatila, fighting between Arafatists and pro-Syrian opposition groups resumed after the War of the Camps ended and intensified during the Internal War from 1989 to 1991, when the last remaining members of Fatah were redeployed from the camps in Beirut to the south and other pro-Arafatist parties were forced into submission. Representatives from the pro-Fatah factions (PFLP and DFLP), who had remained part of the PC until the late 1980s, were gradually edged out under pressure from PFLP-General Command (PFLP-GC), Fatah al-Intifada, and Al-Sa'iqa, the three pro-Syrian factions that have dominated Shatila's PC since 1988. The absence of any arbitrating power—in the form of either Lebanese law or PLO leadership—and the fracturing of the political collective in the camp have created a situation in which competition and partisanship prevail.[26] The chaotic web of partial or "phantom sovereigns" that now controls the camp also serves to underscore the perception that no representative authority exists (Hanafi 2008, 91).

The central role factions play in determining the allocation of camp resources—through the PC, but also through NGOs allied with factions—has extended political rivalry between Fatah loyalists and pro-Syrian parties into the field of service provision. Unlike popular committees in camps farther south—where Fatah continues to remain the primary provider—the pro-Syrian PC in Shatila lacks sufficient resources to fulfill its basic municipal duties. Abu Hani—the PFLP-GC chair of the PC from the late 1990s until his death in January 2005—was the perennial butt of bitter jokes. Accusations against him ranged from claims he was managing brothels and trafficking in drugs and guns, to more routine charges of administrative malfeasance. The most persistent charge, however, was that under his chairmanship, the PC exploited camp resources for the benefit of its members and their political allies in Damascus—aiding and abetting the sale of publicly owned goods (often to Lebanese and Syrian migrants living outside Shatila), at the expense of the camp's residents.[27] Although these allegations were often unverifiable, they circulated with such regularity as to acquire the status of fact.

When people spoke about their disillusionment with camp politics, moral and material disorder went hand in hand; political intimidation and material deprivation were almost always intertwined. Criticizing the PC's failure to address the camp's environmental problems became a way of commenting obliquely on other, more politically sensitive ones. When Abu Ali described his difficulties in getting piped water or expressed outrage at the mounting piles of garbage outside his home, it was also a way of addressing the thorny question of representation and accountability in the camp. "No one is in charge [*ma fi mas'ul mubashir*], and no one is responsible for addressing these problems. It is like herds and mobs here [*qatayi' wa hawash*]!"

For the majority of Shatila's residents, the chaotic mismanagement of the camp's power supply, above all, came to symbolize PC corruption and to bear metonymic relation to other forms of social and political disorder undermining the community from within. When I would visit Abu Qa'id, who owned a grocery store not far from where I lodged, our conversation invariably turned to his problems securing a stable supply of electricity to run the refrigeration unit and the costs entailed for his business by power cuts, which forced him to throw goods away. He was incensed that preferential treatment was given to households and businesses with close ties to the PC and thought basic services should have nothing to do with politics. In an effort to account for the moral failings of the PC, Abu Qa'id once observed that most of the representatives were "strangers"—Palestinians from Syria—who did not share the same values as Palestinians from Shatila:

> The voice you hear when they [the PC] speak is someone else talking. They are not from the camp, and they do nothing for the camp. . . . Look at Abu Hani [originally from Yarmouk camp in Damascus]. When he first came to Shatila, he was wearing flip-flops, and now he's building a villa for himself in Syria. How do you explain this? Real politics don't exist anymore. Now the committee is only PFLP-GC, Fatah Intifada, Al-Sa'iqa [all pro-Syrian]. If there were members from all the factions, as used to be the case, we wouldn't have the problems we have now. For instance, my neighbor, from the PFLP, makes

an illegal connection because he is having problems with his electricity. His neighbor belongs to another political party [i.e., pro-Syrian] and informs on him to the PC. When they find out, the committee will cut the line because he is not from a pro-Syrian faction, or they will demand a bribe. So then my neighbor gets angry and goes out into the street with his gun and threatens the representative from the PC. This is how fights start. There is no longer any authority [*ma fa zimam*]. . . . The other day I saw a big rat outside my house. I wanted to pass and the rat wanted to pass, so we stood there confused about who should pass first. Then a cat walked past us both, and said, "Peace be upon you." I felt the factions should take a lesson from this scene of the cat and rat respecting each other. You see them eating from the same garbage pile. They understand that to survive, they must work together and tolerate each other, in spite of the fact that they are enemies.

The pro-Syrian orientation of the PC has diminished communal loyalty to the institution and encouraged residents to view it as the arm of Syrian intelligence in the camp. Heightened anxieties that residents are spying and informing on one another has further strained relations of trust and cooperation. With the committee increasingly seen as monopolized by pro-Syrian parties, and no longer a mediating force between the various factions, residents have begun resorting to force to settle disputes. The entrenched factionalism and clientelism that have thrived under the PC have fostered parochial loyalties that, as Abu Qa'id suggests in his cat-rat parable, preclude broad solidarity and mobilization.

Examples abound of factional fighting hampering camp improvement initiatives. In 2002, a delegation from the municipal council of Bagnolet (a socialist commune in the suburbs of Paris) met with representatives from the PC in Shatila to establish a twinning committee (*lajnat taw'ami*). In an agreement signed by French and Palestinian committee members, the municipality of Bagnolet committed to providing the camp with substantial material support over several years. In their discussion of what kind of assistance would be most useful, electricity emerged as the most pressing concern. A camp representative who had attended the inaugural party to welcome the French delegates recalled that moments after the group's arrival there had been a power cut, and the entire ceremony had been conducted in semidarkness. The gloom clearly left a lasting impression on Bagnolet's delegates, who subsequently committed to raising funds to purchase a new generator and transformer for the camp.

News of Bagnolet's proposal spread like wildfire, and residents began to refer to the initiative, not without irony, as "Give light to Shatila" (*Aniru Shatila*). Tensions soon emerged, however, between members of the twinning committee affiliated with Al-Sa'iqa and the PC, on the one hand, and those allied with the PFLP, DFLP, and Fatah, on the other, who accused the PC of trying to assume control of the project.[28] In the wake of these disagreements a breakaway committee formed, leaving the representatives of Bagnolet in the unenviable position of having to determine which was the legitimate committee in the eyes of the community.[29] This rift in turn created divisions among the French delegates, and eventually the initiative ground to a halt—not, however, before the municipality of Bagnolet had sent a shipment of long-life bulbs as a final parting gift in lieu of the more ambitious project that had been aborted. I was later informed that some bulbs were distributed to residents, but the remainder had been sold by PC representatives to local vendors in Sabra souk.

The power wielded by the PC in Shatila has come to be understood in literal and spectral terms, both as a series of relations and policies shaping daily experience and as an inscrutable force originating far outside the boundaries of the camp. Residents feel they are subject to powers increasingly remote from their local world, and fear of Syrian influence—at least until Fatah reopened political offices in the camp in 2005—limited candor and set narrow limits on achievable political reform.[30] The sense of intimidation people experience was well expressed by Samar, the elder daughter of Abu Ali, in an account of a confrontation she had with Abu Hani, the chair of the PC, over access to one of the few public sources of potable water, located outside the center in which she worked. Samar recalled that, sitting in her office one day, she heard a commotion in the street below:

> When I went down, I found a young man attaching a long black rubber pipe to the faucet. When I asked him what he was doing, he told me he had been ordered to do so by Abu Hani. I said (jokingly, of course), "Who is this Abu Hani? He is not from the residents [*sukkan*] of Shatila, I don't recognize or respect him, and I won't answer to him."[31] Then I realized someone was standing behind me, and when I turned around, I saw Abu Hani. I felt myself shaking inside, but I didn't want him to see how frightened I was, so I said, "I grew up here and know my rights." He responded, sarcastically, "Thank you, and may your benevolence multiply! [*shukran wa-kaththar khayrak*]."

Of course, in the end there was nothing I could do to stop him, so he continued to pump this supply of fresh water to his home. Afterwards, he made things as difficult as he could for us at the center [an NGO-affiliated with DFLP, a loyalist faction]. One time he accused me of bringing visitors into the camp without seeking permission from the committee. I asked, "What is this committee? Who is with you, and for whom do you speak?" He answered, "Intifada and Al-Sa'iqa." So I said, "Where are DFLP, PFLP, and the camp elders?" He laughed and responded, "They don't agree to join us."

Revealed here is the complex interplay of intimidation, defiance, and grudging consent that has come to characterize relations between residents and the PC. The political power accrued by the PC, undergirded by vivid memories of the brutal suppression of loyalist forces by Syrian-backed factions after the PLO's departure, has created conditions in which the gap between discursive and active resistance is not easily or willingly bridged. While people complain bitterly about camp governance in the privacy of their homes, this critique rarely takes public form. Although verbal accusations did not constitute active opposition to the PC, they enabled speakers to reposition themselves in relation to the institution. Samar's work at the center and her dealings with foreign visitors compelled her to continue to operate within established power structures, and she had little choice but to maintain relations with the committee and with Abu Hani up until his death, even while—as she wryly put it—"he used our drinking water to wash his socks!"

Even though large-scale collective mobilization aimed at challenging or overthrowing the PC was not in evidence, I encountered small-scale acts of resistance taking place all the time. One afternoon while I was sitting with Umm Mahmud, a PC representative stopped by to collect her monthly "service tax" for electricity—in this case the relatively small sum of LBP 5,000 ($3.30). Taking him to task, she made it very clear she would make no such payment. This was within her rights, she explained, not only because the PC had failed to provide power for months but also because she had reason to believe the money was going into the pockets of committee members rather than to the EdL.

Confrontations like this one, which seemed at odds with normative relations between PC representatives and residents, were—I later discovered—occurring in households across the camp. Umm Mahmud's decision not to pay was not only a pragmatic response to inadequate supply but also, given the smallness of the sum involved, a form of protest. As fewer residents were willing to pay the PC for services they were not receiving, these individual acts of defiance snowballed, revealing a collective recognition of common interests at stake. Construed as part of a growing disagreement between camp residents and the PC over the management of electricity, material and ideological grievances began to fuse in more articulate and explicit ways. Although residents often claimed the refusal to pay was a critique of dismal services not received, these actions were also intended as a challenge to Syrian control of the PC.

The fact that these acts of defiance were undertaken independently by individuals, rather than by political factions or established groups, and were couched in mundane material terms rather than overtly political ones, meant those involved were not subject to the same kinds of scrutiny by the PC. However, as these critiques of profiteering and incompetence became more collective, demands for greater efficiency and accountability began to take on momentum. These periodic acts of protest, when camp residents joined forces to defend local interests, represented an alternative mode of political action whose very effectiveness seemed to derive from its ad hoc informality. The absence of any clearly identifiable, organizing structure for these forms of resistance allowed those "protesting" to disappear back into the woodwork as quickly as they had emerged from it, effecting as it were a form of political infiltration and contestation through the seams.

STEALING AND SHARING

When I first began lodging in Shatila, I was struck by the way electrical wiring was a more or less ubiquitous skill. Almost everyone I knew had some idea of how to create a "hookup" should the main supply of electricity fail. The seamless way in which these practices associated with electricity provision have become woven into the fabric of everyday life was revealed during an interview a colleague and I filmed with an elderly blind man. Midway through the interview there was a power cut, and we found ourselves in semidarkness. Assuming we could not continue, we made moves to leave, saying we would return the following day.

Our host, however, had already risen to his feet and, feeling his way over to the window on the other side of the room, called out to his neighbor in the apartment above before proceeding to tug at a wire draped over the windowsill. Fingering the length of the wire until he found a portion covered with a thick layer of protective plumbing tape, he then carefully held onto this unexposed segment and reached through the window, connecting the end (conveniently fashioned in the shape of a hook), to another wire outside. Within seconds power had returned. When I recounted this incident with some amazement (and concern) to a friend, he reminded me that conditions in Shatila were such that camp residents, even the blind, had no choice but to develop some expertise in electrical work.[32]

During the last decade, as problems associated with electricity have become more pronounced, a complex topography of intersecting social networks has developed to deal with shortfalls of supply, grounded in a series of routine practices designed to maximize resources. Technical skill in this sense merges fluidly with skills we might characterize as social and political, such as knowing at any given moment who in each locality has the capacity to source power, broker connections, or bribe officials. Over time it became clear that people's capacity to access power was determined primarily by whom they knew. Indeed, it would seem that people constitute the infrastructure of the camp, operating as nodes within complex networks of shared interests.[33] These alliances, which frequently tap into existent social ties and are based on mutuality and reciprocal exchange, have in modest ways rebuilt the relations of communal trust the PC is accused of undermining. In many cases, the necessarily illicit component of accessing electricity has served to consolidate trust and discretion between the parties involved and strengthen neighborly ties between households.

Umm Mahmud has chosen to supplement her inadequate electricity supply by sharing power with her neighbors and installing an illegal connection to municipal supplies in Ard Jalool, a bordering district. The decision to source electricity from outside the camp was made collectively by residents in her building to reduce the initial costs of buying and installing the cable. A local electrician from the camp set up the connection. Each neighborhood has a number of *kahrabji*—sometimes referred to as "electricity thieves" (*sarraqin kahraba'*)—who make their living by redistributing electric power from outside the camp to their clients within. Residents normally pay a fixed fee of around LBP 15,000 ($10) a month that covers the cost of the materials and labor required to install and maintain the lines, which are regularly dismantled by EdL employees. In cases where electricity brokers are able to bribe EdL staff, a line might stay up for as long as a week; usually, however, hookups will be taken down every few days.

In Umm Mahmud's neighborhood, residents employed a *kahrabji* known affectionately as Abu Sadan (the monkey's father). In contrast to the illegal sales of electricity enriching a handful of PC officials and their cronies, the work of Abu Sadan and his associates was broadly viewed as benefiting the camp. Rather than leech Shatila's limited supply for personal gain, electricity thieves cater to the needs of the community at the expense of the state by sourcing electricity from municipal supplies outside the camp. As a "son of the camp," hailing from one of the founding families, Abu Sadan also has greater legitimacy for many than the Syrian-born Palestinians controlling the PC. As his nickname suggests, he has a reputation as a local trickster, outwitting the EdL inspectors, and he is quick to reconnect wires that have been disconnected, nimbly climbing the pylons with a cummerbund of spare cable and a pair of pliers.

Although he works independently, Abu Sadan collaborates with others in the same line of business, as long as they are not direct competitors. He has a number of partners in Shatila, Bir Hasan, and the Horsh (bordering areas inhabited mainly by Syrian migrant workers and poor Lebanese) with whom he shares information and devises new tactics. By sourcing electricity from more than one area, he has found ways to keep his supplies relatively stable, so when one supply is cut off, others remain operative—a system carefully calibrated to reduce the likelihood of power outages.

Abu Sadan's playfulness in talking about his work belied the very real risks involved. Making the inherent uncertainties of his profession his strength, he has developed a set of skills allowing him to improvise and adapt as his working conditions change from day to day. He memorizes the EdL staff's routes through the surrounding neighborhoods and knows which places to avoid at which times.[34] Sometimes he varies his own work patterns, shifting locations and adopting different strategies to reduce the risk of being caught. In a neighborhood he works, Ard Jallul, he has strategic alliances with several EdL employees and local policemen patrolling the area, paying them bribes to avoid arrest. The strength of Abu Sadan's mode of operating "on the wing" is precisely this ability to seize moments of opportunity as they arise.[35]

While Abu Sadan will tell you he steals electricity because he has to, with few other jobs available to him, these illicit acts also represent a form of resistance in his mind, a kind of "symbolic hijacking" of state power (Bourdieu 2000, 185). The pleasure he derives from his work results partly from his sense that he is engaged in a more equitable distribution of the city's resources. In an interview he told me he preferred to source his electricity from Ard Jallul because of the large number of state officials based there. "I like to take electricity from Ard Jallul because with so many government institutions, like Hariri's clinic and school [established by the former prime minister], the EdL makes sure the supply is good." On a subsequent occasion, he presented his decision to work outside the camp as a conscious critique of electricity theft taking place within the camp under the auspices of the PC. "One bad seed and the whole plate of fruit will rot," he told me, disparaging the work of Abu Hani and other committee members. Stealing from municipal supplies therefore functioned as a threefold critique: of the negligence of the state, the corruption of the PC, and the opportunism of those engaged in piracy within the camp. At other times, Abu Sadan dismissed the political implications of his work, presenting it simply as a source of income, his apparent inconsistency a reminder that everyday tactics become politically valenced only at particular moments and are often marked by indeterminacy and ambiguity.

Power brokers like Abu Sadan generate complex chains of relation—in his case, between EdL staff, local Hezbollah representatives working for the municipality of Ghoubeiry (where Shatila is located), policemen, Lebanese residing in bordering neighborhoods, camp residents, and so on—that extend beyond the camp and therefore work to destabilize not only social and spatial boundaries inscribed by the state but also resource monopolies within Shatila. New networks of exchange and cooperation are continually formed (brokered through fees, bribes, and other informal transactions) between camp residents and diverse elements of the surrounding city. As the government's aggressively exclusionary policies seek to isolate communities like Shatila, these informal and illicit compensatory practices challenge those policies and establish relations of interdependency—both with the surrounding city and within the camp—which in turn can become the basis for other forms of collaboration.

THE ACTIVE ONES

In a context in which people are reluctant to confront the leadership of the PC, and grassroots activism has moved away from the representational structure of formal party politics, to what extent are these informal modes of protest able to feed more sustained forms of political mobilization? Can these same dynamics be deployed in more formal settings? In the course of fieldwork, I encountered a number of informal associations that attempted, with varying degrees of success, to reform camp management. Established in response to specific infrastructural concerns—for example, garbage, sanitation, water and electrical services—these associations would often set out to bring disparate interest groups together through targeted goals. These ostensibly nonpolitical initiatives, however, were often short-lived, as group solidarity was unraveled by political factionalism.

In the late spring of 2003, a group calling themselves "The Active Ones" (Fa'liyyat, literally, the "doers"), comprising camp residents from different political backgrounds, formed an alliance to address the electricity problem.[36] I learned about the initiative when a member delivered a flyer to Umm Mahmud, urging her to join their campaign. "Law and security! We want to systematize conditions in Shatila" (*Haq wa-amaneh! Bidna al-umur tsir nizamiyyeh bi Shatila*) read the announcement. The list of goals seemed straightforward enough: implementing street cleaning and garbage removal, increasing security measures, and improving electricity provision. Umm Mahmud and Munir were nevertheless skeptical, expressing doubts about the group's ability—and even its intention—to deliver reform.

The Fa'liyyat convened its first meeting in an old bomb shelter in the center of the camp. About forty men, mostly in their forties and fifties, gathered in the damp, poorly lit space, some leaning against the walls, others sitting on worn plastic chairs arranged in a circle in the center of the room. A young man introducing himself as Tariq sat next to me, and we struck up a conversation. He told me he had decided to attend because he felt the PC's mismanagement of the camp had reached unacceptable levels and demanded some kind of collective response. Ali al-Khatib, who chaired the meeting, opened the discussion by reminding those gathered that while individuals were welcome, factions were not, and imploring those with factional ties—likely the vast majority—to leave their politics at home. "While it is acceptable to disagree on how to liberate Palestine, we shouldn't be fighting over how to clean up the camp or ensure the safety of our families—we have to work together on this," he concluded.

A lively debate ensued about the cause of and solution to deteriorating conditions in Shatila. There were oblique allusions to the corruption of the PC and to the deleterious impact Syrian influence was having on camp politics, but an emphasis on mismanagement of electricity offered needed camouflage for political critique: "How is it I can see lights on in the Horsh less than ten meters from my house, while I am sitting in the dark?" asked one man, alluding to the recent discovery that the PC had been providing electricity to Syrian migrants living in neighboring squatter settlements. This perception was seconded by Abu Ra'if, a camp elder who had recently returned from the hajj, a gleaming white presence in the dingy gloom. Others were concerned that "guards" appointed by the PC to secure the room where the transformer was kept (under pressure from camp residents) were themselves stealing and selling electricity. Discussion then shifted to how to address these problems, what the group's role should be, and how they should describe their work to others. Many were opposed to becoming a formal, named association, on the grounds that doing so would arouse mistrust and provoke the PC and its allies unnecessarily.

How precisely to confront the PC was clearly a delicate issue. Disagreement centered on whether to compel the PC and other institutions responsible for camp maintenance (municipal authorities, NGOs, UNRWA) to improve existing conditions or to take matters into their own hands. Should the Fa'liyyat deliver a list of complaints and demands to the PC? Should it demand a public meeting, with residents collectively voicing concerns? Or would it be more effective for a select group of representatives to negotiate with committee members behind closed doors? It was decided that rather than confront the PC directly and risk factional conflict, the Fa'liyyat would adopt a strategy of accommodation and dialogue. Responsibility for collecting garbage, patrolling the camp at night, and monitoring Shatila's electricity would rotate among members, with the larger goal of reforming camp management by example. By applying pressure through direct action, Fa'liyyat members hoped to transcend factionalism and force the PC to address pressing community concerns.

While this strategy was embraced enthusiastically at first, doubts began to surface during the weekly meetings. Far from shaming the PC into action, some argued, the Fa'liyyat was doing their work for them, encouraging even greater negligence. Over the course of a number of meetings I attended between April and August 2003, factionalism proved not only revived but more intractable. By July two rival groups had formed—one loosely affiliated with the PFLP, under the leadership of Ali al-Khatib, and the other supporting Sheikh Hassan from Jenin mosque, known to have strong ties with Hamas. Tensions came to a head in August with Sheikh Hassan refusing to recognize a subcommittee elected to meet with the PC, on grounds that he and a number of his associates had not been present when the vote was taken. In the fall of 2003 the Fa'liyyat formally disbanded when it was discovered that several members had been acting as spies for the PC all along.

When I later discussed the demise of the Fa'liyyat with Tariq, he blamed fundamental "misunderstandings" (su'tafahum) between members over how to realize the group's goals. The partisan distribution of camp resources, Tariq pointed out, had left residents little choice but to follow the lead of their political benefactors: "Most people were being pushed from behind by factions; others didn't understand the point of the group and felt there was no clear goal—how could they claim to represent the interests of people in the camp when they themselves were so divided? People say they are independent, but in reality no one can afford to be." While the Fa'liyyat strenuously sought to set itself apart from factional politics, committing to civil reform through action and dialogue, its internal divisions became manifest, and its relationship to the PC, muddied. During the penultimate meeting, Tariq recalled, he accused a member siding with Ali al-Khatib of abandoning the group's original principles: "'Do you want to eat grapes or fight with the watchman (*biddak takul 'inab walla itqatil al-natur*)?,' and he answered, 'Both.' I felt it was a significant thing to say. This was their mistake."

THE ELECTION OF THE PEOPLE'S COMMITTEE

Returning to Beirut in July 2005, after almost a year away, I was greeted with dramatic stories of a power cut lasting from November 2004 to early June 2005. Unable to sustain the mounting pressure placed on it, the main generator managed by the PC had exploded, plunging Shatila into darkness for nearly eight months. Unlike previous power cuts, this one had been "100 percent." Scarcity in the past had been mitigated by siphoning more power from bordering neighborhoods, but this collapse of internal supplies had coincided with a nationwide energy crisis, leaving the entire southern suburbs without electricity. Residents of Shatila found themselves at the mercy of local generator operators and a PC intent on profiting from the situation. Umm Mahmud recounted how—lacking even the glow from the sulfur lights of surrounding neighborhoods—she had seen the stars from her roof for the first time in years. The darkness, in fact, proved enlightening in ways few could have anticipated.

The self-censorship and circumlocution I had come to recognize as veiled critiques of the PC and Syrian hegemony had developed, in the darkroom of an eight-month power cut, into a series of sharp, lucid, forthright attacks. The collective critique of PC incompetence had been clarified and drawn into public discourse. The crisis had also underscored the inability of existing oppositional structures (loyalist factions, unions, shadow committees like the Fa'liyyat, NGOs, and so forth) to deal with the problem or implement change. Factional conflict intensified, as Fatah reopened its office in Shatila and sought to reestablish its power base there. Umm Mahmud described how political rivalries had once again blocked measures to restore the power supply:

> The Syrian factions have controlled this camp for years now. At the beginning of the year Sultan Abu Aynayn [at that time, leader of Fatah in Lebanon], seeing

the problems facing the camp, said the PLO would bring a new generator to Shatila to solve the electricity issue. . . . Fatah said they would install a new generator in the camp if it could be established in their name, so people would know they had paid for the work. Naturally, Abu Hani refused. Abu Hani knew if he let Fatah install a new generator, they would soon implement other improvements, and then they'd have the camp in their hand. This is how our leaders think. The problems we face as a community don't count; it becomes a political game for them.

Umm Mahmud went on to describe how the EU had also become involved—sending engineers from France to assess the needs of the camp and installing a new generator in late January, under the auspices of the PC. Even this failed to switch on the lights, however, because EdL officials and PC representatives demanded residents pay outstanding debts for electricity consumed by unmetered households, estimated at approximately LBP 210 million ($140,000). When it became clear that residents were neither willing nor able to pay, the sum dropped to LBP 32 million ($21,333) and eventually to LBP 3 million ($2,333) over the course of four months. This was taken as further proof that the fines were capricious and illegitimate, a money-making scheme for EdL staff and PC members.

In the time I was away, feelings of being "fed up" (*zah'an*) and disaffected with camp politics had been replaced by more directed forms of political dissent, with electricity frequently the primary source of contention. Friends informed me that by the end of December 2004, different neighborhoods had begun to organize regular protests demanding electricity be restored and calling for new policies to regulate the distribution of power in Shatila.

Intransigent to the last, Abu Hani did little to address these concerns and in early January 2005 suffered a heart attack, viewed by many as the work of divine justice. A new PC chair, Abu Musa, was appointed, who like Abu Hani was a member of the pro-Syrian PFLP-GC. Meanwhile, the demonstrations continued. Ali al-Khatib (the former chair of the Fa'liyyat) recounted that in February he had organized a candle-lit vigil outside the EdL headquarters in Beirut, where a group of thirty residents—including Palestinian and Lebanese residents from Shatila—had distributed leaflets to company employees and passersby, detailing the plight of camp residents and demanding that the government resolve the electricity crisis in the southern suburbs. The efforts of the Fa'liyyat—and various other unsuccessful neighborhood committees—had been hijacked by the political ambitions of one faction or another and were re-placed by a series of spontaneous mobilizations. Just as the decision by Umm Mahmud and others not to pay monthly taxes to the PC constituted an oblique critique of institutional corruption, these protests calling for a radical reorder-ing of Shatila's electricity, both inside and outside the camp, challenged state negligence and were also a demand for internal political reform and greater autonomy from Syrian influence.

While intolerable living conditions had clearly spurred residents to action, the sense of possibility marking this moment was also linked to broader politi-cal transformations in the region. Ali al-Khatib's grassroots initiative to reform the organization of the camp coincided with what seemed to be seismic shifts in Lebanon's political order following the Hariri assassination. In the weeks after Hariri's death, reprisals against Syrians escalated, leading to an estimated three hundred thousand Syrians leaving the country; by the end of April the Syrian army, under mounting international pressure, had withdrawn its forces from Lebanon. In Shatila, pro-Syrian factions, already weakened by the hiatus in their leadership after Abu Hani's sudden death the previous month, strug-gled to retain control of the camp. Having lost the support of its principal ally, the powerbase of the PC and the pro-Syrian factions in the camp visibly weakened.

Though this moment of crisis required political activity to be more self-aware and politically directed, the mobilization of the community was effec-tive precisely because it drew upon the bedrock of political latencies I have described. In February 2005 a group calling themselves the Follow-Up and Reform Committee (FRC) (Lajnat al-Mutaba'a wa al-Islah) emerged, debuting with a leaflet campaign charging the PC with enriching themselves through extortionate fines. The FRC proposed the solution of holding elections for a new People's Committee (Lajnat al-ahali), which might properly represent the interests of the camp. The manifesto stated that the primary responsibility of the People's Committee would be to take charge of electricity provision and improve living conditions in the camp.

The People's Committee was, in fact, an institution dating back to the 1950s and 1960s, which had played an active role in the management of the camp before the arrival of the PLO and the establishment of the PC. Reviving this former civil association marked distance from existing political struc-tures and invoked a period of the camp's history when collective interests had been paramount. The People's Committee also benefited from its perceived autochthony: unlike the PC, which was controlled by "foreigners," representatives elected to the People's Committee had to hail from Shatila's founding families, making the institution a natural extension of local kinship structures. Political neutrality was presented as crucial to the overall success of the initiative, with members of the Reform Committee repeatedly claiming to be acting on behalf of the people of Shatila rather than any particular political faction—a position that for reasons I have outlined is hard to maintain. While the FRC strenuously asserted that the initiative was civil rather than political, and that it did not seek to compete with established institutional structures, the election of a People's Committee was broadly viewed as challenging the authority of the PC, redefining the boundaries of moral and political community in the camp.

The FRC subsequently convened a meeting in the main public hall to discuss the logistics of holding the first democratic elections in Shatila's history and agree upon a list of procedures.[37] The election was scheduled for May 22, 2005, coinciding with the first round of the Lebanese parliamentary elections; the timing seemed deliberate and symbolic, setting the revitalization of camp politics against the ironic backdrop of residents' continuing political disenfranchisement in Lebanon. In the weeks leading up to the election, flyers with the slogan "Voting is your right! Vote for the one who represents you" became ubiquitous, exhorting residents to participate. These official announcements were accompanied by a series of campaign posters promoting individual candidates, which still papered the walls when I arrived in July. Many of these employed standard political tropes ("Enough! 57 years of Nakba!"); others were wittily transgressive, satirizing the whole process as self-promotion. One such poster combined crude, low-tech design with bombastic overstatement and managed to cause a small sensation. The text accompanying the candidate's glum headshot read: "The asphalt gives off light! Why? Because Abu Muhawish is walking on it."

The electoral rules so confidently set down on paper were unevenly enforced. Though two people were barred from registering as candidates because of suspected ties to the PC, of the thirty-two candidates who did register, friends observed, not one could claim political neutrality. Furthermore, while residents were asked to vote for individual representatives rather than a slate (part of the effort to loosen the electoral grip of the factions), by the final week before the election factional coalitions had formed. Thus, initial optimism about what the elections represented was increasingly cut with weariness

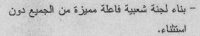

انتخبوا

المهندس: محمد كلّم (أبو عبد الله)

مرشح الكلمة الحرة والشجاعة

مرشح الكفاءات

سأعمل على:

- بناء لجنة شعبية فاعلة مميزة من الجميع دون استثناء.
- رفع الظلم والمعاناة عن أهلنا في مخيم شاتيلا.
- تحسين أوضاعهم الخدماتية والتعليمية والصحية والبيئية.
- تأمين ظروف عمل لهم من خلال المجتمع المدني اللبناني ومن خلال مؤسسات الأونروا ومؤسسات منظمة التحرير الفلسطينية.

* انتخب الإنسان المناسب للمكان المناسب دون تردد فهو في خدمتك.
* لا تنسوا انتخابات اللجنة الشعبية لمخيم شاتيلا.
الأحد ٢٠٠٥/٥/٢٢ من الساعة الواحدة ظهراً ولغاية الساعة الخامسة عصراً.
المكان: قاعة الشّعب.

Abu Muhawish's campaign flyer, May 2005. Photograph by author.

and cynicism; some even began speculating that the entire episode had been orchestrated by the PC to mollify residents with the mirage of electoral reform.

Although the PC hung on for several months, it was clear that its credibility had been irrevocably damaged by the eight-month power cut and by the challenge posed by the election. On June 6, a week after the People's Committee had successfully arranged for the camp to be reconnected to the grid, Abu Musa, the interim chair of the PC, made a statement, which was printed on large posters and affixed to the walls throughout the camp. Thanking the People's Committee for its efforts in resolving the electricity crisis, the statement was widely read as a weak attempt to exculpate PC members:

> The Popular Committee and the Palestinian factions and forces would like to thank the brothers in the People's Committee for their support and resistance and for their financial help in tackling the electricity problem—the problem the people of Shatila have been suffering from for a very long time. In addition, all the people of Shatila would like to salute and greet the brothers in the People's Committee . . . or their brotherly spirit that has put them in the lead position to lift the suffering and injustices undermining the most basic elements of a decent life for Palestinians living in the camps. Although various organizations were approached about this irremediable problem . . . the brothers in the Committee were the only ones to have dealt with it.

Appended to the letter was a copy of a receipt—blown up to a scale that made the figures almost illegible—which the PC claimed was proof of payment made to the EdL. Ultimately, the time and effort the PC spent responding to public reprobation further compromised its legitimacy. Mahmud Kallem, who saved a copy of the poster for me, described how residents interpreted it as proof of the committee's complicity in the collapse of camp services. The People's Committee contacted the EdL to verify the receipt's authenticity, only to be told that in fact no such payment had been made. The brother of one member of the People's Committee later recounted to me that he had reacted to the PC's statement by advising Abu Musa to enlarge the receipt still further. "I told him to make it seven feet by seven feet," Mahmud recalled, with satisfaction; "*then* maybe people will believe you."

After the People's Committee had met with EdL officials and restored electricity to the camp, representatives, intent on securing lower rates and better services for residents, held additional meetings with Lebanese authorities responsible for providing services to Shatila. Subscription to EdL services

بسمه تعالى

رسالة شكر

الإخوة في لجنة دعم المقاومة في فلسطين

السلام عليكم ورحمة الله وبركاته

إن كلاً من اللجنة الشعبية والقوى والفصائل الفلسطينية تتقدمان من الإخوة في لجنة دعم المقاومة في فلسطين بجزيل الشكر والتقدير على دعمهم المالي لمخيم شاتيلا لحل مشكلة الكهرباء التي عانى منها أهالي المخيم خلال فترة طويلة من الزمن. كذلك، فإن الأهالي في مخيم شاتيلا جميعهم يحيّون الإخوة في لجنة دعم المقاومة في فلسطين هذه الروحية الأخوية التي تجعلهم دائماً في موقع الحريص على رفع للمعاناة والمظلومية التي تتحكم بكافة مفاصل مقوّمات الحياة الكريمة عند الفلسطيني في المخيمات.

وإننا في الوقت الذي تقدمنا فيه إلى العديد من المؤسسات لحل هذه المشكلة العضال التي أفاضت هموماً كثيرة على أهالي المخيم بشكل عام، وعلى المؤسسات الاجتماعية والتعليمية والاقتصادية بشكل خاص، لم نجد إلا من الإخوة في لجنة دعم المقاومة سبيلاً لحلّ هذه الأزمة. لذلك، لم تأتِ هذه الرسالة إلا من باب الشكر والتقدير لهذه الجهود الكريمة والطيبة التي قامت وتقوم بها هذه للجنة المباركة.

وكان الله في عون العبد مادام العبد في عون أخيه

والسلام عليكم ورحمة الله وبركاته

اللجنة الشعبية في مخيم شاتيلا

القوى والفصائل الفلسطينية – شاتيلا

10/6/2005

اللجنة الشعبية
مخيم شاتيلا

Abu Musa's statement and the Electricité du Liban receipt, June 10, 2005. Photograph by author.

became incrementally billable, and the EdL agreed to discounted prices for the purchase of meters. Committee members produced a detailed report on the state of Shatila's electrical infrastructure and drew up proposals for needed repair work. A second generator was installed to provide subsidized electricity to households without meters. In the course of documenting the state of Shatila's electricity, committee representatives also gathered information on water, sanitation, and other issues on a neighborhood-by-neighborhood basis. The resulting reports functioned not only as a useful survey of the state of camp services but also as a symbolic counterdiscourse—a "governmentality from below" (Appadurai 2002, 35). By wresting control of the power embedded in technologies of surveillance and enumeration (in this case, both from state officials and inept local institutions), committee members and residents who organized and participated in these surveys sought actively to shape the agenda of local politics.[38]

As the culmination of a protracted struggle between residents and the PC, the election of the People's Committee allowed the community to redefine the terms of political engagement in the camp, confront the corruption and ineptitude of the PC, and reclaim moral leadership. The election also set a precedent for what could be achieved through community mobilization when factional affiliations were sidelined, however fleetingly, and represented a shift in the community's perception of its capacity to implement change and pursue collective goals. During the election itself, but also in the protests leading up to it, residents pooled resources, developed informal neighborhood information campaigns, offered themselves as political candidates, and devised individual and collective strategies for challenging the PC—all, initially at least, outside factional politics. Mobilizing the community while bypassing the factions required residents to draw on local support networks that had formed over the years precisely to deal with problems of service provision.

Ultimately, the success of the election was short-lived and did not radically transform camp politics, root and branch, as residents had hoped. It heralded neither the demise of the factional politics nor the establishment of democratic governance in Shatila. After the People's Committee had resolved the problems related to electricity, interest in further reform waned: the positive change it introduced, in effect, undermined the conditions fostering its existence. Threats by pro-Syrian factions compelled six committee members to withdraw, and within six months the People's Committee had disbanded, and the Syrian-backed PC became once more the primary governing institution in the camp.[39] The election and the events leading up to it, however, revealed a growing awareness that effective camp management could be realized only through a radical revamping of the committee system; it also highlighted how even more traditionally conceived forms of political engagement are being reshaped by everyday material struggles. Tactics for getting by have become a medium of political latency, one not self-consciously ideological or politically self-formulating, to be sure, but one ready to be drawn on in moments of political crisis.

· · ·

Electricity provides an ideal lens through which to examine ontologies of power in Shatila not only because it makes visible the connections between exclusionary state policies and local governance, and the determinative influence of camp politics on resource distribution, but also because the struggle for electricity now represents the ubiquitous backdrop of everyday existence. As the site of intense struggle and improvisation, the field of electricity provision constantly generates new tactical possibilities, new idioms within the local vernacular of informal power. These daily acts of trespass perforate the boundaries between inclusion and exclusion, the legal and the illicit, and as such contribute to a redefinition of political practice in Shatila. Alliances between Palestinians and Lebanese—both within and outside the camp—addressing access to services are suggestive of incipient solidarities forming across ethnic divides, motivated as they are by the shared experience of deprivation and marginalization.

In a context in which residents struggle not only to access the resources of a city that has systematically marginalized them but also to hold their own governing bodies accountable, these forms of "encroachment" are successful precisely insofar as they "do not exhibit any of the characteristic valor or romance of counterpublics" but remain ambivalently positioned (Liang 2005, 13). Configured around a more dispersed logic of everyday consumption and immediate need rather than ideology or factional politics, these practices are nevertheless charged with political meaning, if not always with political intent. As the election revealed, these sporadic actions can cumulatively effect political change by producing structured, harmonized, and articulate movement in times of crisis. Neither explicitly nationalist nor ideological in structure, the significance of the counterpublic that came into being in the course of the eight-month power cut, and consolidated itself in the first democratic election to be held in any Palestinian camp in Lebanon, becomes intelligible only when one considers it in relation to an intricate politics of everyday survival: a supple, unself-conscious, and protean politics that can include practices as subversive and seditious as those described in this chapter, or as intimate and unassuming as those in the next.

Woman at window, Shatila camp. Photograph © Hisham Ghuzlan, 2009.

4 DREAM TALK, FUTURITY, AND HOPE

"OUR VILLAGE WAS NAMED AFTER THE PROPHET SHEIKH DANUN," Umm Jalal began. "There was a shrine for him filled with flags, bowls, and drums. . . . In 1994 I dreamt Sheikh Danun carried me from Lebanon back to my village. Suddenly, I found myself in his shrine [*maqam*] sweeping the floor; everything was covered in dust, as if no one had been there for years. Shortly after that, I went to Palestine and recounted the dream to my sister, and we went to the shrine and swept it." While Umm Jalal's return visit had been facilitated by the International Red Cross, there was no doubt in her mind that it was Sheikh Danun who had truly reunited her with relatives. "He carried me from here to there," she reiterated, matter-of-factly, drawing an arc in the air that mapped her journey over Lebanon's southern border.

When Umm Jalal recounted this dream during an interview for the Nakba Archive, her account of being spirited to Palestine by a saint seemed fantastic—an example of the rural superstitions associated with the worship of saints (*awliya*ʿ). In the urban setting of Shatila it struck me as quaint and anachronistic. The questions I asked in response focused exclusively on the rituals associated with Sheikh Danun's shrine, where barren women went to make vows and young men to shave their beards on the eve of their wedding days. In retrospect I am unsettled by my indifference to the significance of the dream narrative. Katherine Ewing has identified an atheistic "refusal to believe" at the heart of the discipline of anthropology (1994, 571); when I reflect on my own failures of imagination, I am haunted by Ewing's critique, by her diagnostic sketch of the anthropologist as rational skeptic navigating the idiosyncrasies of local lore.[1]

Despite my initial lack of interest, dreams came to figure prominently in my relations with several friends in Shatila. This chapter addresses the significance of what I call "dream talk"—the practice of recounting, interpreting, and enacting dreams.[2] Almost all the dream stories I heard were narrated by women I met through Umm Hadi and Umm Yusuf, who in their different ways both initiated me into the significance of dreams in their community. I came to appreciate dream narrations as a ritual establishing relations of trust and sociality between listeners in the course of everyday life and as a form of prophecy and divination that extended beyond the limits of the visible world. Not reducible to idle yearning or escapism, dream talk introduced possibility and intentionality in everyday relations, allowing desires and afflictions to be articulated and acted upon. In this respect, dream talk represents an intellectual and imaginative resource people can draw on in moments of adversity, allowing them to project themselves into the unknown and make it more tractable.

In treating dream talk as a socially embedded ritual with tangible effects, I regard it as a phenomenon intimately related to other material practices sustaining the community. Dream narratives do not exist in isolation; their meaning necessarily emerges intersubjectively, in the course of social interactions. The social and narrative rituals associated with dream interpretation create room for maneuver and momentum in the lives of the women I describe. In the same way that neighborly networks remake kinship and community, and inventiveness compensates for marginality in the field of electricity provision, dream talk forms the basis of reciprocal relations that can extend beyond the human to include the divine and the invisible. As Amira Mittermaier eloquently argues in her ethnography of dreams in modern Egypt, dreams establish links between the living and the dead, between spirits, saints, and the divine, and in doing so "insert the dreamer into a wider network of symbolic debts, relationships and meanings . . . and enable a mode of being in the world that disrupts the illusion of the autonomous subject, calling attention to in-betweenness and interrelationality instead" (2010, 3). Contending that the practice of dream interpretation informs how people relate to one another, even assert power over one another, I am making a case for its general relevance for social, moral, and political life in Shatila.

While the study of dreams has a long anthropological history, going back to Edward Tylor (1958), who regarded them as the origin of spirits and animism (in dreams the dead come alive), the discipline continues to jealously guard the border between conscious and unconscious states, privileging the observable and material world. For rationalists and secularists, dreams are murky, obscure, and unverifiable. This meticulous separation of ontologies has left what lies on the other side of wakefulness, the darker matter of the night—or even, for that matter, the dialectical relations of the symbolic and the "real"—underexplored. Although it is impossible to undertake an empirical study of the dream experience itself, which is not available to the ethnographer and often eludes even the grasp of the dreamer, it is possible to examine the performative effects of dream interpretation. Because dreams are always reconstructions, communicated and made meaningful by being shared, they take shape through public discourse (Ewing 1994; Tedlock 1991). The focus of this discussion is therefore less on dreams as representations of internal experience than on the social, ethical, and political effects of dream talk. I am interested in dream talk as an intersubjective practice that directs dreamers toward the future and carries the potential to transform experience. Dream talk also makes visible the role Islamic eschatology plays in shaping how people make sense of their existence and the ethical and theological dimensions of religious experience and imagination in everyday life (Hirschkind 2006; Khan 2006; Mahmood 2005; Mittermaier 2010; Pandolfo 1997, 2007).

Two fields of inquiry converge in my analysis of dream talk. The first concerns futurity. Although much has been written on how refugees relate to the past—especially in the historically fraught Shatila—there is comparatively little on how they orient themselves to the future. Ethnographies of camp life rarely address anticipation and foresight. This is understandable on multiple levels: methodologically, it is difficult to research what is yet to be; ethically, it is difficult to ask refugees to probe their future (which can seem like twisting a knife in the wound); and disciplinarily, anthropology tends to see the filaments of culture as rooted in the past rather than vectored into the future. Yet, this reluctance to address futurity has created critical gaps in our understanding of refugee experience.[3] Given that most avenues of social advancement available to Lebanese citizens are unavailable to Palestinians in Lebanon, what are the mechanisms that enable refugees to imagine a future different from their present? Since dream stories exist outside the rational domains of power and access, they represent a site of meaning making—even, therefore, agency—through which refugees imagine and gain purchase on the "forthcoming" (Bourdieu 1977, 76).

The second theme, largely inseparable from the first, concerns hope—the belief that "one can become other or more than one presently is fated to be."[4] If we understand engagement with the future and the possibility of change and renewal primarily in terms of hope, what are the habits of the mind—the "technologies of the imagination" (Sneath, Holbraad, and Pedersen 2009)—that sustain this engagement? In many respects, Palestinian refugees have become experts of hope, existing as they do in a condition of indefinite existential suspension; in this context, I argue, a pragmatics of hope—the resources by which selves remain phenomenologically rooted in futurity—has been not only preserved but even refined in the face of an objectively narrowed range of possibilities.

My interest in dream stories did not grow out of a desire to psychoanalyze friends and interlocutors but from the dawning realization that for many, dreams were experiences one could not ignore. Listening to dream stories became integral to my daily interactions with a number of women. The settings in which dreams were recounted were usually informal, sometimes playful, and normally involved two or three women. Fueled by coffee and cigarettes, sessions of dream talk provided respite and renewal—moments outside the daily grind, where relations were reaffirmed and views were played out, validated, negotiated, or confounded. There was clearly a performative pleasure in exegesis, a shared aesthetics of storytelling and analysis, and narrating dreams was a way of demonstrating cultural competence and knowledge. While these stories were often intensely personal, the conversations that followed invariably referenced communal rather than purely private concerns. Dream talk brought subjective experience into the realm of collective signification.[5] In this respect the hopes and possible futures imagined in dream talk are generated as much by particular constellations of relations as by individuals.

Dream talk represents one of a number of discursive practices used to make life more bearable or facilitate continuity in the face of rupture. Parallel practices with religious, political, and social dimensions would lend themselves equally well to this line of inquiry. I chose to focus on dream talk because it was a pervasive habit among the women with whom I spent my days, but also because I was drawn to what might be called its pragmatics of imagination. As "projective surfaces" (Kilborne 1981, 297), dream narratives represented an ideal medium through which to explore future-oriented thought and imaginative practice, individual and shared, because meaning is constructed and not confined to that which is directly experienced.[6] By interweaving internal and external worlds—the real and the imagined—and blurring temporal boundaries, dream talk allowed people to develop vocabularies for thinking and talking about the future less constrained by present circumstances. Beyond that, my interest in dream talk reflects an intellectual disposition and secondary aim of this book: to uncover the productive pragmatism that often lies behind ritual-ized forms of apparent idleness.

Dream interpretation appears to be a highly gendered activity in Shatila. On the few occasions when I broached the topic of dreams with men, I sensed a reluctance to discuss these experiences or an unwillingness to admit that this was something that they believed in at all. I heard men recount dreams on only two occasions. In both cases the dreams had marked critical turning points in their lives and involved visitations by angels—considered highly significant be-cause they bring divine knowledge and usually call for some particular course of action.[7] Both men described these dreams as "visions" (ru'ya), emphasizing that they were distinct from the kinds of dreams their wives had discussed with me on other occasions. These visions were presented as exceptional moments of revelation, set apart from the more everyday (and by implication, less signif-icant) dream stories they knew me to be interested in. Rather than seek inter-pretive guidance from family or friends, both had consulted a sheikh. Whereas for women, sharing and interpreting their dreams appeared to be a social and egalitarian practice embedded in everyday relations, men tended to be more circumspect and hierarchical in their approach to it.

The fact that women seem more invested in—and adept at—dream talk than men may simply represent the converse of the marginal position they hold in so many of the public institutions that exist for articulating visions of the fu-ture in the camp. Political factions, NGOs, and the like continue to be domi-nated by men; perhaps in a compensatory fashion, women have become highly skilled in informal contexts. Ironically, however, it is precisely the official and institutionalized discourses for thinking about the future that have lost so much credibility and resonance in the community in recent years. Against this back-drop, women's skill at generating meaning and agency has risen in importance.

THE ONTOLOGY OF DREAMS IN SHATILA

When I first expressed an interest in dreams to Umm Mahmud's father, Abu Ali, he seemed taken aback. "Why are you looking at this?" he admonished. "What has this to do with our experience as refugees?" How did I have time for such things, he wondered; surely, the crises facing Palestinians in their waking lives should suffice to keep me occupied. Attending to the imagination, to his mind, seemed almost a breach of trust, one that provoked political and ethical suspicion and threatened to compromise the relevance of my research. "This is fantasy [khayali]; it has nothing to do with how we are living now," he said, also worried that it would present a misleading picture of Shatila as a community of unhinged fantasists. While Abu Ali's skepticism may, in part, be explained by his own doubts about religion, others also expressed surprise about the turn my research had taken, often suggesting that there were more pressing issues to address. Yet, as I reflected on Abu Ali's response, it seemed to me that dreams, and the significance people accord them, says much about how people—women in particular—deal with uncertainty and powerlessness in their daily lives.[8]

In Western discourse there is a tendency to read dreams in psychological terms and to locate the origin of the dream inside the mind of the dreamer. This Freudian model regards dreams as the reworking of past conflicts, childhood desire, and intrapsychic impulses.[9] While the Freudian theory can be helpful for thinking through links between conscious and unconscious processes, the reification of the personal symbolism of dreams limits the range of possible meanings and obscures their potential public and social significance.[10] This erasure is particularly problematic in Islamic contexts like Shatila, where dreams are believed to originate outside the mind of the dreamer.[11] The relationship between one's inner life and the external world is never determined simply by human subjectivity but also by external forces. Because dreams are understood to be divine injunctions from elsewhere that, quite literally, bring to mind other kinds of knowledge and experience not available to the senses, they productively widen the potential realms of apprehension and perception. Muslims regard dreams "not as an escape from but as an engagement with the world" (Mittermaier 2010, 142). In other words, to view Umm Jalal's dream as determined by her past, or as a delusional projection of desire, denies the validity of her experience and the meaning she attributed to it and also the crucial significance of cultural context.

Even if knowing these other dream worlds introduces difficulty and uncertainty, Muslims regard dreams as windows opened briefly onto a reality as ontologically solid as that of material existence.[12] Friends would sometimes introduce a dream narrative by saying, "It came to me in my dream" (*ijani bi manam*), underscoring that the source of a dream was external to the dreamer. While the categories of dream appeared fluid and open to contestation, most of the dreams I heard fell into two broad groups: those thought to be volitional and actively induced by the dreamer through prayer for guidance; and those that came to the dreamer spontaneously, revealing aspects of the unknown and the divine (*al-ghayb*).[13] People also distinguished between daydreams (*ahlam al-yaqza*), which are viewed as close to illusion (*al-wahm*), and dreams experienced during sleep, which are believed to be truthful. Since sleep is viewed as a kind of temporary death (*al-mawt al-saghir*, literally, "a small death")—the moment when meaning is unveiled—it is believed that people experience a form of awakening in sleep.[14] Whereas daydreams are seen as transient experiences produced by the dreamer's everyday preoccupations and desires, dreams encountered in sleep carry divine knowledge and are therefore potentially transformative.

Muslim dream interpretation is related to divination and prophecy, drawing its authority from the Qur'an and hadith literature (Lamoreux 2002; Mittermaier 2010; Oppenheim 1956; Pandolfo 1997). Although I occasionally encountered copies of canonical dream manuals in people's houses—*The Book of Dreams*, by the eighth-century Muslim scholar Ibn Sirin, or *A Compendium of the Words of Dream Interpretation* (*Muntakhab al-Kalam fi tafsir al-ahlam*)—I knew no one who relied on texts for interpretation. My subjects would sooner seek the advice of a friend, neighbor, or sheikh.[15] Generally high levels of illiteracy in Shatila (particularly among older generations) may be a factor in this, but the social dimension of dream talk is key. When discussing dreams, people sometimes invoked established dream typologies. I was told, for instance, that dreams occurring in the middle of the night were dominated by elements of the previous day's activities, or by desires and worries (*hadith nafsi*), and could not therefore be reliable augurs of the future.[16] A nightmare or menacing apparition (*qarineh*) was understood to be inspired by the devil, and associated with *jin* or a ghoul (*ghul*) who appeared in the guise of a friend or lover. They also were believed to come in deep sleep, motivated by an external source. Dream visions by contrast, were regarded as the most reliable for predicting the future because they were experienced in the early morning, representing the clarity of dawn and the Divine. Another commonly held belief, drawing on Qur'anic scripture, is that dream visions can be invoked by praying for divine guidance (the *istikhara* prayer, literally, "seeking the best") and certain ritualized practices, such as sleeping on one's right side, following the example of the Prophet Muhammad.

Belief in the power and prescience of dreams was not uniform. For staunch secularists like Abu Ali, dreams were a form of fantasy. Although dream interpretation has its roots in Qur'anic scripture, certain religious reformers in the camp consider it fundamentally un-Islamic, a dangerous manifestation of irreligious superstition.[17] Even those who believe in the significance of dreams will sometimes begin their stories by acknowledging that only God is all-knowing. The same woman who vigorously critiques dream interpretation in one setting may willingly allow herself to be drawn into a discussion over the meaning of a particular dream in another. The ambiguity surrounding dream talk makes it a liminal space, a corridor of discourse between the latent and the manifest, the concrete and the transcendent, between orthodoxy and heresy, sleep and wakefulness, present and future, life and death.

DREAMS OF MAJID

On a hot afternoon in July 2004, Majid, a robust man in his late fifties, suffered a fatal heart attack while driving home from work. By the time the ambulance reached his car—which was blocking one of the narrow streets running between the neighboring district of Da'uq and Shatila—he was dead. Less than an hour later, Majid's body was carried by his grief-stricken sons into the family's home in preparation for the burial. News of his death spread swiftly, and announcements were made through the mosques. Majid had been a prominent figure in the community and seemingly in good health, and his sudden passing was a shock for many. "But Majid was not ill!" I was told repeatedly. "Majid did not have heart troubles; he did not even have diabetes. By God, he was the healthiest man among us!" remarked one elderly woman. Mourners recalled their disbelief on hearing of his death, some having seen him full of life only the day before, walking and chatting with friends or waving from his car on his way to work. During the three-day wake, the family received a steady flow of visitors to their small apartment, as members of the community and relatives from near and far came to pay their respects. Plastic chairs from neighboring households lined the street to accommodate the overflow. Friends, neighbors, and kin spoke of Majid's valued friendship, his generosity and kindness, and the important role he had played in the life of the camp.

I visited his family again on the third day of mourning and found Majid's wife, Safiyya, sitting with her two daughters in the front room. She looked tired, but the pall of grief seemed to have lifted a little. When I asked her how she was, she told me that a few hours after burying Majid, the family had been comforted by a "visitation" from his spirit in the form of a butterfly (*'ala hay'at farasha*). The butterfly had flown in through the living room's open window after the mourners had left. "We do not have butterflies in Shatila," she said. "This is the first time I have seen a butterfly in the camp. Why would a butterfly come here?" she asked with a wan smile. The butterfly had visited each of his children in turn: "First it rested on Farah's face, then it flew to Ahmed's hand, then it sat on Hana's leg for a long time, and finally it came to me and to Muhammad. We all felt it was Majid's spirit leaving us. The children were so scared that they slept together in the living room with the light on."

Safiyya recounted another remarkable event. In the minutes following Majid's heart attack, the colleague who had been with him in the car had recounted for the family the sudden appearance of a woman from an alleyway. "The woman was carrying a Qur'an and came to him and read the Fatiha and other verses," Safiyya told me. "By the time the ambulance arrived, she was gone." The colleague had not spoken with her and had barely seen her face. On hearing this story, Safiyya and Hana searched Da'uq for the woman, hoping to thank her for her kindness. Residents remembered the ambulance arriving but not the woman reading the Qur'an. Safiyya decided to consult a sheikh. As she suspected, the sheikh believed the woman to be an angel sent by God to ease the passage of Majid's soul from his body. What else could explain her appearance moments after his attack and her disappearance moments before the arrival of the ambulance? "I am grateful for this blessing," Safiyya said, clearly comforted. "It is God's work." Despite this solace, Majid's untimely death continued to haunt his family and friends, in particular his teenage daughter, Hana, who tried in vain to purge her mind of the vision of his dead body laid out in the living room and remained unable to comprehend the transformation of her family's life.

When I stopped by later that week, I found Safiyya and Hana sitting with Majid's sisters and four other women in their front room. As we drank bitter coffee from small plastic cups, one of his sisters from Rashidiyyeh camp, a fierce-looking woman in her sixties, recalled seeing her brother's dead body in a dream, the night before his death, on the threshold of her home. Waking with a start, she believed it to be the workings of a *jin*. She subsequently took the dream to have been a visitation from Majid's soul, which, anticipating its imminent departure, had tried to communicate with her.

This dream story, which seemed less surprising to others present than it did to me, sparked a series of similar accounts of dreams and signs that, retrospectively, were seen to foretell the death of a loved one. Safiyya, who often spoke of her powers of intuition—claiming, for example, always to know precisely when I would visit—described having been unable to eat or sleep the evening before her husband's death. Another of Majid's sisters recalled her sense of impending misfortune. Everyone seemed to be searching for the meaning of his sudden passing, dusting for its teleological tracks.

Hana then narrated two further dream stories, one presaging her father's death and another registering his spirit's efforts to communicate with the family in the days following it. The stories had come from a man named Aref, a blind switchboard operator from UNRWA believed to have visionary gifts. The day before Majid's death Aref had dreamed that he and Majid were sitting in a large tomb, talking and drinking tea as they waited for the angel to make an account of their lives (*yuhasabun*). Both men were hungry and hoped they would soon be in heaven with something good to eat. Hana described the dreams as follows:

> Aref said, "Majid, you can't eat because you're dead, but I am still alive," and with that, he climbed out of the tomb. He told my father about the dream at work the following day but didn't tell him the details, fearing it might harm him. After my father's death, Aref had a second dream in which he saw my father sitting in front of a book, and all the pages in it were blank. At the top of one page was written "Pray for me." When Aref told us this story, we understood it was a message from my father, and so we asked Aref to speak at his *khitma* [third day of mourning]. He spoke for thirty minutes, and everyone was very moved. I could not go [only men were in attendance], but my uncle said many people wept.

An animated debate about the significance of the dreams followed. What was the meaning of the spacious tomb? Surely it was auspicious—an indication of Majid's piety, one woman suggested. But why were both men hungry? A more troubling reading centered on this. The dreams had created room for conjecture, for a reexamination of elements of Majid's life and death.

On of Safiyya's sisters-in-law appeared increasingly uncomfortable with the turn the conversation had taken. As someone who actively cultivated an image of herself as devout, she regarded the discussion of dreams and signs as dangerous and irreligious, stressing that Majid's fate (*nasibu*) was beyond the powers of mortal understanding. To suggest that one could converse with the dead through dreams—or otherwise gain access to the unknown—was to doubt God's omnipotence.[18] She urged the family to pray for Majid and keep their dreams private. Later, after her aunt had left, Hana spoke to me about the fractious exchange: "As people have become more religious, they grow critical of these practices. I understand why people criticize reading signs in coffee or water, but even the Prophet Muhammad (Peace be upon Him) interpreted dreams."[19]

While dream interpretation may be frowned upon in more overtly religious settings, it tends to be condoned in informal, social settings. There is a lack of consensus over its value or veracity, with both supporters and detractors citing hadith and passages in the Qur'an to support their positions. This epistemological ambiguity has not only enabled the practice to continue but has also, arguably, afforded greater room for the creativity and play in the practice of dream interpretation, something I will return to later.

At the most basic level, the discussion of dreams during the days of mourning following Majid's death functioned as a classic pragmatist response to misfortune and uncertainty. As Michael Jackson argues, strategies that modify experience and permit new forms of knowledge allow individuals to counter uncertainty and to "reimagine and surpass the situations in which they find themselves" (2005a, xv). The dream narratives introduced a hermeneutic process, enabling mourners to shift from a state of passive anxiety about sudden loss to one of active engagement and restitution of meaning through a shared reading of signs. It also seems significant that it was primarily Majid's female relatives who were not permitted to attend the burial and days of public mourning in the mosque, who turned to dreams to make sense of his death. The significance of these narratives, however, was not limited to this instrumental role. Aref's dream blurred the boundary between living and dead, opening a realm of imagination and possibility beyond the visible world. The dream in the tomb revealed the workings of the *barzakh*, the limbolike space in Islamic eschatology where the searching souls of dreamers meet the dead as they await judgment.[20] Because the dreams foretold Majid's death and allowed his soul to communicate with the living, their importance had been reaffirmed, both as a source of prophecy and divine knowledge and as a bridge between this world and the afterlife.

Dreams are not only important in negotiating matters of life and death. They are of equal help to the community in interpreting more mundane matters, as demonstrated by two women who draw on dream narratives to engage with—and shape their understanding of—past and future.

UMM YUSUF FORESEES THE FUTURE

Small, quietly self-assured with a piercing gaze, Umm Yusuf is, like Aref, known among friends and family to have the gift of foresight. She reads coffee grounds and water (*tafsir bi may*) and is also considered to be a gifted interpreter of dreams. As a mutual friend put it, "She sees that which is veiled to us" (*makshuf 'anha al-hijab*). Umm Yusuf is Bedouin, and her family hails from the district of Jaffa. She was born in Tel al-Za'tar camp and lived there until the camp was destroyed in 1976, after which she moved with her family to Shatila. When I met her in 2000, she was thirty-four and living in a sparsely furnished room with her husband and three children. A skilled raconteur who drew equally on her past, her dreams—both visions seen while sleeping and consciously held hopes—and the minutiae of daily life, she teased out pattern and meaning not only from momentous events but from the merest ephemera—an unexpected power cut, a visit from a friend, even a headache.

"When I'm convinced of something, it always happens," Umm Yusuf would tell me, recounting examples of her correct predictions. She recalled her vision-ary gifts first emerging in early childhood. "My aunt recognized this ability in me because she also had it. She'd say, 'Don't look at the black coffee grounds; they don't mean anything. The white parts in-between are what's important.'" Although Umm Yusuf has difficulty reading and does not use dream manuals, she occasionally invokes established interpretations associated with particu-lar signs (certain objects or colors, for example). The rare instances when she cited Qur'anic interpretations seemed merely rhetorical invocations of author-ity. Umm Yusuf regards her skill as something given and unlearned, hence to be shared freely and informally with others, never for a fee; a form of everyday reciprocity, it expanded and enriched her social and moral life. Counsel offered to and received from others bound her to neighbors, friends, her children, co-workers, and, at various critical junctures, sheikhs, through relations of obli-gation, trust, and exchange. It nourished her sense of being someone with a unique gift, a player in the larger world.

Umm Yusuf's favored system of dream interpretation relied on opposition, an established system of divination (*al tafsir bi-l-'aks*). Death signifies life, and a birth, illness; the color black heralds joy, while white brings sadness; teeth fall-ing out means death, but cut hair announces "good news"; candles represented divorce, but a dagger, marriage; and so on. The system was reassuring in its lack of ambiguity. "What you see in your dreams will either show you exactly what is going to happen—I mean it's *clear, clear* [*wadih*]—or it will show you ex-actly what is *not* going to happen," Umm Yusuf explained. The logic of reversal worked to her advantage, transforming fear and loss—both of the nocturnal and diurnal mind—into auspicious signs.

Over time I came to appreciate more keenly that for Umm Yusuf her skills were a path both to prophecy and—more prosaically—to social power and influence. Her application of dream talk could be tactical and self-interested. Interpreting the dreams of others enabled Umm Yusuf not only to guide peo-ple's actions but to assert her will and shore up her sense of herself as a person of authority. When a niece she believed to be having an illicit affair with a mar-ried man idly asked Umm Yusuf to interpret her dream, she rendered it as a cautionary tale (acknowledging the interpretive deceit to me later and describ-ing it as a tactful intervention). On another occasion when a neighbor complained of bad dreams, Umm Yusuf suggested a *jin* had been attracted by dirt in her house. "If you have a bad dream, you must spit to your right and say 'I seek refuge in God from the cursed devil'" (*A'uzu billah min al-shaytan al-rajim*).[21] "Then you spit over your left shoulder, where the devil is, and sleep on your right side," she advised, adding, "Make sure you keep your house clean."[22] While Umm Yusuf had no compunction about occasionally using dreams to manipulate situations in ways she deemed morally desirable, it was also clear she regarded them as a source of truth, revelation, and transformative power. The task of interpretation could not be borne lightly.

Sometimes friends and family would come to Umm Yusuf with a particular question or problem. Hiba, a neighbor, recounted a recurrent dream of being pursued by cats. Pregnant after years of trying to conceive, she was anxious that someone had put a curse on her; she assumed the dream was a *qarineh*, which are believed to come to pregnant women and threaten the child. Umm Yusuf confirmed her suspicions, saying the bad dreams were the product of envy. "Put a leaf from the cemetery under your mattress," she advised, assuring her the prophylactic would ward off danger. She, Hiba, and a woman who had accompanied Hiba then discussed who might have eyed her swollen belly with unwitting envy or whether Hiba's own actions had aroused it. "Be careful of those who may envy your good fortune," Umm Yusuf cautioned. Seeking the source of the curse facilitated both critical self-reflection and inquiry into community responsibility. Umm Yusuf made remarks that dramatized tensions and intimacies between Hiba and certain individuals, all the while reaffirming her own solidarity with those present.[23] The exercise, in short, was both a catalyst for neighborly reciprocity and a striking instance of it.

This intersubjective dimension of dream talk, in which meaning was constructed collectively, allowed Umm Yusuf to guide, cast blame, and rebuild and dissolve social ties. Over time it became for me not merely an object of ethnographic study but also a method of relating to others, one that, with increasing frequency, directly implicated me. Description and interpretation of dreams allowed for the cultivation of social selves, making it—however improbably—an instrument of solidarity and influence. Dreams fostered intimacy between dreamers and their audience.

In this respect, dream talk forms an affective counterpart to the other kinds of reciprocal relations I have described. Recognizing fears and aspirations registered in the dreams of others or offering guidance in moments of crisis was a way of signaling membership in a moral community; interpretation bound dreamers to listeners. The belief that recounting a dream makes it come true—sometimes in quite literal ways—raises the stakes further, and since the truth is understood to be revealed in the first reading of a dream, there are profound ethical implications for the person approached for interpretive guidance.[24]

When I first met Umm Yusuf, all three of her children were still in school. Having left school when she was twelve, she placed enormous importance on their education, and her own happiness was tightly bound up with their success. Despite the obstacles Palestinians routinely face, Umm Yusuf had an almost blind faith in the idea of progress through education.[25] She was confident her children would excel in their exams, study at university, and make careers for themselves, and her expectations often found corroboration in her dreams. "At the end of each year I have a dream that tells me whether or not my children will pass their exams," Umm Yusuf explained to me one morning:

> When Yusuf took the *brevé* [national exams] last year, I dreamed we were in Sanayeh. I told him I would wait by the gate while he got his results from an official in the park, but he refused to go alone, so we went together and I waited under a tree. The official called me over and had me sign a paper, and I saw Yusuf was the only one in his class to pass. And that's what came to happen—only Yusuf and one other passed the exam. When Salma took her exams, I knew she would do well because she is a good student. I dreamed she was in a cable car—the one near Jounieh [a wealthy Christian town north of Beirut]—and as she approached the top of the mountain, she began crying. Big tears were falling to the earth, so I knew she would do well but wouldn't get the grades she wanted. When she received her results, she was only one mark away from a top grade. Now, when it comes to Ahmed, Salma and Yusuf say he'll drop out of school before even taking the *brevé*—but I *deny* this; I know he'll do better than both of them. He's the youngest, but he's the cleverest of all.

The significance of these dreams is deepened and clarified in the context of their recounting. Umm Yusuf was preparing lunch with Salma, and her husband and sons were out. I had asked if the end-of-year exam results had been announced, which elicited Umm Yusuf's dream narrative. Soon thereafter she left the room, and Salma confided that the results were in and Yusuf had failed. Devastated and too ashamed to tell her husband or relatives, Umm Yusuf had spent almost a week's earnings on sweets and coffee so that she could invite friends and family to celebrate his fictitious success. When Abu Yusuf eventually discovered the deception, he was furious and refused to speak to any of the family for several days.

In this instance Umm Yusuf's conviction that her eldest son would go to college and not join the ranks of Shatila's unemployed was sustained through recourse to a highly motivated reading of signs. The setting of Sanayeh park also seemed to implicate me in Yusuf's future success, since this was where I was then living—something that became clearer in the course of other conversations we had about his prospects for studying at university and the need to find financial support. The dream sequence not only enabled her to broach the potentially sensitive question of sponsorship but was also a rhetorical device that allowed her to shift between dream and real life and between temporalities: past success pointed to a hoped-for future success over present failure. The interweaving of past and present, dream and real life—what Stephania Pandolfo in her study of dreams in Morocco calls "the uncanny temporality of vestiges" (1997, 183)— provided leverage at a point of impasse, when other forms of agency seemed exhausted or unavailable.[26] Recalling a dream that had correctly foretold Yusuf's success the previous year brought to mind a prior state of optimism.[27] Present failure could then be triangulated by past prophecy and future success.[28] As a discursive practice hinging on opposition, temporal reorientation, and, in some instances, reasoning against the evidence, dream talk constituted a kind of anti-empirical technique for dealing with difficulty and uncertainty by insisting upon a wide and seamless web of causality and signification.

Dreams were also integral to the stories Umm Yusuf told about herself: they marked turning points in her life and informed her understanding of causality, both in terms of external forces acting on her and her own ability to make a life for herself.[29] One dream story in particular, which Umm Yusuf recounted as she and I were drinking coffee on the stairs outside her home, revealed this with great clarity. Just that day, an unexpected visit from a cousin—whom Umm Yusuf had not seen for many months—had brought back joyful memories of childhood and of her mother, from whom she had been inseparable until her mother's death in 1982. Umm Yusuf believes that her death was precipitated by a traumatic visit to the camp in the aftermath of the Sabra and Shatila massacre:

> At the time [1982] we were living in al-Nimsawiyya kindergarten [an Austrian center just south of Shatila]. When we heard about the massacre, we came to search for our relatives. When my mother saw the slaughter in front of her eyes, it broke her heart in two. By God, you could see the line down the middle of the x-ray they made at Al Lahoud Hospital. When the doctors saw her condition, they said she would die in a week and there was nothing they could do. I had

no money to pay for her medication. Umm Nader, a friend who worked with us at SAMED [an institution founded by the PLO in 1970 to provide training and employment for the families of those affected by the national struggle] gave me a little money to buy food for her—two days later she died. . . . My mother was my closest friend; we were more like sisters and we did everything together. When she died, it was like life stopped.

Umm Yusuf paused, overcome with emotion. When she recovered herself, she related a dream she had in the days following her mother's death:

I dreamed that a sheikh came to me and asked me whether I would like to see my mother. I followed him along a path leading underground, and I realized I was in the bomb shelter where we stayed during the Israeli invasion. It was cold, and there were bodies wrapped in white shrouds, their faces covered so I didn't know which was my mother. The sheikh pointed to a body, but when I pulled back the cloth, instead of my mother I saw a young man with a big mustache. I was so shocked I woke up; I felt I had been tricked.

The next day at work I couldn't stop crying. My employer asked me what was wrong. I told her about my dream, and she said I should visit a sheikh in the Ouzai mosque who could interpret it for me. At that time I wasn't religious, so she bought me a headscarf from the market so I could enter the mosque. We went together. When I told the sheikh the dream, he said if I should meet this man, I should marry him, that he was God's gift to me because my mother loved me. He said, "Your mother has sent him to look after you and take her place."

The following week I was walking near al-Wahish, and I saw Abu Yusuf standing in front of a grocer's shop, and I realized this was the man I had seen in my dream! He kept staring at me. After that he used to come and walk me home from work and in the winter drove his red Honda so close to me it would splash my clothes with water from the road. He offered me lifts, but I never accepted. Then after a year he asked me to marry him, and of course I said yes. We didn't marry for three years—we were engaged, but we loved each other so much. He is my life.

The conviction with which she recounted this story was moving. Umm Yusuf told me this dream on two separate occasions, both in the presence of her children, who had clearly heard it many times. Its telling seemed less an imparting of information than a ritual of faith, but each time they listened patiently, never interrupting. I too found myself caught up in its oneiric symmetry, its

emotional dialectic of tragedy and renewal. Narration was folded into interpretation, as the dream story laid the groundwork for a reordering of experience in the wake of an event that had put her entire life into question. For
Umm Yusuf, the dream not only marked a turning point but indeed caused it,
enabling as it did an affective and existential shift both in the days following
her mother's death and as she later recounted this event to me.

Just as Majid's family believe he communicated with them from the *barzakh*
through Aref's dream, Umm Yusuf believes her mother chose her future husband and communicated this choice from the afterlife in a dream. That her
mother selected someone to take her place was of enormous significance for
Umm Yusuf because it represented the continuity of her loving care—even
after death—and carried with it the certitude of the divine. Because souls are
believed to dwell in the realm of truth (*dar al-haq*) and be all-knowing, their
guidance is highly valued and taken to be truthful (Mittermaier 2010, 152). The
dream spoke to her belief that destiny is not simply in one's own hands but
always bound up with one's relations with others, both living and dead. Umm
Yusuf expresses doubt about many things in her life but never questions her decision to marry Abu Yusuf. Her marriage, she once told me, has always been the
basis of the future she can hope for with conviction because it was foreseen by
her mother, prefigured in a dream and blessed by God. The resolution brought
to bear in the words "He is my life" cannot be underestimated and reveals Abu
Yusuf to be both the subject and means of her hope.

UMM HADI: UNCERTAINTY AS POSSIBILITY

During my first year in Shatila I lived in the same building as Umm Hadi and
her family and saw her frequently. Umm Hadi often invited me, along with
other female friends and neighbors, for morning coffee. Unlike Umm Yusuf,
who viewed her marriage as living proof of the enduring and transformative
power of love, Umm Hadi, who was also in her mid-thirties when we first met,
was unhappily married. She believed love had made her vulnerable. Her relations with her husband were strained, and he was rarely around, often returning home after she and her children had gone to bed and leaving early in the
morning before anyone was up. While the circumstances of their estrangement
were complicated and not always clear to me, Umm Hadi's unhappiness became increasingly apparent as the months passed.

By the following summer Umm Hadi had begun to speak about divorce,
though she was clearly anxious about the consequences, fearing social oppro-

brium and the loss of custody of her children. Hania, an older sister visiting from Germany, advised her to pray for a dream that would offer divine guidance (*istikhara*). Umm Hadi followed this advice and a few days later recounted a bad dream involving her children, which she took to be a warning that she should abandon the idea. That the dream's message ran so strongly counter to her own inclinations lent it greater credibility in her mind: it could not be mistaken for the projection of her own desire (*hadith nafsi*).

In the course of our discussion it became clear that this was neither the first time that Umm Hadi had contemplated divorce nor the first time that a dream has dissuaded her. Three years earlier, weeks before the birth of her youngest son, Aziz, she had filed for divorce. In a dream the night before the paperwork was to be finalized, she saw herself walking through the camp. "I heard my sister Randa shouting, and I turned around to see my house collapsing, just falling down in front of my eyes." Deeply disturbed, she took the dream to be a warning and immediately retracted her petition. Several weeks later, in the hours following the birth of Aziz, as she drifted in and out of sleep in the labor ward, she had another vision that suggested she had made the right decision:

> This was a very difficult time for me. If I wasn't so strong, I think I would have gone mad. I was still living by myself most of the time, and my husband was not with me when I went to the hospital. . . . Aziz was born on the Prophet Muhammad's (Peace be upon Him) birthday at midnight, so people were telling me what a good sign this was. They asked me what I would call him—they expected me to say Muhammad. . . . They put Aziz in an incubator, and I fell asleep. I remember it was early morning, a few hours after I'd given birth, and I dreamed that President Lahoud [then president of Lebanon] was standing at the foot of my bed. . . . He was smiling and congratulating me on the birth of my son. When I asked my sister what it meant, she said it was a sign that Aziz would be a successful and important man. I felt this too when I saw Lahoud. . . . It gave me great hope at a time when things seemed very bad for me.

The vision of Christian president Emile Lahoud—a somewhat surprising harbinger of Umm Hadi's changing fortune—seemed to validate her decision to abandon the divorce. The dream took place in the early hours of the morning when, as Umm Hadi put it, "the sky was still gray, streaked black and white," an auspicious time for dreams. Like Umm Yusuf's dream following the death of her mother, it marked a point of transition in Umm Hadi's life and, more particularly, in her relations with her husband and her children. The dream has been validated with time, as Aziz has grown into a precocious and gifted child. When he turned seven, Umm Hadi's Lebanese employer offered to pay for him to study at a well-known private school. Umm Hadi told me this too was part of God's plan, since his success had been prefigured from birth. Her conviction that he is blessed and will succeed sustains her, and her hopes for the future are focused on what he will become. In her account of her life, this particular vision figures prominently in a narrative of willed recovery.

Dreams do not only have evocative power—in the sense that they guide and direct the dreamer—they also have performative power and can make things happen (Mittermaier 2010, 142; Pandolfo 1997, 185). In contrast to Umm Yusuf, Umm Hadi was often reluctant to speak about her dreams for this reason, believing them to be activated by being shared. "If I see something in a dream, I only talk about it after it happens [i.e., after it comes true]," she told me. Making clear just what dreams can *do*, what might be called their performative potency, she recalled a dream that had not simply foreseen disaster but brought it about. The previous Ramadan she had a dream that her husband had a car accident, which she recounted to her mother; three days later it happened exactly as she had seen in her dream. Given the nature of her marriage, intentionality in this instance seemed ambiguous. Where the performative potency of dreams was implicit in my discussions with Umm Yusuf, it became explicit in my conversations with my Umm Hadi. Consider her account of losing her second child:

> I was in a hospital in Jnaah. Abu Hadi was with his family, and my mother was in Germany visiting my sister, so no one was with me. I was in such pain. The nurse didn't believe me when I told her I was about to give birth. I asked her to give me her hand because the pain was so bad, and she laughed and said, "What's this? The first time you've given birth? Cats in the alley give birth by themselves, so you should be able to." She knew from my accent I was Palestinian. . . . Maybe if she had helped me, I wouldn't have lost the child. . . . But I feel she died because of a dream I had in the third month of pregnancy. In this dream Abdel Halim [a famous Egyptian singer] came and kissed me and told me he loved me, and I remember thinking how jealous my neighbor would be. The next morning I told her about it, and we laughed. I said, "You have no luck; you love Abdel Halim, but I meet him in my dreams!" When I lost my daughter, my husband's family said it was because Abdel Halim loved me, so he took my daughter for himself. . . . If I hadn't told my neighbor the dream, I might not have lost my child.

Umm Hadi believed the dream, like Hiba's cat dreams, was the work of a malevolent force jealous of her good fortune and her unborn child. By telling the dream to a neighbor, however, and gloating over her visit from Abdel Halim, she too had become implicated, in effect bringing about what might otherwise have remained only a latent possibility.[30] Recounting the story to me allowed her not only to speculate about the significance of her daughter's death but also to broaden the spectrum of possible causes, alleviating her sense of responsibility. Unlike the dream narratives of Umm Yusuf, Umm Hadi's were not a mechanism for imposing her own interpretive scheme over particular events or transforming them into scenarios of her own making; more often they seemed a technique of deferring closure with regard to painful or unusual events in her life.

If dream talk enables Umm Yusuf to speak with conviction about the future, it allows Umm Hadi to speak conditionally about deeply distressing experiences in her life. The latter's dream narratives open up the possibility of what might be, making available other forms of knowledge that enable her to negotiate her place in the world and redress the balance of "being an actor and being acted upon" (Jackson 2005a, xv). Crucially, however, the dream's meaning invariably escaped determinacy. Paradoxically, it was precisely this indeterminacy—the belief that dreams trigger effects and outcomes that can never be fully known or anticipated—that represented for her the greatest source of comfort. Uncertainty loosened the weave in the fabric of fate, and was productive therefore of agency and hope.[31] Dreams for Umm Hadi hold no promise of assurance but serve instead to sustain "the possibility of diverse readings of what the future might hold."[32]

HOPE AS WAKING DREAM

For both Umm Yusuf and Umm Hadi, dream talk allows traumatic events to be reexamined, other possible futures to be imagined, and hopes to be expressed in contexts that might otherwise seem to militate against it. Loss and suffering are made meaningful, and expectation is detached from the constraints of rational thought, precedent, and present circumstance. Dream talk challenges the limits of reality and the way knowledge of that reality is constructed and communicated to others. Hope—which in Shatila might be defined as belief in tomorrow in spite of today—is nourished and preserved, however fleetingly, in the discursive space of dream talk, a space defined by both ritual and improvisation.[33] As a practice employing the logic of reversal and temporal reorientation, dream talk also allows for a kind of anti-empirical approach to making sense of uncertainty.

While dream talk often operates as a pragmatic coping mechanism, it should not be understood merely in instrumentalist terms: to narrate or interpret dreams is not a means to an end but a way of knowing the world and one's place within it. For my friends and interlocutors, dreams constitute neither interior projections nor imprints of their past, but rather a continuum of perception both physical and metaphysical as well as a realm of speculation and interpretation. Reading dreams in functionalist terms, or finding coherence and logical consistency in experiences that are inherently indeterminate, forecloses the possibility of exploring interpretive frameworks that are not empirically verifiable but are nonetheless profoundly significant to one's interlocutors. To act as arbiter of what constitutes the "real" cannot be the task of the anthropologist. If our mandate is to explore why people do what they do and how they make sense of the world in which they live, then it is incumbent on us to examine not only the normative and self-evident, the "real," but also the imaginative and otherworldly processes that inform perception and apprehension.

This discussion has focused on dream narratives shared with family or intimate circles of friends. We may well ask if these modalities of imagination and hope also operate at a communal level. Can they be scaled up? To return to Abu Ali's question, what bearing do dreams have on the larger political questions and concerns of the community? The unease my interest in dreams initially elicited deserves further scrutiny. In response to his assertion that I should focus instead on issues of social and political relevance, I would argue that dream talk is, in fact, inherently political because it shapes social and moral relations and establishes new forms of connectedness, both in the actual world of the camp and in invisible but meaningful worlds beyond.

The interweaving of dreams into everyday interactions suggests they do not merely reflect or refract everyday life but at certain moments are pulled into it as a form of praxis informing the social in fundamental ways. Dreams also extend the boundaries of community and reciprocity beyond the visible world to include saints, angels, and the dead. The political significance of this expanded notion of community in the context of Shatila is not hard to grasp. As Mittermaier argues, dream stories "destabilize the persistent myth of the autonomous, liberal subject" and "exceed the secular imagined community of the nation-state" (2010, 4–5). As nationalist aspirations lose their gravitational pull and the future seems increasingly uncertain for refugees in Lebanon, these imaginative practices become invested with greater significance precisely because they operate outside a secular, nationalist tradition that has been found wanting. They open up other possible futures.

It would be misleading—even unethical—to romanticize dream talk as enabling people to surmount powerlessness and hopelessness. As opposing poles on the spectrum of expectancy, hopelessness and hopefulness, however, are related categories of experience, in which the former inflects and refines the capacity for the latter. I encountered stoicism and defiance in the face of despair as much as I encountered hope—affective states that, like hope, might also be read as willfulness but are more often understood in terms of passivity, victimhood, and abnegation, or as nationalist tropes of collective steadfastness. This may be partly explained by the fact that agency tends to be defined in ways that conflate "power with purpose and direction" (Lindquist 2006, 7). This presents an awkward fit in Shatila, where the capacity to aspire is rarely accompanied by the means by which to realize aspirations.

To dismiss dream talk as false consciousness, however, is to ignore the ways it sustains people and to artificially segregate material well-being from imaginative well-being. Rational paradigms, moreover, have themselves come to represent a kind of false consciousness for many refugees. A conversation I had with Umm Hadi shortly before I returned to the United States in 2004 captures this. Once again, we found ourselves circling around the fraught question of the right of return and her diminishing expectation that the situation of Palestinians in Lebanon will be resolved anytime soon, if at all:

> People used to be very hopeful. They'd say, "We'll go back, maybe not today or tomorrow, but we will go back at some point." Now, when I look back, I often wonder where that hope came from. . . . Our hope was not just to return; we hoped to get our rights as a people. We believed that one day the international community—or an Arab country—would give us this right . . . but now this right is trampled under foot [*bindar bayn al-ijr*] and no one says anything. Are we not human beings too? . . . I often wish I could wake up to a changed world. . . . We talk about return, and we hope and we talk, and then suddenly one day we realize that this is all an illusion and that we are living in misery [*'aysh bi ka'aaba*]. We understand that everything we have been telling ourselves is a lie, that we have been laughing at ourselves [*nidhak 'a-halna*]. That is why so many people are depressed here and don't want to admit the truth. I can't remember when I realized this, but now when I think about it, I try to return in my mind to the time before I realized this. I try to imagine it [*bitsawwar*] and still to have hope.

The outcome that Palestinians have been told to hold out for as part of final-status negotiations has been revealed to be meaningless, and the "peace process" no longer represents possibility and potential in people's minds. Politics and diplomacy have been semantically hollowed out for refugees and lack the suppleness to accommodate their individual aspirations and affective needs. That their rights continue to be ignored, even after the advent of international advocacy campaigns, has consolidated a sense of indignity and inhumanity once only implicit. In light of growing disenchantment, Umm Hadi finds herself trying mentally to return to a former state of possibility and hope. As in dreams, linear temporality and reality are reconfigured. We see how imaginative capacities refined in one context find application in others and how dreaming—in indirect ways—informs the political.

While the dream stories I have retold may appear to have greater spiritual and affective than material traction, there is a standing need to explore dialectics of imaginative practice and material agency. The argument that belief in a particular outcome can have tangible material effects understandably provokes skepticism.[34] It is not always obvious how belief in remote possibilities or invisible worlds shapes behavior and outlook in the present, how it orients subjects toward the future, or how it offers effective tools for dealing with difficulty and uncertainty. I am well aware that someone else could choose to redescribe the practices at the center of this chapter as forms of mere idleness or escapism. But failed or even futile acts of agency are not the same thing as passivity; they can create conditions for decisiveness and hope. My argument may therefore skirt the periphery of paradox, but it seems a risk worth taking. In a context where the international consensus continues to understand refugee aspirations in highly abstract terms, there is an urgent need to attend to the multiple registers through which refugees imagine and engage with their future. Turning the hopes inscribed by dream talk into a genuinely transformative force in the everyday lives of refugees also requires that we—as researchers and readers—take seriously these experiences and forms of imaginative engagement with the future, an exercise both ethically necessary and politically timely.[35] To be meaningful and effective, the extension of hope from the outside must attend to the structures and practices of anticipation and aspiration already operating within.

Young man in living room, Shatila camp. Photograph © Hisham Ghuzlan, 2009.

5 FUTURES ELSEWHERE

I FIRST MET MAHMUD on one of Shatila's thoroughfares, seated on an old chair that was propped up against the wall of his house, watching three men pour cement into a trench dug to mend a broken sewer. We began talking. Mahmud was in his early twenties. He told me he liked to watch people working with cement because it reminded him of his childhood, of better days, when he would help his father with odd jobs, and because it relieved the boredom of having nothing to do. He had lost his job in a local restaurant and had been unemployed for several months.

"I used to go out a lot," Mahmud told me, "but now I don't like to leave the camp because it feels worse when I return. I feel my heart tighten." Aimless and without resources, he had become debilitated by the sense of confinement and claustrophobia. The image of Mahmud silently watching laborers work in front of his house was a troubling inversion of the classic Marxist definition of labor in which you work to rest, an almost literal equivalent of watching paint dry, when the mind focuses on something constructive in order to generate a sense of momentum where there is none. As the months went by, this particular encounter stuck in my mind and came to symbolize for me the effect of prolonged unemployment and disenfranchisement on Shatila's youth, who feel they live in the shadow of life.[1]

In the preceding chapters I have traced how poverty, chronic unemployment, and political disenchantment conspire to diminish the expectations of refugees. This is experienced most acutely by youth disillusioned by both camp politics and the collective political aspirations of their parents' generation. Lacking opportunity or adequate representation, many of Shatila's youth feel caught in a space of blind waiting. Because they are unable to pursue studies or careers, the provisionality of daily life has produced a particular temporality in which the burdens of the present eclipse past and future. Life is dominated by an unrelenting struggle to get by. The young men and women I knew felt acutely that they had little control over their individual and collective destiny. "We live in the margins, not knowing if we're alive or dead [*nihna bi-l-hamish, ma mna'rif iza 'aayshin aw mayyitin*]," explained one young man. Life in Shatila, I was told, was closed (*musakkara*), strangling (*khanq*), frozen (*jumud*), and stagnant (*rukud*)—spatiotemporal metaphors evoking the ontological continuity between well-being and mobility.[2]

"The quiet is killing! [*'amm bamut min al-hudu*]," Umm Mahmud's husband, Munir, told me over coffee one morning. Compared to the current stalemate, even war seemed preferable: "In war people don't worry about work, food, or tomorrow. They're too busy." People had too much time to dwell on their troubles; days had become tedious and predictable. "Today is like tomorrow," Munir continued, "which was like yesterday, which will be like the day after tomorrow." Without change or progress, the passage of time becomes meaningless, something unproductive, merely to be endured.

When I visited Mahmud the following week, I found him watching the Discovery Channel. The program featured an interview with a retired businessman in Arizona who had invented a hummingbird-feeder hat. When I asked Mahmud if he often watched this channel, he said he found it stimulating. "I eat for my stomach; this is food for the brain. When I watch these things, I feel like I've been somewhere and learned something." However absurd and contrived, novelties like the hummingbird-feeder hat helped ward off introspection and worry. Mahmud went on to explain why he could no longer bring himself to follow the news from Palestine:

> During the Intifada, I watched the news several times a day, and after an attack I would demonstrate in the streets. Now I feel it's useless. When I see news from Gaza, I change the channel. It's not because I don't care—when the baby Iman Hellou was killed, I cried—it's that I feel I can't do anything. It's like your heart is cut in two. . . . Unemployment kills you and you stop thinking. When you don't have work, you have lots of time . . . you despair because you have nothing to do and spend your days worrying. Even if you have a job, you worry because as a Palestinian you earn very little. . . . There are people who don't like to work,

who say they can't make enough to make a difference, so why bother. "What can come of LBP 10,000 [$7]?" they say.

No one has time for politics; everyone is running with empty pockets. One day you go to a demonstration, the next day you feel bored, and the third day it's over, like Eid. You have to start looking for work; Israel can wait but your stomach can't. We have become like those people living in the desert before Islam who ate their god. There was a tribe who worshipped a god made of dates. When the drought came and they were hungry and had no choice but to eat their god.

Despite the odds, young men in Shatila are still expected to carve career paths for themselves, but for a growing number of them, social, political, and economic exclusion have made life in Lebanon seem simply untenable. "No choice but to eat their god" is an arresting metaphor for the near-total encroachment of daily exigencies on nationalist and even community commitments. People are left little room for contemplation. Troubled as Mahmud was by his retreat from political and social life, he had lost faith in his ability to invest his energies profitably in those spheres. Like many of his peers, he was critical of the corruption and clientelism of local factions and the hypocrisy of the national leadership. Military struggle had failed to produce results and was no longer an option for his generation, and at the same time he lacked the resources and opportunities needed to advance personal and professional goals.[3]

There is a gendered dimension to the experience of forced idleness. Unemployment is particularly debilitating for young men because it prevents them from fulfilling the key social expectations of marrying and establishing households of their own and conforming to culturally defined masculinity (Sayre and al-Botmeh 2009, 110). The whole telos of social inclusion—courtship, engagment, marriage, and supporting a family—is in effect economically out of reach for an entire generation.[4] Growing numbers of young men live with their families, dependent on the support of parents often in the same financial predicament. Although education continues to be seen as the primary path to social mobility (Chatty and Hundt 2005), discrimination in the labor market means even those with university degrees are hard-pressed to find work. Those lucky enough to find employment consistently earn lower wages than their Lebanese counterparts (Abdulrahim and Khawaja 2011, 157). The line between youth and adulthood has consequently blurred. Many young men in their early twenties view marriage and independence—and the ability to live up to the responsibilities expected of them—as available only to those who manage to emigrate. This has had profound implications for conceptions of manhood and masculinity in the camp.[5]

Women are not expected to be breadwinners and do not face the same social pressures in this respect. Their days tend to be structured around housework, and they do not experience the same excess of "empty time" (*faraagh*). Men by contrast are often actively discouraged from engaging in housework. Free time became a spiritual burden for the unemployed men I knew, while for women moments of rest—times when one might visit neighbors, drink coffee, and gossip—were savored and anticipated. Umm Mahmud's neighbor's husband once joined us for morning coffee to ease the tedium of sitting at home during a long stretch of unemployment; both his wife and Umm Mahmud later remarked that his presence was inappropriate. "But where is he to go if he doesn't have work?" I bemusedly asked, causing them to repeat simply that it was inappropriate to socialize with women in this way. The tenacity of gender codes in Shatila exacerbates the social and spiritual marginalization of unemployed men, who have neither provisional nor established places to gather, socialize, and relieve the intolerable inner pressure of having nothing to do.

In his study of unemployed Algerians and adolescent "subproletarians" in the Paris *banlieue* (suburbs) Pierre Bourdieu observed that the chronically unemployed are without the "countless tokens of socially recognized *function. . . .* Deprived of this objective universe of incitements and indications which orientate and stimulate action, and through it, social life, they can only experience the free time that is left to them as dead time, purposeless and meaningless" (2000, 222). This describes with unsettling precision the experience of many of Shatila's unemployed. Bourdieu suggests it is in such moments, when the future appears foreclosed, that what he calls *illusio*—the ability to invest oneself in the prospect of a meaningful life—is worn thin. Despite adversity, humans remain inescapably animated by foresight; it is the nature of the "social actor," working "the field of the game," writes Bourdieu, to act in such a way that "social being" and potential are maximized (2000, 240–241). If the field of the game appears bereft of opportunities, *illusio* migrates elsewhere.

FLYING PIGEONS

Close to the building in which I lived was a game room run by the al-Masri family, where young men played pinball and pool. Normally the room had filled to capacity by lunchtime, and small groups would spill outside. By early afternoon, clusters of men huddled around narghilehs spoke animatedly and drank coffee in the narrow alley, where they remained late into the night, despite attempts to sweep them off the street and back to their homes. Many residents, particularly women, complained that these game rooms were generating insecurity, concentrating the tensions and frustations of camp youth in one place to the point where fights would flare up. Game rooms became pathologized for many, a symptom of young men's economic stagnation and social degeneracy.

Besides the game rooms and Internet cafés, rooftops—the scene of pigeon flying (*qshash hamam*)—were another gathering place for the young and unemployed. From my rented aerie I could watch them congregating on surrounding rooftops to talk and tend to their birds or release them into the sky—a mesmerizing sight, especially at twilight. In spring, it was not uncommon to see as many as five flocks of birds circling overhead at dusk, visual echoes of one another. Since the goal is to lure pigeons from a rival's flock into one's own, friends would usually avoid flying their birds at the same time. Retrieving a poached pigeon normally involved a payment, which varied according to the breed of pigeon and the nature of the relationship between owner and poacher. Because pigeon flying, in essence, is a game of theft and ransom akin to gambling, many regard it as illicit. Despite its disrepute, it remains popular among the ranks of Shatila's unemployed.

Ali, who was twenty-two when I first met him, owned a flock of thirty pigeons. He was the nephew of Umm Mahmud's close friend Nadia, whose family I saw frequently before they immigrated to Germany in 2003. Nadia would sometimes joke that her nephew planned his life around his birds, which was not far from the truth. When I met him, Ali had irregular work delivering jerry cans of potable water to houses in his neighborhood but had been without a steady job since leaving school four years earlier. After I expressed interest, he invited me to join him and a small group of friends when they flew his birds. Ali whiled away many hours this way, flying his own and other people's flocks, migrating from one roof to the next: the social rituals associated with the sport introduced structure and anticipation to long days otherwise lacking both. Releasing pigeons into the sky was but one element—albeit the most aesthetically dramatic—of a more involved sociality: card games were played, bets placed, deals made, and stories exchanged; indeed, it sometimes seemed that one illicit activity provided cover for a host of others. Flying pigeons was only intermittently about the birds.

After several afternoons spent on rooftops with Ali and his friends, I began to see the symmetry between avian and human flight, for it was here that young men would imagine their own migrations—to Europe, Canada, or the United States. Their discussions seemed to follow the vectored flight of their flocks as they plotted their own means of escape. The metaphor here is culturally deep and latent—not devised by me—and stirred to vitality by the phenomenology of the sport: it set them apart from the distractions of the street and the entanglements of family, so hours spent on the roof beneath circling birds predisposed young men to thoughts of travel and futures elsewhere. Despite the tremendous risks and costs involved in emigration (now mostly by irregular or "illegal" means), many have come to see it as the only route available to a happy and productive life.[6] For Ali and his companions, planning their journeys was an exercise in geography and imagination. Routes and logistics were mapped out with the zeal (if not always the rigor) of a military campaign. One young man impressed me with his detailed knowledge of the London underground system and the location of well-known historic monuments. His dream was to travel to Britain, and he had spent many hours memorizing maps of the city available online, imagining the places he would visit when he arrived.

While these discussions tended to center on what life would be like at the desired destination—an exercise in hopeful expectation, where luck was always on one's side—they were beaded with tips about visas and traffickers, referred to as "brokers" (*simsar*). Fees, risks, and strategies were assessed; and news of friends en route—or already arrived—aroused interest and sometimes envy. The conviction that lives could be radically transformed through emigration was reinforced by the visits of returning relatives and friends, who brought with them stories of plentitude and possibility. News from abroad (*al-ghurba*, also the term used for homesickness) was followed with interest, circulating through phone conversations, Facebook pages, Internet chat, photos, and videos. When a friend of Ali's sent him a DVD of his wedding in Berlin, he played it for me, marveling at the luxury of his friend's apartment and his expensive clothes. "Look how quickly he has become German," Ali said admiringly, as if the fine furnishings and sharp cut of the groom's suit were proof of the ease with which he had reinvented himself.

Just as dream talk enables prospective thought, broadening horizons of possibility in everyday life, emigration (*hijra*) or "travel" (*safar*)—as it is euphemistically termed—has become a metaphor for the social mobility and citizenship denied Palestinians in Lebanon. Emigration talk, like dream talk, is a "technology of the imagination" (Sneath, Holbraad, and Pedersen 2009); it is dream talk's worldly counterpart, allowing imaginative access to an "elsewhere."[7] Henrik Vigh, in his study of would-be migrants in impoverished Guinea Bissau, observes that "hope in such situations does not die out but migrates—ahead of the migrants that follow it. It becomes temporally or spatially transposed and related to other places or times" (2009, 105). Emigration is tantalizing because it introduces the possibility of discontinuity—both spatial and temporal—between who (and where) one is and what one might become. This radical rupture is often experienced as nothing less than a "migration from the self" (Ali Shariati, cited in Pandolfo 2007, 347). Both in its planning and execution, emigration creates room for fantasy, speculation, and hope, where possible futures are anticipated and pursued.

Most of the young men I met through Ali had chosen destinations based on cost and family connections. It was logical to think first of joining a relative already living abroad. Variations in asylum law rarely figured in people's decisions, and many had only the most rudimentary knowledge, usually based on hearsay, of the asylum process in the countries to which they were proposing to immigrate—the interviews, the extensive paperwork, and the kinds of asylum claims that are successful.[8]

The hardship, loneliness, disorientation, and homesickness many emigrants experience are so rarely discussed as almost to constitute a kind of taboo. Friends and family living abroad, I was invariably told, were happy and had all their needs provided for by the state, unlike Palestinians in Lebanon. They were usually described as either having or not having residency (iqama)—as opposed to citizenship or asylum—making it hard to determine specifics of their legal status with any precision. Passage is often clandestine, and emigrants have little choice but to depend on the "expertise" of smugglers, who rarely convey the real risks for fear of spooking clients and losing business. When discussing the fate of those who had gone or the prospects of those wishing to leave, I was often left with the impression that success was a function of luck rather than planning, that emigration was ultimately a high-stakes gamble.

PALESTINIAN EMIGRATION IN LEBANON

The difficult and dangerous journeys would-be emigrants undertake are often contrasted with previous generations' relative ease of travel. Migration from the camps in Lebanon dates back to the 1960s and is normally broken down into three phases (Carol 2000; Doraï 2003; Hovdenak 1997; Pedersen 1997). The first began in the late 1960s with the oil boom in the Gulf.[9] Revenues generated by the 1973 OPEC (Organization of the Petroleum Exporting Countries) crisis financed rapid development and employment opportunities throughout the region. As Arabic speakers with a comparatively high level of education, Palestinians were ideal candidates for managerial and technical positions. Labor migration helped establish a remittance economy in the camps, with a growing number of families becoming dependent on the incomes of relatives in the Gulf.

During this period, large numbers of Palestinians also migrated to Eastern Europe on PLO-funded scholarships, facilitated by the Palestinian leadership's close ties with socialist governments. Migration for work and education during this initial phase is normally presented as temporary, economically motivated, and voluntary.[10] Few of the Palestinians who went to the Gulf to work or Europe to study left with the intention of permanently resettling, and many returned to Lebanon. Those refugees who did seek asylum in Western countries at this time were categorized not as political refugees but as de facto refugees (Doraï 2003). By the 1980s the demand for Palestinian labor had fallen considerably as Gulf States began actively to recruit cheaper labor from Asia (Sayre and al-Botmeh 2009, 108).

The second major wave of migration began in the 1980s. The Israeli invasion, the Sabra and Shatila massacre, and the War of the Camps displaced thousands of Palestinians inside Lebanon and forced large numbers to seek asylum in Europe.[11] While the security issues facing Palestinians in Lebanon at this time predisposed Western European governments in general to offer them political asylum, Denmark, Sweden, and Germany were favored destinations because they were known to be liberal both in their interpretation of the 1951 Convention Relating to the Status of Refugees and in their reception of Palestinian asylum seekers. Substantial numbers were given residency status and indefinite right to remain in their countries of asylum during this period.

Since the 1990s, however, the avenues for migration just described have been blocked. Following the Gulf War in 1991, about 350,000 Palestinians were expelled from Kuwait (Sayigh 1998a), and severe restrictions were imposed on Palestinians wishing to travel to the Gulf States. Meanwhile, Europe's political turn to the right in the 1990s and rising xenophobia since have led to crackdowns on immigration (legal and illegal), reduced access to asylum, and curtailed economic and social rights for those granted asylum. The creation of an open European market has paradoxically produced more insular and closed political communities.[12] As well as strengthening the monitoring of external border controls, cooperation procedures between EU member states enable countries to deport asylum seekers to the first country of asylum.[13] A growing number of countries of origin now require visas (Triandafyllidou 2010), introducing a further obstacle. In Lebanon it is now effectively impossible for Palestinians with Lebanese travel documents to get visas, and few airlines issue tickets to those without visas, in light of the heavy fines imposed on carriers transporting passengers without appropriate documentation (Bloch, Galvin, and Schuster 2000).

Palestinian migrants are further disadvantaged by a peculiarity of their legal status, the so-called protection gap. Refugees from Lebanon seeking asylum have found their rights compromised by what the UNHCR calls their "irregular movement . . . from a country in which they had already found protection," and by confusion over whether they are covered by the 1951 Convention, the 1954 Convention Relating to the Status of Stateless Persons, or the 1967 Protocol. This ambiguity has allowed receiving states to misinterpret or disregard the entitlements of Palestinians. Article 1D of the 1951 Convention, for example, is often interpreted as excluding Palestinian refugees because they are considered to be receiving assistance from two UN bodies:[14] the United Nations Conciliation Commission on Palestine (UNCCP), created in 1950 to provide legal protection, and UNRWA.[15] However, in 1951 the UNCCP's mandate was radically restricted by the UN General Assembly and its political dealings effectively terminated (Akram 2002, 42). Although UNRWA's mandate is renewed annually by the General Assembly, it has never been authorized to take on the political and legal responsibilities once vested in the UNCCP. No other body has been created to address the political and legal needs of refugees that many (including the authors of a 2002 UNHCR report) argue should bring Palestinians within the scope of the 1951 Convention (Akram and Rempel 2003). The conventional reasoning behind this policy choice is that Palestinians, unlike most refugees, seek repatriation only, not the option of asylum in a third country.[16]

Because most Western signatories to the 1951 Convention and the 1967 Protocol regard Article 1D as an exclusion clause for Palestinians from Lebanon and other areas of UNRWA operation, Palestinian refugees must therefore demonstrate that they are fleeing their place of "last habitual residence" because of a well-founded fear of persecution conforming to the definition of a refugee in the 1951 Convention.[17] This places Palestinians attempting to emigrate from Lebanon in limbo, unable to claim persecution by Israel (since it isn't their "last habitual residence") and assumed to have been afforded protection in Lebanon (Akram 2002). Palestinian applicants for political asylum qualify neither as political refugees nor, often, as stateless persons and are regularly denied the protections afforded other refugees.

Emigration, in other words, has come for many to seem existentially imperative at precisely the moment it has become virtually impossible. Palestinian emigration from the camps in Lebanon is now almost entirely irregular.[18] The few legal routes for obtaining visas to Europe and North America are through marriage to a foreigner (or a Palestinian who has obtained foreign citizenship), visa lotteries, or skilled-worker programs for which most are ineligible due to lack of education and funds.[19] That refugees are willing to pay the exorbitant smuggling fees and brave life-threatening journeys is a measure of the desperation taking hold in camp communities.[20] Those I interviewed between 2002 and 2006 who were planning to leave (or had left and been deported back to Lebanon) paid an average smuggling fee of $5,000, which covered the cost of false travel documents and transport to Europe. The most common smuggling route was through Syria, a relatively simple journey for Palestinians who are able to travel there on their Lebanese travel documents. From Syria, smugglers arranged travel overland to Turkey and from there to Greece, which sometimes involving walking for several days over a mountain range on the northern border (Papadopoulou 2004). Both Greece and Turkey were considered gateways to more desirable European destinations, usually by ship. Another option was to fly from Lebanon to Cuba, Nigeria, or another African country, whose consulates were more likely to issue visas to Palestinians holding Lebanese travel documents. From there one might be able to bribe airport officials to issue transit visas to European countries, where one could claim asylum.

With the emigration process growing far more dangerous and costly since the late 1980s, the number of women leaving the camp has dropped precipitously. Most would-be migrants I met were men. The expectation that male emigrants will earn more than their female counterparts compounds the gender asymmetry.[21] The expenses of emigration are so great that an extended kin group will often pool its resources to fund the journey of a single individual deemed most likely to attain a beachhead abroad. Loans and gifts of money from relatives are often for considerable sums and seen as an investment in the earning power of a family member who will eventually send remittances, as well as sponsor and act as guarantor for others. This collective investment predictably introduces enormous pressures and obligations for the migrant. When an entire family's savings are spent on an unsuccessful journey, the results can be devastating. Even when refugees make it to their destination, their fulfillment of economic expectations abroad (repaying debts, sending remittances, and eventually financing other family members' emigration) remains very much an open question.

EMIGRATION OR RETURN?

Several weeks after Nadia and her four children left Shatila for Berlin in the summer of 2003, Umm Mahmud and I went to visit her husband, Naji, who had stayed behind. He was not at home, but we found Nadia's nephew Ali sitting in his living room. He seemed depressed and recounted a recent conversation with a friend who had left for Germany. Ali told us that his friend had concluded by saying, "Now I know life in Shatila is not life." Clearly chagrined, Ali asked, "How was I supposed to feel?" While he was happy his friend had arrived safely, the conversation had made his own situation seem more intolerable: without savings or wealthy relatives to act as guarantors, the dream of joining his friend in Berlin seemed financially impossible.

Naji soon returned home accompanied by Mustafa, a tall man in his early fifties whom he introduced as a comrade from his days as a Fatah faction leader. After making coffee for us, Naji told us the latest from Berlin: Nadia and the children had been given housing and a weekly allowance by their local municipality in Berlin, and the children had started school and were learning German. The tales of generous state benefits appeared to be true, and their neighbors had been welcoming and kind. Despite this good news, Naji, like Ali, seemed troubled; he missed his family intensely and was worried that as their new lives were beginning, he was in some existential sense being left behind. He told us his days and nights were now consumed by thoughts of travel and little else.

Ali and Naji's anxiety is representative of the social and psychological effects of emigration on those left behind. Keenly missed and imagined to be beginning richer and more rewarding lives elsewhere, the departed enjoy a kind of honorary status, and they give emigration a palpable presence and power in the camp. Both rumors of success and tangible flows of remittance money sharpen the sense of the impoverishment of life in Shatila. The widely held view that one can realize one's potential only by emigrating has transformed "horizons of expectation" not only for those planning to leave but also for those with no choice but to stay (Graw and Schielke 2012). For those like Ali, without resources or benefactors abroad, the deprivation and disenfranchisement of camp life become more intolerable when measured against the imagined rewards of life abroad.

Our discussion also clarified tensions and political costs associated with emigration. Since camps are the visible reminder of the Nakba and the cultural remainder of pre-1948 Palestine, the decision to stay or go is politically charged; both individually and collectively, it raises unsettling questions about identity, belonging, and the pursuit of historic claims. Mustafa sympathized with Naji's desire to join his wife and children but disapproved of the family's initial decision to leave Shatila, which he regarded as tantamount to the abandonment of community and homeland. Addressing his remarks to me, though they were clearly for the benefit of Naji and Ali, he explained why he would never leave the camp:

> In 1985, the Swedish and Danish embassies in Damascus gave Palestinians who applied for emigration visas approval within fifteen days. . . . Many of my friends left, but I refused. I don't regret this decision; on the contrary, I'm happy I stayed and feel that had I gone, I would have come back. A feeling prevents me from going. . . . In 1970 my father turned sixty. I remember him saying, "This revolution [the PLO] looks like the one in Palestine in 1936, and look where that got us." Up to his death in 1998 he was convinced the political organizations representing us would achieve nothing, but he always believed he would return to his village. He lived his life waiting for this to happen. . . . He would tell me, "No right can die if the person still demands it [*ma bimut haq wara mutalib*]." How do you explain this? I am like him. If I am objective, the future looks dark for Palestinians—the Arab League is useless, the international community does not stand by us, and our political organizations do nothing—and yet, like him, I feel I am waiting for this moment.

Like others of his generation who cut their political teeth during the PLO revolution in Lebanon, Mustafa regards the camp as a site of agency and resistance, intimately bound up with his own political awakening and nationalist aspirations. "The camp is the material shape of our political identity," Mustafa continued. "Factions guard the camp and its boundaries because it is the symbol of our cause. Once these boundaries dissolve—as people leave and the population becomes more mixed—our political identity and our right to struggle will also disappear." To his mind, the camp is the material symbol both of Palestinian dispossession and of ongoing popular resistance to displacement and resettlement. To leave the camp is to undermine the right of return and render meaningless years of struggle and sacrifice.

Debates over emigration versus return pit two forms of futurity against one another: one rooted in a vision of nationalist yearning and endlessly deferred return; the other, in personal, familial types of futurity and future planning. While asylum in a third country has long been stigmatized as the betrayal of national interests—taboo both in its symbolic inversion of return and in its apparent privileging of individual aspirations (often understood to be material) over long-term political goals—the majority of camp youth now regard it as the only means of escaping terminal limbo. It is not uncommon, therefore, to encounter individuals who invoke return rhetorically, while simultaneously planning emigration materially. "Everyone wants to leave; this is known," said Ali. "If Canada is hell, better than paradise here. If someone brought a ship tomorrow and offered Palestinians the chance to go to Europe, the lines would reach to Jounieh [a city fifteen kilometers north of Beirut]. Can you blame us? Here we have nothing. Sometimes I have hope," Ali continued, with an air of cynical resignation:

> But most of the time I feel there is none for Palestinians in Lebanon. . . . What is true is that my rights are lost. I feel humiliated. So isn't it better to go abroad and take another nationality and then use this nationality to return to Palestine? It's not that I don't love the camp—I do. I was born and raised here. But conditions are terrible. You die a million deaths each day. You feel buried alive. I have no future here. It is not a beautiful thing for a person to die for the sake of his country; it is more beautiful if he can live for it [*innahu laysa jamilan an yamut al-insan min ajl watanihi, wa ajmal minu an ya'ish li-ajlihi*]. If I travel, maybe I can make enough money to come back here and marry, but I want to live abroad because I don't want my children to taste this bitterness of life. If I can make something for them, then perhaps my life won't seem wasted, but this can only happen if I leave. The only solution is if the gate to emigration [*bab al-hijra*] is opened.

For Ali's generation, the majority of whom have advanced beyond the primary education their parents received, aspirations are rarely framed in collective political terms. Ali is deeply skeptical—much more than his parents' generation—about what might be called the existential efficacy of politics. Holding out for the increasingly remote possibility of a political solution allowing refugees to return to Palestine is, to his mind, tantamount to abject acquiescence to a life of deprivation and servility.[22] This attitude is delicately and difficultly balanced against a rhetorical (albeit feeling) acknowledgment of the sacrifices of his parents' generation and the importance of the armed struggle in the 1970s and 1980s. Shatila ultimately carries for him the residue of failed promise and presents a dystopic counterpoint to the European future he dreams of. His exchange with Mustafa is suggestive of the ontological differences in not only how younger generations understand the history of the community and their place within it but also how they view the future—less as an immutable destiny than as determined by individual will and chance.

While dire conditions inform Ali's sense of urgency, his desire to go to Germany cannot be reduced to economic pragmatism. It springs rather from a sense of existential impasse. There is no future in Shatila; life feels bereft of meaning or promise. Emigration—not only the fact of it but the planning of it, and the discourse surrounding it—offers him and others a teleological praxis that promises the recovery of rights, privileges, and potential. It is about not merely financial security but also meaning and agency, and purpose, reconnecting actions in the present to the prospect of a future yield. Citizenship elsewhere even introduces the possibility of "return" to Palestine, albeit as a tourist on a foreign passport. The regenerative forces associated with emigration pull strongly on the compass needles even of those who, like Ali, lack the resources to achieve it but who nevertheless chart itineraries of the imagination down roads not always leading to Palestine, at least not directly.[23]

"HANGING BETWEEN EARTH AND SKY"

When Naji and Nadia decided to immigrate to Germany in 2002, they were advised not to travel together since it might raise the suspicions of embassy officials and reduce their chance of getting visas. Nadia and their four children were the first to leave, traveling to Italy and then over the border into Germany. Once in Germany Nadia destroyed their travel documents showing passage through Italy (since asylum seekers are expected to seek protection in the first secure state they visit), produced their Palestinian ID cards, and told immigration authorities they had been smuggled from Lebanon and did not know the route taken by their smugglers. The plan was for Naji to join them a few months later. With the help of her sister, who was living in Berlin, and a friend in Beirut who produced a letter of invitation and provided financial support, Nadia and her children were issued Schengen visas.[24] Her luck in all these matters was exceptional, and her asylum claim in Germany succeeded in July 2003.

Naji assumed the hardest part was over, that procuring a visa for one person would be considerably easier than for five. With access to comparatively large reserves of cash and a network of smugglers and middlemen in Beirut and Shatila, he imagined reunion with his family would require a matter of months. "If you have money, you can eat ice cream, even in hell," he joked. The more fraught question was not how to get to Germany but what to tell the authorities when he got there and how to present his case. In the absence of war it would be difficult to claim physical endangerment. In addition to misrecognizing the intrinsic rights of Palestinians to legal status as stateless refugees, European governments have tended to view their migration from Lebanon in the postwar period as economically motivated and therefore voluntary.[25] Friends advised Naji to avoid deportation by devising a compelling political narrative. Before Nadia left, she and Naji had determined what they would tell the immigration authorities to make sure the details of their statements matched. Naji centered his asylum petition on a dispute with Islamic Jihad operatives in Ayn al-Hilweh camp following an explosion outside one of their homes.[26] The attack was blamed on Fatah, and certain individuals from Shatila (including Naji) were named in connection with it. Both chronology and location were changed and certain details embellished to strengthen his case. The incident had in fact occurred years before and did not (as he claimed) involve factions from Ayn al-Hilweh. Naji had been advised to name this camp because of its highly publicized clashes between secular and Islamist factions and its reputation as a haven for Islamic extremism.

Despite having absorbed and assimilated his story, Naji feared that without sufficient proof officials would question its legitimacy. He therefore arranged for an arrest warrant from Islamic Jihad to be created, along with other paperwork demonstrating active membership in Fatah. The process of constructing a case and generating documentation intensified his anxiety, since falsifying papers and warrants would create real dangers if discovered by either political faction. Naji was also ashamed of these deceits, humiliated that he should have to invent a predicament for himself when a real one existed. While economic and political discrimination against Palestinians in

Lebanon amounts to—and is experienced as—persecution, it is not formally recognized as such.[27] Many states refuse to consider persecution by nonstate actors, recognizing only state persecution as grounds for political asylum (Akram 2002). Given their a priori status as refugees with a valid claim to political asylum, Palestinians find the requisite for fictive histories a painful, even grotesque irony.[28]

Because Naji had a friend in France, his first plan was to travel to Paris and make his way from there to Germany. After several months of struggling to get the necessary paperwork for his visa application (including two letters of invitation, one from his friend and the other from the municipal authority of her town of residence), he was notified that his application had been denied. No reason was given. A few months later, in December 2003, Naji tried to get to Germany via Greece. Having traveled first to Turkey by way of Damascus, with the assistance of a smuggler, he made his way up to the border and tried, unsuccessfully, to bribe his way into Greece. After two weeks his money ran out, and he made his way back to Shatila. Naji's next plan, in April 2004, involved traveling to Ukraine. He arranged for a smuggler from Greece and a Palestinian contact from Berlin to join him in Kiev. They would smuggle him through Moldavia, Slovakia, and the Czech Republic into Germany, with the help of middlemen in each country. A friend working in a travel agency in Beirut procured a visa to Ukraine, and Naji booked himself a room in a hotel on the banks of the Dnieper River. The day before he left, we held a small party for him, and friends and family gathered to say their good-byes and wish him luck, many joking—a little unkindly—that we would be holding a homecoming party soon enough. Though I half expected him to succeed, ten days later Naji was back in Shatila. "I got to Kiev airport at about one in the morning," Naji told me:

A Lebanese guy called Adel, whom I met on the plane, gave me a lift to my hotel. Having memorized the number of the broker in Greece—he told me not to take any papers with me—I called him, and he told me to wait for him in the hotel. So I waited and locked the door; I was afraid. Everyone warned me about the mafia there. I watched TV all day. Kiev is beautiful. There was a river right under my window and lots of trees. . . . After two days I tried to call the contact in Germany. Some people told me not to go with him because he has a reputation for running off with money or turning up late after your visa has run out. You have to send the money in advance, and then he comes to collect you, so I gave him only a small amount up front. He never showed up, and neither did the Greek guy. I waited—for five days I did nothing. I ate cheese and crackers in my room. I called the Greek, and he put the phone down on me. . . . On the fifth day I went to a bar and met Adel, and I asked him to help. We went to the airport because he knew one of the officials there and speaks Ukrainian. The official told us there was no chance to get to Germany now, since no one was taking bribes and all the borders were closed, so I came back to Beirut. . . . But I don't give up [*ma bistaslim*]—this is what's important. You can't let yourself feel depressed. If someone offers you a cup of coffee and you say, "I am too depressed; I don't feel like it," and you sit and stare into space, then the hand offering the coffee will withdraw just as quick. You can't feel sorry for yourself, because you won't get anywhere that way.

Naji remained remarkably resourceful and optimistic. When one strategy failed, he soon produced another and would set about preparing for it and gathering resources to fund it. Nevertheless, his failed ventures had begun to take their toll on his finances and friendships. As the months went by, he grew reclusive, spending increasing amounts of time at home and rarely venturing out. Mutual friends complained that he could talk only of his next scheme for getting to Germany; Umm Mahmud commented that his body was in Shatila but his mind had left long ago.

To many of his friends Naji now seemed hopelessly naïve; being swindled out of a small fortune by unscrupulous smugglers had made him a mildly ridiculous and pitiable figure. On one occasion, after I had been away for several weeks, I returned to discover he had left for Turkey. Munir recounted his departure with a friend, Abu Marwan—they had planned to get a visa to Nigeria and from there to France. "He's crazy," Munir told me, shaking his head. "You know what he said? If the customs officials in France take him aside, he will say he is going to see his wife and family in Germany and he has traveled through Syria, Turkey, and Nigeria to get there, and therefore they *must* let him go to Berlin. He believes he can say something like this to a border guard and they will feel compassion!" Unable even to make it to Nigeria, Naji and Abu Marwan returned to Shatila the following week.

Undaunted, Naji and Abu Marwan made a second trip to Turkey a few weeks later. They had been put in touch with a more reliable smuggler they were confident would not let them down. Drawing on his mother-in-law's UNRWA pension, Naji's plan was to purchase tickets to Cuba, transiting through France, where they planned to disembark. He described this new plan in the context of the previous trip to Turkey that had ended in failure:

> Naji: We took the bus to Turkey through Syria. The smuggler was meant to join us and take us on to Nigeria, but he never came. I went with Abu Marwan. He was in Germany before, during the War of the Camps; he was badly injured and was given medical treatment there. . . . It was a thirty-one-hour journey. For Abu Marwan it was a hard trip. He gets pains in his stomach if he doesn't lie flat every few hours. Abu Marwan is a funny guy; we laughed a lot, but he has problems with his eyes, so when we got to Turkey, he was like my child. I had to lead him around by hand, and he was always bumping into things and tripping. We fought about what we would buy to eat and how much money to spend. When I bought a beer, he rebuked me for spending money on alcohol. He feels guilty because of all the money he's borrowed. . . . We phoned the smuggler on Wednesday, and he said, "I'll be there Friday," and then when we called on Friday, it was Sunday and so on. Eventually after a week we came back. We each spent over $500 just on the hotel and the food and everything—all for nothing. When we realized it had fallen through, Abu Marwan cried; he felt ashamed to go back, but he is the kind of person who laughs easily, so I cheered him up. When we got back to Lebanon, I went to Sidon where the smuggler lives and threatened him, so he said he would come with us this time.
>
> DA: Do you believe him?
>
> Naji: They say you don't have beans until you can see them in the balance. I won't believe him until I get to Germany. . . . I feel as if I am hanging between earth and sky, neither here nor there. . . . When I land in the airport in France, I am going to say, "I have to go and see my wife and children. I am not here to take your money or to steal your jobs; I just want to see my family. I can't live without them." I have decided whatever happens, I am not going to let them send me back to Lebanon. . . . Do you know what I am going to do? I am going to take a piece of glass with me, and as soon as I get to the customs, I am going to lift up my shirt and slit my stomach and tell them they *must* let me to go to Germany. . . . Abu Marwan has problems with blood pressure; there are pills he can take that raise his blood pressure and make him collapse. I joked that he mustn't die on me. . . . I am not frightened about cutting my stomach. I am not frightened of dying; only God knows when I will die. I am not scared; I am just very tired.

Naji's resilience had begun to wear thin, and a new state of existential limbo—"neither here nor there"—was replacing the one that had first propelled him and his family to leave Shatila. Because he was faced with the prospect of yet another encounter with rigid and unresponsive border guards, his plan to appeal to their humanity with the simple truth that separation from his wife and family had become intolerable—however poignant and true—seemed desperate and irrational. The months of careful planning, of procuring paperwork and refining his narrative, now seemed utterly irrelevant—the gap between aspiration and reality untenably wide.[29] Naji struggled with the bitter truth that he was powerless to influence the course of events or change his situation and was on the brink of financial ruin. His threat to violate his body to avoid deportation, as a final measure, was a startlingly literal indication of his need for recognition and of the symbolic violence exercised by increasingly restrictive border controls.[30]

The following day I met Abu Marwan walking purposefully down the street near Umm Mahmud's house; he told me he and Naji were hoping to leave that night but were doubtful that the smuggler from Sidon would turn up. Abu Marwan was clearly anxious about the trip and the costs of another failure, both financially and in terms of lost face. I was reminded of Naji's comment that Abu Marwan's many loans had become a source of paralyzing guilt and anxiety. His fear of squandering the savings of relatives and friends, or being unable to repay his debts, was palpably oppressive. Despite these concerns, Abu Marwan—like Naji—remained convinced he could make a life for himself only in Europe. Like Ali, he saw the future as synonymous with emigration. Several days later I learned from Munir that Naji and Abu Marwan had again been forced to return to Lebanon. I did not see either of them again before my own departure to the United States.

Two years later, to my great surprise, Naji phoned me from Berlin. He recounted exuberantly how he had finally managed to get to Germany, via Sweden the year before. After his second abortive trip to Turkey he had found himself destitute, unable to borrow more from friends or relatives in Lebanon. With no remaining alternative, Naji sold his house in Shatila, his last asset; it was a huge gamble but one that paid off. He took pleasure in furnishing me with the details of this final journey, recalling, with characteristic humor, his improbable route, in the last leg of which he was concealed in a lorry filled with household appliances. In the final reckoning, Naji's journey from Lebanon to Germany cost him four years and $20,000. His experience is by no means exceptional.

"For the displaced or the dispossessed, the migrant or the refugee," writes Homi Bhabha, "no distance is more awesome than the few feet across borders" (quoted in Diken 2004, 92). For Palestinians like Naji, living in exile across the Middle East, a history of radical displacement has evolved into one of immobility and containment (Kelly 2008; Shamir 2005). His experiences are a reminder of the obstacles faced by those who, for economic or political reasons, have been left out of the transnational flow of people and capital. For those fortunate enough to make it to Europe or North America, how is the much-anticipated arrival experienced, and what of the inevitable disappointments that often follow? When dreams of self-transformation are not realized and the migrant finds himself facing "a much denser marginalization, in which the impossibility of gaining a worthy life becomes consolidated" (Vigh 2009, 109)? In the remainder of this discussion I turn to Fathi, a young man I met through Umm Mahmud, who claimed asylum in the UK and found himself exchanging one form of statelessness for another.

ARRIVAL

They won't—they will not—permit me
—I'm a shadow's shadow—
they won't let me
be a refugee

Tom Paulin, "Stateless Twice Again," *Love's Bonfire* (2012)

The difficulties refugees experience when they leave Lebanon and try to claim asylum elsewhere offers insight into the uneasy position that they occupy within both Palestinian nationalist discourse and asylum law. The paradoxical experience of the Palestinian refugee who arrives in Britain and is not permitted to be a refugee, the subject of Tom Paulin's poem "Stateless Twice Again," was Fathi's when he arrived at London's Heathrow Airport in October 2004. Then in his late twenties, Fathi grew up in a camp in north Lebanon. He trained as a teacher and worked at an UNRWA school in Shatila for several years. Shortly before I began my fieldwork, Fathi was given a temporary appointment at a school in the north and I began renting his former room, which still contained many of his belongings. I remember looking at his eclectic collection of books, many in English (Pirandello, Beckett, Joyce, Shakespeare, Emile Habibi, and T. S. Eliot among them), and wondering about the person whose room I was sharing. Living with the same family led to many overlaps in our social networks. Fathi had taught the children of Umm Yusuf and Umm Mahmud and was held in high esteem by both families.

Fathi never imagined he would leave Lebanon. Unlike many of his peers, he was not drawn to the idea of emigration. He was devoted to his family and his students; he once told me he could never imagine leaving them. Like Mustafa, Fathi believed his life and destiny were inextricably bound to the camp, where he was born and raised. His departure was therefore unexpected. Apprehensive, with few illusions about what the journey would bring or the transformations that would follow from it, Fathi bought a ticket to the UK and (for reasons I am not at liberty to disclose) was able to travel legally and relatively effortlessly. His experience of the asylum process and of finding his bearings in a radically different cultural and social environment speak to the difficulties facing those lucky enough to arrive, difficulties doubtless experienced even more acutely by those who—unlike Fathi—had imagined migration as the solution to all their problems.

It was not until the following summer, almost a year after Fathi traveled to the UK, that I was able to talk with him about his experience of the asylum process. Shortly after his plane had landed at Heathrow, Fathi recalled asking an airport official where the immigration office was:

> I said I intended to claim asylum. "I am an immigration officer; follow me," the woman answered. It was a very short encounter. She asked me where I was from, and I told her I was a Palestinian from Lebanon. I thought I was being taken to an immigration office, but instead she took me to passport control and I found myself in a long queue. I thought, "How can all these people be claiming asylum?" Then I realized this was customs and I would have to ask for asylum in front of everyone. People were staring at me—it was like a performance, and everyone was keen to know what was going to happen to me. It was hard to talk. I said, "If you want to know the details of my case, I want to speak in a private room." She refused, so I only gave very brief details about where I came from and my age. Then I was taken to another room to be interviewed by an intelligence officer, and he was kind and gave me some juice. They moved me to room B, and I was put with people from Africa, but I was supposed to have been sent to room A, where the people from China, Egypt, and Yugoslavia were, so they moved me again. There were probably about forty people there. . . . I was in room A for several days, though there were people who had been in there for as long as four weeks. The only place you were allowed to go was the bathroom. I could not sleep because it was so crowded. . . . They took an x-ray of my chest. It felt dehumanizing and humiliating.

Fathi's first encounter with UK border officials is a familiar refugee narrative. His description of being shuffled between rooms and people, interviewed, x-rayed, and made to wait for days makes visible the mechanisms of state control, reminding us that a border is not simply a physical line demarcating a point of crossing but an interactive space whose form is determined by the person crossing it.[31] Fathi felt that from the moment he expressed a wish to claim asylum, he became an object of suspicion and scrutiny, the legitimacy of his case preemptively in doubt. The screening centers and "zones" that exist behind the glassy airport facades, to which asylum seekers are swiftly redirected on arrival, place them at the mercy of immigration officials and beyond the "mitigating restraint of law" (Ferme 2004, 98). It is in these administrative areas and *zones d'attente* (waiting areas) that refugees, devoid of their rights and often lacking the linguistic or legal skills to understand or explain their predicament, experience most forcefully the state's policing power.

When would-be refugees apply for asylum on arrival in the UK, they are routinely subjected to long interviews by immigration officers, often within hours of their arrival and before they have a chance to seek legal advice or representation. Many are terrified, disoriented, and unprepared for what is to follow. It is normally on the basis of this first interview that applicant claims are decided. Fathi's account of his own interview with immigration officials reveals the asymmetrical power relations at work:

> First, I had the screening interview at the airport in which they asked about my family, about money, my date of birth, and briefly about my claim. They wouldn't let me tell them more at this point. Then they took my fingerprints. They asked whether I had given my fingerprints before, and I told them UNRWA took my fingerprints as a child, when I collected rations for my mother who was illiterate (they did this for those who couldn't sign). . . . The officer pressed my finger hard. . . . He stared and said, "Well, we have to get it right," and he didn't release the pressure. . . . I was then interviewed by the intelligence officer; another came and started shouting at me; he was the manager of Terminal 4 asylum procedure. He said angrily, "We know all of you are here just to earn money and to have a free education," or something like this. . . . So I said, "I am a teacher, and I don't need your free education. I have a history and I have a claim." And he said, "I don't care about your history or your claim." I answered, "So if you don't care, then I don't want to speak." Then he went away to get my travel documents, and another woman continued to interview me. She apologized for his rudeness

and said it was just his manner. I didn't let him affect my morale, and when he came back and started accusing me again, I said, "You don't know anything." I think this challenge rescued me, because after that he came twice and spoke more calmly. I felt if I hadn't responded in this way, he would have sent me to a detention center. My linguistic skills helped me express myself.

Moving from the camp to a world governed by inscrutable bureaucracy entails a shift of moral orders, where nonnegotiable procedures, indecipherable documents, and the degrading fingerprinting process replace complex reciprocal relations based on trust and familiarity. Fathi's account of being stared down by the officer or, at a later point, told to look an immigration officer in the eye (the assumption being he had something to hide), is redolent of the power relations at the heart of the asylum process, in which border officials, acting as "little sovereigns," establish their own spaces of exception (Agamben [1998], cited in Gehrig 2004, 77). Because Fathi was intimidated and exhausted by his journey, subjected to blatant intimidation as well as slightly more subtle good cop–bad cop routines, it is unsurprising that he muddled certain facts and left out crucial details regarding his circumstances. These blurrings and omissions were to provide the Home Office grounds for subsequently rejecting his asylum application.

Although the refugee determination procedure is presented as a rational, bureaucratic process, Fathi's account suggests it is often arbitrary, determined by contingencies such as linguistic competence, race, gender, class, appearance, and the mood of officials on duty (Nyers 2003). Asylum procedure is rife with strong emotions, and bureaucratic power is often laced with latent prejudice.[32] Others who spoke about their experience of applying for asylum in the UK and Europe recalled the intense fear and intimidation they experienced when confronted with the insolence and power of immigration officers charged with deciding their fate. As in Fathi's case, officials will often attempt to forestall potentially "misleading" expressions of emotion by asylum seekers, particularly when the first statement is taken down, by posing closed questions and demanding yes-or-no answers. The summary dismissal of Fathi's predicament, and the assumption that he was an "illegal immigrant" intent on exploiting state welfare, involved a refusal to recognize the political and emotional components of his narrative, a refusal in itself a breach of the 1951 Convention to which the UK is signatory.[33] To be fair, it can be emotionally stressful for officers whose task is to distinguish fact from fiction, which refugees to admit and which to deport, and it is not surprising that their capacity for empathy is eroded by repeated exposure to narratives of persecution and despair (Fassin 2005; Rousseau et al. 2002).

After several days in room A, Fathi was issued an Application Registration Card (ARC) and allowed to make one phone call. He called a friend, who collected him several hours later. The ARC identification card (a biometric card recently introduced by the HO) contained his fingerprint and photo and a secure chip holding additional information.[34] He was given no formal status but granted "temporary admission" to the UK, which effectively meant the temporary suspension of deportation. No mention was made of legal aid to which he was entitled or of the stages of the asylum process that lay ahead. Fathi was, however, informed that he was eligible for assistance from the National Asylum Support Services (NASS). After filling out the necessary forms, he was given thirty-six pounds a week and told that under the Immigration and Asylum Act of 1999 he was not permitted to work to supplement his welfare allocation.[35] In May 2006, after twenty months of being unable to work legally, under threat of detention or deportation, Fathi was able to apply for a work permit.

Without a formal status Fathi found himself in legal limbo, considered neither a permanent resident (with citizenship rights) nor outside the law, but something in between—a condition not dissimilar to the uncertain position Palestinians occupy in Lebanon. His temporary status effectively enabled the state to acknowledge his claim to protection, while divesting itself of the responsibility to provide it.[36] He was required to register with the local police on a weekly basis, leaving him feeling that he was under constant surveillance. After initially being refused asylum by the HO, Fathi applied for legal assistance, successfully appealed the ruling, and in June 2007 was given Humanitarian Protection (HP) status. This entitled him to remain in the UK for five years, after which time his case would be reviewed. While it is likely that Fathi will, eventually, be granted Indefinite Leave to Remain (ILR) in the UK, his semistatus precludes full personhood (citizenship) and is a reminder that he cannot take his residency for granted. Once again, time appears to be suspended, his future placed on hold as he waits to find out whether he will be permitted to make the UK his home.

Fathi's experience is representative: Palestinians seeking asylum in the UK are categorized as having "indeterminate" status. They are eligible for Discretionary Leave (DL) or HP, but not political asylum, and are treated as recipients of charity rather than political subjects entitled to protection under the law.[37] Both DL and HP operate according to the logic of exception; presented as a privilege rather than a right, they elide the political history and conditions that compel refugees to seek asylum. Misrecognizing the de facto refugee status of Palestinians becomes a way of not acknowledging the events that caused them to become refugees in the first place, ensuring, as Sherene Razack notes, "light need never be shone on First World complicity" (quoted in Ticktin 1999, 36). In the case of Palestinians seeking asylum in the UK, this seems particularly egregious given the role the British Mandate played in the Palestinian tragedy. The reluctance to recognize the legal status and claims of Palestinians who engage in "irregular movement" is symptomatic of the lack of recognition accorded to Palestinians and their cause by the international community.

While Fathi was fortunate enough to make his way out of Lebanon and begin a new life in the UK, he is acutely aware that his family and friends are not so lucky; hope for the future is offset by feelings of guilt not easily assuaged. Although Fathi remains optimistic about his future in the UK, he misses the daily routines and sociality of camp life and is sometimes deeply homesick. The Lebanon-Israel war of 2006 and the political turmoil that followed heightened his anxieties about the safety and well-being of his family. When Nahr al-Bared camp came under attack from the Lebanese army in June 2007, two of his cousins were killed in the crossfire. Without travel documents and unable to return to Lebanon for reasons related to his claim, Fathi could not attend their funerals. It is in such moments—estranged from kin and custom and still a stranger in his new "home"—that the costs of starting a new life are registered most forcefully. During a conversation with Fathi in 2007, almost three years after his arrival at Heathrow, he described his ongoing attachment to his camp in Lebanon and his ambivalence about the decision to leave:

> Fathi: My family has been living in the camp for over fifty years, so not to consider it my anchor is beyond my capabilities as a human being. Many of my childhood memories are negative, but it doesn't detract from the fact the camp represents the place I still consider home; it represents my history, privacy, intimacy, and education. The camps are part of our humanity as Palestinians. I don't think there is a single Palestinian family who left a camp and did not go back and visit. It is not just about personal roots but the

representation of our past. The camps contain the history of the Palestinian community in Lebanon and have transformed from a site of resistance to a sort of normal life. . . . There is no question one day I will go back; we have a saying, "Paradise without the people one loves is pointless" [*janna bidun nas ma btindas*]. I will go back for my friends and family and for the sake of my mother.

DA: Do you ever regret the decision to leave?

Fathi: Sometimes I feel it was my fate, and at other times I think the decision to leave was my own. It's like you go to a furniture shop and you buy a sofa, and then you realize you don't need it, and because you wanted to convince yourself it suits your place and the money wasn't wasted, you bring it home and find a place for it. After a while you get used to it, and you stop thinking about it. This, for me, is traveling and emigration. At some point I wondered if I had made the wrong decision, but I realized I couldn't find my way back and I needed to accept what I had done and take responsibility for it. You need to normalize the situation but can never make it fully normal; it is impossible.

DA: How do you feel your life has changed?

Fathi: I feel as if I am living a different life, not in terms of values but in terms of understanding. Here I have my own opinions about things. . . . In the camp, because of the political dynamics, one ends up associating with one particular group, but now I have a different, independent position from which to look at these issues, and before I didn't have that. This makes me more hopeful, not only about my status here but about expressing my own ideas and in representing Palestinians—though I don't like to use this word—perhaps what I mean by this is representing myself before representing my people. I feel people in the camps have become hostages of hope, whereas people who leave are able to hope in a different way. When you learn another language or start to understand things about another culture, it's important; you feel hopeful; it's new; you change. . . . Here I can develop what I've always had.

The existential gains Ali and his companions imagine emigration bestowing on those who leave seem more or less realized in Fathi's description of life in the UK. Leaving the familiar world of the camp, speaking a different language, and immersing himself in an unfamiliar culture have brought challenges but also an awareness that he is embarking on a qualitatively new life, one he is creating for himself on his own terms. Occupying an independent vantage point removed from the constraining influence of camp politics has given Fathi a new perspective on the strengths and weaknesses of the community he left and the one he joined; he feels able to express himself with greater clarity, to realize himself more fully. Radical departures, which necessarily inform how migration is imagined and experienced, entail "an openness to the future . . . both exhilarating and terrifying" (Jackson 2007, 131). When Fathi was a Palestinian living in a camp in Lebanon, what he could imagine himself becoming had been highly circumscribed, whereas now the future seemed open to extremes of risk and opportunity.

. . .

No family in Shatila is untouched by emigration, and most have at least one member settled elsewhere.[38] The complex transnational networks connecting Shatila to the Gulf, Europe, the Americas, and beyond have not only helped sustain the community materially but have also kept alive the possibility of mobility and opportunity in a context where both now seem lacking. Lives established elsewhere have unsettled and redefined the relationship between home and homeland in subtle but significant ways. As the future has come to seem like something available only to other people, Palestinians in the camps in Lebanon have increasingly turned to emigration as a means of regaining agency and control in their lives and restoring "the delicacies of recognition and positive social being" (Vigh 2009, 95).

Like the survival strategies described in preceding chapters, emigration is intertwined with the economic histories of families over time: those who leave and claim asylum in a third country are often enabled by relatives sponsoring them abroad. They in turn may become providers and guarantors for family members left behind. As such, emigration has come to be viewed as one of the few means by which refugees might carve out better and more secure lives for themselves and their families. While economic security and the prospect of citizenship undoubtedly play a critical role in pushing and pulling refugees into new lives in Europe and beyond, emigration has also come to function as a modality of imagination that in turn reshapes how local life-worlds are perceived. The journeys people plan and undertake—the risk, adventure, and novelty they entail—promise an escape from the repetitive and aimless existence of the camp. For those who emigrate, the borders crossed are understood to be not only physical but metaphoric.[39]

Writing in the wake of the Holocaust, Hannah Arendt famously posited that the condition of the modern refugee presupposes the globalization of the state form. Within this new global order the refugee emerged as the obverse and abject other. Arendt underscored the difference between being outside one's homeland in a politically polymorphous world and being displaced in a politically isomorphic one, where it is necessary for everyone to have a nationality and a passport to prove it.[40] More than a half century later, with increased flow of goods, people, and services perceived to be inexorably eroding the borders of nation-states, the figure of the refugee has once again become the negative image through which new legal-political categories of citizenship and rights are formulated. "The refugee should be considered for what he is," writes Giorgio Agamben, "that is, nothing less than a border concept that radically calls into question the principles of the nation-state and, at the same time, helps to clear the field for a no-longer-delayable renewal of categories" (1995, 117). Building on Agamben's insight, a number of scholars have argued that mobile citizens and noncitizens (illegal aliens, immigrants, and migrants) should be considered agents of political change because the new forms of community and belonging they create cannot be understood in purely territorial terms and expose the limits of juridical nation-state definitions of citizenship.[41] Emigration in the Palestinian refugee community similarly suggests a need for critical scrutiny of assumed categories of identity and belonging and the relationship of citizenship to nationality and territory.

Fathi is a case in point. He is not alone in asserting that the ideal of return has come to seem like a false hope holding refugees "hostage," while emigration to the West introduces the possibility of a "normal life." Though Fathi is now invested in securing British citizenship and building a new life for himself in the UK, he retains a deep attachment to his Palestinian identity and to his roots in Lebanon. These attachments, however, are not mutually exclusive and serve to underscore that citizenship and nationality are not isomorphic. He regards the camp of his birth as the community to which he belongs and will someday return, and his experience of growing up as a refugee in Lebanon as the bedrock of his identity.[42] Fathi's experience—like Naji's and that of others who have left Lebanon to build futures elsewhere—suggests that exile and emigration may be changing the sociospatial coordinates of community and self-identification to produce other geographies of belonging. Seeking asylum and citizenship in a third country complicates the relation of refugees to a Palestinian "homeland" and, by extension, the meaning of "home" and "return." Camps, it seems, are spawning their own diasporas, creating cross-currents of attachment that un-settle our understanding of how Palestinian identity and affiliation should now be conceived. While the establishment of a Palestinian nation-state remains the core demand of the Palestinian struggle, its territorial rendering should not ob-scure other conceptions of home, identity, and belonging that have developed in exile. It is to this matter that I now turn.

"Palestine" mural, Shatila camp. Photograph © Hisham Ghuzlan, 2012.

6 MANY RETURNS

DO PALESTINIAN REFUGEES IN LEBANON still wish to return? This is a question I am often asked. At the rhetorical level the answer is simple: yes. Refugees are eloquent in their yearning for a return to Palestine, for affirmation of their collective right to a material and cultural patrimony unjustly stripped from them, for communion with places they have heard about, imagined, or lived in. Because Palestinian identity is still rooted in territory, and in a traumatic history of expulsion, return to the land of Palestine seems to be the means by which a "natural" order of existence would be restored.[1] The question, however, obscures a more complex relationship between refuge and origin. Return presupposes a fixed relation to territory and home and denies dynamically evolving identity and the cumulative experience of exile. Experiential diversity is lost in the translation of several generations' needs, grievances, and aspirations into the language of formal rights. While the importance and legitimacy of the right of return is not in doubt, what it means for different generations of refugees, in particular those born and raised in exile, is less certain. This chapter, which draws on formal and informal conversations about the right of return with friends and colleagues in Shatila over the past decade, is a modest attempt to examine how it is discussed locally and what it means for different generations and to reflect critically on the practice and politics of solidarity that have arisen around this issue.

Discussion about return is often striking for the absence of voices of camp refugees, those whose lives will be most directly affected by the outcome of final-status negotiations.[2] Within the prodigious body of scholarship, policy literature, and activism addressing the right of return in the years since Oslo, surprisingly little attention has been devoted to the views of refugees themselves, much less to the lines of fragmentation emerging in the Palestinian collective imaginary.[3] The irony is subtle but sharp: the legal, ethical, and cultural right-of-return discourses that surged in strength and purpose after Oslo did so precisely in response to the erasure of refugees' voices from the political discourse of the peace process—but they have, however obliquely, repeated this sin of omission. Both supporters and detractors of the right of return tend to cast refugee sentiments monolithically,[4] and they assume that its implementation would entail the return of *all* refugees (a reading often consonant with their own political agendas).[5] Ideological positions staked out by both sides, in effect, have diverted discussion away from particulars and practicalities and smoothed over differences between the ways justice is defined by the language of policy and international law and by refugees in communities like Shatila.

Shortly after the death of Umm Ali, a conversation I had with her daughter Umm Mahmud was strikingly revealing about this very question—that of belonging, attachment, and desire for return in the context of prolonged exile. The Hasan family was still in mourning. As we sat plucking *mulukhiyyeh* leaves (a type of edible mallow) from their stems for the afternoon meal, Umm Mahmud described the events of the months before:

> At first I couldn't believe my mother was gone. I was waiting for her to wake up, or for myself to wake up. The day she died, I stood by her body thinking, "What is death?" It was as if the life of our family left with her. She would tell us about Palestine, and we grew to love it through her. My father didn't love Palestine like she did. In his thoughts he is here, in Shatila, while she was always in her village, in her memories. At first, when she died, I felt she wasn't happy—that she hadn't wanted to die and she was still holding on to life so she could return [to Palestine]. . . . But about a month later, when I went to clean her grave, I felt she was at peace. It was as if there was a light shining out from her grave, illuminating the graves around it, and I thought maybe she had found comfort after all. We have lost a lot with her death. They say the mother holds the family together [*al-umm bitlimm*], and it's true. But with time it gets better, and we are still living, thanks to God.

This was one of several conversations I had with Umm Mahmud about her mother's death. She spoke about the impact it had had on her, the days of mourning, the conflicts that had arisen between her siblings during the final stages of her mother's illness, and the support she had received from friends and neighbors. Her thoughts had turned increasingly to old age and to her relationship with her own children. All our discussions addressed, in one way or another, her relation to the camp—and the significance of the passing of her parents' generation for those left behind. Because first-generation refugees are seen as the last living link to a lost world, even the literal embodiment of the Palestinian condition, their disappearance, for many, bears synecdochic relation to the political and territorial erasure of the community as a whole.[6]

For Umm Mahmud, her mother's death made transformations in her own family visible, prompting reflection on her ties to extended kin and to the community in which she had grown up. To her mind, it was her mother who had preserved the values of family and fellaheen culture, keeping alive the rhythm and traditions of rural village life in their household. "My mother had the smell of Palestine about her; she carried it with her in everything she did. With her death it feels as if we are losing our own connection to it," Umm Mahmud told me. Umm Ali had sung traditional songs; gone to the mountains above Beirut to collect *za'tar* in the spring, just as she had done as a young woman in Sufsaf (the continuity of practice thereby connecting her to the life of the vanished village); kept close ties with relatives in other camps; and cultivated a reputation for generous hospitality, maintaining relations of reciprocity and goodwill within her extended family and neighborhood. Umm Ali had also ensured that the three children who had emigrated were never far from the thoughts of those who remained in Lebanon; always worrying for their safety and delighting in their successes, she would faithfully relay their news to other family members, preserving emotional intimacy under conditions of diasporic distance.

In recounting her experience to me, Umm Mahmud wove together intimacies of loss with broader reflections about family relations, the future of the camp, and the nature of her attachment to it. The tensions that emerged in the course of her mother's illness and death had destabilized the ties of kinship but also revivified her own social networks in Shatila. Sadness that her mother never returned to Palestine deepened her uncertainty about the nature of her own ties, both to Sufsaf and to Shatila—to her ancestral roots, that is, on the one hand, and to the only home she has known, on the other. Her description of her mother's death as dimming her own connection to Palestine suggested an ontological loss, a loss of belonging to a world and way of life of which she had no direct experience. More generally, this question of what connects refugees born and raised in Lebanon to their villages and towns of origin raises equally fraught questions about the very basis of social and political belonging in exile.

Umm Ali's death brought these latent doubts to the surface, compelling Umm Mahmud to consider her relation to her home and community in Shatila as something more enduring. Umm Ali had lived in anticipation of returning to Sufsaf. Umm Mahmud now found herself questioning the wisdom of investing hope in such a remote possibility and even began speaking candidly about the cost of indefinite deferral: "If I only imagine my kids' future in Palestine, it's like canceling our life here," she told me. Yet to express attachment to home in Shatila could be understood as tantamount to denial of home in Palestine. Ambivalence about identity and belonging vexed friends in my own peer group, and younger generations are increasingly torn between the ideal of a redemptive return to a Palestinian homeland and the pragmatic desire for a secure and meaningful existence in Lebanon or abroad.[7]

Umm Mahmud's reflections dramatized the dissonance between representations of camps in mainstream discourse and policy, as spaces of temporary refuge and unrealized national claims, and the way they are increasingly seen by refugees themselves, as places they authentically belong to and inhabit. Such sentiments also challenge the mainstream assumption that refugees regard *tawtin* and return as mutually exclusive. The importance placed on return—over and above other kinds of individual or familial aspiration—has long shaped conceptions of personhood and community in Palestinian culture (Zureik 2003), but this "culture of return" is increasingly the site of seismic tensions and fault lines.

The canonical response given to researchers and journalists who ask refugees whether they still wish to return to Palestine—"If not me, then my children or my grandchildren"[8]—epitomizes the collective logic in which commitment to resistance and return is equated with living in a camp (maintaining refugee status and refusing to be assimilated) and seen as a birthright automatically passed on and preserved; refugee experiences and aspirations are seen as meaningful insofar as they contribute to the national cause.[9] "Every person becomes an embodiment of The Palestinian, who keeps the struggle going through acts of overt resistance as well as simple steadfastness, stubbornness and resilience" (Taraki 2006, xxi).

Until recently, discussions of the right of return did not address the logistics of implementation.[10] The recovery of lost community was conceptualized in abstract and largely nostalgic terms, obviating the need to acknowledge a new Israeli reality on the ground.[11] Had Umm Ali been able to return to her village, she would have found the landscape of her youth vastly changed, and the neighborly relations and social order grounding her meaning of "home" would no longer exist. For second-, third-, and fourth-generation refugees, return to a place they never left is similarly complicated. For all generations, return involves leaving a community that has become, for better or worse, home.[12]

Even as physical return grows increasingly detached from the daily realities of refugee existence, however, it retains its centrality in nationalist discourse and the collective imaginary, as both a political and existential demand unifying Palestinian society.[13] It is an assertion both of national self-determination (the right collectively to reinhabit lands as a sovereign people) and of Israeli responsibility for the dispossession of Palestinians in 1948 (the right to reclaim personal property unjustly taken from them). As Muna, a woman in her late twenties working in an NGO in the camp explained, recognition of the right of return is important for reasons of justice and existential restoration. For her, however, home was less a particular place than a state of well-being and security, and she had little desire to return to her grandparents' house in Safad, setting her sights instead on Europe or Canada.

While the right of return continues to be the foundation on which Palestinians' understanding of themselves as a people rests, how individuals exercise this right under international law is understood to be a matter of personal choice (Akram 2002; Friedman 2003; Kagan 2007). For younger generations, justice and moral compensation often seem closely tied to the right to determine one's own destiny, what Jackson describes as "the existential imperative to convert givenness into choice, and live in the world as if it were our own" (2005a, xxii). Refugees who expressed reservations about returning to Israel/Palestine, like Muna, or who aspired to citizenship elsewhere, made it clear that this did not imply forgoing their collective political right. A remark Umm Mahmud's husband, Munir, once made, when I asked whether he imagined himself returning to Haifa, captures the curious blend of assertion and letting go that marks much informal discussion of the right of return:

> My life is not in Haifa; what is there for me now? . . . Still, I want the right to knock on the door of my father's house and say to the people living there, "This is my father's house, which you took from him in 1948. I understand that you are living here now, and that's okay. I don't want to live here, but I want you to acknowledge that you took this from him and from me." Then we can sign a paper saying the house now belongs to them and they can give me one dollar to finalize the contract. Then I will feel that my dignity as a human being will be returned. When we talk about return, this is what we are talking about—the return of our dignity.

The significance of Munir's imagined encounter with the current occupants of his father's house lies not in the promise of restoration but in a possibility of closure and renascent dignity. The scholar Mohammed Bamyeh makes a similar point: "The common denominator between all the cleavages within the concept of return, therefore, concerns not its physical allusion as much as the investment in it of an undefined meaning of restoration."[14] While first-generation refugees tend to conceive of return in physical terms (to a particular place, known, lost and yearned for), younger generations tend to view it in more symbolic terms, as the return of a dignity and humanity long denied them.

The imagination and pragmatism I constantly encountered on the question of return among refugees contrasted sharply with the zero-sum logic of political factions and activists who claim to represent them and who are unanimous in their rejection of resettlement (anti-*tawtin*). Tariq, the young man I met in 2003 at the Fa'liyyat meeting to resolve Shatila's electricity crisis, once remarked that Oslo—a bitter betrayal in the minds of most 1948 refugees—might also be seen as an achievement of a sort:[15]

> During Oslo I thought, "Good! Arafat and the PLO are now in Palestine and not in Tunis—we are a step closer to our goal of statehood." Many believe Palestine should be from the Jordan River to the sea, but can we actually realize this? No. To move forward may require hard compromises [*tanazulat*]. I believe in the right of return since it is our collective right as a people; it is only natural that we should demand it. This is part of a national and religious feeling we can't deny; it is part of our humanity. But return for everyone is not realistic. America and Israel will never let it happen. I have an uncle and aunt in Sweden now; they have Swedish nationality and could return to Palestine [on their Swedish passports] but don't. I have two aunts married to Lebanese who took nationality here, and now they don't think of going back, and if all the Palestinians from Jordan were to go back to their lands, Jordan would be empty. So you have to think about the matter in relation to what is happening on the ground.

Views like these, in my experience, are as commonplace in the daily vernacular of the camp's coffee tables as they are taboo in its official channels of political discourse.[16] Tariq's plea for candor about the transformations Palestinian society has undergone since 1948 (and their implications for the implementation of return) is not an admission of defeat; it signals "a refusal to telescope time to 1948," a resistance to the romance of "return to an unmediated past" (Peteet 2005, 219). It calls for realism—and a reconceptualization of justice—in the wake of recognition that comprehensive return and "absolute justice" are no longer possible. For Tariq, the real risk lay in a failure to live up to the demands of present and future, not simply in the inability to realize historic claims.

I found opinions on return to be fluid and dynamic, sometimes shifting dramatically as visiting delegations and political initiatives kindled and dashed hopes for imminent solutions. When US president George W. Bush—in his letter of April 14, 2004, to Israeli prime minister Ariel Sharon—described it as "unrealistic to expect that the outcome of final status negotiations will be a full and complete return," Tariq, having previously spoken of the need for compromise, now vigorously reasserted the right of return as something not to be bargained away at any price. "We want peace as much as they [Israelis] do," he exclaimed, angrily, "but when you are challenged like this, you find yourself forgetting peace, whatever the cost. Bush does not have the right to decide my future. . . . This is not his right to give away."[17] When others are seen to be making compromises on behalf of refugees—which happens with predictable regularity—staunchly nationalist positions resurge. These rhetorical shifts, which express refugees' frustration at being excluded from decision-making processes, suggest that on the ground, right-of-return discourse is as much about recognition of rights—of refugees as rights-bearing individuals—as about implementation of a physical return.

In a conversation with Fatima in her shop, shortly before her death in 2005, she echoed Tariq's call for candor about what is practically possible as opposed to ideologically ideal. "I want to return, but let's be realistic; it's not likely. And if I do go back, it will probably be to a Palestinian state in the West Bank or Gaza, not to Khalisa where my family is from." She then added, "Jews are humans like us, and I believe we can live together."[18] Although the prospect of resettlement in Lebanon was not something she embraced, like Tariq she believed that naturalization of the majority, as part of an internationally brokered deal, was inevitable. If accompanied by civic rights, such an eventuality might not be so bad. "Lebanon is my home—my life is here," she continued. "I sometimes forget I am a refugee—that is, until the Lebanese remind me."

Fatima described herself as cautiously optimistic, saying that not to be open to the possibility for change would make life intolerable. Her investment in making Shatila livable was an expression of both faith in community and feelings of ownership and entitlement. While Fatima also spoke of her very real desire to return to Khalisa, it was her business—the financial independence and social networks she had created through it—that animated and sustained her. As Edward Said observed, Palestinians have learned to see home as "the place whose identity is retained only in the repeated experience of staying and then moving on." Going back to a place one has never left involves a "constantly postponed metaphysics of return" (1999, 150). The relationship between home and homeland is deeply vexed, and any account of refugee aspirations, of longing and belonging, must factor in the cumulative experience and attachments of exile.

THE CULTURE OF RETURN

Rosemary Sayigh was among the first to examine the tenacity of peasant culture and rural values in the camps in Lebanon in the 1970s; she found that village ties were "built into the personality of each individual villager to a degree that made separation like an obliteration of self" (1979, 107). Charting neighborhoods according to pre-1948 ties—down to a street-by-street spatial fidelity—was understood as a tactic of cultural resistance, enabling refugees to sustain ways of life, social matrices, and kinship ties in readiness for their eventual return to Palestine.[19] It also signaled continued refusal of permanent resettlement in Lebanon.

While cultural authenticity and "Palestinianism" are still associated with the "metaphorical universal 'original village'" (Zureik 2003, 10), a history of dynamic adaptation in the camps has weakened mnemonic communities more than is generally recognized.[20] With the relocation of the PRM to Lebanon in 1970, there was a conscious shift away from primordial attachments in the camps, which subsequently began to be organized around the political offices (*makatib*) and divided into bases or axes (*mahawir*). Village networks accommodated the arrival of resistance fighters from Jordan and elsewhere, and traditional social structures were overlaid with new political allegiances. While the national movement actively cultivated rural customs and accommodated traditional structures of authority in an effort to underscore its autochthonous, grassroots nature (Peteet 1987), it also privileged a unified national identity over regional attachments, thereby attenuating local ties.[21] Camp residents sometimes recall this period as the moment when "we became one village and Palestine was the name" (Peteet 2005, 134).

The evacuation of the PLO in 1982 (and consequent backlash against the nationalist rhetoric of the 1960s and 1970s) effected a partial return to local solidarities. The trend became even more pronounced after the 1993 Oslo Accords, when the commemoration of ancestral villages became a way for refugees in the diaspora to reaffirm their right of return. Village committees were reestablished and village memorial books produced, amid a general renewal of interest in origins and ancestry (Davis 2010; Khalili 2004; Sayigh 2004). The creation of al-'Awda and the Palestinian Right of Return coalition (PRC) in 1998, both as a response to Oslo and to commemorate the fiftieth anniversary of the Nakba, exemplified and nourished this renewed interest in a "culture of return," which marked a new era of international activism around refugee rights.[22]

After Oslo, the PA (which superseded the PLO as the institutional body representing Palestinians, in theory if not in practice) lost all semblance of credibility among Palestinians in exile. The vacuum created by its failure to advance refugee interests was filled by Palestinian factions, international organizations like al-'Awda and PRC, an assortment of (mostly politically affiliated) NGOs, and a vocal Palestinian intelligentsia in Europe and the United States.[23] The Right of Return Movement (RoRM) raised awareness about history and the plight of refugees languishing in camps in exile, threw their history into sharp relief against the willed amnesia of the peace process, and reaffirmed the right of return's nonnegotiability. In May 2000, South Lebanon was liberated after twenty years of Israeli occupation, allowing refugees to visit the border and see Palestine, many for the first time. This event, like the start of the Al-Aqsa Intifada four months later, raised refugee hopes of an imminent return.

When I began working in Shatila in 2001, I had expected to find an active right-of-return movement. The RoRM had gained momentum in Europe and North America, and activist mobilization during the second Intifada had renewed the connection between Palestinians in exile and those living under Israeli occupation. During that year I attended many demonstrations and rallies in the camp, which were held in solidarity with the Palestinian struggle in the OPT. While the right of return was often invoked during these events, it was not itself the subject of sustained grassroots activism.[24] There was no unified position on return: opinion was divided between pro-Syrian groups, who were vocally critical of the PA's failure to uphold the right of return, and pro-Fatah groups, whose delicate task was to assert national rights without questioning the party leadership. Because calls for right of return were folded into other political activities (rallies, solidarity events, and commemorations), they were subject to the rivalries I have described elsewhere. They were, moreover, sometimes regarded in a cynically entrepreneurial light, much as NGOs and factions were sometimes accused of profiting off the Nakba or using commemorative projects to generate funds for their own institutions.[25]

Reception of the Geneva Accords, the unofficial Palestinian-Israeli peace plan launched with much fanfare in October 2003, provided a useful lens through which to examine refugee opinion about return. Initially, I was struck by the indifference with which people greeted the news. Few seemed surprised to find surrender of the right of return once again presented as the precondition for peace, and their own notions of a "lasting and comprehensive peace" unsolicited and tacitly deemed irrelevant. Umm Mahmud cursed at the TV and switched channels. Others observed that the two-state solution—in which the future Palestine would comprise only the West Bank and Gaza, and not the villages and towns in the northern Galilee and along the coast from which most refugees in Lebanon hail—would at best facilitate the true return of very few refugees in Lebanon anyway. "Return," in this context, seemed more like another form of displacement.[26] Umm Mahmud summed it up succinctly: "If our leadership no longer believes in return, how can we?"

When I later asked Abu Qa'id, an elderly man who operated a small grocery store in the camp, what he thought of this latest peace plan, he shrugged his shoulders. "You adjust your body to the length of the mattress" ('ala ad frashak mid rijlayk) was his wry response, which has lingered in my mind as a pithy example of the irony, fatalism, and detachment with which refugees register the cumulative existential costs of not only their purported leadership's endless concessions but, more important, their near-total exclusion from deliberations about their own fate and future. Public response to the Geneva Accords was indeed characterized by general indifference and exhaustion. As one middle-aged man put it, "Talk of return is meaningless" (bala 'awda, bala batikh). A phrase I heard over and over to describe the peace process was "empty talk" (haki fadi). For refugees, the opacity, futility, and interminability of the process had made it a kind of synecdoche for their general political and economic disenfranchisement.

Palestinians do not have "the right to have rights," to borrow Hannah Arendt's formulation.[27] Refugees sometimes question the wisdom of pursuing national claims through international law at all, given its apparent toothlessness in the context of their conflict with Israel. Since the UN is not itself empowered to implement laws and is governed by the veto rules of the Security Council, refugees argue that periodically reaffirming the existence of this right is pointless and simply compounds the political deadlock.[28]

Meanwhile, the heady mix of revolution and armed resistance that galvanized older generations is gone. For many of Shatila's residents, return now seems unrealistic and utopian, their ancestral villages literally and figuratively a property of the past.[29] There is little faith in local or national leadership on this score, and the skepticism is unsurprising. The consensus that emerged at Camp David (2000) and Taba (2001) was clear: refugees would not simply have to yield their right of return in any peace process endgame; they and their claims were to be left out of the negotiating framework altogether.[30]

Several weeks after the Geneva Accords were made public, I found myself at a rally in downtown Beirut to protest their failure to uphold the right of return. The protest had been coordinated by the DFLP and PFLP, both pro-Syrian factions whose vocal support of the right of return is bound up with their critique of Fatah and the PA. In a moment that seared itself into my mind, a protester from Shatila broke suddenly and discordantly from the rhythmic regularity of the demonstrators' chants and began shouting, "Shit to the right of return; we want to live" (*khara 'a-l-'awda; biddna n'ish*). She was swiftly rebuked and silenced by a DFLP faction leader, but her brief blasphemy elicited a murmur of recognition and muted nods of assent from others present.

For an observer in my position, it was as if a window had been suddenly and subversively thrown open, then no less violently again thrust shut—a window into the ambivalence evoked by "return" in the very refugees whose claims and grievances it presumes to articulate. While the outburst seemed paradoxical given the context, it is less puzzling when one considers that return—as the only right of Palestinians in Lebanon to be formally recognized by the government or vigorously championed by activists abroad—has come to signify all *and* nothing for refugees: the affirmation of legitimate political rights under international law but also the negation of civil rights in their host country (whose citizenry sees extension of rights to Palestinians as a prelude to their naturalization).

After the protest, on the bus back to the camp, I was seated next to a middle-aged woman. "It is understandable people feel fed up when you consider how the Lebanese government uses our rights against us," she reflected. "When Walid Jumblatt [at that time minister for the displaced] was asked, 'Why don't you allow the Palestinians to build ceilings?,' he replied, 'When Palestinians live with a roof over their head, they'll settle down and forget Palestine.'" She continued:

> The government refuses to give us civil rights, and meanwhile they talk about return. When we want to buy property or demand our civil rights, the government responds by more talk of return. They connect issues that shouldn't be connected. It's like someone is hitting you hard and telling you not to say what you want and then stops beating you and asks you what you want—of course,

you're not in a position to say what you want. On one side the government puts unbearable pressure on us by refusing to give us civil rights, and on the other side they say that we must have the right of return. I think before talking about return, they should allow us to work.

Sentiments like these are, in my experience, very widely held if only privately expressed. Few refugees regard socioeconomic integration as a genuine threat to their political rights, and many, like Abu Yusuf, will vigorously endorse the counterargument: greater economic security can strengthen the hand of refugees in their national struggle. The zero-sum logic of government policy has also undermined attempts to build a civil rights movement for refugees, deepening their economic vulnerability and obfuscating discussion of their return.[31] While there have been various attempts over the past decade to build a civil rights movement in Lebanon, none have gained traction.[32] The belief that national struggle should take precedence over class or gender issues—an idea shared by the resistance groups in the 1970s—continues to inform how factions regard the question of socioeconomic justice (Sayigh 2011b). Indeed, faction representatives often cite the poverty and isolation of camp communities as proof of refugees' political steadfastness and their continued refusal to assimilate.

The furor generated by Khalil Shikaki's 2003 study of refugee attitudes to return is further evidence of the perceived conflict of interest between nationalist orthodoxies and local material concerns. Carried out under the auspices of the Palestinian Centre for Policy and Survey Research in the OPT, Lebanon, and Jordan, the Shikaki study was the single largest survey ever conducted of refugee opinion on the question of return. It found that if the legal situations and material conditions of refugees in Lebanon were to improve, the majority would prefer to remain, with only 23 percent electing to return to their ancestral villages (2003a, 160–162). Approximately one hundred Palestinian organizations denounced the survey, arguing that the questions were designed to encourage refugees to opt for permanent resettlement over return.[33]

Shortly after its publication, a colleague of mine recounted a conversation he had with a Palestinian legal scholar in Beirut. The latter had suggested that refugee opinions could not be trusted since, overwhelmed as they are by the exigencies of daily life, they would all too readily give up their inalienable rights for an immediate improvement of their situation. The comment is revealing, both of the depth of refugee disenfranchisement (not only do they not have the right to have rights; they are not even reliable sources for their own ambitions and subjective desires) and of the tacit complicity between institutional stakeholders on the Palestinian political scene and the Lebanese government in maintaining the status quo. In February 2011, a delegation of British MPs who visited camps in Lebanon as part of a PRC-organized fact-finding mission were shocked to discover that Palestinian factions rejected any improvements to conditions in the camps, fearing that it would diminish leverage of the right of return. Instead, they proposed that international aid budgets be brought under their control.[34] In light of the stalled peace process and the looming specter of UNRWA's dismantlement, both the Lebanese government and the Palestinian leadership in the camps seem to prefer "the preservation of a sub-optimal status quo . . . to the uncertainties related to any in-depth overhaul of the refugees' status" (Husseini and Bocco, 2009, 274).

THE MARCH OF RETURN, MAY 2011

At first glance, the direct actions of May 15, 2011—when Palestinian refugees from Lebanon, Syria, and Jordan marched to their respective borders with Israel—would seem to represent a striking and significant departure from the trend I have been describing. Inspired by the Arab uprisings of that year, an estimated forty thousand Palestinians from all over Lebanon gathered at Maroun al-Ras on the border with Israel to commemorate the sixty-third anniversary of the Nakba.[35] In the words of Aluf Benn (2011), editor-in-chief of the Israeli newspaper *Haaretz,* "The nightmare scenario Israel feared since its inception became real—that Palestinian refugees would simply start walking from their camps towards the border and would try to exercise their right of return." Six Palestinians were killed and more than one hundred injured during the protest, when Israeli soldiers fired on a large crowd of unarmed protesters after several people tried to scale the border fence.

Unlike previous Nakba commemorations, the March of Return united Palestinians in Lebanon, bringing together the middle class and elite from the cities with camp refugees. The terms used to describe the event registered a shift in thinking, presenting the anniversary as an occasion not for mourning the past but rather celebrating return as a realizable future goal.[36] Promotion of the march was playful, including the erection of signs stating the distance to Palestine and Jerusalem along the major southbound highways out of Beirut. As I walked the last stretch of road to Maroun al-Ras, I met an elderly man I had interviewed for the Nakba Archive several months earlier. He had come by bus with a group of friends and relatives and was walking arm in arm with his cousin, a frail man also in his eighties. "We are returning home," he said joyfully, before urging me to visit him at his home outside Tyre with a copy of his interview. His invitation was a reminder of how overlapping conceptualizations of home are often seamlessly woven together in refugee experience, and the sight of them walking slowly down the dirt track in their faded jackets and kaffiyehs was moving. As they retraced their fateful steps of sixty-three years before, it seemed for a brief moment as if they were actually returning.

The march was coordinated by a committee of independent activists (the majority of them university-educated Palestinians not from the camps, along with some Lebanese), under the banner of national unity and political neutrality. Strategy and goals were emphasized over ideology and party commitments. While much of the mobilization of camp communities occurred through independent channels, factions, political parties, and NGOs were invited to the planning meetings in an effort to incorporate all institutional players. All factions participated with the exception of Fatah. Committee members I spoke with described painstaking discussion and consensus decision making in the months leading up to the march. It was the first time so many Palestinian factions and organizations had worked together. When faction representatives tried to take over the preparations in the weeks prior to the march, committee members were able to mediate and reassert control. Although political posters were circulated in the final week before the march, and the factions indeed came to dominate the speakers' platform at Maroun al-Ras, only the Palestinian flag was flown that day. The event was striking both for the broad spectrum of participants and low visibility of factions.

Grassroots activism and preparations for the March of Return suggested both a strengthening of refugee identification with Palestine and a growing desire for avenues of political expression outside party politics. There was an upsurge of political engagement among camp youth in Lebanon, spurred on by the previously unthinkable gains of protesters in Tunisia, Egypt, Libya, and Yemen. The March of Return Facebook group had tens of thousands of followers in a matter of weeks, and the teenage children of friends in the camp discussed the new material uploaded daily. Revolution-related news from around the region was accompanied by debate about issues affecting Palestinians in Lebanon and discussion of the urgency of political reform.

Ahmed, Umm Yusuf's youngest son, who learned about the march through Facebook, initially imagined a hidden political agenda and intended not to participate. Like his father and elder brother, Ahmed is not a member of any party and is deeply skeptical about the factions. He nevertheless could not help finding the idea of the march compelling. "I had never once been to the border. That refugees from everywhere would go to the borders was great," Ahmed admitted. "Everyone was involved. Islamic Jihad, communists, independents, and so on were all united around the idea of Palestine and not their own political agendas; that was something new." Against his parents' wishes, Ahmed joined a bus from Shatila at the last minute, drawn by a desire to see Palestine with his own eyes. Soon after reaching Maroun al-Ras, he found himself running up to the border with a group of protesters and was shot in the stomach by an Israeli soldier as he tried to scale the fence. "When I saw my country, my heart took over my mind," he explained.

Several weeks later I visited the family in Shatila. Ahmed's older brother Yusuf recounted that, moments after the ambulance reached the hospital in Beirut, the family was visited by Sheikh Ali Shaheem from Islamic Jihad, who tried to pay for Ahmed's treatment. The family had been informed that the Ministry of Health might pay for Ahmed's hospitalization; their decision to refuse Islamic Jihad's financial assistance was a serious risk. Over the next few days, leaders from every single pro-Syrian faction involved in the march came to the hospital to offer help (an ironic reversal of Abu Yusuf's situation years before, when despite his long-standing membership in the DFLP the party refused to pay for treatment of an injury he sustained fighting for them during the civil war). "You know how factions operate here," Yusuf told me with distaste. "If you take money, you are tied. When I refused help from the Hamas official, he seemed annoyed and said, 'Even the Prophet (Peace be upon Him), accepted gifts.' I told him I was not the Prophet.... The parties said they wanted to help, but they would have eaten us." Yusuf went on to compare his own family's experience with that of the Hasanayn family after Hasan Hasanayn was killed during a border demonstration in 2000. "The factions fought to claim him as a martyr even though, like Ahmed, he didn't belong to any party. If you are shot by the enemy, you become a hero."

When I later asked Ahmed whether, in hindsight, he regretted his decision to attend the march, he began by reiterating the critique of factional politics so familiar to me:

When I think six people died and so many were injured for nothing, I feel angry. Blood was wasted. Has anything changed for us since the march? No. There was no plan, and as usual it is the people from the camps who bear the cost. The faction leaders from Shatila encouraged youths to go to the fence but didn't go themselves. After the march, neither the Palestinian embassy nor the factions made any formal objection to the UN about Israel's actions—they simply called for a day of mourning and closed schools.[37] It pains me to say this, but none of our political parties will liberate Palestine. There will be no return until we regain a pure longing for Palestine, one that isn't shaped by political parties: like there was before 1965 and after 1948. Now the parties are divided, and 10 percent of what they do is for Palestine, and the other 90 percent just fighting for power, for their own interests. They have lost their way. . . . While I was in hospital Abdullah Abdullah [the PLO representative in Lebanon] visited me and said, "You're a hero! You've made us proud [*rafa't rasna*] and brought us closer to Palestine. You are the generation of the liberation!" What he said seemed meaningless to me.

Pausing, he then returned to my question:

Would I go back down to the border again? Yes, if it was for Palestine. When I heard Rafik Nasrallah [the director of a Lebanese media center with ties to Hezbollah] saying that Palestinians, directed by their factions, were simply following the orders of Syria, it made me furious. You think I would have done this for Syria? When I saw Palestine, I wanted to be there. I lost my mind and tried to get in. . . . Israelis are spending millions to protect people in settlements near the border. . . . Are our lives worth less than theirs? Every Palestinian can work for this goal, for Palestine, in their own way—through work, through education, with whatever tools they have.

Umm Yusuf, who had been listening attentively and with evident pride in her son, added provocatively: "All people look out for their own interests here. I swear, every day I pray God shall not make us victorious [*Allah ma yunsurna*]— why? Because we are not together."

Conversations with the Nasser family and others about the march revealed a sharpened awareness of the relation between means and ends, as well as the need for strategy. Yusuf and Ahmed's political positions were often idiosyncratic and generally shaped by personal experience rather than commitment to party politics or nationalist doctrine. "The generation of the Nakba didn't understand what they were doing when they left," Yusuf argued. "Although my father believes he fought for Palestine, the revolution was about the struggle for survival and control here [Lebanon]. Palestine was far from their minds." Yusuf contrasted this naïve romanticism with his own generation's sober realism—"we are more aware"—but also its disillusion. With regard to the march, he spoke of a despair verging on nihilism: "Young people here are lost—without opportunities, leadership, or direction. I was against going to the border, but had I gone, I would have done the same. Running across a field of mines is crazy, but it shows that people feel they have nothing to lose. I don't know what he [Ahmed] was thinking. Maybe he saw Jerusalem or Jaffa before him?" Yusuf's point about a politics born of despair and frustration as much as political conviction was seconded by Ahmed. His description of initial indifference, followed by idle curiosity, then emotional turmoil—of being drawn to the fence, viscerally and inexorably, as if by a magnet—echoed descriptions of that day by a number of my friends. It suggested their actions were neither a simple expression of nor an inevitable consequence of their political beliefs. Although the march was a commemoration highlighting the right of return, it brought forth and crystallized emotions that went beyond that, grievances that transcended the Israeli-Palestinian context to include the experience of exclusion and marginalization in Lebanon. Ahmed's euphoria as he approached the border resulted not only from seeing Palestine for the first time but also from the sense that for once he was the protagonist, able to assert himself and make his feelings known.

I was subsequently struck by how formal descriptions of the march—both by media and by activists (in refugee organizations as well as external solidarity groups)—evoked precisely the singularity and purity of political purpose I had found notably absent in the informal firsthand accounts of friends. Foregrounding sacrifices of the martyrs and stressing only those claims addressed exclusively to Israel, they downplayed both internal critiques of the march and the general sense of powerlessness and despair that had also fueled refugee participation. Right-of-return advocates, factions, and political spokespersons invoked the march as indisputable proof of the centrality of return for refugees (and by extension, the relevance of their work); meanwhile, however, the clearest consensus to emerge from my discussions in Shatila was rejection and rebuke of the institutions claiming to represent refugees and their political appropriation of return. The fact that this upsurge in political engagement and identification in the camps could not be sustained—or developed into a mass movement—may well be due to this failure to adequately address or even recognize the questions of social justice that arose.

In the weeks following the march I heard passionately opposed views about its significance. The polarity of opinion reflected an underlying uncertainty about what exactly *had* happened at the border or how to describe it. For some of the organizers, the march heralded the dawn of a new era in grassroots political mobilizing among Palestinians in Lebanon (see Ali Nayel 2011b; Blumenthal 2011). For others it was a bitter disappointment, with the goal of faction-free politics undone by organizational weaknesses, in turn allowing political parties to wrest control at the eleventh hour. Many believed that refugees had been set up by Hezbollah and their own (pro-Syrian) factions to create a distraction from events in Syria following the massacre carried out by pro-Assad forces in Daraa weeks before. One committee member said that the experience revealed the extent to which socioeconomic conditions in the camps have depoliticized refugees and argued that future grassroots mobilization would have to prioritize socioeconomic justice. Like Ahmed, many in Shatila blamed the deaths and chaos at the border on the incompetence of the organizing committee and the factions and thought the march revealed their chronic lack of political vision and strategy. The fact that the committee dissolved after the march, without any formal public evaluation, compounded the perception that it had not followed through and lacked accountability.

However short-lived the suprafactional politics cultivated by the organizing committee proved to be, the March of Return signifies a potentially significant shift in Palestinian politics in Lebanon. By challenging political hierarchies in the camps and tapping political possibilities outside factional agendas, the march represented a rupture in the dominant order and—albeit fleetingly—opened up a new political space in which refugees could express grievances, make claims, and articulate political belonging. Against the backdrop of revolutionary change and the reimagining of political practice throughout the region, there emerged a palpable sense of possibility: when the two elders spoke of returning home, they seemed momentarily to inhabit this position of "what might be." The decision of several protesters to take matters in their own hands, scale the fence, and enter Palestine illegally, though a priori an act of irrational recklessness, might represent—in however flawed a form—a newly performative approach to activism in which refugees "enact" their rights rather than wait for them to be conferred.[38]

As pure political performance, the march was indeed powerful. The sight of tens of thousands of refugees gathered on the border, unified in their demand for recognition and return, was a show of force that challenged the inviolability of Israel's de facto borders and literalized claims that had become increasingly abstract. The 2011 march was seen by many as a critical turning point that promised an alternative to "the limited imaginings of both realpolitik and rights discourses" (Barclay and Qaddumi 2012, 1). Though explicitly addressed to Israel and the international community, in its local Lebanese context—with Palestinians lacking political rights and even freedom of movement (they cannot travel to the border without a permit)—the march necessarily also represented a powerful if tacit challenge to a status quo in which refugees do not even have the "right to have rights."[39] Exploiting precisely what refugees are stereotypically thought to lack (voice and political agency), refugees asserted themselves within a Lebanese national context and a diasporic Palestinian one.[40] While not demanding Lebanese citizenship, the show of force—in which refugees demanded recognition as rights-bearing claimants—constituted them as a newly visible political collective and cast a harsh light on the dehumanizing and exclusionary policies of the Lebanese government.[41]

.   .   .

Critical consideration of right-of-return discourse and practice among refugees in Lebanon inevitably raises questions about the nature and legitimacy of representation in camp communities. Who now speaks on behalf of refugees? What are their priorities, and how are they conveyed? To what extent are camp institutions (factions, popular committees, NGOs) and local advocacy groups accountable and responsive to their supposed constituencies? Given the exclusion of camp populations from the negotiating table, and from discussion and debate about issues directly affecting them, can their opinions shape and direct national politics or local advocacy?

In recent years the question of representation has become a key topic of debate in the Palestinian diaspora.[42] While proposals to revive and reform the PLO and the PNC—thereby enabling all Palestinians to participate in national politics and decision-making processes—have been mooted, these efforts to reverse representational fragmentation remain preliminary and have yet to have any discernible impact on camp populations.[43] When I asked a colleague involved in organizing a 2012 workshop on PNC elections as a mechanism for enfranchising refugee communities why the event had not been advertised in the camps, she explained that once the parameters for discussion were established, a second round of debates would be held that would involve camp communities. The exclusion of camp refugees seemed a conscious omission rather than an oversight. Echoing the legal scholar's remark after the Shikaki survey, her comment implied that poverty and marginalization limited the ability of camp refugees to recognize their own political predicament. The fact that they are poor and disenfranchised disqualifies them from representation—thus goes the implicit and troublingly circular logic.

Despite growing awareness of the need for direct engagement with refugee communities, with their needs and aspirations and the political solutions they envision, it has yet substantially to happen. Camp populations are spoken for variously by the national leadership, competing local factions and NGOs, researchers, self-appointed spokespersons, and a vocal international solidarity movement.[44] Over the past decade the most fervent and vocal support for the right of return has often come from middle-class Palestinians and international activists based in the West—individuals, in other words, who have the security and means to think and speak in principled absolutes, a luxury shared by few of those being thought and spoken for.

Although many I have spoken with in Shatila regarding the right of return express openness to solutions that would bring immediate relief of their dire living conditions, faction representatives, activists, and advocacy groups tend to regard proposals including compensation or citizenship elsewhere as politically and morally compromised.[45] The unacknowledged logic seems to be that recognition of contemporary suffering of refugees effaces its historical dimension; those championing the rights of Palestinians are often more invested in their struggle with Israel than with the Lebanese state.[46] Scholars, public intellectuals, and activists in sympathy with the national struggle are also sometimes wary of addressing diversity of opinion on return, seeing it as undermining the unity of the national movement—and therefore its political leverage—precisely when both are most needed. A recent lecture at the American University in Beirut emphasizing the need to "produce knowledge for social justice," and how "blurr[ing] the lines [demarcating contemporary and historical suffering] . . . benefits Israel and Zionism and should be avoided," is fairly representative of the politically committed scholarship that prevails in Palestine studies.[47]

It is significant that many recent projects invoking the right of return are in English and implicitly addressed to Palestinians in the West and frame the work of return as an exercise of "imagination," "speculation," and "visualization"—effectively circumventing the one thing that might actually allow for a return, or the resolution of the refugee predicament: politics.[48] Omitted in these visionary discourses is a rigorous rethinking of not only the political mechanisms that might potentially bridge idealism and practice but also—and more glaringly—the perspectives of camp dwellers themselves. Although commitment to the inalienable right of Palestinians to return and live in their homeland is both justified and laudable, the analytical and ethical closure often accompanying it is not. The activists, scholars, and refugee advocates who insist on the sacrosanct nature of return—to the point of categorically resisting discussion of alternatives—have become, paradoxically, implicated in the very systems of exclusion and marginalization they set out passionately to challenge.

In raising such questions, I hope to avoid replacing one dogma with another. Refugee rights are enshrined in international law and cannot be casually or rhetorically dismissed, and in any case it is the prerogative of refugees themselves to champion or abrogate them. In this latter respect the events of May 2011 may indeed prove to be a turning point. I neither contest the essential legitimacy and historic importance of these claims nor wish to belittle the efforts of activists, who have tirelessly advocated for refugee rights. Finally, Israeli intransigence on the question of refugee return does not make the application of international law any less relevant.[49]

In scrutinizing the moral ambiguities of the discourse of return for communities like Shatila, or the costs incurred for refugees, I am not being morally prescriptive: they can of course choose to bear them. My argument is directed rather at the scholars, writers, and activists who constitute a kind of loose-knit international solidarity group for Palestinians. There is a need here for more supple and reflective forms of solidarity, forms that engage and integrate the range of refugee perspectives on this issue (in Lebanon and elsewhere) and thereby open up new arenas for thought and action.[50] It should not be the role of solidarity to demarcate or enforce discursive taboos. The absence of critical discussion of what return means for different communities of refugees, and what its fulfillment would entail, may be compounding the sense of stalemate and blocking other political solutions. Dislodging this taboo might enable refugees to tap into potentialities embedded in everyday life; camp residents, as I have argued throughout this book, are well practiced at finding small-scale, resourceful solutions to bigger problems in order to get by and at inhabiting a hopeful politics of what might or ought to be. As Bamyeh cautions: "Superior ethical visions should not need to keep us from considering the smaller ethics of something more workable" (2003, 833).

Baking bread, Shatila camp. Photograph © Hisham Ghuzlan, 2009.

CONCLUSION

The Roots of Exile

"THE WORLD IS LOST BETWEEN THE MOUTHS OF PEOPLE" (*il-dunya day'a bayn atmam al-nas*). Umm Yusuf said this, in passing, as we discussed the upcoming UN bid for Palestinian statehood in the fall of 2011—the latest (at that point) proposal to silently jettison the rights of refugees in exile. We were drinking coffee on the stairs, taking in the familiar early-morning bustle. It struck me then as now as an apt description, not only of the low signal-to-noise ratio of the peace process but of the heft and pathos of the lives thrown aside in service of it. To spend time in a camp is to feel the painful meaninglessness of the peace process for refugees, caught as they are between the world of international law, so distant and abstract, and the world of material want and desperate lack of traction directly underfoot. After six decades of exile, their condition has managed to calcify into permanence while retaining its provisionality.

But a different, more personally unsettling take on Umm Yusuf's formulation soon stole over me like a shadow. The world of refugees is lost between the mouths of scholars, activists, and chroniclers—people *like me*, in short—who set out to give voice and end up taking it away. The contrast between the dense multitudinousness of refugee experience—with its knotted undergrowth of vertical roots gripping down into Lebanon and runners reaching waywardly into Palestine—and the airy purity of solidarity rhetoric, with its clean geometries of longing and belonging arcing over the decades, had come, over the course of my time in Shatila, to seem stark and intolerable; addressing it became the core motivation for this book. In the late stages of composing it, Umm Yusuf's words came to haunt me, as I wondered if it was possible to avoid repeating the very problem I had set out to redress.

With my ethnographic material—and these authorial misgivings—in the mind of the reader, I want to revisit the questions and concerns of my project and explain and justify its method. Central to it is the perception, informed by my fieldwork and my conversations in Shatila, that refugee experience can no longer be adequately understood through the ideological lens of national attachment. The strong tendency is to see refugees as historical and ideological subjects, but not contemporary material ones—and that emphasis, I argue, has become deeply distortive. The archetype of the refugee waiting to return, so iconic in the literature and scholarship on Palestinians in exile, has come to resemble Walter Benjamin's "angel of history," with gaze fixed on the past, bearing the lost origin of paradise, and back turned toward the future into which he is blown; a figure for whom the passage of time ceases to have meaning, for whom unfolding events simply are the latest instantiation of things past rather than the earliest instance of things to come (2003, 292). For the angel of Shatila, the catastrophic past is a moral condition, an unchanging reality she must inhabit to preserve her political identity. For the people of Shatila, however, it is a sequence of historical contingencies on a dynamic continuum with present and future, a sequence to be added to and altered, rebraided, turned in the light of different necessities.

I have argued in this book that what now constitutes home, homeland, and the basis of identity and belonging for Palestinian refugees is no longer adequately captured by nationalist *doxa*.[1] Identity is not simply a fixed, reified conceptual order individuals inherit, narrate (Bhabha 1990; E. Said 1984b; Slyomovics 1998), or imagine (Anderson 1983), but a lived condition that is processual and open-ended. The empirical thrust of this study has therefore been to explore camp life as it is experienced and known—in a phenomenological and material sense—by refugees themselves, to trace the fine grain of life lived. How do local material conditions shape the way refugees think, feel, and act? How are identity and belonging perceived and enacted by refugees themselves? How are social relations—the interdependencies and solidarities that hold people together—created and sustained? How is home conceptualized? While the significance of transnationalism and diaspora for the formation of deterritorialized Palestinian identities has been explored (see Aouragh 2011; Doraï 2002; Hanafi 2005; Mason 2007; Zaidan 2011), less attention has been paid to the local and rooted dimensions of Palestinian identity in exile. A core assertion of this book is that identity and belonging do not float above the local, material world refugees inhabit but are constituted through it and enmeshed within it.

In describing culture and identity as illuminated by rather than transcending daily life, I make claims not for the latter's unique authenticity but for the insights it offers into the constitution of selves and community. History, politics, and culture play an irreducible role in shaping refugee existence; the significance of what people do and say loses all meaning without an appreciation of those forces. In the course of my discussions with refugees, however, it became clear that concepts like "identity" (*hawiyya*) and "belonging" (*intima'*) had little significance for them in the abstract.[2] They became meaningful in and through local routines, bound up with Shatila's infrastructure and institutions, its political economy; with neighborly networks and rituals; and with the micropolitics of camp life. Writers like Jackson (1996) and Desjarlais have set out to "convincingly link modalities of sensation, perception, and subjectivity to pervasive political arrangements and forms of economic production and consumption" (Desjarlais 1997, 25). The former's "radical empiricism" and the latter's "critical phenomenology" have profoundly influenced my own dialectical method.

Sensorial experience and embodied memory have been recognized in recent scholarship as important to recollections of Palestine but have yet to figure centrally in studies of camp life itself.[3] My view is that the "felt immediacies" (Desjarlais 1997) of the latter are ignored because in a nationalist context they are quasi-taboo; they do not advance collective claims and can even seem to undermine them. The camps have been valued variously as a staging ground for revolution; a point of leverage in peace negotiations; and a compound symbol of Israeli guilt, international indifference, and Palestinian steadfastness. But the notion that camp life has intrinsic value, a cultural rootedness and integrity of its own, is threatening insofar as it is seen as weakening the moral weight of the demand for return. The ethnographic blind spots created by this unspoken taboo are quite startling. In much of the literature refugees are noble sufferers, vivid in the act of memory and in the depth of their yearning for the past, but abstract subjects, even ciphers, in the cultural and socioeconomic topographies of contemporary Lebanon. They exist in order to—and insofar as they—signify something about Israel/Palestine.

In camps like Shatila, however, the coordinates for knowing and being are as much embodied and emotional as cognitive; refugees experience identity and belonging not just at the ideological level of symbol and doctrine but at the visceral level of embodied practice. These emotional and introspective dimensions of refugee experience have been addressed only when charged with political or religious significance and symbolism. The chapters of this book reveal a social somatics of attachment in places where theorists have not yet looked for it.

The ordinary—and not so ordinary—activities of daily camp life reveal pragmatism and resourcefulness in the face of adversity, complex processes of meaning making and reflection, and fine-grained particularity of local knowledge. "Experience-near" approaches challenge the fetishization of culture and fixed categories of knowing by engaging the multifaceted and dynamic ways in which individuals make sense of their situations and actions, and the embodied, affective and imaginative dimensions of lived experience. As Abu Lughod suggests, retaining the flux and inconsistency of people's lives can serve as a reminder that others "live as we perceive ourselves living—not as automatons programmed according to 'cultural' rules or acting out social roles, but as people going through life wondering what they should do, making mistakes, being opinionated . . . enduring tragic personal losses, enjoying others, and finding moments of laughter" (quoted in Jackson 1996, 23). Recovering complexity, contingency, and ambivalence not only deepens our understanding of what is existentially at stake for Palestinians in Shatila but also introduces diversity and possibility into discussion of their case.

A single anecdote may provide a cross-sectional view of the complexities of attachment and belonging now animating camps. Following the Israeli withdrawal from South Lebanon in 2000, busloads of Palestinian refugees from camps all over the country flocked to Fatima's Gate (a former border crossing near the village of Kafr Kila) to see Palestine, many for the first time. Like participants in the March of Return more than a decade later, those who made the pilgrimage described the experience as renewing their sense of connection with each other and with Palestine and raising their hopes for an imminent return. The liberation of South Lebanon—and the subsequent eruption of the second Intifada in the West Bank—were seen as signs of a quickening, of history coming to a head. The euphoria also provoked unexpected anxieties. Mayssun Sukarieh, a Lebanese anthropologist and educator who worked for many years in Shatila, was on one of the buses and recounted to me that on the journey back to Beirut, several teenagers expressed concern about what an actual return to Palestine would entail—specifically, an end to their lives in Shatila.[4] "'We love the camp,' they were telling me," Sukarieh recalled. "'This is our home and where all our friends are. What will happen to it if we leave?' Then one of them came up with an idea: 'Let's move Shatila to Palestine.'"

This image—of a kind of community tissue transplant—is strikingly rem-
iniscent of practices employed by first-generation refugees during the early
years of exile in Lebanon, when camps were organized around village and clan
networks carried over intact from Palestine. That a young girl would propose to
consecrate her return to Palestine by preserving within it the conditions of exile
seemed winsomely paradoxical, a piece of Hegelian wit. In the aftermath of
the 2011 border protest, an almost identical comment circulated on Facebook:
a young man from Burj al-Barajneh camp proposed that the camp should be
made into a village.[5] In hindsight I see these comments as a kind of overture to
this book. They speak to the dissonance between mainstream and nationalist
representations of the camps and the way they are experienced by the refugees
who live in them. They are not anomalous spaces awaiting obsolescence in the
moment of return, and they should not be seen as constituting the symbolic
order of nation through their abject otherness.[6] Like the villages that preceded
them, camps like Shatila form part of the warp and woof of refugee identity
and humanity. Loyalties, intimacies, loss, knowledge of self and other—all have
been wrought from camp life and refugee existence. Exclusion and ambivalence
complicate but do not obviate these ties.

These tectonic shifts in the alignment of people and place, and the recon-
figuration of "home," have introduced tensions to nationalist orthodoxies. Evidence of realignment is threaded through this book: Nidal's admission that
there is a "difference of experience" that separates him from his father ("I've
learned about Palestine, but I *know* and *love* Lebanon"); Fathi's longing for the
camp he has left; Umm Mahmud's admission that her mother's passing shifted
her center of existential gravity from origins to exile; the comment Umm
Mahmud's neighbor Huda made to a visiting journalist: "Shatila is our land
too; we grew up here. When I die, this is where I want it to happen." Just as we
saw that return is now invested with a plurality of meanings for refugees, we are
reminded that they now have not one conception of home but many.

Human experience, Hannah Arendt wrote, is always conditioned by both
a desire to preserve the past and the prospect of new beginnings, a disposition she calls "natality."[7] This yearning for the new is central to Arendt's theory
of the *vita activa*, in which action—rather than a posteriori contemplation of
life—forms and reveals our sense of ourselves, our humanity, and our relations
with others. Arendt presents identity as an emergent rather than antecedent
property of experience and action. By necessity, Shatila has been and continues
to be a site of social, political, and material innovation and renewal. During the

civil war, Shatila survived a number of brutal onslaughts designed to obliterate it. Its ability to rebuild and recover is a vigorous affirmation of its natality. Not long after I moved in with Umm Mahmud and her family, her husband, Munir, described his pride in the camp's resilience: "Because we have suffered and survived here," he explained, "Shatila, for us, is a dynamic place. It represents the transformations of our community. Here we have fought the Lebanese, the Syrians, and each other. We were resistance fighters; now we are trying to lead a kind of normal life."

These feelings of attachment to the camp involve the interplay of history and affect.[8] One young man put it in these terms: "The hardship we have lived is very important. It is this suffering that draws us to the camp—not happiness, because when you are happy, you don't need to reflect on your situation. When you're sad, you focus on your sadness and try to transcend it. It becomes part of you this way." Just as organizing the camp around village and family kept Palestine alive in the daily lives of refugees after the Nakba, the symbolic and spatial reorganization of Shatila in the wake of the civil war memorialized the sacrifices of the community and the histories of particular families and neighborhoods. This fractured, materially prismatic quality of collective memory is overlooked by those who describe Shatila as a "mnemonic community" only with reference to Palestine and the Nakba. Sites like the mass grave beneath Shatila's primary mosque (where those killed in the War of the Camps were buried) or the memorial grounds for the victims of Sabra and Shatila form "a palimpsest of violently crafted historical layers" (Peteet 2005, 18). They are also evidence of identification and group consciousness rooted in camp residence and the specificities of refugee experience and constitute local renderings of the national in exile (Sayigh 2011a).

Ties between refugees and their camps are increasingly acknowledged (Doraï 2010; Misselwitz and Hanafi 2009; Peteet 2005; Sayigh 2011a, 2011b), but these are heavily qualified.[9] Camps still "do not count as places that bestow identity,"[10] and there is a concomitant tendency to overlook the intimate histories of struggle and survival that have sustained and transformed refugee communities. Abu Yusuf, who came of age during the revolution, recounted how the struggle to defend camp and home triggered a shift in his attachments: "We were brought up to say, 'I am from Jaffa,' or 'I am from Haifa.' That changed when Tel al-Za'tar camp was attacked in 1976. Then we started to hear people say, 'I am from Za'tar'; then after the massacre in 1982, 'I am from Shatila'; and so on." Abu Yusuf went on to recall that under siege conditions during the War of the Camps Shatila had to accommodate the dead. "We had no choice but to bury our relatives and neighbors beneath us," he said. "When you pay with blood for a piece of land, a new kind of feeling grows."

Shatila's history, like that of other camps in Lebanon, is defined less by continuity than by periodic rupture and ongoing processes of adaptation, transformation, and renewal. The PLO's arrival in 1970 transformed Shatila from a marginal and downtrodden community into a hub of revolutionary activity and patronage. After 1982, the camp once again found itself without protection and representation, embattled and impoverished. These conditions have worsened since 1989, when the Ta'if Accords sought to excise Palestinians from the Lebanese mind and body politic, casting them into the metaphorical desert in which, as Mahmud put it, they have been forced to "eat their god." Poverty and disenfranchisement, however, have kindled new forms of solidarity and subjectivity. Shatila's residents have become bound to the camp and to each other through the shared experience of insecurity and exclusion and through the forms of improvisation and innovation that have enabled them to survive. In his words quoted earlier, Munir declares his allegiance to the camp on the grounds of its history of resistance, its demonstrated capacity for transformation, and its potential for further change. Here the figure of the refugee pivots to face the future and—looking to the possibility of "a normal life"— offers a counterimage to that of Benjamin's angel, enthralled by its originary banishment.

Even as refugees feel the weight of worsening social and economic conditions bear down upon them—the "structuring structures" of *habitus*—this openness to possibility remains (Bourdieu 1977, 90). It is a "dispositional" form of agency in precisely the way Bourdieu (2000, 130) envisioned it, where contingencies of the past condition how refugees imagine and invest in the "forthcoming," where ambiguity and uncertainty become sources of agency and aspiration as much as of doubt and despair. As I have suggested in this book, this disposition—in which uncertainty also creates conditions of possibility— informs every aspect of refugees' experience, shaping their social relations and moral life, their political and economic environment, their relationship to the past, and their orientation toward the future.

.   .   .

Corollary to this decentering of nationalism in my ethnographic work is an expanded—and I hope, demystified—notion of the political. One finds in Shatila pervasive disillusionment with—and disengagement from—camp politics, widely regarded as morally and pragmatically bankrupt. My contention is that political energies and impulses since the failure of the revolution and the departure of the PLO have been redirected into small-scale, nonideological activities, what Bayat in another context calls the "pragmatic politics of the poor" (2010, 16). Individual and collective strategies for acquiring and controlling electricity; resisting demolition; and improving camp security, water provision, garbage collection, sewer maintenance, winter flooding measures, and so on represent an informal politics of survival that is bound up with structures of governance, both at the microlevel of camp neighborhoods and the macrolevel of the state. How refugees express grievances and tackle immediate material concerns reveals emergent forms of agency and activism that do not fit prevailing models for political subjectivity.

The political and legal claims of Palestinians in Lebanon are almost always discussed with reference to Israel, despite the fact that their lives, and the viability of their communities, are determined in an irreducible way by Lebanese government policies.[11] As I demonstrated in the previous chapter, this political disconnect reflects how refugees' civil rights under Lebanese law have been set in invidious tension with their political rights under international law, so straightforward assertions of the former can be rebuffed on grounds that they undermine the latter. Refugees nevertheless engage in practices that—however obliquely and subversively—contest their exclusion and, in doing so, contribute to a redefinition of their political subjectivity and status within Lebanon.

Ethnographic attention to local ontologies of power (including not only moments of dramatic political rupture, like those created by the border protest of 2011, but also seemingly mundane struggles over access) allows for a more intimate understanding of the politics of practice, in which the abstractions of law, disenfranchisement, and factional politics find purchase, become visible, and are contested. Recent work on "acts of citizenship" has described how strategies of interruption and dissensus can bring into being new political identities and relations to citizenship (Isin 2008; McNevin 2011); acting as if one *were* a citizen, one constitutes oneself *as* a political subject meriting the rights and entitlements of citizens.[12] Daily struggles to secure access to services and the growing (if still hesitant) movement for Palestinian civil rights in Lebanon are two examples of how refugees challenge and make demands on the Lebanese state. These claims are based on their moral entitlements as a subject population and, significantly, are framed as a demand not for citizenship per se (which is often actively rejected by refugees) but rather for basic rights and recognition as a political community within Lebanon.[13]

Mundane material struggles may lack political intentionality, concerned as they are with housekeeping rather than homeland, but they often open up significant political possibilities and weaken the false dichotomy between nationalist politics and civil rights. These moments of contestation often involve Palestinians and Lebanese working together, against the policies of the state (as happened when Palestinians rallied to the defense of Lebanese squatters in Shatila as the squatters' homes were demolished, or when Abu Sadan alerts his Lebanese associates that their hookups have been dismantled), suggesting emergent forms of political subjectivity that transcend identity and ethnicity to encompass class struggle—forms that might well go unnoticed when considered solely through a nationalist lens. The political influence of Palestinians during the PLO era of the 1970s is incontestable, but the converse does not follow: it is *not* true that the departure of the leadership in 1982 and the consequent fracturing of the national movement have left refugees passive and powerless. Political energies have instead become more dispersed and rhizomic—weaker at present, yes, but also more critical of clientelism and more charged with possibility.

Against the present backdrop of revolutionary upheaval in the region, the kind of small-scale mobilization I have described may seem inconsequential. Yet, as Bayat (2010) and Chatterjee (2004) have argued, the imperatives that drive it, the forms it takes, and its cumulative force over time can be rich with significance. The protester at the 2003 rally who shouted, "Shit to the right of return; we want to live," challenged not only the faction leaders who had organized the demonstration but also the activists there to support the right of return (like me) as well as a broader Lebanese audience. This startling intervention seemed directed at some still-inchoate future audience—one that would be able to recognize her as a political subject in Lebanon with legitimate needs and demands.[14] I would argue that refugees question the terms used to describe their political condition and constitute themselves as political subjects in moments such as this.

In a context in which solidarity activists aim to present community claims with moral clarity, ambiguity can seem risky. This "strategic essentialism," however, incurs serious costs for refugees.[15] It forecloses the space of politics and elides the plurality and diversity that political action postulates.[16] Louis Althusser's seminal account of interpellation should give us pause for thought here. The individual is transformed, argues Althusser, through recognition: "Hailed, the individual will turn around. By this mere one-hundred-and-eighty-degree physical conversion, he becomes a subject" (1971, 174).

In refugee communities, the subject hailed by nationalist ideology in all its various permutations—in political rhetoric, international diplomacy, solidarity campaigns, scholarship, and so on—no longer recognizes it as addressed to him; the self that turns around is one from which he is now dissociated. In Shatila, there is no longer (and perhaps never has been) a neat fit between the refugee as nationalist signifier and signified: while the former exists discursively (untouched by the passage of time or by material realities), the latter is confounded by the environment in which she finds herself. What is at stake for refugees is the misrecognition of the specific conditions that constitute life as a Palestinian in Lebanon. Umm Rabbiya's sense of alienation following the Civitas meeting—the very purpose of which, after all, was to reconnect diasporic communities—is a signal instance of this misrecognition. Her image of the refugee as a barking dog to whom no one will respond is an elegant inversion of Althusserian hailing.

. . .

This book has aimed in part to critique the politics of solidarity, the "romance of resistance" (Abu Lughod 1990), and the analytical elisions that sometimes accompany it. Activist scholarship, in aligning itself with its subjects and their cause, often closes avenues of inquiry and leaves too many assumptions unquestioned. In the case of Palestinians in Lebanon, it has produced awkward distortions; as ethnographers, we need to refer back to the local worlds refugees inhabit and the particular predicaments they face. The process of learning to perceive anew requires that we loosen our conception of refugees from the larger ideological questions to which they are conventionally tied.[17]

If the failure and departure of the PLO and the subsequent deterioration of nationalism have obviously deepened deprivation and disillusionment in Shatila, on another level they are generating new forms of social and political subjectivity. If we subscribe to the view that local moral worlds are continually created by situated actors (Jackson 2005a; Kleinman 1995; Whyte 1997), ethnographic realism requires that we attend to the ways refugees deal with difficulty and desire in their daily lives and to the terms in which they describe their predicament; in doing so, we come to recognize refugees as agents creatively negotiating their local environment. They do so through the supple and dynamic practices this book has attempted to document, practices that now do more to sustain them than officially sanctioned political activity and the promise of return.

This very opposition, however—between the reified and the codified, on the one hand, and the resilient, the pragmatic, and the quotidian, on the other—is clarifying but not impermeable. Indeed, in the course of writing this book, I have become conscious of not only the stakes but also what might be called the ethical perils of my argument. For instance, to critique official commemorative practices (in contradistinction to both private rituals of remembrance and the pragmatic demands of everyday survival) is also to become aware of the critical role these very practices play in securing international funds, NGO involvement, and bonds of solidarity and sympathy with outsiders, without which the economic and spiritual life of the camp would be truly abject. In suggesting that the conceptual potency of nationalism for refugees in exile has been overemphasized, I am not saying it is obsolete. This would be analytically distortive and ideologically presumptuous; refugees remain fiercely proud of their identity as Palestinians. To some extent, therefore, the *performance* of what I have critiqued as reified nationalist tropes is itself part of the supple, dexterously responsive grammar of everyday practice, the pragmatic vernaculars of hope and survival that have been the subject and the muse of this study. A proper acknowledgment of the moral stakes and dangers that commemoration entails requires both recognizing and scrutinizing this paradox.

When I began to move in the direction of this analysis, my misgivings were political and ideological. By a peculiar ethical conflation I have never known quite how to question, the moral status of what happened in 1948 is generally understood to be indexed to the level of present attachment of the Palestinian refugee diaspora to the land of Palestine. If that attachment is weakened, or partly supplanted, the logic goes, their grievances, both historical and contemporary, are seen to lose purchase. I am still haunted by a question put to me by an early (and supportive) reader: "Does this mean Zionism has won?" I have never quite dispelled these political misgivings. Even with the acknowledgment that national identity structured rigidly around the logic of return implies a devaluation of everyday life, hardly compensated by whatever phantasmal leverage against Israel it offers, there are still very real ethical risks entailed by too eagerly welcoming the sunset of exilic nationalism. Some readers may feel that my arguments have gone too far in this direction, that they risk further undermining the rights and claims of refugees. While I have reservations about the way my work may be interpreted and used, as an anthropologist, my first duty is to represent the concerns and experiences of my interlocutors and friends, as they have described them to me.

If refugees in Shatila no longer represent a "community of memory" in the sense of being connected to Palestine and to each other through inherited attachments or the belief that they are "a returning people" (Rabinowitz 2008, 227), how *should* we understand community and identity there? If we conceptualize Palestinian refugees in Lebanon not simply as an anomalous, out-of-place group but as a community with complex, locally embedded structures of affiliation, how do we address the impact of deterritorialization without deepening or legitimizing it? Because refugee rights are defined in terms of a particular event and ties to territory, questioning the coherence of nationalism or pointing to a decoupling of people and land could have far-reaching consequences.[18] As Beshara Doumani cautions, "Questioning the territorial dimension of peoplehood and the meaning of sovereignty while the conflict is still 'hot' could be understood by some as challenging the very right of Palestinians to Palestine, as well as undermining the political language of self-determination." Yet Doumani goes on to conclude that in light of the increasing transnationalism of the Palestinian community, "statehood might not be the only or even the best form of self-determination . . . just as nationalism may not be the most fruitful form of realizing justice, equality, and freedom" (2007, 60, 62). Creating a new mobilizing political discourse necessarily involves rethinking the relationship between nation, people, and place and recognizing increasingly disjunctive trajectories of belonging.[19]

What role can researchers, engaged scholars like me, and activists play in this process? Bringing refugee voices and opinions to the fore, in all their multivalent complexity, and creating conditions in which local agendas can shape advocacy, research, and policy would allow for new thinking about identity and political mobilization to emerge. A chastened and critically self-aware solidarity might bring about an ethical repositioning, one that relies less on sympathy with a national cause, which produces problematic essentialisms, than on empathy, which recognizes alterity and the distances separating refugees, ethnographers, and their readers (Stamatopoulou-Robbins 2008). Empathy and understanding in this context together require a recognition of Palestinian refugees as doubly dispossessed—not only by the creation of Israel in 1948 but also by a national movement that first abandoned them and then commandeered their identity and memory for political purposes. Because of the contradictions and internal tensions involved, what is required is solidarity of a more versatile kind than we have generally seen, one that balances its commitments between the private and political, the individual and the collective, and the ideological and material. The empathy and solidarity we extend to Palestinian refugees—in our various capacities as activists, ethnographers, representatives of NGOs, members of the international community—and the terms by which we agree to extend these have measurable, even profound, consequences for both the moral and material economies of camp life. This book has been, in part, an effort to rethink and renegotiate those terms.

REFERENCE MATTER

NOTES

INTRODUCTION

1. I lived, worked, and carried out research in Shatila intermittently from 2002 to 2006, returning for brief visits up until 2009. Between 2010 and 2012 I was based in Beirut.

2. The concept of *sumud* represents an iconic trait of Palestinian identity. Traditionally used to describe Palestinians who stayed on their land and resisted Israel in 1967, the term now refers generally to the refusal of Palestinian refugees in exile to relinquish their right of return and be naturalized.

3. Following "Black September" in 1970, when the Jordan-based PRM was defeated by King Hussein's army, many thousands of guerrilla fighters and their families fled to Lebanon.

4. Refugees often describe their situation post-1982 in terms of "loss," "betrayal," and "abandonment," and accounts of the PLO's evacuation often explicitly mimic and build on the "before and after" quality of Nakba narratives. However, while the title of this book invokes the historical irony that the revolution aimed at territorial restoration for refugees left them newly dispossessed, the social, economic, and psychological aftermath of a failed movement is obviously not morally equivalent to the deliberate removal of an entire people from their homeland by colonial occupiers.

5. Because some Zionist scholars continue to claim the mass displacement of Palestinians during the Nakba was not the result of ethnic cleansing by Jewish paramilitaries but poor political leadership and the absence of nationalist sentiment, scholars of Palestine have felt the need to shine a bright light on the rich and complex forms of Palestinian national culture and collective belonging prior to 1948.

6. This project was co-directed with Mahmud Zeidan and funded by the Ford Foundation, the Welfare Foundation, and private donations. Over five years we collected more than five hundred interviews with refugees from 135 villages in Mandate Palestine. See http://www.nakba-archive.org.

7. First coined by the literary critic Van Wyck Brooks in his seminal essay, "On Creating a Usable Past" (1918). The phrase has since been used influentially by the historians Hobsbawn and Ranger (1992).

8. For this reason I have chosen not to write about the 1982 massacre, which was the subject of a number of studies published following the 2001 indictment of the former prime minister of Israel, Ariel Sharon, for war crimes (Borneman 2004; al-Hout 2004; Kallem 2003; Shahid 2002).

9. A communiqué detailing Civitas's progress released in April 2006 extended its mandate to include the development of bridging structures with host countries and humanitarian agencies serving refugees in the camps. The Civitas report is available at http://www.forcedmigration.org/research-resources/thematic/palestinians-register-laying-foundations-and-setting-directions.

10. The exact number of refugees from 1948 is the subject of debate. Benny Morris writes of "some 600,000–760,000 refugees" (1987, 1).

11. Originally there were fifteen camps in Lebanon. Nabatiyyeh, Tel al-Za'tar, and Jisr al-Basha were destroyed during the Lebanese civil war.

12. It is generally recognized that the actual number is between 260,000 and 280,000, since many refugees who emigrate and gain citizenship elsewhere retain their refugee residency status in Lebanon (Chaaban et al. 2010, 10).

13. Of the 230,000 Palestinian refugees registered as living outside the camps, approximately 40,000 live in forty-two unofficial "gatherings" around the country (Norwegian Refugee Council 2009); a significant proportion reside outside the country but retain refugee residency status; and the remainder tend to be middle-class Palestinians (primarily Christian) living in the cities.

14. In the early 1950s, under the presidency of Camille Chamoun, approximately 3,000 Christian Palestinians were naturalized and given Lebanese citizenship (Hudson 1997, 250).

15. The insecurity and deprivation experienced by Palestinians are more pronounced in Lebanon than in Jordan (and in Syria, at least until the civil war that began in 2012), where refugees enjoy civil rights and are integrated into socioeconomic life (Brand 1988).

16. The Abu Nidal Organization, part of the secular, left-wing Palestinian Front formed in 1974, was in fact the responsible party, not the PLO.

17. Al-Hout 2004. Sabra is the name often used, erroneously, to refer to the unofficial Palestinian gathering living in Da'uq, an area that borders the neighborhood and market of the same name.

18. It is estimated that anywhere between 3,781 and 6,787 Palestinians were killed during this struggle, which is considered the most bloody and brutal in the history of the Beirut camps. During this period the camps of Shatila and Burj al-Barajneh were essentially razed to the ground (Giannou 1992; Sayigh 1994; Stork 1985).

19. Allowances given to the families of martyrs, student scholarships, medical care, salaries for faction members, and retirement payments all decreased markedly after 1982.

20. Lebanese government approval for UNRWA's Camp Improvement Program

(CIP) in 2006 marked a shift in state policy toward the rehabilitation and upgrading of camp infrastructure (Misselwitz and Hanafi 2009, 360).

21. Knudsen 2009. The Shi'ite party, Hezbollah, is the only party that does not regard granting civil rights as a threat to the right of return and instead argues (like the majority of Palestinians) that improving the living conditions of refugees would enable them to campaign more effectively for their political rights.

22. The Lebanese rejectionist stance can be summarized as the "refusal to participate in the multilateral negotiations on refugees [the Refugee Working Group formed in 1991], refusal to co-operate with or permit any measures that would result in further entrenchment of the Palestinians, and the rejection of permanent settlement" (al-Khazen 1997, 80).

23. Khalidi and Riskedahl 2007. Although the Lebanese Parliament ratified a new labor law to facilitate the employment of Palestinians in August 2010, it has yet to be formally implemented.

24. Interview with Suhail al-Natour, Merlias camp, July 15, 2004.

25. Since 1962, Palestinians have been banned from seventy high-status professions, to which a further forty-six were added in a decree issued by the Ministry of Labor in 1995. In 2005, Hezbollah's labor and agriculture minister, Trad Hamade, lifted the ban on clerical and manual jobs (Knudsen 2009, 66).

26. Addressing the inherent paradox of humanitarian practice, Ilana Feldman writes: "Its nonpolitical stance is often what makes humanitarianism possible—permitting access to populations in need of aid, convincing countries to sign on to refugee conventions—but it also gives humanitarianism a sometimes cruelly narrow focus, able to keep people alive but entirely incapable of changing the conditions that have put them [refugees] at such great risk" (2007, 139).

27. Liisa Malkki observes that the refugee regime that developed after World War II defined refugees as a universal category—a dehistoricized "object of knowledge, assistance and management" (1996, 377). While Palestinians accuse UNRWA of turning a political condition into a humanitarian one, Israeli critics have frequently taken the opposite view, blaming the organization for politicizing refugee communities by perpetuating their refugee status, claiming that had UNRWA not existed, refugees would have been assimilated into Arab societies long ago.

28. Peteet 2005, 74. UNRWA's policy of providing services only to refugees living in the camps discourages refugees from moving out. Lebanon has the highest percentage of camp-dwelling refugees (55.4 percent) of all countries hosting Palestinians (Knudsen 2005, 218).

29. In the 1950s, Gordon Clapp, advisory chairman of the Economic Survey Mission, proposed a series of economic initiatives to promote resettlement of refugees and "halt the demoralizing process of pauperization" in the camps. This plan was rejected both by the Lebanese government and by officials representing refugee interests (Johnson and O'Brian 2003, 78).

30. Since UNRWA first established its microfinance program in 1991, no loans have been awarded to Palestinians in Lebanon, but $85,882,170 has been awarded to Palestinians in Gaza; $4,249,893 to refugees in Syria; $33,435,274 in the West Bank; and $7,524,717 in Jordan (UNRWA 2003).

31. Refugees' suspicion of aid derives from the belief that by accepting it, they have "initiated a deal exchanging rations for acquiescence to displacement and denativization" (Peteet 2005, 80).

32. In particular, refugees regard UNRWA as beholden to the political interests of the United States (the largest donor), and by extension, the interests of Israel, believing it to be engaged in a thinly disguised program of resettlement (Akram 2002).

33. Feldman's analysis of how aid informs the construction of political subjects in Gaza is again applicable: "Relief services came to serve as 'evidence' both of dispossession and of international responsibility for it. . . . Receiving aid seemed the only way to formally claim dispossession and, perhaps, even to claim the right to Palestine" (I. Feldman 2007, 144).

34. There are forty-six registered Arab NGOs and twenty foreign organizations working in the camps in Lebanon. While Arab NGOs tend to be more involved in the provision of services to refugees, the role of foreign organizations is primarily one of funding (Hanafi 2010, 52). In 1994, a Palestinian NGO Forum was created to increase coordination between institutions operating in the camps and as a means of facilitating cooperation and efficiency. In general, however, NGOs continue to work independently and do not coordinate their activities.

35. The fact that formal registration and charitable status require that Palestinian NGOs be headed by a Lebanese citizen has also placed constraints on the scope of NGO activities (J. Suleiman 1997, 401).

36. The demise of the Soviet Union and the crisis of the secular left also gave new impetus to the creation of an alternative public forum for political leaders from these parties.

37. The two most prominent NGOs in Shatila—the Youth Center run by Abu Mujahed, and Beit Atfal al-Sumud—are affiliated with the Popular Front for the Liberation of Palestine (PFLP). The directors of both organizations were formerly prominent members of the PFLP who embarked on humanitarian work after the civil war ended.

38. UNRWA 2012. UNRWA defines SHCs as the most disadvantaged and vulnerable refugees, primarily widows, orphans, the elderly, the chronically ill, and those with disabilities. SHCs are eligible for food, cash assistance, and shelter rehabilitation. For a detailed discussion of SHCs, see Hejoj and Badran 2006.

39. A fall in remittance income following the 1991 Gulf War also narrowed the margin of survival in the camp. The expulsion of Palestinians living in Kuwait and other Gulf States resulted in the loss of a significant source of income for many Palestinian families.

40. For more on the debates surrounding UNRWA's camp improvement program, see Gabiam 2012; and Misselwitz and Hanafi 2009.

41. In the field of higher education, the 2002 classification of Palestinians as "foreign students" led to dramatically increased fees for Palestinians that few can afford.

42. A history of spies and collaborators infiltrating camp society has led to a suspicion of outsiders. I was told of a number of cases in which Mossad agents, working as volunteer doctors in the late 1970s, had produced detailed maps of the camp and gathered information about Shatila's military capacities. This information was put to use in the Israeli invasion of 1982 and during the Sabra and Shatila massacre. In addition, it is well known that Syrian intelligence (Mukhabarat) has deep roots within the community.

43. Al-Ahbash (the Ethiopian) is a Sunni group espousing a political ideology of nonviolent quietism, with strong Syrian ties. The Habashi theology blends Sufism with elements of Sunni and Shi'a belief (Knudsen 2005).

44. Hezbollah, now considered the Palestinians' closest political ally in Lebanon, has close ties to Palestinian Islamist groups and enjoys widespread support in the camp for the same reasons (Khalili 2007).

45. Protests at the border meanwhile grew more heated. During a demonstration next to the Fatima Gate on October 7, 2000, Shadi Anas from Burj al-Barajneh camp and Hasan Hasanayn from Shatila were killed by Israeli fire, and a number of other protesters were wounded. This led to restrictions preventing Palestinians in camps north of Sidon from traveling to the south without official authorization.

46. The World Bank estimates that external support for Palestinian NGOs during the early 1990s dropped by around 40 percent, from $170 million to $100 million (Hammami 1995, 51–63).

47. Originally a kind of tent city, Shatila has since the 1950s gradually but decisively shifted to using permanent materials for its architecture and infrastructure. It is now a mixed community, with Palestinians constituting less than half the population. As of 2005, around 12 percent of that Palestinian minority represented first-generation refugees born in Palestine (Tiltnes 2005).

48. Hannah Arendt (1973) observed that the condition of the modern refugee presupposes the globalization of the state form and becomes the pathological foil through which new legal-political categories of citizenship and rights could be formulated. Camps, by extension of this logic, have tended to be regarded not only as refuges for "people out of place" but as spaces of containment and control, enabling governments to cordon off and monitor undesirables, enforcing boundaries of belonging and exclusion. See Agier 2011; Diken and Lausten 2005; Fassin 2005; Ticktin 2011.

49. Giorgio Agamben's (1998, 2000) concept of the "bare life" in a state of exception—where the *homo sacer* exists in a liminal zone neither fully within nor outside the legal political order—is regularly cited in texts dealing with camps, theories of citizen-

ship, and refugee rights, often to make starkly visible the powerlessness of refugees and the biopolitical apparatuses employed by host governments to control them.

50. There are a few notable exceptions. See, for example, Abu Nahleh 2006; Johnson 2006; Kuttab 2006; Taraki 2006.

51. Khalili 2007; Klaus 2003; Peteet 1991, 2005; Roberts 2010; Sayigh 1979, 1994. Rosemary Sayigh's work in particular has been invaluable. Her ethnography, *Too Many Enemies* (1994), which charts the history of Shatila through a palimpsestic layering of oral testimonies, has inspired this work in many ways.

52. Dewey and William James argued that all experience is relational and creatively engaged rather than passively received. Radically empiricist, they challenged Cartesian rationalism and the view that philosophy should consist of unchanging, a priori postulates, arguing that it should be guided rather by the particularities of personal experience. Reality was not to be regarded as transcendent but rather subject to the contingencies of practice, with given truths tested "within the stream of experience" (James 1907, 53).

53. See also Bourdieu 1990, 2000, and Desjarlais's theory of "critical phenomenology," which links the phenomenal and the political (1997, 24–27).

54. Like the "informal politics" of direct action in squatter communities in Iran and Egypt described by Asef Bayat (1997, 2010), the activities I discuss develop outside institutional settings, are motivated by immediate needs, and rarely adopt the long-term goals of social or political movements. See also Partha Chatterjee's (2004, 2008) work on "the politics of the governed," which explores informal political practices occurring outside electoral politics among India's urban and rural poor.

CHAPTER 1

Portions of the following previously published material are included in this chapter: "Commemorative Economies and the Politics of Solidarity in Shatila Camp," *Humanity* 4, no. 1 (2013): 133–148; "The Politics of Witness: Remembering and Forgetting 1948 in Shatila Camp," in *Nakba: Palestine, 1948, and the Claims of Memory*, edited by Lila Abu-Lughod and Ahmad Sa'di (New York: Columbia University Press, 2007), 253–284; "Mythologizing the *Nakba*: 1948 Narratives in the Production of Collective Identity and Cultural Practice among Palestinian Refugees in Lebanon," *Journal of Oral History* 33, no. 1 (2005): 47–56.

1. Najdeh was established in 1976 by the Democratic Front for the Liberation of Palestine (DFLP) to provide vocational training for women widowed during the siege and destruction of Tel al-Za'tar Camp.

2. The War of the Camps, when the Lebanese Shi'a militia, Amal, attacked and besieged the camps in Beirut and the south, lasted three years (1985–1988); during this time much of Shatila was razed.

3. This mass grave, said to hold between eight hundred and twelve hundred bodies, was a garbage dump until 1999, when it was turned into a commemorative site by Hez-

bollah, the Lebanese Shi'a political party that controls the municipality of Ghoubeiry (where Shatila is located).

4. Davis 2010. See also the work of 'A'idun (The Returnee), founded in 1998, http://www.aidoun.org; Al-Jana and the Arab Resource Center for Popular Arts (ARCPA), http://www.al-jana.org; the Palestinian Human Rights Organization (PHRO), http://www.palhumanrights.org; and the research initiative on Palestinian memory conducted by Institut français du Proche-Orient, http://www.ifporient.org/node/321.

5. Although refugees are normally not permitted to organize demonstrations outside the camps, that year the Internal Security Forces (ISF) issued permits to camp representatives, enabling them to hold right-of-return rallies in Beirut.

6. In his introduction to an edited volume on the case brought against Ariel Sharon by survivors of the Sabra and Shatila massacre, John Borneman observes that it has become increasingly necessary for powerless victims to "manage and organize suffering so that outsiders identify with their pain" (2004, 9). Stories like the one recounted by Mazen and Samar are clearly intended for circulation and consumption in settings far removed from the contexts of their telling. See also Allen 2006; Farah 1999; Fassin 2008; I. Feldman 2008; Hill 2005; and Khalili 2005 on the role memorial and testimonial play in shaping legal and political practice.

7. With the notable exception of the unprecedented mobilization of camp refugees during the 2011 commemoration of the Nakba, when an estimated fifty thousand Palestinians went to demonstrate at Maroun al-Ras, on the Lebanese border with Israel.

8. Some scholars argue that the use of the term "returners" is still favored over "refugees" because the latter normalizes the status quo and the possibility of resettlement. Julie Peteet writes that in referring to themselves as "returners," "they were constructing a lexicon of both refusal and resistance" (1995, 177).

9. The repressive measures of the Lebanese Sûreté Générale, and later the Deuxième Bureau, also muted nationalist expression and politically motivated remembrance of the Nakba at this time.

10. During the 1970s, the day marking the creation of the State of Israel (May 15) was not called "the day of the catastrophe" (*yawm al-Nakba*) as it is now, but *yawm Balfour*, with reference to Lord Balfour's 1917 declaration calling for the establishment of a Jewish homeland in Palestine.

11. International awareness of the events of 1948 (as well as historical consensus about the causes) increased during this period partly as a result of the Israeli New Historians, who—making use of Israeli government documents declassified in the 1980s— wrote demystified and nonhagiographic histories of Israel's founding and the displacement of the Palestinians. See Morris 1987; Pappé 1997, 2001, 2003, 2006; Piterberg 2001; Segev 1994; Shlaim 1995, 2000, 2002; as well as the work of the Palestinian-American historian R. Khalidi 1997.

12. Idealized depictions of pre-1948 Palestine dominate nationalist discourse and

are often fetishized in ways that appear to bring them closer to myth. The structure of nationalist narrative in this context bears relation to the mythico-histories Liisa Malkki encountered among Hutu refugees living in camps in Tanzania. Malkki notes that these historical narratives represented a "reinterpretation of [the past] in fundamentally moral terms. In this sense, it cannot be accurately described as either history or myth. It was what can be called a mythico-history." She goes on to suggest, "What made the refugees' narrative mythical, in the anthropological sense, was not its truth or falsity, but the fact that it was concerned with *order* in a fundamental, cosmological sense" (1995a, 54–55).

13. In addition to Said, these figures include Mahmoud Darwish, Ghassan Kanafani, Raja Shehadeh, Fadwa Tuqan, Salim Jubran, Naji Ali, and Ismail Shammout.

14. Quoted from the *New England Psychological Association Newsletter* in a personal communication, December 2005.

15. In particular, see Walid Khalidi's monumental work *Kay la Nansa* (Lest we forget), published under the English title *All That Remains* (1992), which documents the histories of depopulated villages in pre-1948 Palestine. Other notable examples are the meticulous cartographic works of Salman Abu Sitta (2000, 2004), detailing the origins of Palestinian refugees and the current state of properties and estates in pre-1948 Palestine, and Shukri Arraf's (2004) research on place-names. In each case, geographic and toponymic histories are woven into a narrative of return.

16. Karma Nabulsi has argued that refugees represent the core of Palestinian national identity. In an editorial for the *Guardian*, on the twentieth anniversary of the Sabra and Shatila massacre, Nabulsi writes: "The Palestinians' strength always resides inside the refugee camps themselves, be they in Gaza and the West Bank, South Lebanon or Amman. It is also where, should anyone desire to discover it, one finds the will of the Palestinian people" (2002).

17. Litvak 1994, 45. See also Bardenstein 1999; Bowman 1994; Hammer 2001; Khalili 2004, 2005; Parmenter 1994; Sa'di 2002; Siddiq 1995; and Slyomovics 1998.

18. Y. Suleiman 2011, 206. On the political significance of naming in Palestinian oral poetry and wedding songs in the Galilee, see Yaqub 2007; and the work of Zochrot, an Israeli NGO that has worked extensively on raising awareness about destroyed Palestinian villages, at http://www.zochrot.org/en.

19. For a discussion of this phenomenon in oral history, see Dakhlia 2001.

20. Tracing the relation between what James Young calls an "invented" psychiatric discourse and the flourishing field of memory politics, Paul Antze and Michael Lambek observe how "memory worth talking about—worth remembering—is trauma" (1996, xii). They argue that far from being an unmediated process, in which facts about traumatic pasts are naturally brought to light, the concept of "trauma" should instead be viewed as a cultural and intellectual phenomenon—a model for understanding suffering and self that has been shaped by political, cultural, and economic forces structuring Western society.

21. Pappé 2006. There is widespread Israeli resistance to reexamining the origins of the State of Israel, and claims for the ontological uniqueness of the Holocaust are often used to justify past and current oppression of Palestinians (Finkelstein 2000). In this sense bearing witness to the events of 1948 involves the delicate task of proving the latter without denying the former.

22. In their analysis of the politics of testimony and "humanitarian psychiatry" in Palestine, Didier Fassin and Richard Rechtman write that the gathering of testimonies has produced "histories without history." They go on to argue that "what is gained in familiarity, by bringing those experiencing violence closer to the public whose awareness needs to be raised, making the cause of the former less abstract and more accessible, is lost in terms of genuine understanding. The social effectiveness of trauma does not necessarily produce the historical truth of the victims" (2009, 214–215). See also Redfield 2006.

23. In his critique of Holocaust discourse in America, Peter Novick suggests that the increased circulation of books, testimonials, and films about the Holocaust was not "the return of the repressed" but a political move. Interest in the Holocaust increased during the Six-Day War, at a point when the State of Israel felt threatened, and its invocation was an attempt to frame the war as the product of a new strain of violent anti-Semitism and a justified means of self-defense. The fashioning of Holocaust discourse as a "cult" and "fetish," Novick argues, has essentially heralded the destruction of critical historical consciousness of this event. The exceptionalism that it claims for itself also becomes a way of foreclosing the possibility of seeing Palestinians as victims (2000, 14).

24. Writing about the sacralization of the Holocaust, LaCapra suggests that the linking of this traumatic event with the sublime—as beyond any ability to name or to know—produces a spiritual uplift (2004, 65). This derives from a belief in the essential resilience and dignity of humans and their ability to endure all hardship and emerge on a higher level of spirituality. This perspective holds many parallels for the ways in which the Nakba has become the symbol not only of loss but also of great fortitude in the face of prolonged suffering.

25. See Tom Hill's (2005) analysis of the historical narratives and commemorations deployed during the fiftieth anniversary of the Nakba, and the impact that a renewed interest in survivor testimony had on Palestinian historiography.

26. See Tom Segev (1994).

27. "The Palestinian People's Appeal on the 50th Anniversary of the Catastrophe, May 14, 1998." Cited in Benvenisti (2000, 308).

28. While I distinguish between institutional and everyday forms of remembrance, I am not claiming that public commemoration of 1948 or 1982 in Shatila lacks resonance for its residents. In opposing nationalist commemoration with subjective, everyday forms of remembering, I realize that I am in danger of reifying the latter as somehow "authentic" or unmediated. I should therefore point out that I do not view personal memories as free of social, political, and moral calculations.

29. See the Nakba Archive, http://www.nakba-archive.org.

30. Cf. A. Feldman 2004, 163–202.

31. Jayyusi has written about this relationship between the lived body and place in Palestinian memory—which she calls "*in-vivo* subjectivity"—where former ways of life are recalled through reference to embodied memories of work and sensory experience. "We can say that it is *in* and *through* this (mindful) body that we are in 'place.' . . . And it is in and through the body that place is therefore experienced, shaped and navigated; and it is through this relationship to the body that it is remembered and narrated" (2007, 121).

32. The involuntary quality of this form of recollection resembles Henri Bergson's theory of duration (*durée*), in which past experiences move, ceaselessly, by "reciprocal interpenetration" into present consciousness. "Memory," he writes, "is not a faculty of putting away recollections in a drawer or of inscribing them in a register. . . . In reality . . . all we have felt, thought and willed from our earliest infancy is there, leaning over our present, which is about to join it, pressing against the portals of consciousness that would fain leave it outside" (1960, 5).

33. Samera Esmeir regards the fractured quality of 1948 narratives itself as a form of witness: "Death generates present absence and nonexistence. It is something that lives on with its survivors. . . . Incoherence, contradictions and absences should be understood as signifiers of something that is still present" (2003, 45).

34. See Khalidi and Riskedahl 2010, 6. The assumed automaticity of memory transmission among Palestinian refugees in exile remains a staple of much academic and activist literature.

35. Drawing on research in Burj al-Barajneh camp, Khalili writes: "To insist on the trope of intergenerational transmission of memory—even if now the primary medium of transmission is the Internet or television—is another way in which the refugees insist that memory legitimates their belonging to the nation" (2004, 7).

36. On October 29, 1948, Sufsaf was occupied by Israeli forces. Seventy men from the village were rounded up, blindfolded, and shot. Three cases of rape were also documented.

37. Interview, December 16, 2003.

38. This trend has been observed by other scholars working in the Palestinian camps. In a recent study of Palestinian children and adolescents, Chatty and Hundt note that "historical consciousness appears to be waning as the younger generations learn less about their past" (2001, 41).

39. These findings contrast to those of Sayigh, who in her study of life histories of Palestinian women in Shatila found that the starting point of narratives was invariably 1948, not only among those who had actually experienced the events of the expulsion but also among generations too young to have personal recollections. If, as I suggest, the political context of remembering is central to what is highlighted, the political context for Sayigh's piece published in 1998—when the commemoration of the Nakba was at its height—might in part explain the discrepancies in our results (1998c, 45).

40. Valentine Daniel (1996) and Liisa Malkki (1995a) both argue that this is an essential component of political agency for refugees—who by foregrounding who they were prior to displacement challenge official representations of what they have become.

41. Interview, June 17, 2004.

42. Writing in the wake of September 11, 2001, Judith Butler observed that the process of mourning and accepting loss is always at some level about submitting to transformation: "There is losing, as we know, but there is also the transformative effect of loss" (2004, 21).

43. Since I was a British woman, studying at an American university, suspicion was sometimes accentuated by a sense of ethnohistorical resentment.

44. Interview, July 28, 2004.

45. Among the key theorists of trauma, Shoshana Felman and Dori Laub (1992) argue that the Shoah is an event without witnesses, beyond representation, a quagmire of aporias. In their rather circular argument, which almost fetishizes lacunae, all that can be witnessed is the fact of the breakdown of witnessing. Cathy Caruth describes this latency of traumatic memory more helpfully, as positioned "between the elision of memory and the precision of recall" (1995, 153).

46. Das makes a similar argument in her discussion of the silence of Indian women about their experiences of violence during the Partition. Silence, Das suggests, should be interpreted as a conscious act of agency, and efforts to break the silence can deny the power and meaning of this choice (2007, 57).

47. It is important to bear in mind that the estrangement of the physical and social spaces of memory is particularly pronounced in Shatila because of the violent disruptions that followed the Israeli invasion of Beirut in 1982, the War of the Camps between 1985 and 1988, and internal interfactional disputes during the late 1980s and early 1990s.

48. Marc Augé argues suggestively that memory and forgetting are not antithetical: "To praise oblivion is not to revile memory; even less is it to forget remembrance, but rather to recognize the work of oblivion in the first one and to spot it in the second" (2004, 14).

49. Battaglia 1992, 14. Battaglia's "willed transformation" of memory is similar to Nietzsche's theory of "active forgetting." The capacity to "feel unhistorically," to forget, Nietzsche suggests, enables people to avoid a condition in which an excess of memory precludes action or future development ([1873] 1983, 62). "Active forgetting" is presented as intentioned—a mechanism regulating both the individual and society, balancing memory with oblivion, knowledge with ignorance, and a past that is reflected upon with a present that is lived.

50. Sylvain Perdigon encountered a similar critique of "fantastical" (*khayal*) descriptions of Palestine in his research in Jal al-Bahar in South Lebanon. He writes that the use of the term *khayal* is significant, "in that it associates the plight of refugee status

not only with the actual denial of rights, but also with a certain psychic curse on the imagination: as though your imagination, struck on fire by the awareness of injustice and uprooting, always threatened to come and stand between you and the world, blocking you from seeing the world as it is, a form of refugee melancholia" (2010, 103).

51. Raja Shehadeh writes that a standardized vocabulary of national belonging may be engendering an altered perception of homeland: "Sometimes when I am walking in the hills, say Batn el-Hawa, unselfconsciously enjoying the touch of the hard land under my feet, the smell of thyme and the hills and trees around me, I find myself looking at it, it transforms itself before my eyes into a symbol of *samidin*, of our struggle, of our loss. And at that very moment, I am robbed of that tree; instead, there is a hollow space into which anger and pain flow" (quoted in Parmenter 1994, 86–87).

52. Among them, the Israeli air raid that destroyed Nabatiyyeh (1973); the attack on Tel al-Za'tar—carried out by Lebanese Christians, with Syrian backing (1976); the War of the Camps; and the "Internal Wars" (1989), when Arafat loyalists were pitted against a coalition of ten pro-Syrian Palestinian factions (al-Tahaluf).

53. Allan and Brown 2010. For a nuanced discussion of the role the Internet has played in cross-border, Palestinian political activism and identity formation, see Aouragh 2011.

CHAPTER 2

This chapter includes portions of a previously published article, "From Nationalist to Economic Subjectivity: A Study of Emergent Economic Networks among Shatila's Women," *Journal of Palestine Studies* 38, no. 4 (2009): 1–16.

1. Although remittances from wealthier relatives living elsewhere are an acknowledged lifeline for many families, they have introduced friction, and local forms of authority—most obviously, seniority—are sometimes disregarded because they lack economic clout. While emigration has helped to sustain families in the camps through transnational support networks, it has also weakened local kin structures, both through physically displacing family members and destabilizing established power hierarchies within camp communities (Hanafi 2007; Ugland and al-Madi 2003; Zureik 1997).

2. Family and kin have long occupied a privileged place within Palestinian nationalist discourse as synecdoches of stoicism, resilience, and resistance in Palestinian society (Hovdenak 1997; Jean-Klein 2001; Latte Abdallah 2006; Rosenfeld 2004; Taraki 2006). As in other prestate societies, the family continues to be viewed as the basic unit of social, economic, and political organization, enabling the day-to-day survival of refugees, creating moral community, and instilling nationalist values. In the camps in Lebanon, economic insecurity, political repression, and weak governance worked to reinforce kin relations and informal ties, which have historically provided an economic safety net in periods of adversity and functioned as a local source of power, leverage, and mediation (Sayigh 1979; J. Suleiman 1999).

3. I was told that the village committee of Majd al-Krum has been sustained thanks to yearly contributions from former residents now living in the Gulf States.

4. "Moral familism" refers to the central role that the family has traditionally played in sustaining structures of solidarity in peasant society, where loyalty to the *hamula* (clan) and to male elders shapes social relations (Sayigh 1979, 17–25).

5. Sayigh (2008) notes that the tension between the needs of the family and the national movement goes back to the PLO revolution in Lebanon, when reidentification of the camps as bases of national struggle raised an identity dilemma for families. Support for the resistance might entail releasing sons and daughters from familial obligations, a loss that could jeopardize a household's future.

6. This contradiction of gender roles and expectations has become more pronounced in recent years as a growing number of women support their families and provide for their children. While gender norms dictate that men should be providers, the declining resources of factions and discriminatory labor laws implemented in the post-Ta'if period have dramatically increased male unemployment. Shatila's economy has therefore become increasingly dependent on alternative sources of income and support generated by women, both through the neighborhood networks I have been describing and through their work outside the camps, primarily as cleaners, nannies, and service workers. Social and familial controls that once placed strict limits on the movement of women have been relaxed, allowing their labor, both in and out of the camp, to be recognized as essential for the survival of family and community (Allan 2009).

7. Employing kinship as a pragmatic form of sociality resembles theories of "idiomatic" (Geertz and Geertz 1975) and "practical" kinship (Bourdieu 1977), where relatedness is strategically invoked to include neighbors and friends in reciprocal circuits of exchange. While rule-based, patrilineal models foreground the importance of group representation and legitimate a particular sociopolitical order, "practical kinship" includes strategic, nongenealogical relations oriented toward a politics of everyday survival (Bourdieu 1977, 33–34).

8. Since women tend to spend more time at home and traditionally have had less power and influence in male-centered kinship structures and other male-dominated institutions, they tend to be better practiced at forming neighborly connections extending beyond traditional kin boundaries. In Shatila this has given women greater responsibility and influence in managing the domestic economy.

9. This willingness to support others through adversity resembles what Haydar al-Mohammad (2010), in his study of struggle for everyday existence in Basra, has called an ethics of "being-with," where living with others creates bonds of care guided not by social norms of how one should act but rather by a pragmatics of everyday life.

10. The growing importance of these alternative structures of solidarity reaffirms the salience of concepts like "wealth in people" (Guyer and Eno Belinga 1995; Ntombi 2004; Simone 2004), in which social power and the capacity for survival are determined

not simply by fixed assets but by relations of mutual dependency that can function as safety nets in moments of financial crisis.

11. This broader definition of kinship is built into the etymological roots of the Arabic term for kin, *qaraba*, which simultaneously is used to mean relationship, proximity, and kinship. In her study of marriage practices in Jabal Nablus in the West Bank, Annelies Moors describes how kinship is understood in social and biological terms. Moors found marriage preference to be determined not solely by blood ties but by the shared experience of class, culture, and spatial proximity, and by what she calls "sameness," which is "associated with 'closeness' [*qaraba*], a relative rather than an absolute term" (cited in Johnson 2006, 76).

12. The same ethic can be found structuring the *blat* networks that helped Russians survive the vicissitudes of a postsocialist economy, in which relations were often formed for strategic reasons and it was more useful to be part of a social network in which "sanctions are imposed by the 'people of the circle' where one wants to belong rather than 'family' where one belongs with no choice" (Ledeneva 1998, 57).

13. Ghawarni Bedouin hail from the Hula Valley swampland in the northern Galilee. There has traditionally been a certain amount of animosity between the Bedouin and the fellaheen, who regard Bedouins as not being "fully Palestinian" in their cultural practices.

14. The corrupting influence of great infusions of Arab oil wealth from the Gulf in the 1970s and 1980s was a recurrent theme in conversations about the revolution. In an interview, a former PLO cadre described the irrational and irresponsible habits wealth produced: "We were perhaps the most wealthy revolutionaries in the world. After years of poverty, people in the camps were suddenly exposed to comfort and luxury living. Corruption took people over, top down. People sold themselves. I remember a scene from Jean Genet's *Prisoner of Love*, where he writes that he followed the fedayeen through the Jordanian desert, eating Gruyère cheese. At first I wondered what he meant by this, but later I realized he was showing how thoughtless they were to the poverty of the Jordanian peasants around them. Whatever aid they were sent they flaunted, and they didn't bother to share the bounty or win over the Jordanians. No wonder they hated us."

15. From 2002 until his death in November 2004, the Israeli army confined Arafat to his compound in Ramallah.

16. Fatima was not alone in speaking about the phenomenon of concealing resources from family. A friend of Umm Mahmud's recounted the shock of seeing relatives who lived in the same building hiding groceries from one another to avoid having to share them. Another woman freely admitted to hiding savings from her husband and putting aside gifts sent from siblings abroad, in the hope of amassing enough to send her daughter to university. She feared her husband would appropriate her savings to pay off debts.

17. A recent study conducted by Marwan Khawaja and Laurie Blome Jacobsen in the camps in Lebanon similarly found that "the usual cultural argument about the unique-

ness of the Arab extended family in nurturing exchange" no longer holds, with familial support extending only to "those who can reciprocate" (2003, 599).

18. Credit relations have long played an important role in Palestinian society. In his study of the changing political economy of the Jabal Nablus region in the eighteenth and nineteenth centuries, Beshara Doumani (1995) examines how money-lending practices, in particular *salam* contracts (in which cash is paid in advance of the delivery of the purchased goods), structured rural-urban relations between merchants and peasants and led to the emergence of a rural middle class, transforming land regimes in the Palestinian hinterland.

19. Some Muslims consider this to be the only type of loan that does not violate the prohibition on interest (*riba*) since it does not compensate the creditor for the time value of money (Maurer 2005).

20. Sometimes outstanding bills are paid by wealthier members of the community, who cover the debts of poorer neighbors either through a voluntary donation (*sadaqa*) or as alms (*zakat*) during Ramadan.

21. Fatima was attentive to shifts in patterns of consumption in the camp: "Now people buy small bottles of olive oil and a kilo of sugar every few days. Before, people would buy ten-kilo bags of sugar and twenty liters of oil for the year. No one can afford this anymore. In the end the poor get hit twice."

22. Marcel Mauss (1990) was the first to identify the importance of gift giving as a mechanism for forging and sustaining social relations, since gifts generate the obligation to reciprocate, binding people together through reciprocal relations.

23. Janet Roitman's research on the productivity of debt in Cameroon, which builds on Mauss's insights into debtor-creditor relations, offers a useful model for understanding indebtedness as creating conditions for new forms of sociability. Roitman describes debt as "not opposition, but diversion of appropriate paths and modalities of exchange; [it] represents a moment when particular truths about social relations are revealed" (2005, 75). See also Clara Han's (2012) work on debt relations in Chile.

24. In his analysis of gift exchange, Pierre Bourdieu (1977) focuses on the lapse of time separating the gift and its return. In instances in which it is returned too quickly, the social symbolism of the gift is nullified and exchange resembles commodity exchange between strangers, and can therefore be interpreted as an insult. In this sense, gifts are always in some respect about giving time itself.

25. More recently I have encountered young men participating in *jam'iyyat* to raise funds to marry.

26. Diane Singerman (1995) and Homa Hoodfar (1997) have written about similar women-run savings associations that function as a parallel banking system among Cairo's poor.

27. While decisions about the management of a *jam'iyya* are usually taken collectively, a person is often nominated as arbitrator and overall coordinator at the outset.

28. Like the savings associations Daniel Fessler describes in Indonesia, the *jam'iyya* "is embedded in relationships of reciprocity [that] use the ethic of sharing as a defense against having to share" (2002, 40).

29. While *jam'iyyat* have become a lifeline for many families, they continue to be viewed by some as morally suspect, given the difficulties in determining with any precision how money is sourced or spent. Umm Walid, in spite of her enthusiasm for savings associations, recognized the moral risks: "You can never know with certainty how the money given through savings associations will be used."

30. Although it was easier for this generation of men to find unskilled manual labor in the 1980s and 1990s, as they age, the opportunities for waged work diminish, increasing their vulnerability in the labor market.

31. This phenomenon of family ties faltering, or being willfully severed, under conditions of economic duress has been observed by other anthropologists and sociologists working in deprived communities. See Biehl 2005; Desmond 2012; Fessler 2002; Han 2011; Hoodfar 1997; al-Mohammad 2010; Povinelli 2006; and Simone 2004.

32. Amartya Sen's (1989, 2000) work on relational deprivation offers a helpful model for rethinking the abstractions of economic analysis in the context of the camps. Sen argues that it is important not to view concepts such as "standard of living" simply in material, money-metric terms but rather as bound up with social values and "capabilities." The perception of deprivation is relative, defined according to normative standards of living in any given context. Sen contends that poverty is experienced not only as a physical and economic reality but also as an acute lack of well-being and agency, and makes a persuasive case for the importance of placing questions of respect, dignity, and moral well-being at the heart of economics (2000, 87–111).

33. Since the departure of the PLO, competition between Fatah loyalists and Syrian-backed rejectionist factions has also increased clientelism, as scarce resources are fought over ever more furiously.

34. For an in-depth discussion of factionalism and political practice in the camps in Lebanon, see Sari Hanafi and Taylor Long's (2010) article on camp governance.

35. Because aid parcels are standardized and do not vary according to the needs of the recipient, there are often surplus or unwanted items, which are sold or exchanged. An elderly neighbor of Umm Mahmud, for instance, would sell her milk rations to the local store.

36. Bourdieu writes that aid undermines the autonomy and independence of the recipient because it "exclude[s] the possibility of an equivalent return, the very hope of an active reciprocity, which is the condition of possibility of genuine autonomy" (2000, 200). See also Harrell-Bond (2002).

37. I knew of a number of individuals who had shifted political allegiances in order to access a range of services not currently available to them.

38. While faction membership was understood to be a precondition for participa-

tion in the resistance and central to Palestinian identity during the 1970s, the perception that factions are corrupt and inept has meant that adopting a nonpartisan position is often regarded as the most principled choice among younger generations of refugees.

39. Abu Yusuf's relations of indebtedness stand in stark contrast to the *jam'iyyat*, which are normally structured around future goals. While participation in a *jam'iyya* is often taken as a sign of financial stability, impromptu debts that are unregulated and oriented toward meeting daily needs as they arise are compensatory rather than constructive.

40. Because poverty has absolute and relative dimensions, any analysis of basic needs must take into account not only biological necessities, such as food and shelter, but also socially constructed requirements for social and psychological well-being (Sen 1989, 2000).

41. Refugees reject the Lebanese government's claim that discriminatory policies are designed to protect their national rights and will often argue that greater social and economic integration would do more to further their political rights. A recent comparative survey conducted by Near East Projects in 2005 in camps in Syria, Lebanon, and the OPT supports this view, showing that greater socioeconomic security in the case of refugees in Syria correlated with an increased desire for return (Bocco and Husseini 2010, 282).

CHAPTER 3

"Welcome to the Camps" (first epigraph to this chapter) is quoted in Nicholas Puig's article on Palestinian rap in the camps in Lebanon (2010, 113).

1. The establishment of the Infrastructure and Camp Improvement Program (ICIP) in 2006 signaled a significant shift in UNRWA's policy toward camp rehabilitation and sustainable development. Shatila has yet to see any significant improvement in the field of water and electricity provision.

2. Given the sensitive nature of the subject of this chapter, I have tried by various means (not limited to the use of pseudonyms) to preserve the anonymity of those directly involved in providing stolen electricity in Shatila.

3. Recent studies of camp governance draw on the work of Giorgio Agamben (1998) to argue that camps in Lebanon constitute "spaces of exception" and "bare life," since refugees are subject to repressive, exclusionary laws, without being subjects of the law (Hanafi 2008; Hanafi and Long 2010). Responding to these claims, Perdigon (2011) argues that while this formulation may make legal sense, invoking the concept of "bare life" to describe refugee experience ignores the complex social and moral worlds refugees inhabit, a position I share. By focusing on the politics of electricity distribution in Shatila—both as a form of resistance to state neglect and an expression of new political formations—this chapter also challenges the view that refugee existence is irredeemably subjugated by technologies of state power.

4. Camps in Beirut are rarely recognized as part of the city. During a weeklong series of debates at the American University of Beirut (AUB) in May 2004, titled "La Meen Beirut?" (Whose Beirut?), camps did not feature. It is not uncommon for Lebanese who have never seen or visited a camp to claim, with considerable conviction, that they are lawless and dangerous places that need to be controlled or eradicated altogether.

5. Exaggerated claims that camps are "security islands" (*juzur amniyya*) beyond the law have also contributed to the perception that camps threaten Lebanese sovereignty and are havens for extremists and criminals (J. Suleiman 1999, 72). This portrayal of the camps as beyond the law is politically motivated and conceals the true extent to which Lebanese security forces in fact control the camps (Knudsen 2009, 61).

6. The most startling deviation from the government's policy of nonintervention was the Lebanese army's assault on the northern camp of Nahr al-Bared during the summer of 2007. Fighting between the army and Fatah al-Islam, a largely non-Palestinian political group, resulted in the destruction of much of the camp, the killing of many soldiers and civilians, and the mass displacement of thirty-three thousand people, setting a deeply troubling precedent for other communities like Ayn al-Hilweh camp, which have also been accused of harboring extremists (Abboud 2009).

7. Bayat 1997, 57. See also Heyman and Smart 1999; Willen 2007.

8. See also Lawrence Liang's (2005) work on "porous legalities" and the clandestine means by which marginalized urban communities in Delhi and São Paulo access civic amenities and create avenues of participation.

9. These tactics for acquiring essential resources resemble James Scott's "weapons of the weak," because they are characterized by an "implicit disavowal of the state" and a "focus on immediate gains" (1985, 33) rather than longer-term strategic interests. However, while Scott and others in the field of subaltern studies locate political agency in everyday acts they regard as politically motivated, Bayat attends to strategies so unassuming as to seem free of conscious political intent but that nonetheless produce effective reciprocal networks based on shared interests.

10. Diane Singerman's work on the varieties of popular participation among Cairo's poorer *sha'b* communities is helpful for thinking through the power struggles and informal politics of ordinary people (1995).

11. Recent development projects on Shatila's periphery, notably the Sport City Stadium and the Rafiq Hariri clinic and school, are visible reminders of the government's threat to redevelop the land.

12. Bayat 1997, 10. Bayat's analysis is concerned less with ideology than with direct action. He writes: "While new social movements are said to focus largely on identity and meaning, my protagonists concern themselves primarily with action. Therefore, in a metaphorical sense, these everyday encroachments may be seen as representing a movement in itself, becoming a social movement per se only if and when the actors become conscious of their doings by articulating their aims, methods and justifications" (1997, 7).

13. In focusing on illegal acts, I am not trying to romanticize these strategies of making do, nor am I suggesting they constitute a deviant or "abnormal" subculture associated exclusively with Beirut's poorer suburbs. Illegality is not the preserve of the marginalized but also involves powerful players, including municipal representatives and state officials.

14. Refugees were forbidden to use durable materials, such as concrete, and the *barqiyyat* dwellings, which replaced the tents that first sheltered refugees, were made from sheets of tin. Piped water was introduced only in 1969, once again thanks to the entrepreneurial skills of Abu Turki. This private water supply—along with a number of communal wells that were dug inside Shatila in the 1970s—sustained the community through the worst sieges during the War of the Camps (Sayigh 1994, 39). The importance of establishing internal water supplies, to avoid dependency on municipal sources that could be cut off, was made starkly clear in the siege of Tel al-Za'tar camp in 1976, when Christian Phalangist militias cut off all supplies. The lack of wells is generally regarded as a crucial factor in the defeat of the camp (Giannou 1992, 66).

15. The 1969 Cairo Agreement allowed for the creation of local committees, which preceded the establishment of the Popular Committee in 1973. The agreement also extended employment and residency rights to Palestinians and sanctioned Palestinian armed struggle against Israel from Lebanese soil. The Lebanese government unilaterally abrogated the Cairo Agreement in 1987 (al-Natour 1997; J. Suleiman 1999).

16. Laurie Blome Jacobsen and Aziza Khalidi estimate that 6–15 percent of the infrastructure and facilities destroyed during the 1980s have never been repaired or restored (2003, 183). UNRWA has tended to avoid large-scale rehabilitation projects because of inadequate funds and because such initiatives are often interpreted as a precursor to resettlement and therefore politically fraught (Gabiam 2012).

17. In 2005, a line bearing a current of about five amperes at 220 volts for an average of six hours a day cost approximately $12 per month.

18. I am indebted to Karim al-Sabbagh and Amer Saeddine for sharing their report on Shatila's services, which helped clarify the different sources of electricity now available.

19. A World Bank report from 2007 estimated that EdL's deficit in 2006 was close to US $1 billion, more than a fifth of the total government revenues. The report also revealed that as many as 40 percent of households in Lebanon are without meters and do not pay bills (7).

20. This theory was given further credence when, several months later, the EdL levied a number of large fines for electricity brokers who had been illegally sourcing electricity outside the camp and arrested several camp residents.

21. In subsequent parliamentary elections in May and June 2005, Hezbollah increased its parliamentary seats to fourteen. No longer purely a resistance movement, but a political force within the government, Hezbollah assumed responsibility for the Ministry of Energy and Water up until the Lebanon/Israel war in July 2006. Assigning

Hezbollah this role was viewed as a strategic move to compel the party to reform its protectionist policies in the field of energy, notably in Beirut's southern suburbs.

22. State policies often assume "native credulity" to justify the differential treatment and management of the "irrational" poor, while establishing themselves as the source of sovereign rationality (Das 2004, 248).

23. Partha Chatterjee's theory of "political society"—as distinct from civil society— is useful for theorizing political mobilization that occurs outside rights-based electoral politics (2004, 53–78). Relations of governmentality, he suggests, shape not only state policies but also the "politics of the governed." Chatterjee considers how illegal squatter communities in Calcutta, which exist outside state law but are nonetheless subject to it, make claims based on their collective rights as a "demographic category of govern-mentality" (59). By "appealing to the moral rhetoric of a community striving to build a decent social life under extremely harsh conditions" (59–60), marginal sectors of Indian society—like disenfranchised Palestinians—are able to invest the empirical categorizations of government policy with moral content.

24. Syria's interest in retaining control over the Palestinian community in Lebanon is often seen as linked to its efforts to regain the Golan Heights. Supporting the right of return and preserving the Palestinian "refugee file" in Lebanon would allow Syria to use Palestinian refugees as a bargaining chip in future negotiations with Israel (Knudsen 2009, 64).

25. As Bernard Rougier observes, Syrian policy toward Palestinians in Lebanon has been one of "encouraging inter-Palestinian rifts and blocking any possibility of direct negotiation between the Lebanese government and the [Palestinian Authority's] local representatives" (quoted in Hanafi and Long 2010, 138).

26. J. Suleiman 1999, 76. This changed somewhat after the Syrian withdrawal in 2005. During that year the Palestinian embassy was reopened and PLO ambassador Abbas Zaki became responsible for supervising the work of PCs throughout Lebanon and reconciling the factions. The retreat of pro-Syrian factions in Shatila was temporary, however, and Syrian influence was swiftly reasserted.

27. The PC is also accused of issuing building permits for construction that does not conform to code as a way of generating further kickbacks.

28. Doubts were expressed about the selection of twinning committee members and who in the camp stood to benefit from the alliance. Many were concerned that pro-Syrian political factions dominating the committee would use their influence to secure privileges for their own parties.

29. This second committee was led by Abu Mujahed, the founder of Shatila's youth center and a former PFLP leader.

30. After 2000, as relations between Damascus and the PA improved, Fatah reen-tered the camp: its presence was formally recognized in 2005, with the opening of factional offices. The Syrian withdrawal in 2005 and the strengthening of ties between the

PA and the ruling March 14 coalition, under Prime Minister Fouad Siniora, both helped to consolidate Fatah's presence in Beirut.

31. As the context here suggests, the term *sukkan* normally denotes more than the simple fact of residency and refers to the original families, who are presented as the rightful "owners" of the camp.

32. The predictable cost of this local knowledge is the alarming number of electrocutions that occur. During the winter months, overloaded lines, rising floodwater, and exposed wires make electrical work particularly hazardous.

33. In his study of the urban poor in South Africa, Abdoumaliq Simone traces the existence of comparable networks that enable marginal communities to compensate for their disenfranchisement—a phenomenon he calls "people as infrastructure" (2004, 409).

34. Learning how to deal with provisionality and risk produces a "specific economy of perception and collaborative practice . . . constituted through the capacity of individual actors to circulate across, and become familiar with, a broad range of spatial, residential, economic and transactional positions" (Simone 2004, 407).

35. In his analysis of everyday tactics, de Certeau suggests that since these tactics do not have a "proper" place or institution from which to operate, their power is critically dependent on timing (1988).

36. The concept of the Fa'liyyat is an old one. Over the years there have been a number of similar "independent" groups that have tried to resolve everyday concerns. While these shadow committees have intermittently afforded camp residents greater voice and collective force, they have also made political and social authority more diffuse, further complicating the process of problem solving (J. Suleiman 1999).

37. This included guidelines for candidacy applications, voting regulations, and the duties and terms of office for those elected. Only Palestinian men over the age of twenty-one, whose permanent home and place of work was Shatila, and who were not members of any political faction, could register as candidates. Those eligible to vote were Palestinian men and women at least eighteen years of age, and an identification card was required to prove residence to ensure that factions did not send voters from outside the camp (Kortam 2011, 201).

38. Such strategies, which are adopted by the urban poor from Mumbai to Shatila, are "animated by the social relations of shared poverty, by the excitement of active participation in the politics of knowledge," and by an "openness to correction through other forms of intimate knowledge and spontaneous everyday politics" (Appadurai 2002, 35).

39. Following the collapse of the People's Committee, a rival PC was created by Fatah. Since 2005 these competing committees, one led by pro-Syrian Tahaluf parties and the other by PLO-Fatah, have continued to vie for control of the camp. The January 2006 electoral victory of Hamas in the OPT brought further complications for camp governance, as tensions between Fatah loyalists and a growing constituency of Hamas supporters have grown.

CHAPTER 4

1. Ewing argues that the anthropologist's "refusal to believe," in the name of objectivity, raises ethical concerns: "To rule out the possibility of belief in another's reality is to encapsulate that reality and, thus, to implicitly impose the hegemony of one's own view of the world" (1994, 572).

2. "Dream talk" is a concept I have coined to describe an array of discourses and practices associated with dream stories and is not how dreamers themselves refer to these activities.

3. A bias toward the past is arguably a structural principle of anthropology, a discipline that privileges custom, heritage, tradition, and habit over calculation, hope, and expectation. See Arjun Appadurai for more on anthropology's relationship to the past (2004, 60).

4. Jackson 2011, xi. Recent anthropological studies of hope argue that what people hope for and how they hope are socially determined (Hage 2003; Jansen 2006; Lindquist 2006; Miyazaki 2004, 2006). Appadurai (2004) argues that with the growth of global capitalism the "capacity to aspire" has increasingly become conditioned by the capacity to consume, the implication being that the inability of the poor to alter or challenge their material conditions debilitates their aspirational resources in general. Hope is increasingly understood as a function of the ability to save, invest, or engage in financial speculation (Miyazaki 2007). This instrumentalist view of hope, however, reduces complex social and psychological factors to a simple economic logic and occludes other kinds of aspiration and alternative modalities for imagining the future. My analysis of hope here is concerned less with its economic than its existential dimension (not that the two can ever be extricated).

5. The practice of sharing dreams resembles storytelling in Kuranko culture in Sierra Leone. "Storytelling," observes Michael Jackson, "simply by virtue of its being a shared action ... makes possible the momentary semblance of a fusion of disparate and often undisclosed private experiences. It is, therefore, not so much the *substance* of what is said or suggested in a story ... but the very act of participating in a shared event and referring separate experiences to a common source" (2005b, 359).

6. In his study of the Tangu of New Guinea, Kenelm Burridge observed that in Tangu culture dreams "tend to pull a future into current sensible reality; they give definition to hope, adding faith, thereby putting the dreamer in touch with a verity shortly to be manifest" (quoted in Crapanzano 2001, 254).

7. In Islam, angels are thought to be spiritual beings created from light by God, and belief in their existence is one of the six articles of faith: "The Messenger believes in what has been revealed to him from his Lord and so do the believers. All believe in Allah, His Angels, His Books and His Messengers" (Qur'an 2:285).

8. By contrast, in contexts where such opportunities for personal advancement are more readily available, dreaming is often stigmatized as antithetical to work, progress, capitalism, even sanity, encouraging a more private culture of dream.

9. Sigmund Freud writes: "In every sense a dream has its origin in the past. The ancient belief that dreams reveal the future is not indeed entirely devoid of truth. By representing a wish as fulfilled the dream certainly leads us into the future; but this future, which the dreamer accepts as his present, has been shaped in the likeness of the past by the indestructible wish" (1999, 452).

10. Phenomenological and existential critiques of Freudian dream theory offer potentially helpful models for thinking through the limits of a subject-centered, psychoanalytic model and also for conceptualizing dream stories as an anticipatory, future-oriented practice. The existential psychoanalyst Ludwig Binswanger (1986) argues that dreaming is a way of *being* in the world, as much as a means of *thinking* about it. In his introduction to Binswanger's text, Michel Foucault suggests that dreams are a source of imaginative potential that cannot be reduced to mechanistic symbolism or psycho-physiological models; they represent a way of knowing the world (1986, 21).

11. Citing John Lamoreaux's study of Muslim dream literatures, Mittermaier argues that dream visions are valued because they imply access to an external reality, "providing insight not into the dreamer's psyche but into the hidden affairs of the world" (2010, 14).

12. As Al Ghazâli, the twelfth-century Iranian philosopher, writes: "God most high . . . has favored His creatures by giving them something analogous to the special faculty of prophecy, namely dreams. In the dream-state a man apprehends what is to be in the future, which is something of the unseen" (cited in Pandolfo 1997, 355).

13. The distinction between volitional and involuntary dreams can be ambiguous, particularly in cases where the dream appears both to speak to particular concerns and desires of the dreamer and to carry a divine message whose significance extends beyond these concerns.

14. Albert Hourani writes that dreams were believed to "open a door onto a world other than that of the senses." Hourani cites Ibn Khaldun's claim that dream interpretation should be regarded as one of the religious sciences: "When ordinary sense-perception was removed by sleep, the soul could catch a glimpse of its own reality; released from the body, it could receive perceptions from its own world, and when it had done so it could return to the body with them; it could pass its perceptions on to the imagination" (2002, 105).

15. The two terms commonly used for dream interpretation are *ta'bir* and *tafsir*. The former is commonly used in everyday settings and can also refer to verbal expression (particularly of feelings); the latter is associated with the Qur'an and textual commentaries on the meanings of dreams.

16. The word *nafsi* comes from *nafs*, which is usually translated as "self." *Nafs* is associated with emotions, desire, and self-interest. Islamic thought posits an opposition between *nafs* and *'aql* (reason, mind) as integral to human nature (Graw 2006, 100).

17. The influence of Wahhabi and Salafist thinking in Shatila has grown significantly during the last decade, primarily through Saudi-funded mosques and religious initia-

tives. As part of its doctrine of purification and reform through a return to the Qur'an and the *sunna*, Wahhabism contends that since only God has access to the unknown (*al-ghayb*), all forms of divination are irreligious and blasphemous.

18. The belief that the living and dead can communicate is contested. For Wahhabi reformists the separation between the living and the dead is absolute until Judgment Day.

19. The Prophet Muhammad is believed to have interpreted the dreams of his followers, a fact noted in a hadith: "Whenever the Prophet finished the (morning) prayer, he would face us and ask, 'Who amongst you had a dream last night?' So if anyone had seen a dream he would narrate it. The Prophet would say: 'Mashallah'" (Bukhari 2:468).

20. Stephania Pandolfo describes the *barzakh* as "the intermediate resting place of the soul between this world and the other; and there it awaits the last judgment. If the journey—and the absence—is temporary, its memory is the dream" (1997, 184).

21. This supplication is believed to ward off the temptations of Satan and is usually made after having a bad dream or when encountering someone doing something evil (Qur'an 114:1–6).

22. A hadith says that in cases where dreams are inspired by the devil, the dreamer must spit over her left shoulder and seek refuge in God: "A good dream is from Allah, and a bad or evil dream is from Satan; so if anyone of you has a bad dream of which he gets afraid, he should spit on his left side and should seek refuge with Allah from its evil, for then it will not harm him" (Bukhari 9:168).

23. In this instance, dream talk provided a space of other-directed deliberation and speculation, what Susan Reynolds Whyte (in her study of divination and healing in southeastern Uganda) calls "extrospection" (1997, 30).

24. In his study of Moroccan dream practice, Vincent Crapanzano writes: "They [Moroccans] recognize the way this goodness and badness [of dream images] can be transferred to another in at least the first recounting of the dream. They say that to neutralize its effect one should first tell a bad dream to a rock" (2001, 239).

25. The 2002 classification of Palestinians as "foreign students" led to dramatically increased fees for them that few families can afford, preventing the vast majority of Palestinians from studying at university.

26. Pandolfo argues that the evocative ambiguity of dreams often entails "a beading of stories in which real-life situations, the circumstances of dreaming, and the dreams themselves [are] so tightly interwoven as to become inseparable. They were all real" (1997, 185).

27. This attempt to recapture an earlier state of hopefulness and possibility resonates with Henri Bergson's theory of bodily memory, later elaborated in Bourdieu's (1977) notion of *habitus*, in which the body records its own history of sensation and affect separately from the mind. Bodily memory, Bergson argued, continues to exert energy in the present; it is "lived and acted, rather than represented" (1988, 81). In other words, one might be pessimistic in one's analysis of a particular situation yet still retain

a visceral ability to be joyful, or as Gilles Deleuze describes it, in his analysis of Francis Bacon's method of painting, "cerebrally pessimistic but nervously optimistic, with an optimism that believes only in life" (2003, 43).

28. Benedict Anderson argues that prophetic temporalities allow dreamers to reconfigure the real by rupturing "the steady onward clocking of homogenous, empty time" (quoted in Mittermaier 2010, 236).

29. Crapanzano's (1975) study of dream practices in Morocco similarly identifies ways in which dreams can be foundational in the histories people tell about themselves, both in terms of what the dream symbolizes in the trajectory of a person's life and also through the imagery and context that it conjures. See also Pandolfo 1997, 184–185.

30. This fear of making something bad happen by speaking about it can also be aroused by ordinary speech; it is not limited to dreams.

31. Primo Levi (1989), writing about his experiences in a Nazi concentration camp during World War II, notes that what sustained people was not certainty. Levi speculates that had they known what fate awaited them, they would not have been able to carry on from day to day. It was precisely the sense of uncertainty that left space for hope.

32. In his study of illness narratives, Byron Good applies the linguistic analogy of "subjunctivity" to describe this strategy for "trafficking in human possibilities rather than in settled certainties" (1994, 153).

33. Aristotle's definition of hope, as reported by Diogenes Laertius: "What is hope? The dream of an awakened man" (quoted in Desroche 1979, 12).

34. An ethnographic study of hope presents particular methodological difficulties. Hope is often associated with passivity rather than with intentionality and can seem too nebulous a phenomenon for empirical study (Hage 2003); it can also be hard to distinguish from other affects, such as optimism, wishing, and desire (Crapanzano 2004).

35. Recognizing the humanity these aspirations express also requires that we *give* hope. As Ghassan Hage acknowledges, "There is no doubt this is partly what we are talking about when it comes to discussing hospitality towards asylum seekers, or compensation for the colonized indigenous people of the world, or compassion towards the chronically unemployed: the availability, the circulation and the exchange of hope" (2003, 9).

CHAPTER 5

1. Two of every three unemployed Palestinian males are between the ages of eighteen and thirty-five, and 43 percent of unemployed are under twenty-five (Tiltnes 2006).

2. Zygmunt Bauman's (2007, 46) description of refugee camps as spaces of "frozen transience," where there is time but no history, captures the paradoxical state of permanent temporariness and resonates with the terms residents themselves use to describe camp life.

3. Since the abrogation of the Cairo Agreement in 1987, Palestinians have been pro-

hibited from owning weapons and engaging in military activities. Refugees are also prohibited from going to the southern border.

4. In a report produced by Fafo on the living conditions in the camps, the inability to marry or provide for one's family was cited as the primary cause of depression among young men (Tiltnes 2006).

5. Gender research among Palestinians in Lebanon has tended to focus on the experience of women (Peteet 1991; Sayigh 1994). Relatively few scholars have examined men's lives through a gendered lens, though there are some exceptions (Barbosa 2008; Perdigon 2010).

6. These risks are very real and can be life-threatening. In July 2002, a month before I started working in Shatila, a boat bound for Italy capsized off the coast of Greece and more than one hundred people drowned. Four young men from Shatila were among the victims. This incident was often mentioned when people spoke of the dangers of illegal travel.

7. Acknowledging the centrality of imagination in social and cultural life, David Sneath, Martin Holbraad, and Morten Axel Pedersen write, "Imagination can be defined in terms of its irreducibly indeterminate relationship to the processes that precipitate it (i.e., its 'technologies')" (2009, 6). I take the social and material practices associated with emigration to be technologies through which particular imaginings are generated in this context.

8. Due to the particularities of the Palestinian refugee case, and the absence of any institution responsible for protecting the individual rights of Palestinians, interpretation of their status tends to be ad hoc, and decided on a case-by-case basis, making it harder for refugees to comprehend or anticipate what awaits them (Akram 2002, 43).

9. In a recent study of migration from the camps as a coping strategy, Are Hovdenak (1997) lists Kuwait, Saudi Arabia, and the smaller Gulf States of the United Arab Emirates, Qatar, Bahrain, and Oman as the primary destinations for Palestinian emigrants during this period.

10. The tightening of employment restrictions for Palestinians in Lebanon in the 1970s and poor living conditions, however, raise the question of how "voluntary" the decision to migrate was (Shami 1993).

11. There is a lack of reliable statistics on the number of refugees who migrated during these two phases. Many emigrants never declared citizenship elsewhere, fearing they would lose their right to compensation and return in any final settlement, and therefore retained their UNRWA refugee status and residency permits. Illegal emigration in recent years has also made reliable figures elusive. Household surveys conducted by Fafo, however, suggest that the majority of Palestinian households in camps and gatherings have close relatives abroad (Hovdenak 1997).

12. The growing concern about increased numbers of unwanted migrants and asylum seekers is normally attributed to the European Union Act (1985), which abol-

ished internal border controls within the EU and allowed for free movement between member states, and conflicts in the Balkans, which led to an influx of asylum seekers from southeastern Europe to Western Europe (Bloch, Galvin, and Schuster 2000; Fassin 2005; Hollifield 1992).

13. The agreements between EU member states, such as the Schengen Agreement (1985) and the Dublin II regulation (2003), aimed at preventing asylum seekers from submitting multiple applications to EU member states, have served to intensify surveillance of migrants and played an important role in management and control of irregular migration.

14. Article 1D of the 1951 Convention states that it "shall not apply to persons who are at present receiving from organs or agencies of the United Nations other than the United Nations High Commissioner for Refugees protection or assistance" (UNHCR 2007, 11). See also Akram 2002; Takkenberg 1998.

15. The UNCCP's role was to protect the political rights of Palestinian refugees and implement a durable solution by ensuring Israel's recognition of internationally binding agreements regarding the right of return.

16. W. Said 2003. Since Lebanon is not a signatory to the 1951 Convention, the 1967 Protocol, or to conventions protecting the rights of stateless people, the government has also been able to deny basic civil and human rights to Palestinians. Whatever benefits are granted to Palestinians are therefore framed as "privileges" rather than rights and can be revoked at any time (Akram 2002, 42).

17. Article 1A(2) states that a refugee is a person with a "well-founded fear of being persecuted for reasons of race, religion, nationality, membership in a particular group or political opinion, is outside the country of his nationality, and is unable, or, owing to such fear, is unwilling, to avail himself of the protection of that country; or who, not having a nationality and being outside the country of his former habitual residence as a result of such events, is unable or, owing to such fear, is unwilling to return to it."

18. A number of scholars (Anderson and Ruhs 2010; De Genova 2002) rightly argue that terms like "illegality" and "clandestine" in refugee and migration law are social and political constructs used by governments and state institutions to criminalize irregular or undocumented migrants. In seeking to distinguish between citizens and noncitizens, immigration law determines "sanctioned identities" (Collier, Maurer, and Suárez-Navez 1995), naturalizes and criminalizes contingent categories of "illegality," and works to conceal the complex processes that compel people to move as well as the geopolitical contexts that define who belongs and who does not (Bloch and Chimienti 2011; Coutin 2000; Tyler 2006).

19. The drive to emigrate has led to an increasing number of arranged marriages in camp communities. Sylvain Perdigon's study of intimacy and kinship in Jal al-Bahar, a Palestinian Bedouin gathering in South Lebanon, examines how the ideal of marriage guided by the moral codes of *al-ma'rifah* (the mutual knowledge of both parties) is giving way

to a more instrumental understanding, in which marriage to a foreigner or first cousin is validated "by the escape it permits from the biopolitics of the refugee regime" (2010, 104).

20. This desire to emigrate is shared by Lebanese youth. In a recent study of Lebanon's postwar generation, Jad Chaaban (2009) found that one-third of youth wished to emigrate.

21. The few women I met who were able to leave legally were either sponsored by relatives abroad or had obtained residency elsewhere through marriage.

22. As camp communities have come increasingly to rely on remittances, émigrés sometimes counter the charge of abandoning cherished national goals by suggesting that emigration offers a more tangible way of supporting the national movement, even if it may be revising its terms in the process.

23. Sayigh encountered a similar desire to emigrate among youth in Burj al-Barajneh camp. In field notes from January 2010, she records the despair of one young man from the camp: "We can do nothing now, we can barely take breath. . . . We need to secure our economic situation. Young people think only of emigration but there's no road open. No one has thought for Palestine. The factions that represent the Palestinian people can't do anything—they express the helplessness of the leadership. Everyone dreams of return but they know it's not possible" (2011b, 8).

24. The Schengen Agreement was first signed by Germany, France, Belgium, the Netherlands, and Luxembourg in 1985, as the first step in dismantling border controls within Europe to facilitate free movement of labor, goods, and services. In 1990, the convention applying the Schengen Agreement was signed by all EU member states, with the exception of the UK and Ireland (Bloch, Galvin, and Schuster 2000).

25. The question of volition is central to the definition of who is a "refugee." In both legal and scholarly definitions, economic reasons for migrating are normatively viewed as voluntary, and political ones as involuntary (Hayden 2006; Zolberg, Suhrke, and Aguayo 1989).

26. Ayn al-Hilweh camp is about forty kilometers south of Beirut, on the outskirts of Sidon.

27. As the Lebanese minister of foreign affairs openly acknowledged in 1994, discrimination against Palestinians is part of an official state policy to compel them to emigrate permanently (Bocco and Husseini 2010, 270), making the recent surge in emigration simply another instance of forced displacement.

28. My own experience of working for a UK-based solicitor on a number of appeal cases of Palestinians from Lebanon denied asylum by the British Home Office (HO) revealed the extent to which claims centering on factional feuds within the camps—now one of the few bases on which a case for political asylum can be made—are increasingly not recognized as valid. As an "expert witness," my task was to examine and assess the reasons for the HO's refusal. In all the cases I worked on, the HO ignored the political discrimination faced by Palestinians in Lebanon and rejected evidence supporting

claims of torture and other persecution. When petitions were dismissed on grounds that the reasons for migration were economic rather than political, the political discrimination producing chronic unemployment and poverty in the first place was ignored. HO refusal statements read like checklists for exclusion and betrayed an ingrained skepticism about the applicant's claims. This skepticism was also reflected in the way that applicant statements were closely scrutinized for discrepancies and inconsistencies, however slight, and in the distrust elicited by narratives of misfortune and physical suffering, often deemed to be "inauthentic" and overstated. Evidence of suffering and persecution was necessary, but it seemed there shouldn't be too much of it.

29. Jackson writes that it is at such moments that "the logic of imagination loses touch with the logic of social practice [and] desperate fantasies are born" (2005a, xxiv).

30. Invoking the work of Agamben (1995, 1998), a number of scholars argue that the political rights of refugees are increasingly superseded by a globalized humanitarianism, in which it is the supposedly apolitical "bare life" of the suffering body that counts rather than the political body (Chávez 2011; Diken 2004; Fassin 2001, 2005; Tyler 2006). Miriam Ticktin's work on the "sans papiers in France, and the growing number of refugees willing to self-infect with HIV in order to gain asylum under the 'illness clause' (a recent addition to French asylum law), offers the most striking example of the way asylum seekers and undocumented immigrants are being forced to 'trade biological integrity for political recognition'" (2006, 33).

31. As Steve Caton and Bernardo Zacka observe, a border "can strip a person naked. . . . Or, it can, instead, flatten itself out and become a simple line that can be easily crossed without any loss of dignity" (2010, 209).

32. Mariane Ferme writes that the arbitrariness with which sovereignty is exercised at borders "tell[s] us much about the shifting contours of state interests in different subjects and territories" (2004, 89), the meaning of citizenship, and who belongs and who doesn't.

33. This particular anecdote, in which the asylum officer accused Fathi of being a freeloader before having heard his testimony, is a measure of the shifts in the popular perception of asylum seekers in the UK. The figure of the "illegal immigrant" has become the bogeyman of the current refugee regime. The language used to describe asylum seekers in the mainstream media often employs images of greed and duplicity: they are presented as "queue jumpers" and "leeches" with "bogus" claims who threaten to "swamp" the system (Tyler 2006).

34. ARC cards are an automated fingerprint technology introduced in December 2000, replacing the Standard Acknowledgement Letter previously issued to asylum seekers, which was considered too easy to forge.

35. The revisions to welfare assistance provided to asylum seekers introduced under the Immigration and Asylum Act 1999 (implemented November 1999) were designed to be harsh enough to deter asylum seekers from claiming asylum. The changes to the right

to work after making an asylum application have had a particularly devastating impact (Bloch, Galvin, and Schuster 2000).

36. This semilegal status is similar to the Temporary Protected Status (TPS) granted to certain nationalities, or to stateless aliens in the United States, or the temporary residence permits granted in Germany and elsewhere in Europe. Tina Gehrig (2004) has examined the performative work of legal categories, in particular how "temporary" status has been used by the German state to classify and manage Afghan asylum seekers and delegitimize their claims.

37. Fassin 2005; Malkki 1996. DL is a status that, along with Humanitarian Protection (HP), replaced Exceptional Leave to Remain (ELR) in April 2003.

38. A recent study by Marwan Khawaja found that nearly 80 percent of refugee households in the camps in Lebanon have relatives abroad (2003, 51).

39. The existential aspects of migration and the role that expectation and imagination play in the migratory project have been addressed in recent anthropological works by Ferguson (1999, 2007); Graw (2012); Graw and Schielke (2012); Hage and Papadoulos (2004); Jackson (2007, 2008); Mains (2007); Pandolfo (2007); Potts (2010); and Vigh (2009).

40. Arendt 1973. "We became aware of the existence of a right to have rights . . . and a right to belong to some kind of organized community," Arendt observed, "only when millions of people emerged who had lost and could not regain these rights because of the new global political situation" (296). It is one of many ironies that the events leading to the creation of the modern refugee regime, and an awareness of the importance of protecting the rights of stateless persons, produced in their wake the Palestinian refugee community, one of the largest and longest-standing refugee populations in the world today, whose rights the international community have consistently misrecognized and failed to uphold.

41. Balibar 2004; Isin 2008, 2009. Engin Isin writes that the intensification of flow of people has "generated new affinities, identifications, loyalties, animosities and hostilities across borders. . . . Various processes have combined to produce new, if not paradoxical, subjects of law and action, new subjectivities and identities, new sites of struggle and new scales of identification" (2008, 16).

42. Roger Zetter, writing about Cypriot refugees, observes that home "represents not just physically bounded space, but a living organism of relationships and traditions stretching back into the past" (1999, 12). See also Jansen 2006.

CHAPTER 6

1. Dan Rabinowitz critiques the logic of return, describing it as Augustinian: "Contemporary physical reality is but a corridor to a metaphysical universe where the important business of salvation can actually take place" (2008, 229). See also Malkki on the construction of refugees as people "out of place" in nationalist discourse (1995b, 512).

2. There are some exceptions: see Gabiam 2012; al-Hardan 2012.

3. There is a vast body of scholarship and policy literature on the right of return. Among the more prominent texts are Abunimah 2006; Abu Sitta 1997, 2001, 2006; Akram 2002; Aruri 2001; Chiller-Glaus 2007; Dumper 2007; Ghandour 2001; Hanafi 2002, 2005; Jarrar 2003; W. Khalidi 1992; Lustick and Lesch 2005; Masalha 2003; Nabulsi 2001; Qumsiyeh 2004; Rempel 1999; W. Said 2001; Shikaki 2003a; J. Suleiman 2001; Takkenberg 1998; Tamari 1996; Zureik 2002.

4. Abu Sitta writes, "The Right of Return is sacred to all Palestinians. It has remained their fundamental objective since 1948" (2001, 15).

5. The talismanic prominence of the key to lost homes in both discourses exemplifies the reification of refugee aspirations. For right-of-return activists, the key represents steadfastness; for many Israelis, it represents existential fears; for both, the monolithic intention of all refugees to return is unquestioned, a given.

6. In a 2005 study, Tiltnes estimated that first-generation refugees represent about 12 percent of the population.

7. Avishai Margalit's work on the ethics of memory in the wake of the Holocaust, and the tension between the duty to remember and the desire to forget, resonates with my own findings on attitudes toward return in Shatila. Reconstructing an argument between his parents, Margalit recalls his mother's assertion that the "only honorable role for Jews that remain is to form communities of memory—to serve as 'soul candles.'" Margalit's father responds by questioning this obligation to keep alive memories of injustice: "We, the remaining Jews, are people, not candles. . . . Better to create a community that thinks predominantly about the future and reacts to the present, not a community that is governed from mass graves" (2002, viii–ix).

8. In his study of kin networks and rural attachments among Palestinians in Kuwait, Shafeeq Ghabra writes, "It is meaningless . . . to identify a Palestinian family in isolation from its village of origin" (quoted in Johnson 2006, 56).

9. In their recent study of Beirut's Burj al-Barajneh camp, Rima Afifi and Maya El Shareef found that Palestinian youth "spoke of identity in relation to a collective movement for a Palestinian state, rather than the 'I' as other youth did" (2010, 36).

10. In recent years, activists, scholars, and NGOs working to advance refugee rights have begun to focus, in a more rigorous and detailed way, on what return might actually look like if implemented. The stated goal of a 2013 Right of Return Conference held at Boston University—to "open the floor to a multiplicity of visions" and "grapple with the practical implications of the Right's fulfillment"—is representative of this shift from justification to logistics. (The full text of the mission statement is available at http://rightofreturn.net/mission-statement.) See also Hanafi (2010), Husseini and Bocco (2009), Salih (2013), and the joint initiative of BADIL and the Israeli activist organization Zochrot to explore the specific stages of return, published in 2012.

11. Rabinowitz 2008, 230. Abu Sitta (2001), the Palestinian geographer and right-

of-return advocate, argues for the physical feasibility of comprehensive return for all refugees, but he doesn't say how it would be implemented.

12. Roger Zetter's (1999), Stef Jansen's (2006), and Daniel Warner's (1994) work on the meaning of "home" and "return" in exilic communities raises important questions about the disarticulations and transformations that repatriation often entails.

13. Although the right of return has consistently been a core component of the national struggle, its meaning and political symbolism have evolved over time. Introduced into the PLO charter in 1967 and formally recognized by the Palestinian National Council (PNC) in 1974, it was only in 1988 that the PLO articulated return as a legal right to be achieved through negotiations rather than military liberation (Klein 2005, 91).

14. Mohammed Bamyeh makes a similar point when he argues that return should be understood less literally as a concept "used by various generations of Palestinians not as a standard reference to a necessary physical eventuality, but more like a 'common heuristic or a candlelight, to summarize or shed light on common suffering'" (2003, 842).

15. Tariq's views are, doubtless, in part shaped by his own loyalty to Fatah and the Palestinian Authority.

16. Refugee doubts about return date back as early as 1951, when the director of UNRWA observed that desire for it was "general among all classes" but added a significant caveat: "Many refugees are ceasing to believe in a possible return, yet this does not prevent them from insisting on it, since they feel that to agree to consider any other solution would be to show their weakness and to relinquish their fundamental right" (quoted in Husseini and Bocco 2009, 282).

17. "Letter From President Bush to Prime Minister Sharon," April 14, 2004, The White House Archive, http://georgewbush-whitehouse.archives.gov/news/releases/2004/04/20040414-3.html.

18. Given Fatima's own history of loss—her fiancé was killed during the Israeli bombardment of Nabatiyyeh camp in 1973, and she lost eight members of her immediate family during the Sabra and Shatila massacre in 1982—this recognition of a common humanity and a shared destiny seemed particularly remarkable.

19. The sociologist Bassem Sirhan wrote in 1975 that refugees "have lost neither their social consciousness nor their family ties, and if they returned tomorrow, this extraordinarily tenacious social factor would be of the greatest importance in the rapid reconstruction of Palestinian society" (1975, 101). See also Peteet 1995.

20. Mohammad Doraï argues that camps no longer function as preservers of Palestinian national identity: "Far from being only spaces of memory, the camps became the place of social change and construction of a Palestinian society in exile, reinforcing its cohesion, but also rich in their multiple experiences in various locations" (2010, 90). See also Hanafi 2010.

21. This "peasantization" campaign also enabled the national resistance movement to establish ties to the leaders of the Great Revolt of 1936–1939, as well as promote greater

unity by obscuring persistent class differences and the predominantly urban middle-class male orientation of the national leadership (Sayigh 2008). During this period the figure of the "peasant as signifier" (*fellah*), bound to land, family, and rural tradition, became pervasive in nationalist discourse and culture (Swedenburg 1990).

22. Rabab Abdulhadi has written about the impact of the Oslo Accords on Palestinian activism and identity in exile, arguing that "it was a time for Palestinians to regroup and take stock. . . . No longer viewed as part of inclusive Palestinianness, Palestinians on the outside (of the areas controlled by the Palestinian Authority) were now seen as marginal to the Palestinian collectivity. . . . Oslo signaled a need to reconfigure what Palestinianness meant to displaced Palestinians" (2004, 250–251).

23. In 2001, only two independent right-of-return organizations existed in Lebanon: 'A'idun (The Returnee), founded in 2000, and the PHRO. While 'A'idun's goal was to raise political awareness about return and, more broadly, to create a "culture of return" through cultural activities and grassroots mobilization, the collective was run by volunteers with limited resources and its impact was small. 'A'idun's membership, mainly Palestinian intellectuals and activists based outside the camps, may also have contributed to its low profile. In the case of PHRO, its broad mandate (documenting all rights abuses in the camps in Lebanon) also limited its focus on return.

24. This stands in sharp contrast to the situation in Syria, where there has been an active RoRM in the camps (Gabiam 2012; al-Hardan 2012).

25. In her study of the RoRM in Palestinian camps in Damascus, Anaheed al-Hardan noted similar perceptions of RoRM initiatives as entrepreneurial: "The abundance of RoRM groups—fully or semi-independent, factionally affiliated or not—has led many to remark on (private) 'right-of-return corner shops [*dakakin*]' that 'trade' on the right of return" (2012, 70).

26. The UN bid for statehood in 2011 was met with skepticism by refugees for the same reason. See Ali Nayel 2011a.

27. In a much-cited passage in *The Origins of Totalitarianism*, Arendt argued that during the interwar period the world became aware of the right to have rights only through the emergence of a new category of human being, the stateless refugee. Deprived of citizenship and forced to live outside recognized political and legal structures, refugees had not simply had their rights violated but lost them altogether. To live outside the political community, in other words, was to be expelled from humanity (1973, 295–297).

28. Elazar Barkan argues that the PLO's decision to reframe return as a legal right under international law—thereby placing it on the "higher moral plateau" of rights—has only served to increase the stakes and compound the deadlock over the responsibility for the refugees (2005, 88).

29. Sari Hanafi (2002) argues for the need to distinguish between what he calls "the sociology of return" (i.e., the political and historical symbolism that has come to be associated with this right) and its physical implementation.

30. The Palestine Papers, leaked in January 2011 and detailing Israeli-Palestinian peace negotiations from 1999 to 2010, revealed the PA's readiness to cede the right of return, consider the permanent resettlement of refugees, and accept the return of only a token number of refugees (Swisher 2011), as did the PA's bid for statehood in November 2011, which if territorially rendered would comprise less than 10 percent of historic Palestine (Massad 2011).

31. A number of advocacy campaigns centered on the right to work—notably, the UNRWA-backed Committee for the Employment of Palestinian Refugees in Lebanon (CEP) and the Palestinian-Lebanese Coalition for the Right to Work—have challenged the government's claim that giving Palestinians the right to work would undermine their political rights, or lead ineluctably to their permanent resettlement. In October 2005, the government established the Lebanese-Palestinian Dialogue Committee (LPDC), an interministerial consultative advisory body, to address poor living conditions in the camps and initiate discussion on sensitive refugee-related issues; though this indicated a growing willingness to address the question of Palestinian civic rights, it has yet to produce results. Few refugees in Shatila seemed to have heard of the LPDC, and those who had were skeptical of its ability to implement change. For more on the LPDC's work, see http://www.lpdc.gov.lb/HomeLPDC.aspx?lang=en-us.

32. In 2010 a group of independent activists, under the direction of Palestinian sociologist Sari Hanafi, coordinated a march for civil rights in Beirut. While organizers tried to involve the factions, political leaders condemned the march and refused to participate, viewing the initiative as a challenge to their authority. The march was timed to coincide with a proposal put before the Lebanese Parliament that sought to improve living conditions in the camps by granting Palestinian refugees the right to work. This legislation was passed in Parliament, but it has yet to be implemented.

33. Shikaki argued that his research in no way undermined the right of return but merely suggested that its recognition did not carry the kinds of risks Israel has long claimed. In a *Wall Street Journal* editorial responding to his critics, Shikaki wrote: "Some among the Palestinians and the Israelis will resist the logic embodied in the findings of my surveys. By doing so, they will perpetuate the conflict indefinitely. Those . . . seeking to prevent the release of the surveys' findings acted on the belief that sacred rights cannot be tampered with, not even by other refugees, let alone researchers. This unhealthy obsession with idealized rights at the expense of vital, or even existential, needs threatens to perpetuate the suffering of millions of refugees. Rights and suffering need not go together, not for so long" (2003b, A12).

34. When the delegation met with Prime Minister Najib Mikati, he acknowledged the need to improve humanitarian conditions in the camps, adding that if the PA were to issue refugees with identity papers, he would propose that Lebanon grant them work permits. MP Michael Connarty passed Mikati's comments on to faction representatives and found himself immediately rebuffed: "The instant plea that 'Israel would not allow it' from Pales-

tinian organizations opened my eyes further to the degree to which the ability to deal with, or use the Palestinians as victims in Lebanon may be preferred to actually viewing their abused position as a problem that requires workable solutions" (quoted in Charles 2011).

35. For descriptions of the march, see Ali Nayel 2011b; Cassel 2011; Samaha 2011.

36. A representative online editorial maintained that "in this moment of seemingly unlimited possibility, where Al-Awda ('The Return') suddenly moves from a nostalgic imaginary to something both tangible and realisable, we are forced to engage in new ways with the spatial, political and social landscapes of Israel-Palestine. Instead of asking 'can we return?' or 'when will we return?' Palestinians are suddenly allowed to ask 'what kind of return do we want to create for ourselves?'" "Planning Al-Awda: Reimagining the Spatial Contours of Israel-Palestine," http://arenaofspeculation.org, May 18, 2011.

37. The only formal complaint came from Mounib Al Masri, a wealthy and influential figure in Palestinian politics, who filed a case against Israel after his grandson was shot during the march.

38. The border protests' power to inspire new forms of activism was manifest in the rebuilding of the village of Iqrit in August 2012, when a group of third-generation refugees returned to their ancestral village (Sherwood 2013).

39. In Ruba Salih's article published in *Jadaliyya* on March 26, 2013, she argues that Palestinian refugees are once again becoming the political vanguard, articulating a new political vision that challenges an earlier liberal consensus of state-civil relations. Salih writes: "Palestinian refugees are forming a 'political society,' composed of new claims, narratives, and political practices, which they base on a broader moral and political ground than that of nationalism and the nation-state." The 2011 border protests would seem to be an expression of the new political society Salih describes. See http://www.jadaliyya.com/pages/index/10814/reconciling-return-and-rights_palestinian-refugees.

40. Isin 2008; McNevin 2011; Nyers 2003; Rancière 2004. Peter Nyers (2003, 1078) has examined how noncitizen communities (refugees and nonstatus migrants) challenge their characterization as invisible, voiceless victims through "acts of citizenship" that assert their right to speak and be heard—and by extension, their right to exist as political subjects by embodying qualities associated with citizens. Isin also makes a case for the performative dimension of citizenship and regards acts of citizenship as those moments when "regardless of status and substance, subjects constitute themselves as citizens—or, better still, those to whom the right to have rights is due" (2008, 18). See also McNevin's analysis of the limitations of citizenship as a rubric for imagining paralegal political contestation and emergent forms of political practice and belonging (2011, 99–102).

41. William Walters's idea of "acts of demonstration" is also helpful for theorizing political interventions in which noncitizen subjects contest the political status quo but do not make claims in the name of citizenship. Acts of demonstration occur when "injustice is revealed, a relationship to power is contested, or a particular wrong is protested, but when the identity of the subjects at the heart of the protest is left relatively open" (2008, 194).

42. For more about current debates regarding representation and the role of the PLO, see Abdulhadi 2012; Khalil 2013; Nasrallah 2012.

43. The 2006 Civitas Project, directed by Karma Nabulsi at Nuffield College, Oxford, sought to facilitate communication between the PA and its constituencies in the diaspora and revive the PLO. More recently the Kamel al-Sawt al-Falasteeni Campaign, organized by a network of local and international activist groups, civil society organizations, and academics based in Lebanon, called for PNC elections as a way of involving refugee communities in the political process and as a first step to reforming the PLO.

44. A Palestinian American friend (and an activist herself) made the point that these individuals also often claim to speak on behalf of Palestinians in their own communities. "It isn't exclusive to Lebanon. It is a dynamic of pro-Palestinian organizing that has emerged in the aftermath of the dissolution of popular mobilization within Palestinian communities across the diaspora. The cynicism of Palestinians in the camps regarding self-anointed advocates is similar to that of a Palestinian in Chicago facing FBI surveillance, and finding everyone wanting to talk on his behalf but no one wanting to help pay his legal bills."

45. In his account of a 1999 workshop convened as part of the Ottawa process on refugee compensation, Terry Rempel (a researcher from BADIL, a right-of-return center based in Bethlehem) noted that many of the participants found the very topic distasteful. In the words of one discussant, "The homeland [is] not for sale" (1999, 41).

46. Hage has described how "a specific politico-affective conception of the sources of society's ills that a radical subjectivity has invested itself in struggling against" can count for more, in that subjectivity's estimation, than an empirical analysis of same (2012, 291).

47. The lecture took place in January 2012 and was given by Rabab Abdulhadi, a self-identified activist scholar.

48. See the work of Allesandro Petti, Sandi Hillal, and the Decolonizing Architecture and Art Residency (DAAR) collective, and the online project Arena of Speculation (arenaofspeculation.org), both of which explore architecture and urban planning as forms of spatial resistance; Visualizing Palestine, which uses creative visual practices as advocacy (http://visualizingpalestine.org/Disappearing-Palestine); al-Shabaka's newly created policy circle for "reframing return" (Barclay and Qaddumi 2012); a practical "Manual of Return" published by #3awda: Palestine, Present and Future (3awda.org), an online collective that "calls on activists, artists, creative professionals, community organisers and entrepreneurs to engage in initiatives and to share in the shaping of a new vision towards return"; and the online campaign "When I Return" (http://wheni return.uspcn.org), which is coordinated by the US Palestinian Community Network and solicits testimonials registering "the daily resonance of the Nakba, as not only a vanishing memory to be commemorated but a persistent moment binding us to our past, our present and to each other."

49. Joseph Massad argues that de facto acceptance of Israel's rejectionist position in mainstream discourse on the right of return has led to the troubling view that "everything Israel rejects is 'not pragmatic,' while everything it accepts is 'pragmatic'" (2001, 108).

50. In his essay "Secular Criticism," Edward Said insists that critical thinking is not opposed to solidarity but essential to it: "The history of thought, to say nothing of political movements, is extravagantly illustrative of how the dictum 'solidarity before criticism' means the end of criticism. I take criticism so seriously as to believe that, even in the very midst of battle in which one is unmistakably on one side against another, there should be criticism, because there must be critical consciousness if there are to be issues, problems, values, even lives to be fought for" (1983, 28).

CONCLUSION

1. What Bourdieu calls "the paradox of doxa" allows dominant conceptual orders to appear natural and immutable, simultaneously a product of the social order and beyond its influence (2001, 1).

2. Sylvain Perdigon argues that the category of identity is less pertinent to Palestinian refugees than usually imagined. "We should be wary of the self-evident relevance that the category of identity has gained in the language of social science. . . . [It] pertains to a specific genealogy: the liberal imaginary of a self-making subject anxiously apprehending the constraints placed upon her by various kinds of inheritances. . . . When we assume that our interlocutors . . . share our concerns for, referents for, and ways of inheriting the category of 'identity,' we might be assuming a lot" (2010, 97).

3. Drawing on the work of phenomenologist Maurice Merleau-Ponty, the Palestinian scholar Lena Jayyusi has coined the term "*in-vivo* subjectivity" for states of being in which places in Palestine are remembered through reference to bodily experience (2007, 121).

4. This particular trip was recorded in Mai Masri's 2001 documentary *Dreams of Exile* (*Ahlam al Menfa*), and forms the climactic scene. The uncertainties generated by the experience do not form part of the film's narrative.

5. This proposal to re-create Shatila in Palestine appears to be a recurrent motif representing the strength of communal ties. Peteet describes a similar story that circulated in the 1990s, in which a young boy dreams of refugees from Shatila returning to Palestine and choosing not to resettle in their ancestral villages but rather to rebuild Shatila. Peteet traces the origin of this dream narrative back to a documentary made by Syrian director Mohammed Malas in the 1980s (2005, 217).

6. Philip Misselwitz and Sari Hanafi have written of the need to reconceptualize refugee camps. In light of recent "de-tabooization" of camp rehabilitation programs, they argue that camp improvement projects might be the first step toward greater civil and economic integration of refugee communities. Refugees, they suggest, would be able to live in appropriate living conditions in these "refugee cities," without losing their status as refugees (2009, 361–388).

7. Arendt writes: "The new beginning inherent in birth can make itself felt in the world only because the newcomer possesses the capacity of beginning something anew, that is, of acting. In this sense of initiative, an element of action, and therefore of natality, is inherent in all human activities" (1958, 9).

8. As the phenomenologist Edward Casey argues, the physical place of community is of enduring significance because it draws together "experiences and histories, even languages and thoughts" (1997, 24).

9. Given the larger political and rhetorical contexts of the Israel-Palestine conflict, the wariness regarding any analytical rubric that could be seen to question the essential unity of national belonging is understandable. Sayigh, meanwhile, points out that in the absence of national institutions, "subjective feelings of 'commonality,' 'sameness' and 'unity' must substitute for a fully recognized 'identification'" (2011b, 2).

10. Sayigh 2004, 9. In a recent collection of essays on Palestinians in Lebanon, Muhammad Ali Khalidi and Diane Riskedahl recognize local loyalties but conclude that refugees "do not regard such links as competing with their identification with Palestine or their specific places of origin in Palestine. . . . Refugees express pride in their camps and the lives they have built in them, all the while stressing their impermanence and temporary character" (2010, 7).

11. The assault on the northern camp of Nahr al-Bared in 2007, which essentially razed it, belied claims that camps exist beyond the reach of Lebanese sovereignty. The conflict between the Lebanese army and the largely non-Palestinian group that sought cover in the camp revealed in dramatically brutal fashion the extent to which camp communities are subject to government force and surveillance.

12. Isin's (2008) theory of acts of citizenship, when new forms of citizenship are brought into being by being enacted, is useful for theorizing how subjects outside a formal political order of entitlements and rights go about rupturing it.

13. Chatterjee's theory of the "politics of the governed" provides a useful model for examining the political agency of marginalized "paralegal" groups. Questioning the usefulness of a Western liberal political tradition, or the "utopian politics of classical nationalism," for understanding political agency in marginalized communities (2004, 23), Chatterjee analyzes how squatters, migrants, and the homeless in Calcutta are able to challenge normative politics by basing their demands not on their rights as citizens but on their moral entitlements as a subject "population." The form their resistance takes, in other words, is an outgrowth of the techniques of governmentality through which the state has sought to classify and control them.

14. This particular incident resembled what William Walters calls "an act of demonstration," where subjects contest a particular relationship with power but do not act in the name of citizenship, or where citizenship is explicitly refused. Such acts occur when the presence of the witness cannot be taken for granted and when the act "appeals to an audience which is not already there" but yet to come (2008, 203).

15. The phrase "strategic essentialism" is attributed to postcolonial, feminist theorist Gayatri Spivak, who argued that while essentialist categories of identity should be subject to vigorous critique, they are sometimes necessary to retrieve subaltern consciousness and to promote minority rights, so long as they are applied "in a scrupulously visible political interest" (1987, 205).

16. Addressing the "pitfalls" of identity politics in cultural studies, historian Paul Gilroy calls on scholars to recognize that "identity formation . . . is a chaotic process that can have no end. In this way, we may be able to make cultural identity a premise for political action rather than a substitute for it" (1996, 238).

17. Dewey, in his seminal book *Art as Experience*, differentiates between perception that is "fresh and alive" and what he calls "recognition," which is perception that has been "arrested at the point where it will serve some *other* purpose." While the former is about learning to appreciate the significance of a particular work through an intimate, sensory engagement with the medium itself, the latter involves learning to read the cues of cultural convention: "We recognize a man on the street in order to greet or to avoid him," writes Dewey, "not so as to see him for the sake of seeing what is there" (1934, 54).

18. In his essay on the role played by transnationalism, diaspora, and deterritorialization in the Palestinian-Israeli conflict, Rabinowitz questions the feasibility of nonterritorial notions of belonging, identity, and affiliation in a context where both sides are "in the thick of nation-building frenzy" and far from what could be called a "postnational" position (2000, 767).

19. Arguing for the political importance of a "deeper and more differentiated politics of identification," James Clifford writes: "Effective democratic mobilizations begin where people are (not where they 'should be'): they work through the cultural discourses that situate groups, that provide them with roots (always spliced), with narrative connections between past and present (traditions), with distinctive social habits and bodies" (2000, 97).

REFERENCES

Abboud, S. 2009. "The Siege of Nahr al-Bared and the Palestinian Refugees in Lebanon." *Arab Studies Quarterly* 31 (1–2): 21–48.

Abdulhadi, Rabab. 2012. "Debating Palestine: Representation, Resistance, and Liberation." Al-Shabaka, April 5. Available at http://al-shabaka.org/debating-palestine-rep resentation-resistance-and-liberation?page=show.

———. 2004. "Activism and Exile: Palestinianness and the Politics of Solidarity." In *Local Actions: Cultural Activism, Power and Public Life*, edited by Melissa Checker and Maggie Fishman, 231–253. New York: Columbia University Press.

Abdulrahim, Sawsan, and Marwan Khawaja. 2011. "The Cost of Being Palestinian in Lebanon." *Journal of Ethnic and Migration Studies* 37 (1): 151–166.

Abufarha, Nasser. 2009. *The Making of a Human Bomb: An Ethnography of Palestinian Resistance*. Durham, NC: Duke University Press.

Abu Lughod, Lila. 1991. "Writing against Culture." In *Recapturing Anthropology: Working in the Present*, edited by R. Fox, 137–162. Santa Fe, NM: School of American Research Press.

———. 1990. "The Romance of Resistance: Tracing Transformations of Power through Bedouin Women." *American Ethnologist* 17 (1): 41–55.

Abu Nahleh, Lamis. 2006. "Six Families: Survival and Mobility in Times of Crisis." In *Living Palestine: Family Survival, Resistance and Mobility under Occupation*, edited by Lisa Taraki, 103–184. Syracuse, NY: Syracuse University Press.

Abunimah, Ali. 2006. *One Country: A Bold Proposal to End the Israeli-Palestinian Conflict*. New York: Henry Holt.

Abu Sitta, Salman. 2006. "Reversing Ethnic Cleansing: The Right to Return Home." Palestine Land Society, June 6. Available at http://www.plands.org/articles/020.html.

———. 2004. *The Atlas of Palestine*. London: Palestine Land Society and Palestinian Return Center.

———. 2001. *The End of the Palestinian-Israeli Conflict: From Refugees to Citizens at Home*. London: Palestinian Return Center.

———. 2000. *The Palestinian Nakba 1948: The Register of Depopulated Localities in Palestine*. London: Palestine Return Center.

———. 1997. "The Feasibility of the Right of Return." In *The Palestinian Exodus*, edited by Ghada Karmi and Eugene Cotran, 171–196. Reading, UK: Ithaca Press.

Afifi, Rima, and Maya El Shareef. 2010. "How Do Palestinian Youth in the Diaspora Self-Identify? The Case of Burj al-Barajneh Camp in Lebanon." In *The Lived Reality of Palestinian Refugees in Lebanon*, edited by Muhammad Ali Khalidi, 35–45. Beirut: Institute of Palestine Studies.

Agamben, Giorgio. 2000. *Means without End: Notes on Politics*. Translated by V. Binetti and C. Casarino. Minneapolis: University of Minnesota Press.

———. 1998. *Homo Sacer: Sovereign Power and Bare Life*. Translated by D. Heller-Roazen. Stanford, CA: Stanford University Press.

———. 1995. "We Refugees." Translated by Michael Rocke. *Symposium* 49 (2): 114–119.

Ager, Alastair. 1999. *Refugees: Perspectives on Forced Migration*. London: Continuum.

Agier, Michel. 2011. *Managing the Undesirables: Refugee Camps and Humanitarian Government*. Translated by David Fernbock. Cambridge, UK: Polity Press.

———. 2008. *On the Margins of the World: The Refugee Experience Today*. Translated by David Fernbock. Cambridge, UK: Polity Press.

Akram, Susan. 2002. "Palestinian Refugees and Their Legal Status: Rights, Politics and Implications for a Just Solution." *Journal of Palestine Studies* 31 (3): 36–51.

Akram, Susan, and Terry Rempel. 2003. "Temporary Protection for Palestinian Refugees: A Proposal." Paper presented at IDRC Stocktaking II: Conference on Palestinian Refugee Research, Ottawa, June 17– 20.

Ali Nayel, Moe. 2011a. "Palestinian Refugees in Lebanon Eye Statehood Bid with Skepticism." *Electronic Intifada*, September 19. Available at http://electronicintifada.net/content/palestinian-refugees-lebanon-eye-statehood-bid-skepticism/10398.

———. 2011b. "Thousands at the Border." *Electronic Intifada*, May 17. Available at http://electronicintifada.net/content/thousands-border/9971.

Allan, Diana. 2013. "Commemorative Economies and Politics in Shatila Camp." *Humanity* 4 (1): 133–148.

———. 2010. "From Archive to Art Film: A Palestinian Aesthetics of Memory Reviewed." *Cairo Papers in Social Science* 31 (3–4): 149–166.

———. 2009. "From Nationalist to Economic Subject: Emergent Economic Networks among Shatila's Women." *Journal of Palestine Studies* 38 (4): 1–16.

———. 2007. "The Politics of Witness: Remembering and Forgetting 1948 in Shatila Camp." In *Nakba: Palestine, 1948, and the Claims of Memory*, edited by Lila Abu-Lughod and Ahmad Sa'di, 253–284. New York: Columbia University Press.

———. 2005. "Mythologizing the *Nakba*: 1948 Narratives in the Production of Collective Identity and Cultural Practice among Palestinian Refugees in Lebanon." *Journal of Oral History* 33 (1): 47–56.

Allan, Diana, and Curtis Brown. 2010. "Media's Messengers: The Mavi Marmara at the Frontlines of Web 2.0." *Journal of Palestine Studies* 40 (1): 1–15.

Allen, Lori. 2009. "Martyr Bodies in the Media: Human Rights, Aesthetics, and the Politics of Immediation in the Palestinian Intifada." *American Ethnologist* 36 (1): 161–180.

———. 2006. "The Polyvalent Politics of Martyr Commemorations in the Palestinian Intifada." *History & Memory* 12 (2): 107–138.

Althusser, Louis. 1971. *Lenin and Philosophy, and Other Essays.* Translated by Ben Brewster. New York: Monthly Review Press.

Anderson, Benedict. 1983. *Imagined Communities: Reflections on the Origin and Spread of Nationalism.* London: Verso.

Anderson, Bridget, and Martin Ruhs. 2010. "Researching Illegality and Labour Migration." Guest editorial, in "Researching Illegality and Labour Migration: The Research/Policy Nexus." Special issue, *Population, Space and Place* 16 (3): 175–179.

Antze, Paul, and Michael Lambek. 1996. *Tense Past: Cultural Essays in Trauma and Memory.* New York: Routledge.

Aouragh, Miriyam. 2011. *Palestine Online: Transnationalism, the Internet and the Reinvention of Identity.* London: I. B. Tauris.

Appadurai, Arjun. 2004. "The Capacity to Aspire: Culture and the Terms of Recognition." In *Culture and Public Action: A Cross-Disciplinary Dialogue on Development Policy*, edited by Michael Walton, 59–84. Stanford, CA: Stanford University Press.

———. 2002. "Deep Democracy: Urban Governmentality and the Horizon of Politics." *Public Culture* 14 (1): 21–47.

———. 1996. *Modernity at Large: Cultural Dimensions of Globalization.* Minneapolis: University of Minnesota Press.

Arendt, Hannah. 1973. *The Origins of Totalitarianism.* New York: Harcourt. First published in 1951.

———. 1958. *The Human Condition.* Chicago: University of Chicago Press.

Arraf, Shukri. 2004. *Al-Mawaqi'a al-Jougrafiyya fi Filasteen: al-Asma' al-'arabia wa al Tasmiyat al 'ibria* [Geographic sites in Palestine: Arabic and Hebrew denominations]. Berkeley: Institute of Palestine Studies and University of California Press.

Aruri, Naseer. 2001. "Towards Convening a Congress of Return and Self-Determination." In *Palestinian Refugees: The Right of Return*, edited by N. Aruri, 260–272. London: Pluto Press.

Augé, Marc. 2004. *Oblivion.* Translated by Marjolijn de Jager. Minneapolis: University of Minnesota Press.

BADIL-Zochrot. 2012. "Thinking Practically about Return." *Al-Majdal* 49 (Spring–Summer): 39–55.

Balibar, Étienne. 2004. *We, the People of Europe? Reflections on Transnational Citizenship.* Translated by James Swenson. Princeton, NJ: Princeton University Press.

Bamyeh, Mohammed. 2003. "Palestine: Listening to the Inaudible." *South Atlantic Quarterly* 102 (4): 825–849.

Barbosa, Gustavo. 2008. "Back to the House: Becoming a Man in the First Palestinian Intifada." *Vibrant–Virtual Brazilian Anthropology* 5 (2). Available at http://www.vibrant .org.br/issues/v5n2/gustavo-barbosa-back-to-the-house/.

Barclay, Ahmad, and Dena Qaddumi. 2012. "Reframing Palestinian Return: A New Al-Shabaka Policy Circle." Al-Shabaka, November 12. Available at http://al-shabaka.org/ sites/default/files/BarclayQaddumi_Commentary_En_Nov_2012.pdf.

Bardenstein, Carol B. 1999. "Trees, Forests and the Shaping of the Palestinian and Israeli Collective Memory." In *Acts of Memory: Cultural Recall in the Present*, edited by Mieke Bal, Jonathan Crewe, and Leo Spitzer, 148–171. Hanover, NH: Dartmouth College Press.

Barkan, Elazar. 2005. "Negotiating Truth: The Holocaust, Lehavdil, and al-Nakba." In *Exile and Return: Predicaments of Palestinians and Jews*, edited by Ann Lesch and Ian Lustick, 85–106. Philadelphia: University of Pennsylvania Press.

Battaglia, Debbora. 1992. "The Body and the Gift: Memory and Forgetting in Sabari Mortuary Exchange." *American Ethnologist* 19 (1): 3–18.

Bauman, Zygmunt. 2007. *Liquid Times: Living in an Age of Uncertainty*. Cambridge, UK: Polity Press.

———. 2002. *Society under Siege*. Cambridge, UK: Polity Press.

Bayat, Asef. 2010. *Life as Politics: How Ordinary People Change the Middle East*. Stanford, CA: Stanford University Press.

———. 1997. *Street Politics: Poor People's Movement in Iran*. New York: Columbia University Press.

Beck, Ulrich. 1999. *World Risk Society*. Cambridge, UK: Polity Press.

———. 1994. "The Reinvention of Politics: Towards a Reflexive Theory of Modernization." In *Reflexive Modernization: Politics, Tradition and Aesthetics in the Modern Social Order*, edited by Ulrich Beck, Anthony Giddens, and Scott Lash, 1–55. Stanford, CA: Stanford University Press.

Benjamin, Walter. 2003. *Selected Writings*. Vol. 4, *1938–40*, edited by Howard Eiland and Michael W. Jennings. Cambridge, MA: Harvard University Press.

Benn, Aluf. 2011. "The Arab Revolution Is Knocking on Israel's Door." *Haaretz*, May 16. Available at http://www.haaretz.com/print-edition/news/the-arab-revolution-is -knocking-at-israel-s-door-1.361969.

Benvenisti, Meron. 2000. *Sacred Landscape: The Buried History of the Holy Land since 1948*. Berkeley: University of California Press.

Bergson, Henri. 1988. *Matter and Memory*. Translated by Nancy Margaret Paul and W. Scott Palmer. New York: Zone Books. First published in 1896.

———. 1960. *Time and Free Will: An Essay on the Immediate Data of Consciousness*. Translated by F. L. Pogson. New York: Harper. First published in 1889.

Bhabha, Homi K. 1990. *Nation and Narration*. London: Routledge.

Biehl, João. 2005. *Vita: Life in the Zone of Social Abandonment*. Berkeley: University of California Press.

Binswanger, Ludwig. 1986. "Dream and Existence." Translated by Forrest Williams. *Review of Existential Psychology and Psychiatry* 19:79–107. First published in 1954.

Bloch, Alice, and Milena Chimienti. 2011. "Irregular Migration in a Globalizing World." *Ethnic and Racial Studies* 34 (8): 1271–1285.

Bloch, Alice, T. Galvin, and L. Schuster, eds. 2000. "Editorial Introduction." *Journal of Refugee Studies* 13 (1): 1–10.

Blome Jacobsen, Laurie. 2000. *Finding Means*. Vol. 2, *The Persistence of Poverty among Palestinian Refugees*. Fafo report 415. Oslo: Fafo Institute for Applied Social Science.

Blome Jacobsen, Laurie, and Aziza Khalidi. 2003. "Housing and Environment." In *Difficult Past, Uncertain Future: Living Conditions among Palestinian Refugees in the Camps and Gatherings in Lebanon*, edited by Ole Fr. Ugland, 183–201. Fafo report 409. Oslo: Fafo Institute for Applied Social Science.

Blumenthal, Max. 2011. "Interview: Planning the Nakba Day Movement in Lebanon." *Electronic Intifada*, June 5. Available at http://electronicintifada.net/content/interview-planning-nakba-day-movement-lebanon/10046.

Bocco, Riccardo, and Jalal Husseini. 2010. "The Status of the Palestinian Refugees in the Near East: The Right of Return and UNRWA in Perspective." *Refugee Survey Quarterly* 28 (2–3): 260–285.

Boltanski, Luc. 1999. *Distant Suffering: Morality, Media and Politics*. Translated by Graham Burchell. Cambridge: Cambridge University Press.

Borneman, John. 2004. "Introduction: The Case of Ariel Sharon and the Fate of Universal Jurisdiction." In *The Case of Ariel Sharon and the Fate of Universal Jurisdiction*, edited by John Borneman, 1–30. Princeton, NJ: Princeton Institute for International and Regional Studies Monograph Series.

Bourdieu, Pierre. 2001. *Masculine Domination*. Translated by Richard Nice. Stanford, CA: Stanford University Press.

———. 2000. *Pascalian Meditations*. Translated by Richard Nice. Stanford, CA: Stanford University Press.

———. 1990. *The Logic of Practice*. Translated by Richard Nice. Stanford, CA: Stanford University Press.

———. 1977. *Outline of a Theory of Practice*. Translated by Richard Nice. Stanford, CA: Stanford University Press.

Bowman, Glenn. 1994. "A Country of Words: Conceiving the Palestinian Nation from a Position of Exile." In *The Making of Political Identities*, edited by Ernesto Laclau, 138–170. London: Verso.

Brand, Laurie. 1988. *Palestinians in the Arab World: Institution Building and the Search for State*. New York: Columbia University Press.

Brooks, Van Wyck. 1918. "On Creating a Usable Past." *Dial* 64 (April): 337–341.

Brynen, Rex. 1997. "Imagining a Solution: Final Status Arrangements and Palestinian Refugees in Lebanon." *Journal of Palestine Studies* 26:42–58.

————. 1990. *Sanctuary and Survival: The PLO in Lebanon*. Boulder, CO: Westview Press.

Bukhari, Sahih al-. 1979. *The Translation of the Meanings of Sahih al-Bukhari*. Translated by Muhammad Muhsin Khan. Riyadh, Saudi Arabia: Darussalam.

Butler, Judith. 2004. *Precarious Life: The Powers of Mourning and Violence*. London: Verso.

Carol, Colin. 2000. "Resistance Movements: Migration, Kinship Networks and Palestinian Refugees in Lebanon." Master's thesis, Culture, Development and Environment Center, University of Sussex.

Caruth, Cathy. 1995. *Trauma: Explorations in Memory*. Baltimore: Johns Hopkins University Press.

Casey, Edward. 1997. "How to Get from Space to Place in a Fairly Short Stretch of Time: Phenomenological Prolegomena." In *Senses of Place*, edited by S. Feld and K. H. Basso, 13–52. Santa Fe, NM: School of American Research Press.

Cassel, Matthew. 2011. "Palestinians in Lebanon, at the Lonely End of the Arab Uprisings." *Guardian*, May 16. Available at http://www.guardian.co.uk/commentisfree/2011/may/16/palestinian-refugees-lebanon-right-to-return.

Caton, Steven C., and Bernardo Zacka. 2010. "Abu Ghraib, the Security Apparatus, and the Performativity of Power." *American Ethnologist* 37 (2): 201–211.

Certeau, Michel de. 1988. *The Practice of Everyday Life*. Translated by Steven Rendall. Berkeley: University of California Press. First published in 1980.

Chaaban, Jad. 2009. "The Impact of Instability and Migration on Lebanon's Human Capital." In *Generation in Waiting: The Unfulfilled Promise of Young People in the Middle East*, edited by Navtej Dhillon and Tarik Yousef, 120–142. Washington, DC: Brookings Institution.

Chaaban, Jad, Hala Ghattas, Rima Habib, Sari Hanafi, Nadia Naamani, Nadine Sahyoun, Nisreen Salti, and Karin Seyfert. 2010. *Socio-Economic Survey of Palestinian Refugees in Lebanon*. Beirut: UNRWA and American University of Beirut.

Charles, Tom. 2011. "The Unknown Hell of Palestinian Refugees in Lebanon." *Jadaliyya*, December 12. Available at http://www.jadaliyya.com/pages/index/3490/the-unknown-hell -of-palestinian-refugees-in-lebano.

Chatterjee, Partha. 2008. "Democracy and Economic Transformation in India." *Economic and Political Weekly* 43 (16): 53–62.

————. 2004. *The Politics of the Governed: Reflections on Popular Politics in Most of the World*. New York: Columbia University Press.

Chatty, Dawn. 2010. *Displacement and Dispossession in the Modern Middle East*. Cambridge: Cambridge University Press.

————. 2009. "Palestinian Refugee Youth: Agency and Aspiration." *Refugee Studies Quarterly* 28 (2–3): 318–338.

Chatty, Dawn, and Gillian Lewando Hundt. 2005. *Children of Palestine: Experiencing Forced Migration in the Middle East*. London: Berghahn Books.

————. 2001. *Children and Adolescents in Palestinian Households: Living with the Effects of Prolonged Conflict and Forced Migration.* Oxford: Refugee Studies Center, University of Oxford.

Chávez, Sergio. 2011. "Navigating the US-Mexico Border: The Crossing Strategies of Undocumented Workers in Tijuana Mexico." *Ethnic and Racial Studies* 34 (8): 1320–1337.

Chiller-Glaus, Michael. 2007. *Tackling the Intractable: Palestinian Refugees and the Search for Middle East Peace.* Bern: Peter Lang AG, International Academic Publishers.

Clifford, James. 2000. "Taking Identity Politics Seriously: 'The Contradictory Stony Ground. . . .'" In *Without Guarantees: In Honour of Stuart Hall*, edited by Paul Gilroy, Lawrence Grossberg, and Angela McRobbie, 94–113. London: Verso.

Collier, J. F., B. Maurer, and L. Suárez-Navez. 1995. "Sanctioned Identities: Legal Constructions of Modern Personhood." *Identities* 2 (1–2): 1–28.

Coutin, S. B. 2000. *Legalizing Moves: Salvadoran Immigrants' Struggle for U.S. Residency.* Ann Arbor: University of Michigan Press.

Crapanzano, Vincent. 2011. *The Harkis: The Wound That Never Heals.* Chicago: University of Chicago Press.

————. 2004. *Imaginary Horizons: An Essay in Literary-Philosophical Anthropology.* Chicago: University of Chicago Press.

————. 2001. "The Betwixt and Between of the Dream." In *Hundert Jahre "Die Traumadeutung": Kulturwissenschaftliche Perspektiven in der Traumforschung*, edited by Burkhard Schnepel, 232–259. Studien zur Kulturkunde, vol. 119. Cologne, Germany: Rüdiger Köppe Verlag.

————. 1975. "Saints, Jnun, and Dreams: An Essay in Moroccan Ethnopsychology." *Psychiatry* 38 (2): 145–159.

Dakhlia, Jocelyne. 2001. "New Approaches in the History of Memory? A French Model." In *Crisis and Memory in Islamic Societies*, edited by Angelika Neuwirth and Andreas Pflitsch, 59–74. Beirut: Orient Institute.

Daniel, E. Valentine. 1996. *Charred Lullabies: Chapters in an Anthropography of Violence.* Princeton, NJ: Princeton University Press.

Darwish, Mahmoud. 1995. *Memory for Forgetfulness: August, Beirut, 1982.* Translated by Ibrahim Muhawi. Berkeley: University of California Press.

Das, Veena. 2007. *Life and Words: Violence and the Descent into the Ordinary.* Berkeley: University of California Press.

————. 2004. "The Signature of the State: The Paradox of Illegibility." In *Anthropology in the Margins of the State*, edited by Veena Das and Deborah Poole, 225–252. Santa Fe, NM: School of American Research Press.

Davis, Rochelle. 2010. *Palestinian Village Histories: Geographies of the Displaced.* Stanford, CA: Stanford University Press.

De Genova, Nicholas. 2002. "Migrant 'Illegality' and Deportability in Everyday Life." *Annual Review of Anthropology* 31:419–447.

Deleuze, Gilles. 2003. *Francis Bacon: The Logic of Sensation.* Translated by Daniel W. Smith. London: Continuum.

Desjarlais, Robert. 2003. *Sensory Biographies: Lives and Deaths among Nepal's Yolmo Buddhists.* Berkeley: University of California Press.

———. 1997. *Shelter Blues: Sanity and Selfhood among the Homeless.* Philadelphia: University of Pennsylvania Press.

Desmond, Matthew. 2012. "Disposable Ties and the Urban Poor." *American Journal of Sociology* 117 (5): 1295–1335.

Desroche, Henri. 1979. *The Sociology of Hope.* Translated by Carol Martin-Sperry. London: Routledge and Kegan Paul.

Dewey, John. 1934. *Art as Experience.* New York: Penguin.

Diken, Bülent. 2004. "From Refugee Camps to Gated Communities: Biopolitics and the End of the City." *Citizenship Studies* 8 (1): 83–106.

Diken, Bülent, and Carsten Bagge Lausten. 2005. *The Culture of Exception: Sociology Facing the Camp.* Abingdon, UK: Routledge.

Doraï, Mohammed K. 2011. "Palestinian Refugee Camps in Lebanon: Migration, Mobility and the Urbanization Process." In *Palestinian Refugees: Identity, Space and Place in the Levant,* edited by Are Knudsen and Sari Hanafi, 67–80. London: Routledge.

———. 2010. "From Camp Dwellers to Urban Refugees? Urbanization and Marginalization of Refugee Camps in Lebanon." In *The Lived Reality of Palestinian Refugees in Lebanon,* edited by Muhammad Ali Khalidi, 75–93. Beirut: Institute of Palestine Studies.

———. 2003. "Palestinian Emigration from Lebanon to Northern Europe." *Refuge* 21 (2): 23–31.

———. 2002. "The Meaning of Homeland for the Palestinian Diaspora: Revival and Transformations." In *New Approaches to Migration: Transnational Communities and the Transformation of Home,* edited by N. al-Ali and K. Koser, 87–96. New York: Routledge.

Douglass, Ana, and Thomas A. Vogler, eds. 2003. *Witness and Memory: The Discourse of Trauma.* London: Routledge.

Doumani, Beshara. 2007. "Palestine versus the Palestinians? The Iron Laws and Ironies of a People Denied." *Journal of Palestine Studies* 38 (4): 49–64.

———. 1995. *Rediscovering Palestine: Merchants and Peasants in Jabal Nablus.* Berkeley: University of California Press.

Dumper, Michael. 2007. *The Future for Palestinian Refugees: Toward Equity and Peace.* Boulder, CO: Lynne Rienner.

Esmeir, Samera. 2003. "1948: Law, History, Memory." *Social Text* 21 (2): 25–48.

Ewing, Katherine P. 1994. "Dreams from a Saint: Anthropological Atheism and the Temptation to Believe." *American Anthropologist* 96 (3): 571–583.

Farah, Randa. 2010. "UNRWA: Through the Eyes of Its Palestinian Employees." *Refugee Studies Quarterly* 28 (2–3): 389–411.

———. 1999. "Popular Memory and Reconstruction of Palestinian Refugee Identity: Al Ba'qa Refugee Camp in Jordan." PhD diss., Department of Anthropology, University of Toronto.

Fassin, Didier. 2008. "The Humanitarian Politics of Testimony: Subjectification through Trauma in the Israeli-Palestinian Conflict." *Cultural Anthropology* 23 (3): 531–558.

———. 2005. "Compassion and Repression: The Moral Economy of Immigration Policies in France." *Cultural Anthropology* 20 (3): 362–387.

———. 2001. "The Biopolitics of Otherness: Undocumented Foreigners and Racial Discrimination in French Public Debate." *Anthropology Today* 17 (1): 3–7.

Fassin, Didier, and Richard Rechtman. 2009. *The Empire of Trauma: An Enquiry into the Condition of Victimhood*. Translated by Rachel Gomme. Princeton, NJ: Princeton University Press.

Feldman, Allen. 2004. "Memory Theaters, Virtual Witnessing and the Trauma-Aesthetic." *Biography* 27 (1): 163–202.

Feldman, Ilana. 2008. "Refusing Invisibility: Documentation and Memorialization in Palestinian Refugee Camps." *Oxford Journal of Refugee Studies* 21 (4): 498–516.

———. 2007. "Difficult Distinctions: Refugee Law, Humanitarian Practice, and Political Identification in Gaza." *Cultural Anthropology* 22 (1): 129–169.

Felman, Shoshana, and Dori Laub, eds. 1992. *Testimony: Crises of Witnessing in Literature, Psychoanalysis, and History*. New York: Routledge.

Ferguson, James. 2007. *Global Shadow: Africa in the Neoliberal World Order*. Durham, NC: Duke University Press.

———. 1999. *Expectations of Modernity: Myths and Meanings of Urban Life on the Zambian Copperbelt*. Berkeley: University of California Press.

Ferme, Mariane. 2004. "Deterritorialized Citizenship and the Resonances of the Sierra Leonean State." In *Anthropology in the Margins of the State*, edited by Veena Das and Deborah Poole, 81–116. Santa Fe, NM: School of American Research Press.

Fessler, Daniel. 2002. "Willpower: The Psychocultural Dynamics of Rotating Savings and Credit Associations in a Bengkulu Village." *Ethos* 30 (2): 25– 48.

Finkelstein, Norman. 2000. *The Holocaust Industry: Reflections on the Exploitation of Jewish Suffering*. London: Verso.

Fisk, R. 1991. *Pity the Nation: Lebanon at War*. London: André Deutsch.

Foucault, Michel. 1986. "Dream, Imagination, and Existence." Translated by Forrest Williams. *Review of Existential Psychology and Psychiatry* 19:19–78.

Freud, Sigmund. 1999. *The Interpretation of Dreams*. Translated by Joyce Crick. Oxford: Oxford University Press. First published in 1900.

Friedman, Adina. 2003. "Unraveling the Right of Return." *Refuge* 21 (2): 30–45.

Frykman, Jonas, and Nils Gilje. 2003. "Being There: An Introduction." In *Being There: New Perspectives on Phenomenology and the Analysis of Culture*, edited by Jonas Frykman and Nils Gilje, 7–51. Lund, Sweden: Nordic Academic Press.

Gabiam, Nell. 2012. "When Humanitarianism Becomes 'Development': The Politics of International Aid in Syria's Palestinian Refugee Camps." *American Anthropologist* 114 (1): 95–107.

———. 2006. "Negotiating Rights: Palestinian Refugees and the Protection Gap." *Anthropological Quarterly* 79 (4): 717–730.

Geertz, Clifford. 1993. *Local Knowledge: Further Essays in Interpretative Anthropology.* London: Fontana Press.

Geertz, Hildred, and Clifford Geertz. 1975. *Kinship in Bali.* Chicago: University of Chicago Press.

Gehrig, Tina. 2004. "The Afghan Experience of Asylum in Germany: Towards an Anthropology of Legal Categories." *Tsantsa* 9:72–80.

Ghandour, Nahla. 2001. "Meeting the Needs of Palestinian Refugees in Lebanon." In *Palestinian Refugees: The Right of Return*, edited by N. Aruri, 152–165. London: Pluto Press.

Giannou, Christopher. 1992. *Besieged: A Doctor's Story of Life and Death in Beirut.* New York: Olive Branch Press.

Gilroy, Paul. 1996. "British Cultural Studies and the Pitfalls of Identity." In *Black British Cultural Studies: A Reader*, edited by Houston Baker, Manthia Diawara, and Ruth Lindeborg, 223–239. Chicago: University of Chicago Press.

Good, Byron. 1994. *Medicine, Rationality and Experience: An Anthropological Perspective.* Cambridge: Cambridge University Press.

Graw, Knut. 2012. "On the Cause of Migration: Being and Nothingness in the African European Borderzone." In *The Global Horizon: Migratory Expectation in Africa and Beyond*, edited by Knut Graw and Samuli Schielke, 23–43. Leuven, Belgium: Leuven University Press.

———. 2006. "Locating *Nganiyo*: Divination as Intentional Space." *Journal of Religion in Africa* 36 (1): 78–119.

Graw, Knut, and Samuli Schielke. 2012. Introduction to *The Global Horizon: Migratory Expectation in Africa and Beyond*, edited by Knut Graw and Samuli Schielke, 7–23. Leuven, Belgium: Leuven University Press.

Guyer, Jane, and M. Eno Belinga. 1995. "Wealth in People as Wealth in Knowledge: Accumulation and Composition in Equatorial Africa." *Journal of African History* 33 (1): 91–120.

Hage, Ghassan. 2012. "Critical Anthropological Thought and the Radical Political Imaginary Today." *Critique of Anthropology* 32 (3): 285–308.

———. 2003. *Against Paranoid Nationalism: Searching for Hope in a Shrinking Society.* Annandale, New South Wales: Pluto Press.

Hage, Ghassan, and Dimitris Papadoulos. 2004. "Ghassan Hage in Conversation with Dimitris Papadoulos: Migration, Hope and the Making of Subjectivity in Transnational Capitalism." *International Journal for Critical Psychology* 12:95–117.

Hammami, Rita. 1995. "NGOs: The Professionalisation of Politics." *Race & Class* 37 (2): 51–63.

Hammer, Juliane. 2001. "Homeland Palestine: Lost in the Catastrophe of 1948 and Recreated in Memories and Art." In *Crisis and Memory in Islamic Societies*, edited by Angelika Neuwirth and Andreas Pflitsch, 453–482. Beirut: Orient Institute.

Han, Clara. 2012. *Life in Debt: Times of Care and Violence in Neoliberal Chile.* Berkeley: University of California Press.

———. 2011. "Symptoms of Another Life: Time, Possibility and Domestic Relations in Chile's Credit Economy." *Cultural Anthropology* 26 (1): 7–32.

Hanafi, Sari. 2010. "Palestinian Refugee Camps in Lebanon: Laboratory of Indocile Identity Formation." In *The Lived Reality of Palestinian Refugees in Lebanon*, edited by Muhammad Ali Khalidi, 45–74. Beirut: Institute of Palestine Studies.

———. 2008. "Palestinian Refugee Camps in Lebanon: Laboratories of State-in-the-Making, Discipline and Islamist Radicalism." In *Thinking Palestine*, edited by R. Lentin, 82–100. London: Z Books.

———. 2007. "Social Capital, Transnational Kinship and Refugee Repatriation Process." In *Israel and the Palestinian Refugees*, edited by Sari Hanafi, Eyal Benvenisti, and C. Gans, 3–40. Berlin: Springer and Max-Planck Institute.

———. 2005. "Rethinking the Palestinians Abroad as Diaspora: The Relationships between the Diaspora and the Palestinian Territories." In *Homelands and Diasporas: Holy Lands and Other Places*, edited by André Levy and Alex Weingrod, 97–122. Stanford, CA: Stanford University Press.

———. 2002. "Opening the Debate on the Right of Return." *Middle East Report* 222 (March): 2–7.

Hanafi, Sari, and Taylor Long. 2010. "Governance, Governmentalities, and the State of Exception in the Palestinian Refugee Camps in Lebanon." *Journal of Refugee Studies* 23 (2): 134–159.

Hardan, Anaheed al-. 2012. "The Right of Return Movement in Syria: Building a Culture of Return, Mobilizing Memories for the Return." *Journal of Palestine Studies* 41 (2): 62–79.

Harrell-Bond, Barbara. 2002. "Can Humanitarian Work with Refugees Be Humane?" *Human Rights Quarterly* 24:51–85.

Hayden, Bridget. 2006. "What's in a Name? The Nature of the Individual in Refugee Studies." *Journal of Refugee Studies* 19 (4): 471–487.

Hejoj, Ibrahim, and Adnan Badran. 2006. *A Socio-economic Analysis of Special Hardship Case Families in the Five Fields of UNRWA Operation.* Gaza: UNRWA Public Information Office. Available at http://www.unrwa.org/userfiles/20100118135535.pdf.

Herzfeld, Michael. 1997. *Cultural Intimacy: Social Poetics and the Nation-State.* New York: Routledge.

Hesford, Wendy. 2004. "Documenting Violations: Rhetorical Witnessing and the Spectacle of Distant Suffering." *Biography* 27 (1): 104–144.

Heyman, Josiah, and A. Smart. 1999. "States and Illegal Practices: An Overview." In *States and Illegal Practices*, edited by J. Heyman, 1–24. Oxford: Berg.

Hill, Tom. 2005. "Historicity and the Nakba Commemorations of 1998." Florence, Italy: European University Institute Working Papers, Robert Schuman Center for Advanced Studies, Mediterranean Programme Series No. 2005/33.

Hirschkind, Charles. 2006. *The Ethical Soundscape: Cassette Sermons and Islamic Counterpublics*. New York: Columbia University Press.

Hobsbawn, Eric, and Terence Ranger, eds. 1992. *The Invention of Tradition*. Cambridge: Cambridge University Press.

Hollifield, J. F. 1992. *Immigrants, Markets and States: The Political Economy of Post-war Europe*. Cambridge, MA: Harvard University Press.

Hoodfar, Homa. 1997. *Between Marriage and the Market: Intimate Politics and Survival in Cairo*. Berkeley: University of California Press.

Hourani, Albert H. 2002. *A History of the Arab Peoples*. Cambridge, MA: Belknap Press of Harvard University Press.

Hout, Bayan N. al-. 2004. *Sabra and Shatila: September 1982*. London: Pluto Press.

———. 1998. "Oral History: Continuous, Permanent Connection." *Al-Jana* (May): 10–12.

Hovdenak, A. 1997. "On the Gulf Road: Palestinian Adaptations to Labour Migration." In *Constructing Order: Palestinian Adaptations to Refugee Life*, edited by A. Hovdenak, J. Pedersen, D. H. Tuastad, and E. Zureik, 19–78. Fafo report 236. Oslo: Fafo Institute for Applied Social Science.

Hudson, Michael. 1997. "Palestinians and Lebanon: The Common Story." *Journal of Refugee Studies* 10 (3): 243–260.

Husseini, Jalal al-, and Riccardo Bocco. 2009. "The Status of Palestinian Refugees in the Near East: The Right of Return and UNRWA in Perspective." *Refugee Studies Quarterly* 28 (2–3): 260–285.

Isin, Engin F. 2009. "Citizenship in Flux: The Figure of the Activist Citizen." *Subjectivity* 29 (1): 367–388.

———. 2008. "Theorizing Acts of Citizenship." In *Acts of Citizenship*, edited by Engin Isin and Greg M. Nielsen, 15–43. London: Palgrave Macmillan.

Jackson, Michael. 2011. *Life within Limits: Well-Being in a World of Want*. Durham, NC: Duke University Press.

———. 2008. "The Shock of the New: On Migrant Imaginaries and Critical Transitions." *Ethnos* 73 (1): 57–72.

———. 2007. "Migrant Imaginaries: With Sewa in Southeast London." In *Excursions*, 102–134. Durham, NC: Duke University Press.

———. 2005a. *Existential Anthropology: Events, Exigencies and Effects*. New York: Berghahn Books.

———. 2005b. "Storytelling, Events, Violence, and the Appearance of the Past." *Anthropological Quarterly* 78 (2): 355–375.

————. 1996. "Introduction: Phenomenology, Radical Empiricism, and the Anthropological Critique." In *Things As They Are*, edited by Michael Jackson, 1–50. Bloomington: Indiana University Press.

————. 1989. *Paths towards a Clearing: Radical Empiricism and Ethnographic Inquiry.* Bloomington: Indiana University Press.

James, William. 1907. *Pragmatism: A New Name for Some Old Ways of Thinking: Popular Lectures on Philosophy.* New York: Longmans, Green.

Jansen, Stef. 2006. "The Privatization of Home and Hope: Return, Reforms and the Foreign Intervention in Bosnia-Herzegovina." *Dialectical Anthropology* 30:177–199.

Jarrar, Najeh. 2003. *Palestinian Refugee Camps in the West Bank: Attitudes towards Repatriation and Integration.* Ramallah: Palestinian Diaspora and Refugee Center, Shaml.

Jayyusi, Lena. 2007. "Iterability, Cumulativity and Presence: The Relational Figures of Palestinian Memory." In *Nakba: Palestine, 1948, and the Claims of Memory*, edited by Lila Abu-Lughod and Ahmad Sa'di, 107–134. New York: Columbia University Press.

Jean-Klein, Iris. 2001. "Nationalism and Resistance: The Two Faces of Everyday Activism in Palestine during the Intifada." *Cultural Anthropology* 16 (1): 83–126.

Johnson, Penny. 2006. "Living Together in a Nation of Fragments: Dynamics of Kin, Place and Nation." In *Living Palestine: Family Survival, Resistance and Mobility under Occupation*, edited by Lisa Taraki, 51–102. Syracuse, NY: Syracuse University Press.

Johnson, Penny, and Lee O'Brian. 2003. "Perpetual Emergency: The Persistence of Poverty and Vulnerability among Palestinian Camp Populations in Jordan, Lebanon, West Bank and Gaza." In *Finding Means*, vol. 2, *The Persistence of Poverty: UNRWA's Financial Crisis and Refugee Living Conditions*, edited by Laurie Blome Jacobsen. Fafo report 427. Oslo: Fafo Institute for Applied Social Science.

Kagan, Michael. 2007. "Restitution as a Remedy for Refugee Property Claims in the Israeli-Palestinian Conflict." *Florida Journal of International Law* 19 (2): 421–489.

Kallem, Mahmoud. 2003. *Sabra wa Shatila: Dhakira al-Damm* [Sabra and Shatila: The memory of blood]. Beirut: Bisan Books.

Kapferer, Bruce. 1997. *The Feast of the Sorcerer: Practices of Consciousness and Power.* Chicago: University of Chicago Press.

Kelly, Tobias. 2008. "Returning to Palestine: Confinement and Displacement under Israeli Occupation." In *Struggles for Home: Violence, Hope and the Movement of People*, edited by Stef Jansen and Staffan Löfving, 25–42. New York: Berghahn Books.

Khalidi, Muhammad Ali, and Diane Riskedahl. 2010. "The Lived Reality of Palestinian Refugees in Lebanon." In *Manifestations of Identity: The Lived Reality of Palestinian Refugees in Lebanon*, edited by Muhammad Ali Khalidi, 1–13. Beirut: Institute for Palestine Studies.

————. 2007. "The Road to Nahr al-Barid: Lebanese Political Discourse and Palestinian Civil Rights." *Middle East Report* 244 (Fall). Available at http://www.merip.org/mer/mer244/road-nahr-al-barid.

Khalidi, Rashid. 1997. *Palestinian Identity: The Construction of Modern National Consciousness.* New York: Columbia University Press.

———. 1992. "Observations on the Right of Return." *Journal of Palestine Studies* 21 (2): 29–40.

Khalidi, Walid. 1992. *All That Remains: The Palestinian Villages Occupied and Depopulated by Israel in 1948.* Washington, DC: Institute of Palestine Studies.

Khalil, Osamah. 2013. "Who Are You? The PLO and the Limits of Representation." Al-Shabaka, March 2013. Available at http://www.al-shabaka.org/sites/default/files/Khalil_PolicyBrief_En_Mar_2013.pdf.

Khalili, Laleh. 2007. *Heroes and Martyrs of Palestine: The Politics of National Commemoration.* Cambridge: Cambridge University Press.

———. 2005. "Commemorating Contested Lands." In *Exile and Return: Predicaments of Palestinians and Jews,* edited by Ann Lesch and Ian Lustick, 19–40. Philadelphia: University of Pennsylvania Press.

———. 2004. "Grassroots Commemorations: Remembering the Land in the Camps of Lebanon." *Journal of Palestine Studies* 34 (1): 6–22.

Khan, Naveeda. 2006. "On Children and Jinn: An Inquiry into an Unexpected Friendship during Uncertain Times." *Cultural Anthropology* 21 (2): 234–264.

Khawaja, Marwan. 2003. "Demographic Characteristics." In *Finding Means: UNRWA's Financial Crisis and Refugee Living Conditions,* edited by Laurie Blome Jacobsen, 20–56. Fafo report 427. Oslo: Fafo Institute for Applied Social Science.

Khawaja, Marwan, and Laurie Blome Jacobsen. 2003. "Familial Relations and Labor Market Outcomes: The Palestinian Refugees in Lebanon." *Social Science Research* 32:579–602.

Khazen, F. el-. 1997. "Permanent Settlement of Palestinians in Lebanon: A Recipe for Conflict." *Journal of Refugee Studies* 10 (3): 275–293.

Kilborne, Benjamin. 1981. "Moroccan Dream Interpretation and Culturally Constituted Defense Mechanisms." *Ethos* 9 (4): 294–311.

Klaus, Dorothée. 2003. *Palestinian Refugees in Lebanon—Where to Belong?* Berlin: Klaus Schwartz Verlag.

Klein, Menachem. 2005. "The Palestinian Refugees of 1948: Models of Allowed and Denied Return." In *Palestinian Refugee Repatriation: Global Perspectives,* edited by Michael Dumper, 87–105. London: Routledge.

Kleinman, Arthur. 2006. *What Really Matters: Living a Moral Life amidst Uncertainty and Danger.* New York: Oxford University Press.

———. 1995. *Writing at the Margin: Discourse between Anthropology and Medicine.* Berkeley: University of California Press.

———. 1980. *Patients and Healers in the Context of Culture.* Berkeley: University of California Press.

Kleinman, Arthur, and Joan Kleinman. 1997. "The Appeal of Experience; The Dismay of Images: Cultural Appropriations of Suffering in Our Times." In *Social Suffering*, edited by Arthur Kleinman, V. Das, and M. Lock, 1–24. Berkeley: University of California Press.

Knudsen, Are. 2009. "Widening the Protection Gap: The 'Politics of Citizenship' for Palestinian Refugees in Lebanon." *Journal of Refugee Studies* 22 (1): 51–74.

———. 2005. "Islamism in the Diaspora: Palestinian Refugees in Lebanon." *Journal of Refugee Studies* 18 (2): 216–234.

Kortam, Manal. 2011. "Politics, Patronage and Popular Committees in the Shatila Refugee Camp, Lebanon." In *Palestinian Refugees: Identity, Space and Place in the Levant*, edited by Are Knudsen and Sari Hanafi, 193–205. London: Routledge.

Kuttab, Eileen. 2006. "The Paradox of Women's Work: Coping, Crisis and Family Survival." In *Living Palestine: Family Survival, Resistance and Mobility under Occupation*, edited by Lisa Taraki, 231–276. Syracuse, NY: Syracuse University Press.

LaCapra, Dominick. 2004. *History in Transit: Experience, Identity, Critical Theory.* Ithaca, NY: Cornell University Press.

Lamoreux, John. 2002. *The Early Muslim Tradition of Dream Interpretation.* Albany: State University of New York Press.

Latif, Nadia. 2008. "Making Refugees." *New Centennial Review* 8 (2): 253–272.

Latte Abdallah, Stéphanie. 2006. *Femmes réfugiées palestiniennes.* Paris: Presses Universitaires de France.

Ledeneva, Alena V. 1998. *Russia's Economy of Favors: Blat, Networking, and Informal Exchange.* Cambridge: Cambridge University Press.

Levi, Primo. 1989. *The Drowned and the Saved.* Translated by Raymond Rosenthal. London: Abacus.

Liang, Lawrence. 2005. "The Other Information City." World Information.org, February 5. Available at http://world-information.org/wio/readme/992003309/1115043912.

Lindquist, Galina. 2006. *Conjuring Hope: Healing and Magic in Contemporary Russia.* New York: Berghahn Books.

Litvak, Meir. 1994. "A Palestinian Past: National Construction and Reconstruction." *History & Memory* 6 (2): 24–56.

Lustick, Ian S., and Ann M. Lesch. 2005. "The Failure of Oslo and the Abiding Question of the Refugees." Introduction to *Exile and Return: Predicaments of Palestinians and Jews*, edited by Ann M. Lesch and Ian S. Lustick, 3–18. Philadelphia: University of Pennsylvania Press.

Mahmood, Saba. 2005. *Politics of Piety: The Islamic Revival and the Feminist Subject.* Princeton, NJ: Princeton University Press.

Maier, Charles. 1993. "A Surfeit of Memory? Reflections on History, Melancholy and Denial." *History & Memory* 5:136–151.

Mains, Daniel. 2007. "Neoliberal Times: Progress, Boredom, and Shame among Young Men in Urban Ethiopia." *American Ethnologist* 34 (4): 659–673.

Malaby, Thomas. 2002. "Odds and Ends: Risk, Mortality, and the Politics of Contingency." *Culture, Medicine and Psychiatry* 26:283–312.

Malkki, Liisa. 1996. "Speechless Emissaries: Refugees, Humanitarianism and Dehistoricization." *Cultural Anthropology* 11 (3): 377–404.

———. 1995a. *Purity and Exile: Violence, Memory and National Cosmology among Hutu Refugees in Tanzania.* Chicago: University of Chicago Press.

———. 1995b. "Refugees and Exile: From 'Refugee Studies' to the National Order of Things." *Annual Review of Anthropology* 24:495–523.

Margalit, Avishai. 2002. *The Ethics of Memory.* Cambridge, MA: Harvard University Press.

Masalha, Nur. 2003. *The Politics of Denial: Israel and the Palestinian Refugee Problem.* London: Pluto Press.

Mason, V. 2007. "Children of the 'Idea of Palestine': Negotiating Identity, Belonging and Home in the Palestinian Diaspora." *Journal of Intercultural Studies* 28 (3): 271–285.

Massad, Joseph. 2011. "State of Recognition." *Al Jazeera,* September 15. Available at http://www.aljazeera.com/indepth/opinion/2011/09/20119158427939481.html.

———. 2001. "Return or Permanent Exile?" In *Palestinian Refugees: The Right of Return,* edited by Nasser Aruri, 105–122. London: Pluto Press.

Maurer, Bill. 2005. *Mutual Life, Limited: Islamic Banking, Alternative Currencies, Lateral Reason.* Princeton, NJ: Princeton University Press.

Mauss, Marcel. 1990. *The Gift: The Form and Reason for Exchange in Archaic Societies.* Translated by W. D. Halls. London: Routledge. First published in 1950.

McNevin, Anne. 2011. *Contesting Citizenship: Irregular Migrants and New Frontiers of the Political.* New York: Columbia University Press.

Misselwitz, Philipp, and Sari Hanafi. 2009. "Testing a New Paradigm: UNRWA's Camp Improvement Programme." *Refugee Survey Quarterly* 28 (2–3): 360–388.

Mittermaier, Amira. 2010. *Dreams That Matter: Egyptian Landscapes of the Imagination.* Berkeley: University of California Press.

Miyazaki, Hirokazu. 2007. "Between Arbitrage and Speculation: An Economy of Belief and Doubt." *Economy and Society* 36 (3): 397–416.

———. 2006. "Economy of Dreams: Hope in Global Capitalism and Its Critiques." *Cultural Anthropology* 21 (2): 147–172.

———. 2004. *The Method of Hope: Anthropology, Philosophy and Fijian Knowledge.* Stanford, CA: Stanford University Press.

Mohammad, Haydar al-. 2010. "Towards an Ethics of *Being-With*: Intertwinements of Life in Post-invasion Basra." *Ethos* 75 (4): 425–446.

Morris, B. 1987. *The Birth of the Palestinian Refugee Problem, 1947–1949.* Cambridge: Cambridge University Press.

Nabulsi, Karma, ed. 2006. *Palestinians Register: Laying Foundations and Setting Directions.* Report of the Civitas Project, Nuffield College, Oxford University. Available at

http://www.forcedmigration.org/research-resources/thematic/palestinians-register
-laying-foundations-and-setting-directions.

———. 2002. "Our Strength Is in the Camps." *Guardian*, September 17. Available at http://www.guardian.co.uk/world/2002/sep/17/comment.

———. 2001. *Right of Return: Joint Parliamentary Middle East Councils Commission of Enquiry—Palestinian Refugees*. London: Labour Middle East Council, Conservative Middle East Council, and Liberal Middle East Council.

Nasrallah, Tayseer. 2012. "Reclaiming the PLO: An Urgent Call to Unite All Palestinians." *Electronic Intifada*, July 14. Available at http://electronicintifada.net/content/reclaiming-plo-urgent-call-unite-all-palestinians/11488.

Natour, Suhail al-. 1997. "The Legal Status of Palestinians in Lebanon." *Journal of Refugee Studies* 10 (3): 360–377.

Nietzsche, Friedrich. 1983. *Untimely Meditations*. Translated by R. J. Hollingdale. Cambridge: Cambridge University Press. First published in 1873.

Norwegian Refugee Council (NRC). 2009. *Needs Assessment in the Palestinian Gatherings of Lebanon: Housing Water and Sanitation*. Beirut: NRC.

Novick, Peter. 2000. *The Holocaust and Collective Memory: The American Experience*. London: Bloomsbury.

Ntombi, Ngwenya Barbara. 2004. "Evading Household Indebtedness through Participation in Group Solidarity Coping Strategies in Contemporary Botswana." *East Africa Social Science Research Review* 20 (2): 1–30.

Nyers, Peter. 2006. *Rethinking Refugees: Beyond States of Emergency*. New York: Routledge.

———. 2003. "Abject Cosmopolitanism: The Politics of Protection in the Anti-deportation Movement." *Third World Quarterly* 24 (6): 1069–1093.

Oppenheim, Leo. 1956. "The Interpretation of Dreams in the Ancient Near East: With a Translation of an Assyrian Dream-Book." *Transactions of the American Philosophical Society* 46 (3): 179–373.

Pandolfo, Stephania. 2007. "'The Burning': Finitude and the Politico-theological Imagination of Illegal Migration." *Anthropological Theory* 7 (3): 329–363.

———. 1997. *The Impasse of Angels: Scenes from a Moroccan Space of Memory*. Chicago: University of Chicago Press.

Papadopoulou, Aspasia. 2004. "Smuggling into Europe: Transit Migrants in Greece." *Journal of Refugee Studies* 17 (2): 167–183.

Pappé, Ilan. 2006. *The Ethnic Cleansing of Palestine*. Oxford: Oneworld Publications.

———. 2003. "Humanizing the Text: Israeli 'New History' and the Trajectory of the 1948 Historiography." *Radical History Review* 86:102–122.

———. 2001. "The Tantura Case in Israel: The Katz Research and Trial." *Journal of Palestine Studies* 30 (3): 19–39.

———. 1997. "Post-Zionist Critique on Israel and the Palestinians." Pt. 1, "The Academic Debate." *Journal of Palestine Studies* 26 (2): 29–41.

Parmenter, Barbara. 1994. *Giving Voices to Stones: Places and Identity in Palestinian Literature*. Austin: University of Texas Press.

Paulin, Tom. 2012. *Love's Bonfire*. London: Faber and Faber.

Pedersen, Jon. 1997. "Introduction: Migration, Homecoming and Community." In *Constructing Order: Palestinian Adaptations to Refugee Life*, edited by A. Hovdenak, J. Pedersen, D. H. Tuastad, and E. Zureik, 7–18. Fafo report 236. Oslo: Fafo Institute for Applied Social Science.

Perdigon, Sylvain. 2011. "The One Still Surviving and Viable Institution." In *Palestinian Refugees: Identity, Space and Place in the Levant*, edited by Are Knudsen and Sari Hanafi, 165–179. London: Routledge.

————. 2010. "Bachelors' Corniche: Transnationality and the Unmaking of Intimacy among Palestinian Youths in Jal al-Bahar, South Lebanon." In *Manifestations of Identity: The Lived Reality of Palestinian Refugees in Lebanon*, edited by Muhammad Ali Khalidi, 93–109. Beirut: Institute for Palestine Studies.

Peteet, Julie. 2005. *Landscape of Hope and Despair: Palestinian Refugee Camps*. Philadelphia: University of Pennsylvania Press.

————. 1996. "From Refugees to Minorities: Palestinians in Post-war Lebanon." *Middle East Report* 26 (3): 27–30.

————. 1995. "Transforming Trust: Dispossession and Empowerment among Palestinian Refugees." In *Mistrusting Refugees*, edited by E. Valentine Daniel and John Chr. Knudsen, 168–186. Berkeley: University of California Press.

————. 1991. *Gender in Crisis: Women and the Palestinian Resistance Movement*. New York: Columbia University Press.

————. 1987. "Socio-political Integration and Conflict Resolution in a Palestinian Refugee Camp." *Journal of Palestine Studies* 16 (2): 29–44.

Picard, Elizabeth. 2002. *Lebanon: A Shattered Country*. Translated by Franklin Philip. New York: Holmes and Meier.

Pieterse, Edgar. 2005. "At the Limits of Possibility: Working Notes on a Relational Model of Urban Politics." In *Urban Africa: Changing Contours of Survival in the City*, edited by Abdoumaliq Simone and Abdelghani Abouhani, 138–176. London: Zed Books.

Piterberg, G. 2001. "Erasures." *New Left Review* 10:31–4.

Potts, Deborah. 2010. *Circular Migration in Zimbabwe and Contemporary Sub-Saharan Africa*. Woodbridge, UK: Boydell and Brewer.

Povinelli, Elizabeth A. 2006. *The Empire of Love: Toward a Theory of Intimacy, Genealogy, and Carnality*. Durham, NC: Duke University Press.

Puig, Nicholas. 2010. "'Welcome to the Camps': The Emergence of Palestinian Rap in Lebanon, a New Social and Political Song." In *Manifestations of Identity: The Lived Reality of Palestinian Refugees in Lebanon*, edited by Muhammad Ali Khalidi, 109–125. Beirut: Institute for Palestine Studies.

Qumsiyeh, M. B. 2004. *Sharing the Land of Canaan: Human Rights and the Israeli-Palestinian Struggle.* London: Pluto Press.

Rabinowitz, Dan. 2008. "Israel and the Palestinian Refugees." In *Waging War, Making Peace: Reparations and Human Rights,* edited by Barbara R. Johnston and Susan Slyomovics, 225–240. Walnut Creek, CA: Left Coast Press.

———. 2000. "Postnational Palestine/Israel? Globalization, Diaspora, Transnationalism and the Israeli-Palestinian Conflict." *Critical Inquiry* 26 (4): 757–772.

Rancière, Jacques. 2004. "Who Is the Subject of the Rights of Man?" *South Atlantic Quarterly* 103 (2–3): 297–310.

Redfield, Peter. 2006. "A Less Modest Witness: Collective Advocacy and Motivated Truth in a Medical Humanitarian Movement." *American Ethnologist* 33 (1): 3–26.

Rempel, Terry. 1999. "The Ottawa Process: Workshop on Compensation and Palestinian Refugees." *Journal of Palestine Studies* 29 (1): 36–49.

Roberts, Rebecca. 2010. *Palestinians in Lebanon: Refugees Living with Long-Term Displacement.* London: I. B. Tauris.

Roitman, Janet. 2005. *Fiscal Disobedience: An Anthropology of Economic Regulation in Central Africa.* Princeton, NJ: Princeton University Press.

Rosenfeld, M. 2004. *Confronting the Occupation: Work, Education and Political Activism of Palestinian Families in a Refugee Camp.* Stanford, CA: Stanford University Press.

Rougier, Bernard. 2007. *Everyday Jihad: The Rise of Militant Islam among Palestinians in Lebanon.* Translated by Pascale Ghazaleh. Cambridge, MA: Harvard University Press.

Rousseau, C., F. Crépeau, P. Foxen, and F. Houle. 2002. "The Complexity of Determining Refugeehood: A Multidisciplinary Analysis of the Decision-Making Process of the Canadian Immigration and Refugee Board." *Journal of Refugee Studies* 15 (1): 43–70.

Sa'di, Ahmad. 2002. "Catastrophe, Memory and Identity: Al-Nakbah as a Component of Palestinian Identity." *Israel Studies* 7 (2): 175–198.

Said, Edward. 2003. "At the Rendezvous of Victory." In *Culture and Resistance: Conversations with Edward Said,* interviews by David Barsamian, 159–196. Cambridge, MA: South End Press.

———. 1999. *After the Last Sky: Palestinian Lives.* Photographs by Jean Mohr. New York: Pantheon. First published in 1986.

———. 1984a. "The Mind of Winter: Reflections on Life in Exile." *Harper's* 269 (September): 49–55.

———. 1984b. "Permission to Narrate." *Journal of Palestine Studies* 8 (3): 27–48.

———. 1983. "Secular Criticism." In *The World, the Text, and the Critic,* 1–31. Cambridge, MA: Harvard University Press.

Said, Wadie E. 2003. "Palestinian Refugees: Host Countries, Legal Status and the Right of Return." *Refuge* (21) 2: 89–95.

———. 2001. "The Obligations of Host Countries to Refugees under International

Law: The Case of Lebanon." In *Palestinian Refugees: The Right of Return*, edited by N. Aruri, 123–152. London: Pluto Press.

Salih, Ruba. 2013. "Reconciling Return and Rights: Palestinian Refugees and the Emergence of a 'Political Society.'" *Jadaliyya*, March 26. Available at http://www.jadaliyya .com/pages/index/10814/reconciling-return-and-rights_palestinian-refugees.

Samaha, Nour. 2011. "On Our Way to Palestine: An Eyewitness Account of Nakba Day at the Lebanese Border." *Jadaliyya*, May 22. Available at http://www.jadaliyya.com/ pages/index/1644/on-our-way-to-palestine_an-eyewitness-account-of-n.

Sanbar, Elias. 2001. "Out of Place, out of Time." *Mediterranean Historical Review* 16 (1): 87–94.

Sanyal, Romola. 2010. "Squatting in Camps: Building and Insurgency in Spaces of Refuge." *Urban Studies* (June): 1–14.

Sayigh, Rosemary. 2011a. "Palestinian Camp Refugee Identifications: A New Look at the 'Local' and the 'National.'" In *Palestinian Refugees: Identity, Space and Place in the Levant*, edited by Are Knudsen and Sari Hanafi, 50–64. London: Routledge.

———. 2011b. "Palestinian Refugee Identity/ies: Generation, Class, Region." Birzeit University Working Paper 2011/55, Conferences and Public Events Module.

———. 2008. "Palestinians: From Peasants to Revolutionaries a Quarter of a Century On." In *Temps et espaces en Palestine*, edited by Roger Heacock, 247– 262. Beirut: Institut français du Proche-Orient.

———. 2006. "Back to the Center: Post-Oslo Revival of the Refugee Issue." In *The Struggle for Sovereignty: Palestine and Israel, 1993–2005*, edited by Rebecca Stein and Joel Beinin, 130–140. Stanford, CA: Stanford University Press.

———. 2005. "A House Is Not a Home: Permanent Impermanence of Habitat for Palestinian Expellees in Lebanon." *Holy Land Studies* 4 (1): 17–39.

———. 2004. "House: Loss, Refuge and Belonging." In *Forced Migration Review*, conference report, Trondheim, Norway, September 16–18.

———. 2001. "Palestinian Refugees in Lebanon: Implantation, Transfer or Return?" *Middle East Policy* 8 (1): 95–105.

———. 1998a. "Dis/Solving the 'Refugee Problem.'" *Middle East Report* 207:19–23.

———. 1998b. "Oral History for Palestinians: The Beginning of a Discipline." *Al-Jana* 1 (May): 6–12.

———. 1998c. "Palestinian Camp Women as Tellers of History." *Journal of Palestine Studies* 27 (2): 42–58.

———. 1995. "Palestinians in Lebanon: Harsh Present, Uncertain Future." *Journal of Palestine Studies* 25 (1): 37–53.

———. 1994. *Too Many Enemies: The Palestinian Experience in Lebanon*. London: Zed Books.

———. 1979. *Palestinians: From Peasants to Revolutionaries*. London: Zed Books.

Sayre, Edward, and Samia al-Botmeh. 2009. "In Search of a Future: The Struggle of

Young Palestinians." In *Generation in Waiting: The Unfulfilled Promise of Young People in the Middle East*, edited by Navtej Dhillon and Tarik Yousef, 95–119. Washington, DC: Brookings Institution.

Schiff, Benjamin. 1995. *Refugees unto the Third Generation: UN Aid to Palestinian Refugees*. Syracuse, NY: Syracuse University Press.

Scott, James C. 1985. *Weapons of the Weak: Everyday Forms of Resistance: Hidden Transcripts*. New Haven, CT: Yale University Press.

Segev, Tom. 1994. *The Seventh Million: The Israelis and the Holocaust*. Translated by Haim Watzman. New York: Hill and Wang.

Sen, Amartya. 2000. *Development as Freedom*. New York: Knopf.

———. 1989. "Development as Capabilities Expansion." *Journal of Developmental Planning* 19:41–58.

Sfeir, Jihan. 2010. "Palestinians in Lebanon: The Birth of the 'Enemy Within.'" In *Manifestations of Identity: The Lived Reality of Palestinian Refugees in Lebanon*, edited by Muhammad Ali Khalidi, 13–35. Beirut: Institute for Palestine Studies.

Shahid, Leila. 2002. "The Sabra and Shatila Massacres: Eye-Witness Reports." *Journal of Palestine Studies* 32:36–58.

Shami, Seteney. 1993. "The Social Implications of Population Displacement and Resettlement: An Overview with a Focus on the Arab Middle East." *International Migration Review* 27 (101): 4–33.

Shamir, Ronen. 2005. "Without Borders? Notes on Globalization as a Mobility Regime." *Sociological Theory* 23 (2): 197–217.

Sherwood, Harriet. 2013. "Return to Iqrit: How One Palestinian Village Is Being Reborn." *Guardian*, May 15. Available at http://www.guardian.co.uk/world/2013/may/15/return-iqrit-palestinian-village-israel.

Shikaki, Khalil. 2003a. "Results of Palestine Survey Research Unit Refugee Polls in the West Bank/Gaza Strip, Jordan and Lebanon on Refugees' Preferences and Behavior in a Palestinian-Israeli Permanent Refugee Agreement." Palestine Survey Research Unit, July 18. Available at http://www.pcpsr.org/survey/polls/2003/refugeesjune03 .html.

———. 2003b. "The Right of Return." *Wall Street Journal*, Eastern ed., July 30, A12.

Shlaim, Avi. 2002. "A Betrayal of History." *Guardian*, February 21. Available at http://www.guardian.co.uk/world/2002/feb/21/israel.

———. 2000. *The Iron Wall: Israel and the Arab World*. London: Penguin.

———. 1995. "The Debate about 1948." *International Journal of Middle East Studies* 27 (3): 287–304.

Siddiq, Muhammed. 1995. "On the Ropes of Memory: Narrating the Palestinian Refugees." In *Mistrusting Refugees*, edited by E. Valentine Daniel and John Chr. Knudsen, 87–101. Berkeley: University of California Press.

Simone, AbdouMaliq. 2004. "People as Infrastructure: Intersecting Fragments in Johannesburg." *Public Culture* 16 (3): 407–429.

Singerman, Diane. 1995. *Avenues of Participation: Family, Politics and Networks in Urban Quarters of Cairo*. Princeton, NJ: Princeton University Press.

Sirhan, Bassem. 1975. "Palestinian Refugee Camp Life in Lebanon." *Journal of Palestine Studies* 4 (2): 91–107.

Slyomovics, Susan. 1998. *The Object of Memory: Arab and Jew Narrate the Palestinian Village*. Philadelphia: University of Pennsylvania Press.

Sneath, David, Martin Holbraad, and Morten Axel Pedersen. 2009. "Technologies of the Imagination: An Introduction." *Ethnos* 74 (1): 5–30.

Spivak, Gayatri Chakravorty. 1987. *In Other Worlds: Essays in Cultural Politics*. London: Routledge.

Stamatopoulou-Robbins, Sophia. 2008. "The Joys and Dangers of Solidarity in Palestine: Prosthetic Engagement in an Age of Reparations." *CR: The New Centennial Review* 8 (2): 111–160.

Stork, Joe. 1985. "The War of the Camps, the War of the Hostages." *MERIP* Reports 133 (June): 3–7, 22.

Strathern, Marilyn. 1988. *The Gender of the Gift: Problems with Women and Problems with Society in Melanesia*. Berkeley: University of California Press.

Students for Justice in Palestine, Boston University Chapter. 2013. Mission Statement for the Right of Return Conference, Boston University, April 6–7. Available at http://rightofreturn.net/mission-statement/.

Suleiman, Jaber. 2001. "The Palestinian Liberation Organization: From the Right of Return to Bantustan." In *Palestinian Refugees: The Right of Return*, edited by N. Aruri, 87–105. London: Pluto Press.

———. 1999. "The Current Political Organization and Security Situation in the Palestinian Refugee Camps of Lebanon." *Journal of Palestine Studies* 29 (1): 66–80.

———. 1997. "Palestinians in Lebanon and the Role of Non-governmental Organizations." *Journal of Refugee Studies* 10 (3): 397–410.

Suleiman, Yasir. 2011. *Arabic, Self and Identity: A Study of Conflict and Displacement*. Oxford: Oxford University Press.

Swedenburg, Ted. 1995. *Memories of Revolt: The 1936–1939 Rebellion and the Palestinian National Past*. Minneapolis: University of Minnesota Press.

———. 1990. "The Palestinian Peasant as National Signifier." *Anthropological Quarterly* 63:18–30.

Swisher, Clayton. 2011. *The Palestine Papers: The End of the Road*. London: Hesperus Press.

Takkenberg, Lex. 1998. *The Status of Palestinian Refugees in International Law*. Oxford: Clarendon Press.

Tamari, Salim. 1996. *Palestinian Refugee Negotiations: From Madrid to Oslo II*. Washington, DC: Institute of Palestine Studies.

Taraki, Lisa. 2006. Introduction to *Living Palestine: Family Survival, Resistance and Mo-*

bility under Occupation, edited by Lisa Taraki, xi–xxx. Syracuse, NY: Syracuse University Press.

Tedlock, Barbara. 1991. "The New Anthropology of Dreaming." *Dreaming* 1:161–178.

Ticktin, Miriam. 2011. *Casualties of Care: Immigration and the Politics of Humanitarianism in France*. Berkeley: University of California Press.

———. 2006. "Where Ethics and Politics Meet: The Violence of Humanitarianism in France." *American Ethnologist* 33 (1): 33–49.

———. 1999. "Selling Suffering in the Courtroom and Marketplace: An Analysis of the Autobiography of Kiranjit Ahluwalia." *PoLAR* 22 (1): 24–41.

Tiltnes, Åge A. 2006. *Characteristics of the Palestinian Labour Force in Lebanon: Some Findings*. Fafo Study on the Employment of Palestinian Refugees in Lebanon. Oslo: Fafo Institute for Applied Social Science.

———. 2005. *Falling Behind: A Brief on the Living Conditions of Palestinian Refugees in Lebanon*. Fafo report 464. Oslo: Fafo Institute for Applied Social Science.

Triandafyllidou, A., ed. 2010. *Irregular Migration in Europe: Myths and Realities*. Farnham, UK: Ashgate.

Tuastad, Dag H. 1997. "The Organization of Camp Life: The Palestinian Refugee Camp of Bureij, Gaza." In *Constructing Order: Palestinian Adaptation to Refugee Life*, edited by A. Hovdenak, J. Pedersen, D. H. Tuastad, and E. Zureik, 103–157. Fafo report 236. Oslo: Fafo Institute for Applied Social Science.

Tyler, Imogen. 2006. "'Welcome to Britain': The Cultural Politics of Asylum." *European Journal of Cultural Studies* 9 (2): 185–202.

Tylor, Edward B. 1958. *Primitive Culture*. New York: Harper. First published in 1871.

Ugland, Ole Fr., and Yousef al-Madi. 2003. "Household Economies." In *Difficult Past, Uncertain Future: Living Conditions among Palestinian Refugees in the Camps and Gatherings in Lebanon*, edited by Ole Fr. Ugland, 155–182. Fafo report 409. Oslo: Fafo Institute for Applied Social Science.

UNGA (United Nations General Assembly). 1951. *Convention Relating to the Status of Refugees*, 28 July. United Nations Treaty Series, vol. 189, p. 137. Available at http://www.refworld.org/docid/3be01b964.html.

UNHCR (United Nations High Commissioner for Refugees). 2007. *Collection of International Instruments and Legal Texts concerning Refugees and Others of Concern to UNHCR*. Geneva: United Nations Publications.

UNRWA (United Nations Relief and Works Agency). 2012. *Population Statistics as of 1 January 2012*. Gaza: UNRWA Public Information Office.

———. 2011a. *Palestine Refugees: A Special Case*. Beirut: UNRWA Public Information Office. Available at http://www.unrwa.org/userfiles/20111002306.pdf.

———. 2011b. *The Right to Work*. Beirut: UNRWA Public Information Office. Available at http://www.unrwa.org/userfiles/2011100225615.pdf.

———. 2003. *Twelve Years of Credit to Microenterprise.* Gaza: UNRWA Public Information Office.

Vigh, Henrik. 2009. "Wayward Migration: On Imagined Futures and Technological Voids." *Ethnos* 74 (1): 91–109.

Walters, William. 2008. "Acts of Demonstration: Mapping the Territory of (Non-)Citizenship." In *Acts of Citizenship*, edited by Engin Isin and Greg M. Nielsen, 182–207. London: Palgrave Macmillan.

Warner, Daniel. 1994. "Voluntary Repatriation and the Meaning of Return to Home: A Critique of Liberal Mathematics." *Journal of Refugee Studies* 7 (2): 160–174.

Weine, Stevan. 1999. *When History Is a Nightmare: Lives and Memories of Ethnic Cleansing in Bosnia-Herzegovina.* New Brunswick, NJ: Rutgers University Press.

Whyte, Susan Reynolds. 1997. *Questioning Misfortune: The Pragmatics of Uncertainty in Eastern Uganda.* Cambridge: Cambridge University Press.

Willen, Sarah S. 2007. "Toward a Critical Phenomenology of 'Illegality': State Power, Criminalization, and Abjectivity among Undocumented Migrant Workers in Tel Aviv, Israel." *International Migration* 45 (3): 8–36.

World Bank Report. 2007. *Lebanon Economic and Social Impact Assessment: From Recovery to Sustainable Growth.* Document of the World Bank, Middle East and North Africa, Social and Economic Development Group Publication. Washington, DC: World Bank.

Yaqub, Nadia G. 2007. *Pens, Swords and the Springs of Art: The Oral Poetry Dueling of Palestinian Weddings in the Galilee.* Leiden, Netherlands: Brill Studies in Middle Eastern Literatures.

Zaidan, Ismat. 2011. "Mobility and Transnationalism: Travel Patterns and Identity among Palestinian Canadians." PhD diss., Department of Geography, University of Waterloo, Canada.

Zetter, Roger. 1999. "Reconceptualizing the Myth of Return: Continuity and Transition amongst the Greek-Cypriot Refugees of 1974." *Journal of Refugee Studies* 12 (1): 1–22.

Zolberg, Aristide R., Astri Suhrke, and Sergio Aguayo. 1989. *Escape from Violence: Conflict and the Refugee Crisis in the Developing World.* New York: Oxford University Press.

Zureik, Elia. 2003. "Theoretical and Methodological Considerations for the Study of Palestinian Society." *Comparative Studies of South Asia, Africa and the Middle East* 23 (1): 3–13.

———. 2002. "The Palestinian Refugee Problem: Conflicting Interpretations." *Global Dialogue* 4 (3): 92–102.

———. 1997. "The Trek Back Home: Palestinians Returning Home and Their Problem of Adaptation." In *Constructing Order: Palestinian Adaptation to Refugee Life*, edited by A. Hovdenak, J. Pedersen, D. H. Tuastad, and E. Zureik, 79–102. Fafo report 236. Oslo: Fafo Institute for Applied Social Science.

INDEX

Abboud, S., 246n6

Abdulhadi, Rabab, 261n22, 264n47

Abdullah, Abdullah, 206

Abdulrahim, Sawsan, 26, 163

Abu Aynayn, 126–27

Abu Aziz, 57, 58

Abufarha, Nasser, 4

Abu Faruq, 112–13

Abu Hani, 115, 118, 119, 123, 127, 128

Abu Lughod, Lila, 22, 216, 222

Abu Mujahed, 232n37, 248n29

Abu Musa, 127, 131

Abu Nahleh, Lamis, 234n50

Abu Nayef, 46–48, 53, 54, 57, 62, 106–7

Abu Nidal Organization, 230n16

Abunimah, Ali, 259n3

Abu Qa'id, 117

Abu Sitta, Salman, 236n15, 259nn3,4,11

Abu Turki, 107, 247n14

acts of citizenship, 220–21, 263n40, 266n12

Afifi, Rima, 259n9

Agamben, Giorgio, 183, 188; on bare life, 25, 233n49, 245n3, 257n30

agency of refugees, 6, 25, 29, 34, 39, 59, 66, 96, 99, 139, 151, 156, 158, 159, 172, 174, 219, 244n32; acts of citizenship, 220–21, 263n40, 266n12; and emigration, 33, 187; as political, 45, 106, 172–73, 209, 220–21, 239n40, 246n9, 263n40, 266nn12,13; as pragmatic, 2, 30, 62, 222–23; and silence, 56, 239n46; women's agency, 79, 141

Ager, Alastair, 25

Agier, Michel, 25, 233n48

Aguayo, Sergio, 256n25

'A'idun (The Returnee), 235n4, 261n23

Akram, Susan, 16, 169, 170, 176, 195, 232n32, 254n8, 255n16, 259n3

Al-Ahbash movement, 23, 233n43

Al-Aqsa Intifada, 23, 24, 63, 199, 216

Al-'Awda, 199

Algerian Harkis, 51

Al Ghazâli: on God and dreams, 251n12

Ali, Naji, 236n13

Ali Nayel, Moe, 208

Al-Jana and the Arab Resource Center for Popular Arts (ARCPA), 235n4

Allan, Diana, 64

Allen, Lori, 40

Stanford Studies in Middle Eastern and Islamic Societies and Cultures

---

Shira Robinson, *Citizen Strangers: Palestinians and the Birth of Israel's Liberal Settler State*
2013

Joel Beinin and Frédéric Vairel, editors, *Social Movements, Mobilization, and Contestation in the Middle East and North Africa*
2013 (2nd ed.), 2011

Ariella Azoulay and Adi Ophir, *The One-State Condition: Occupation and Democracy in Israel/Palestine*
2012

Steven Heydemann and Reinoud Leenders, editors, *Middle East Authoritarianisms: Governance, Contestation, and Regime Resilience in Syria and Iran*
2012

Jonathan Marshall, *The Lebanese Connection: Corruption, Civil War, and the International Drug Traffic*
2012

Joshua Stacher, *Adaptable Autocrats: Regime Power in Egypt and Syria*
2012

Bassam Haddad, *Business Networks in Syria: The Political Economy of Authoritarian Resilience*
2011

Noah Coburn, *Bazaar Politics: Power and Pottery in an Afghan Market Town*
2011

Laura Bier, *Revolutionary Womanhood: Feminisms, Modernity, and the State in Nasser's Egypt*
2011

Samer Soliman, *The Autumn of Dictatorship: Fiscal Crisis and Political Change in Egypt under Mubarak*
2011

Rochelle A. Davis, *Palestinian Village Histories: Geographies of the Displaced*
2010

Haggai Ram, *Iranophobia: The Logic of an Israeli Obsession*
2009

John Chalcraft, *The Invisible Cage: Syrian Migrant Workers in Lebanon*
2008

Rhoda Kanaaneh, *Surrounded: Palestinian Soldiers in the Israeli Military*
2008

Asef Bayat, *Making Islam Democratic: Social Movements and the Post-Islamist Turn*
2007

Robert Vitalis, *America's Kingdom: Mythmaking on the Saudi Oil Frontier*
2006

Jessica Winegar, *Creative Reckonings: The Politics of Art and Culture in Contemporary Egypt*
2006

Joel Beinin and Rebecca L. Stein, editors, *The Struggle for Sovereignty: Palestine and Israel, 1993-2005*
2006